Journal of the American Revolution

JOURNAL

OF THE

AMERICAN REVOLUTION

ANNUAL VOLUME 2019

WESTHOLME
Yardley

Westholme Publishing, LLC
904 Edgewood Road
Yardley, Pennsylvania 19067
Visit our Web site at www.westholmepublishing.com

ISBN: 978–1–59416–325–8

Printed in the United States of America.

CONTENTS

Contents

EDITOR'S INTRODUCTION

When the *Journal of the American Revolution* was created in 2013, it took a great deal of inspiration from the newspapers of the eighteenth century. Although JAR is produced and presented using thoroughly modern technologies, the inspiration and even some of the content came directly from the pages of America's early newspapers. It is fitting, then, that the first article in this, the fifth annual compilation volume of JAR articles, is a study of the most iconic of all newspaper images of the era: Benjamin Franklin's famous "Join, or Die" cartoon, still a staple of patriotic iconography.

The *Journal of the American Revolution* also captures the spirit of newspapers in bringing something for every interest. This year's annual features politics, from Benjamin Franklin's efforts to effect reconciliation before war began, to diplomatic recognition of the United States by other nations; warfare, from a refugee crisis at the Siege of Boston to a massacre of civilians on the Pennsylvania frontier; romance, from the prenuptial sparring of John and Abigail Adams to a wife's plot to murder her husband; espionage, in books and in daring spies; women's studies, from soldiers' wives accused of crimes to a wealthy Loyalist woman left to protect her estate; naval actions, from a cantankerous captain to an encounter with Horatio Nelson; opinions, from a Loyalist perspective on France's alliance with the United States to Benedict Arnold's proposals for British victory; personalities, from the famous John André to the almost unknown Elias Hasket Darby; slavery, from the attitudes of American generals to the service of freed slaves in the Royal Navy; international affairs, from Minorca to China; scandals, from the burning of Norfolk, Virginia, to terrorism in the dockyards of England.

It's been another great year for exciting new studies of the American Revolution. Enjoy this sampling of what JAR has presented in the last twelve months, and keep an eye on even more to come.

Join, or Die: Political and Religious Controversy Over Franklin's Snake Cartoon

❀❂ DANIEL P. STONE ❂❀

On May 9, 1751, Benjamin Franklin published a satirical article in the *Pennsylvania Gazette* commenting on British laws that allowed convicted felons to be shipped to the American colonies. As an equal trade, Franklin wryly suggested that the colonists should send rattlesnakes to Great Britain and carefully distribute them among "Places of Pleasure."[1] Although these reptiles seemed to be the most suitable returns, Franklin nonetheless lamented on one disadvantage of the trade. In Franklin's mind, even if Britain received these venomous pests, the risk was not comparable to the one the colonists' bore. According to Franklin, "the RattleSnake gives Warning before he attempts his Mischief; which the Convict does not."[2] Notwithstanding his sardonic wit, this American entrepreneur did not know that he would eventually unleash a literary rattlesnake upon Britain and its American colonies. Precisely three years later, on May 9, 1754, Franklin published a political cartoon depicting a rattlesnake with the admonishing title, "JOIN, or DIE."[3]

This graphic masterpiece, originally representing the inevitable death of the American colonies if they failed to unite during the impending French and Indian War, later stirred political and religious

1. Editorial, "Rattle-Snakes for Felons," *Pennsylvania Gazette*, May 9, 1751.
2. Ibid.
3. Benjamin Franklin, editorial, *Pennsylvania Gazette*, May 9, 1754. Although some historians question whether Franklin's original cartoon displayed a rattlesnake, J. A. Leo Lemay conjectures that this was probably Franklin's intention. Also, by referencing rattlesnakes in his articles published by the *Pennsylvania Gazette* (May 9, 1751) and *The Pennsylvania Journal* (December 27, 1775), it seems likely that Franklin meant for the cartoon to portray this type of serpent.

controversy between Loyalists and Patriots during the American Revolution. To Loyalists, the serpent represented Satan, deception, and the spiritual fall of man, proving the treachery of revolutionary thought. To Patriots however, the snake depicted wisdom, vigor, and cohesiveness, especially when the colonies united for a common purpose. By closely examining colonial newspapers and images, one notices that Franklin's cartoon not only represented the political unity of the American colonies, but evoked religious ideals during the Revolution. Newspaper articles adopted the infamous words, "JOIN, or DIE!" to stir colonial citizens to join the revolutionary cause, renditions of Franklin's cartoon were published on mastheads of newspapers, and conflicting editorials were published to teach the correct religious interpretation of the "American Serpent."[4] Due to the cartoon's prominent influence and the controversy that it created, the snake inevitably became the first national symbol for the newly created United States. Loyalists and Patriots eventually synthesized biblical imagery with Franklin's political cartoon to articulate their positions for the revolutionary cause, creating religious controversy while solidifying the serpent as America's first national emblem. This is an intriguing subject that has received little analysis, requiring further investigation.[5]

BIRTH OF THE SNAKE CARTOON

To fully appreciate the political and religious controversy that Benjamin Franklin's snake cartoon generated, it is important to first relate the history of the illustration as well as discuss the symbolism that Franklin hoped it would portray. By reexamining some historical details, it is possible to show how the political history and religious story of Franklin's cartoon are inherently linked.

During early May 1754, when England and France competed for territory in the Ohio River Valley, Benjamin Franklin was a staunch advocate for British colonial unity. Writing an article in his newspaper, the *Pennsylvania Gazette*, Franklin reported the tragedy of Ens. Edward Ward's surrender to Capt. Claude-Pierre Pecaudy. He wrote that Ward's troops, while trying to build an English fort in the area of mod-

---

4. Editorial, "Extract of a letter from New London, Feb. 27, 1779," *The New-Hampshire Gazette*, March 9, 1779. See also, editorial, "Boston, March 4," *The New Jersey Gazette*, March 31, 1779.

5. The most comprehensive examination of Franklin's snake cartoon was written by Albert Matthews in his article, "The Snake Devices, 1754-1776, and the Constitutional Courant, 1765," *Publications of the Colonial Society of Massachusetts* 11 (1910): 408-453. However, Matthews' article is more of a bibliographic discourse, and he did not examine the religious connotations found in Loyalist and Patriot editorials.

"JOIN, OR DIE." Cartoon by Benjamin Franklin from the *Pennsylvania Gazette*, May 9, 1754.

ern-day Pittsburgh, were surrounded by Pecaudy's French force of over four hundred men.[6] Then after describing the hardships the colonists would suffer if the French continued to seize Pennsylvania's western territory, Franklin inserted his snake cartoon. Displaying a rattlesnake cut into eight parts, the forewarning phrase "JOIN, OR DIE." loomed beneath the image.[7] This illustration, as scholar J.A. Leo Lemay asserted, was the first published symbol for colonial unity.[8]

In addition, as Lemay revealed, this probably was not a foreign image to some English citizens. The serpent was a classical symbol and had been presented in religious and mythological literature for centuries. Lemay wrote, "Franklin knew the various symbolic meanings of the serpent, and when he wanted to portray colonial union, he recalled the image of a serpent cut into two that appeared in a seventeenth-century emblem book."[9] This book was Nicolas Verrien's *Recueil d'em-*

6. J.A. Leo Lemay, *The Life of Benjamin Franklin: Soldier, Scientist, and Politician 1748-1757* (Philadelphia: University of Pennsylvania Press, 2009), 3: 363.
7. Ibid.
8. Ibid., 3: 364.
9. Ibid., 3: 367.

blemes, displaying a cut snake with the motto, "Un Serpent coupé en deux. Se rejoindre ou mourir' (A serpent cut in two. Either join or die)."[10] Also, throughout the years a superstition had widely circulated among the British colonies that a cut serpent would come alive if the pieces were joined back together before sundown. This also may have been another influence to help Franklin concoct the cartoon.[11] Franklin most likely knew about the French snake emblem and the mythological folklore behind the serpent. Some of his readers, no doubt, would have been familiar with these representations as well.

It is no surprise, therefore, that Franklin's image quickly became a popular symbol for colonial unity. Four colonial newspapers published versions of the cartoon in May 1754, with the most dramatic modification by the *Boston Gazette* on May 21.[12] Although the cartoon exhibited the motto "JOIN, or DIE," the image of the snake was more detailed, displaying a scroll with the maxim, "Unite and Conquer."[13] Franklin's cartoon became a reoccurring symbol during the upcoming months, especially when the *Virginia Gazette* reported the defeat of Col. George Washington's forces at Fort Necessity. The article concluded by referencing the cartoon, stating, "Surely this will remove the infatuation of security that seems to have prevailed too much among the other colonies" and "inforce a late ingenious Emblem worthy of their Attention and Consideration."[14] Within a short period of time, colonials started to appreciate Franklin's cartoon. Individuals, whether interpreting the snake emblematically or superstitiously, understood its message — if the colonies did not unite to defend themselves against foreign encroachments, they would perish and become subject to other nations. Although Franklin's cartoon became a popular symbol before the French and Indian War, it would not become a national emblem until the American Revolution.

REVOLUTIONARY RESURRECTION

To scholars such as J.A. Leo Lemay and Gordon S. Wood, Benjamin Franklin's snake cartoon ultimately became a national emblem due to its unifying aspects and powerful political imagery. These historians are correct to assert that the cartoon encapsulated the political and social struggles of the American Revolution, especially when Britain began enforcing new taxation laws on its North American colonies. However,

---

10. Ibid.

11. Ibid. See also Donald Dewey, *The Art of Ill Will: The Story of American Political Cartoons* (New York: New York University Press, 2008), 2.

12. For examples of these renditions, see Matthews, "The Snake Devices," 416-17.

13. Editorial, *Boston Gazette*, May 21, 1754.

14. Quoted in Lemay, *The Life of Benjamin Franklin*, 3: 366.

the story turns much more captivating when reading the newspaper editorials.[15] By examining these writings within the political context of the time, a fascinating history emerges. Franklin's cartoon was resurrected as a potent call for colonial unity against Great Britain, ultimately giving momentum to the religious controversy that would soon follow when Loyalists and Patriots began writing their opinions on what the snake symbolized.

Once word reached the colonies that Parliament passed the Stamp Act in March 1765, a surge of protests spread throughout the continent. The lieutenant governor of Massachusetts, Thomas Hutchinson, feared for his life, and lamented to Franklin about the mobocracy that was forming in Boston.[16] The home and office of Massachusetts's stamp distributor was attacked, and Hutchinson's mansion was invaded. These acts made Hutchinson hope for a speedy repeal of the tax, but as Franklin suggested in a private letter, this was not likely to happen. Hutchinson also informed Franklin how Bostonians protested the new tax.[17]

According to Hutchinson, opponents resurrected Franklin's motto, "JOIN, or DIE" to promote their insurgency. He wrote to Franklin, "When you and I were at Albany ten years ago, we did not Propose an union for such Purposes as these."[18] Franklin had published his snake cartoon two months before he and Hutchinson met at the Albany Congress in July 1754 to attempt to form an intercolonial government under British authority. Franklin's cartoon had been originally intended to support this type of union under the British Crown.[19] But a decade later, angry colonists started to use Franklin's cartoon to encourage unification against Britain's encroachments, transforming the original intention of the image by making it a call for revolutionary ideology. Hutchinson recognized the significance of this transformation, and as others would later realize overtime, Franklin's cartoon would radically influence revolutionary protests.

When Parliament passed the Boston Port Act at the end of March 1774, riots swept the city and other colonies lent moral and economic support to Boston.[20] As the act declared, Boston's harbor was closed

15. See Lemay, *The Life of Benjamin Franklin*, 3: 362-368; Gordon S. Wood, *The Americanization of Benjamin Franklin* (New York: Penguin Press, 2004), 110.

16. Wood, *The Americanization of Benjamin Franklin*, 110.

17. Ibid.

18. Quoted in ibid.

19. Thomas S. Kidd, *Benjamin Franklin: The Religious Life of a Founding Father* (New Haven, CT: Yale University Press, 2017), 180-81.

20. Robert Middlekauff, *The Glorious Cause: The American Revolution, 1763-1789* (New York: Oxford University Press), 237-40.

on June 15, 1774 and was expected to be tightly regulated until the East India Company received compensation for the merchandise that was lost during the Boston Tea Party.[21] This act outraged several colonists and induced them to further adopt Franklin's famous motto. With the admonishing title, "JOIN or DIE," Rhode Island's *Newport Mercury* published an article that rebuked Parliament and declared that the American colonies needed to unite. The article stated:

> The act of parliament for blockading the harbour of Boston, in order to reduce its spirited inhabitants to the most servile and mean compliances ever attempted to be imposed on a free people, is allowed to be infinitely more alarming and dangerous to our common liberties, than even that hydra the Stamp Act (which was destroyed by our firmness and union) and must be read with a glowing indignation by every real friend of freedom, in Europe and America— ... The Generals of despotism are now drawing the lines of circumvallation around our bulwarks of liberty, and nothing but unity, resolution, and perseverance, can save ourselves and posterity from what is worse than death—SLAVERY.[22]

Parliament's acts were seen by angry colonists as reducing Bostonians to a form of slavery, and if the colonies did not unite, these insurgents claimed that every province would soon be subjected to tyranny. Franklin's motto now became imbedded in revolutionary ideology and began to exemplify the cause. A rendition of this article was printed in *The Massachusetts Spy* on May 26, 1774, demonstrating that the forewarning title, "JOIN or DIE" continued to spread throughout the colonies.

One month later, Franklin's motto again appeared in the *Newport Mercury*, this time promoting the unification of the colonies to create a Continental Congress. On June 27, 1774, the paper reported:

> The freeholders and inhabitants of New Jersey, had a meeting at Newark in said country, the 11th of June inst. when they passed resolves nearly similar to those of most other towns and colonies on the continent, and were very zealous for having a congress appointed, as soon as possible; and according to present appearances such a congress will certainly take place ... notwithstanding the enemies of American freedom, in this town and other places, have boasted that the other colonies would not join the province of Massachusetts Bay. The colonies know they must 'JOIN, or DIE.'[23]

21. Ibid., 355.
22. Editorial, "JOIN or DIE!" *The Newport Mercury*, May 16, 1774. See also editorial, JOIN or DIE!" *The Massachusetts Spy*, May 26, 1774.
23. "NEWPORT, JUNE 27," *The Newport Mercury*, June 27, 1774.

As the article claimed, there were individuals who boasted that the colonies would not unify for the revolutionary cause. Yet as this Patriot declared, a congress was being summoned for that very purpose. This article demonstrated the tensions that stirred between Loyalists and Patriots during the tempestuous months of 1774. Colonists of several ideological backgrounds began to contemplate their political views, and many resolved to determine which side they would support. This year, known for the Intolerable Acts that were imposed on the colonies, is when Franklin's cartoon became the embodiment of the revolutionary cause and aroused the most heated controversy. This is when Franklin's cartoon would begin to be synthesized with biblical literature, affixing it a religious icon and America's first national emblem.

By July 1774, several colonial newspapers placed renditions of Franklin's cartoon on their mastheads. The *New-York Journal* displayed an image of a snake cut into nine parts with the maxim "UNITE or DIE."[24] However, the most detailed alteration was created by the *Massachusetts Spy*. This newspaper already had an ornate masthead, but when it added Franklin's image, the front page became a crest for revolutionary fervor. The newspaper displayed a snake separated into nine parts contending with a dragon.[25] This creative version of Franklin's cartoon attempted to portray the contest between the American colonies and Great Britain. The same motto "JOIN or DIE" was printed above the snake, but it was accompanied by another adage: "Do THOU Great LIBERTY inspire our Souls—And make our Lives in THY Possession happy—On our Deaths glorious in THY just Defence."[26]

CONTROVERSY OVER THE SNAKE

These mastheads adopted Benjamin Franklin's snake cartoon for two purposes: to purport revolutionary ideology and to encourage unity against Great Britain. As a result, Loyalists became unsettled and began to synthesize Franklin's image with biblical literature to undermine the Patriotic campaign.

The first Loyalist satirization of Franklin's cartoon appeared in *Rivingston's New York Gazetteer* on August 25, 1774. Entitled, "On the SNAKE, depicted at the head of some American NEWS PAPERS," the epigram read:

> YE Sons of Sedition, how comes it to pass,
> That America's typ'd by a SNAKE—in the grass?
> Don't you think 'tis a scandalous, saucy reflection,

---

24. Masthead, *The New-York Journal*, July 7, 1774.
25. Masthead, *The Massachusetts Spy*, October 6, 1774.
26. Ibid.

That merits the soundest, severest Correction,
NEW ENGLAND's the HEAD, too; —NEW-ENGLAND's abused;
For the Head of the Serpent we know should be BRUISED.[27]

Adopting language from the third chapter of Genesis, the rhyme manipulated the curse that God had placed on the serpent. Genesis reads, "And I will put enmity between thee and the woman, and between thy seed and her seed; it shall bruise thy head, and thou shalt bruise his heel."[28] Typifying revolutionary America as a "SNAKE" and its citizens as "Sons of Sedition," this poem paralleled God's curse with the inevitable defeat of the colonies. By combining political ideals with biblical literature, this poem associated revolutionary America with Satan. However, the fact that this author tried to condemn the illustration proves that Franklin's cartoon had now become a powerful symbol for colonial unity. This epigram was later reprinted in the *Boston News-Letter* on September 8, 1774, demonstrating that Loyalist fervor was growing to condemn the revolutionary cause.[29]

Inspired by the Loyalist poem found in *Rivington's New York Gazetteer*, a competing rhyme was published in the Patriot newspaper, the *New-York Journal*, on September 1, 1774. With the heading, "For the New-York Journal. On reading the Lines in Mr. Rivington's last Paper, on the Snake at the Head of several American News Papers, the following occurred, viz.," the poem read:

Ye Traitors! The Snake ye with Wonder behold,
Is not the Deceiver so famous of old;
Nor is it the Snake in the Grass that ye view,
Which would be a striking Resemblance of you,
Who aiming your Stings at your Country's Heel,
Its Weight and Resentment to crush you should feel.[30]

Referencing the same biblical verse of the previous Loyalist epigram, this anonymous Patriot author associated Loyalists with the treachery of Satan. By equating Loyalist fervor to "Stings" aimed at the colonies' "Heel," the author used the same biblical story to declare that the Patriots would "crush" any Loyalist backlash. Using religious imagery, this

27. Epigram, *Rivington's New-York Gazetteer*, August 25, 1774.
28. Genesis 3:15.
29. Epigram, "On the Snake, depicted at the Head of some American NEWS PAPERS," *The Boston News-Letter*, September 8, 1774.
30. Epigram, "For the NEW-YORK JOURNAL. On reading the Lines in Mr. Rivington's last Paper, on the Snake at the Head of several American News Papers, the following occurred, viz." *The New-York Journal*, September 1, 1774.

Patriot hoped to highlight the literary power of Franklin's cartoon. Also, by publishing this poem in a newspaper that proudly displayed a rendition of the image on its masthead, the author tried to convince Patriotic readers that the revolutionary cause was sacred.

In the same issue of the *New-York Journal*, another Patriot article appeared to explain Franklin's cartoon. Although the editor claimed that the piece was written "about two or three months" before the current edition, he stated that he was not reminded of it until the first Loyalist poem was published in *Rivington's New York Gazetteer*.[31] The author, known only as "SPECULATOR," introduced the article by stating that he hoped to explain "the Design of the emblematical Figure at the Head" of *The New-York Journal*.[32] The author wrote, "The Serpent has been from the earliest Ages, used as an Emblem of Wisdom—We are told in the 3rd Chapter of Genesis, that the Serpent was more subtil than any Beast of the Field, and the Apostle exhorts us to be wise as Serpents."[33] Instead of associating the serpent with Satan, this author linked Franklin's cartoon to positive religious connotations. Referencing the third chapter of Genesis in beneficial terms, this article again combated *Rivington's* Loyalist editorial which had drawn upon the same biblical chapter. Also, by referencing the tenth chapter of Matthew, the author associated Franklin's cartoon with the words of Jesus Christ, which read, "Behold, I send you forth as sheep in the midst of wolves: be ye therefore wise as serpents, and harmless as doves."[34] The religious connotations the Patriot author related to Franklin's cartoon were virtuous and emulated the teachings of the Christian savior. By synthesizing Franklin's cartoon with biblical virtues, the author demonstrated that the snake was a choice emblem for the revolutionary campaign. The author also stated that the serpent represented "Life and Vigour," as well as "a watchful Dragon" that guarded the colonists' "Rights and Liberties."[35]

After *The New-York Journal* published its Patriot rebuttals, the *Boston Post Boy* decided to join the debate and reprinted a satirical poem found in the *London Magazine*. On September 26, 1774, the newspaper published the following:

---

31. SPECULATOR, editorial, "The following Piece was written about two or three Months ago, but laid aside and forgot, till brought to Remembrance by some Lines in Mr. Rivingston's last Paper. TO THE PRINTER. July 1, 1774," *The New-York Journal*, September 1, 1774.
32. Ibid.
33. Ibid.
34. Matthew 10:16.
35. SPECULATOR, editorial, T*he New-York Journal*, September 1, 1774.

A BOSTONIAN EPIGRAM.

To the Ministry
YOU'VE sent a Rod to Massachusetts,
Thinking the Americans will buss it;
But much I fear, for Britain's Sake,
That this same Rod may prove a Snake.[36]

Referencing the fourth chapter of Exodus, this poem drew upon the imagery of God transforming Moses' rod into a serpent.[37] In the story, God used the transformation of the rod as a warning and example of his power. Yet what makes this epigram so intriguing is that it characterized the British ministry as Moses, who when first experiencing the transformation of his rod, became afraid.[38] When the British Crown imposed the Intolerable Acts, it hoped to suppress the colonists into obedience. Yet, as the poem suggested, instead of this "rod" convincing Americans to respect British power, the rod turned into a snake, showing the Crown that it needed to be mindful of its actions.

As the poem alleged, Britain's repressive actions created the American snake, making the Crown face serious consequences. This epigram directly referenced Franklin's cartoon, but it also helped solidify the image of the snake as a symbol for revolutionary thought. The snake was not portrayed as a symbol of evil, but as a retribution for Britain's harsh treatment. Franklin's image was used as an emblem of power and it cast a moral light upon the Patriotic cause. By giving this image religious and ethical overtones, Patriots hoped to demonstrate that their ideology was righteous; they wanted Franklin's cartoon to represent the virtue of God's holy word.

Since Franklin's cartoon had started to become a hallowed emblem, Loyalists continued to write articles hoping to undermine its Patriotic symbolism. In an article published by the *Norwich Packet* on October 6, 1774, Samuel Peters, a well-known reverend and Loyalist, complained about the persecution inflicted by the Sons of Liberty and connected this activity with Franklin's cartoon. Peters wrote, "The Riots and Mobs that have attended me and my House, set on by the Go_ _ _ _ _ _ of Connecticut, have compelled me to take up my Abode here; and the Clergy of Connecticut must fall a Sacrifice with several Churches, very soon, to the Rage of Puritan Mobility, if the Old Ser-

---

36. Epigram, "From the LONDON MAGAZINE, for June, 1774. A BOSTONIAN EPIGRAM. To the Ministry." *Boston Post Boy*, September 26, 1774.
37. Exodus 4:3.
38. Ibid.

pent, that Dragon, is not bound."[39] Peters attached the satanic conno-
tation of Franklin's snake cartoon to Patriots, simply referring to them
as "the Old Serpent, that Dragon." In his article, Peters insinuated that
Patriots were possessed by the devil and that the revolutionary cause
needed to be "bound." Peters not only referenced the biblical image of
Satan, but applied verbiage found in the first two verses of chapter
twenty in the book of Revelation. The verses read, "And I saw an angel
come down from heaven, having the key of the bottomless pit and a
great chain in his hand. And he laid hold on the dragon, that old serpent, which is the Devil, and Satan, and bound him a thousand years."[40]
Alluding to this scripture, Peters attempted to demonstrate the sinful
state of Patriots.

As the years progressed, Loyalists continued to write commentaries
that rebuked American Patriots. Samuel Peters, as well as others, proceeded to link Franklin's cartoon to the evils of Satan.[41] By consistently
synthesizing negative biblical imagery with Franklin's illustration, however, they unwittingly solidified the cartoon as a venerated Patriotic
emblem and provoked revolutionaries to redeem their reputations. Patriots continued to attack Loyalist propaganda by publishing their own
writings, and by applying positive religious imagery with Franklin's cartoon, they made the snake a virtuous symbol of their campaign.

When the fall of 1774 arrived, colonial condescension of British authority was imbedded in Massachusetts. However, as Loyalist compo-
sitions continued to be printed, Patriots persisted with their
countercharges. Magnifying the importance of Franklin's snake as a religious and Patriotic emblem, an epigram published in the *Massachusetts
Spy* advanced the editorial campaign. Entitled, "On the BRITISH MIN-
ISTRY, and NEW-ENGLAND, the Head of the American Snake. AN EPI-
GRAM, 1774," the poem read:

> BRITAIN's sons line the coast of Atlantic all o'er,
> Great of length, but in breadth they now wind on a shore.
> That's divided by inlets, by creeks, and by bays,—

39. Samuel Peters, editorial, "BOSTON, October 1, 1774," *Norwich Packet*, October 6, 1774.
40. Revelation 20:1-2.
41. For further examples of Loyalist editorials and propaganda, see also Editorial, "BOSTON.
MASSACHUSETTS continu'd. To the INHABITANTS of the Province of MASSACHUSETTS-BAY."
The New-Hampshire Gazette, March 10, 1775; Editorial, "Parnassian Packet," *Essex Journal*,
March 22, 1775; Poem, "(Continued from our last.)" *Essex Journal*, May 6, 1775; LEONATUS,
editorial, "LONDON, From the General Evening Post, of August 5, 1777. To the EDITOR."
The New-York Gazette, November 3, 1777.

A Snake* cut in parts, a pat emblem conveys—
The fell junto at home—sure their heads are but froth -
Fain this snake would have caught to supply viper broth
For their worn constitutions—and to it they go,
Hurry Tom, without hearing his yes or his no,
On the boldest adventures their annals can show:
By their wisdom advised, he their courage displays,
For they seized on the tongue 'mong their first of essays;
Nor once thought of teeth when our Snake they assail -
Though the prudent catch Snakes by the back or the tail -
To direct to the head! our good King must indite 'em -
They forgot that the head would most certainly bite 'em.[42]

The rhyme suggested that Loyalists, while trying to curb Patriots from promoting their cause, forgot that the American snake had metaphorical "teeth" that could "bite" them. These "teeth" were the poems and articles that Patriots continued to publish to refute Loyalists that branded revolutionary ideology as evil. This epigram, although using common snake imagery, also contained religious symbolism, referencing several passages from the Bible. Using words such as "wisdom" and "head" to reference the American snake, the author evoked imagery from the books of Genesis and Matthew, as well as others throughout scripture.[43] Furthermore, by stating that the American snake was going to "bite" the hasty British Crown, the author noted the political tensions that existed in the colonies. Franklin's serpent, which began as a political call for colonial unity, had now become a religious embodiment of the American Revolution.

By continuing to reference Benjamin Franklin's snake cartoon, Patriots and Loyalists increased its literary power. However, it might seem odd that the man who created the cartoon and who was known for his contributions to journalism, would remain silent during this widely publicized controversy. Franklin was an ardent Patriot for the revolutionary cause, and as the creator of the cartoon, he surely would have known what the image symbolized. Therefore, in a manner that was common for Franklin, he surreptitiously joined the editorial contest by submitting an article to the *Pennsylvania Journal*.

On December 27, 1775, using the pseudonym "An American Guesser," he published an article entitled, "The Rattle-Snake as a Symbol of America."[44] With a whimsical tone, he wrote that his wishes

---

42. Poem, "Parnassian Packet." *The Massachusetts Spy*, October 27, 1774.
43. See Genesis 49:17, Numbers 21:6-9, Psalms 140:3, and Jeremiah 8:17.
44. Benjamin Franklin (AN AMERICAN GUESSER), "The Rattle-Snake as a Symbol of America," *The Pennsylvania Journal*, December 27, 1775.

were "to guess what could have been intended by this uncommon device."[45] Franklin penned: "I took care, however, to consult on this occasion a person who is acquainted with heraldry, from whom I learned, that it is a rule among the learned in that science 'That the worthy properties of the animal, in the crest-born, shall be considered,' and, 'That the base ones cannot have been intended;' he likewise informed me that the antients considered the serpent as an emblem of wisdom, and in a certain attitude of endless duration—both which circumstances I suppose may have been had in view."[46] Interestingly enough, Franklin wrote that people of ancient times had recognized the serpent as an emblem of "wisdom" and "endless duration." Similar to Patriots who countered Loyalist editorials, Franklin related the serpent to positive ancient writings, which of course, included biblical literature. This is not surprising. After all, according to historian Thomas S. Kidd, Franklin had constantly referenced the Bible to support his ideas and arguments. "Franklin knew the Bible backward and forward," Kidd affirmed. "It framed the way he spoke and thought. Biblical phrases are ubiquitous in Franklin's vast body of writings. Even as he embraced religious doubts, the King James Bible colored his ideas about morality, human nature, and the purpose of life. It served as his most common source of similes and anecdotes. He even enjoyed preying on friends' ignorance of scripture in order to play jokes on them."[47] Franklin was broad in his assertion, but when he connected the serpent to ancient notions of "wisdom" and "endless duration," he probably referenced the books of Matthew and Numbers. As previously stated, in the book of Matthew, Jesus Christ had declared that men should be wise as serpents. In the book of Numbers, the story of the brazen serpent conveyed the allegory of timeless duration. To heal the ancient Israelites who had suffered from snake bites as a punishment for their sin and unbelief, God had commanded Moses to craft a "fiery" or brass serpent and fasten it to a pole. All the Israelites had to do to receive healing was cast their eyes on the serpent. Later on, many Christians interpreted this story as a foreshadowing of Christ's atonement for mankind—Jesus had died for the sins of the world so that people could look on him to receive eternal life.[48] Just like Moses's brazen serpent which represented extended life, Franklin suggested that the rattlesnake

45. Ibid.
46. Ibid.
47. Kidd, *Benjamin Franklin: The Religious Life*, 5-6.
48. Numbers 21:4-9; John Wesley, *Wesley's Notes on the Bible* (Grand Rapids, MI: Christian Classics Ethereal Library, n.d.), 905.

symbolized the vigor of the American colonies. If Patriots continued to seek what the snake cartoon exemplified, Franklin subtly insinuated, the Revolution would endure.

CONCLUSION

As the Revolutionary War dragged on, Benjamin Franklin's snake cartoon continued to function as America's holy national symbol. In an article published by the *New-Hampshire Gazette* on March 9, 1779, a journalist wrote, "The British Lion, unable to bruise to any purpose the head of the American Serpent is now playing with its tail."[49] Reporting the southern campaign of the British army, this newspaper again represented the colonies as a serpent with biblical connotations. Nevertheless, as the war drew closer to an end, the image of the American serpent dissipated. The bald eagle became the new national emblem in 1782, forever replacing Franklin's political and religious illustration that had gained its prominence during the American Revolution.[50]

The image of the American serpent was first conceived by Franklin in 1754, then contested by Loyalists and Patriots from 1774 to 1779.[51] Yet through this controversy, the cartoon became a political and religious ensign. Loyalists represented the snake as a symbol of evil, while Patriots endowed the snake with honorable qualities. All these allusions came from biblical literature—literature which carried divine clout for justifying the political positions of both parties. By synthesizing Franklin's snake cartoon with religious imagery, the illustration became not just a call for colonial unity, but a holy embodiment of the American Revolution. As *The New-Hampshire Gazette* claimed, Great Britain could not bruise the head of the revolutionary campaign, and similar to Moses lifting the brazen serpent to the ancient Israelites, so too did Patriots raise Franklin's snake during the Revolution, calling for colonists to "JOIN, or DIE."

49. Article, "Extract of a letter from New London, February 27, 1779," *The New-Hampshire Gazette*, March 9, 1779; See also, Article, "Boston, March 4." *The New Jersey Gazette*, March 31, 1779.
50. Lemay, *The Life of Benjamin Franklin*, 650, footnote 34.
51. It seems that 1779 was the last year when Franklin's cartoon was referenced using religious connotations. However, further research could potentially uncover more articles, editorials, epigrams, and poems that connected Franklin's snake to biblical literature. Nonetheless, the controversial climax between Loyalists and Patriots occurred between 1774-1775.

John Adams Lists Abigail's Faults and Abigail Replies!

JOHN L. SMITH, JR.

As a young country lawyer, John Adams thought he seemed to lack focus. "Ballast is what I want, I totter, with every Breeze. My motions are unsteady."[1]

History has shown that he eventually would find his "Ballast" in the steady personage of Abigail (Smith) Adams, his almost-equally-famous better half. Over the course of their fifty-four year long marriage, they exchanged nearly 1,100 letters which chronicled the entire birth of the United States up to John Adams' presidency.[2] Though Abigail was home schooled by her mother, her father, Rev. William Smith of Weymouth, Massachusetts, had a parsonage library of hundreds of books which Abigail had free access to—and which she used. At an early age, Abigail became an avid reader and writer . . . good qualities if you'll be hooking up with John Adams.

But Abigail wasn't the first heart throb of John. That title would have to go to twenty-two year old Hannah Quincy, the witty, flirtatious daughter of Col. Josiah Quincy of Braintree. Hannah was very popular

---

1. "[A Letter to Richard Cranch about Orlinda, a Letter on Employing One's Mind, and Reflections on Procrastination, Genius, Moving the Passions, Cicero as Orator, Milton's Style, &c., October–December 1758.]," Founders Online, National Archives, founders.archives.gov/documents/Adams/02-01-02-0010-0001-0003, accessed June 4, 2018 (original source: *The Adams Papers, Earliest Diary and Autobiography of John Adams, June 1753–April 1754, September 1758–January 1759*, ed. L. H. Butterfield (Cambridge, MA: Harvard University Press, 1966), 69–82).

2. Their famous letters extended from 1763 during their courtship to 1797, the first year of Adams' presidency. Abigail died on October 28, 1818. The last letter Abigail is thought to have written was to their daughter, Louisa Catherine Johnson Adams, dated August 21, 1818. In it, Abigail references Andrew Jackson: "I have just been reading the Life of Genll Jackson—and I admire the Man; as his character is represented—I esteem him, much more highly than I did before, I read it."

within the social club of eligible bachelors that John was part of, which included the future Declaration of Independence signer Robert Treat Paine. But Hannah let it be subtly known that she had found young John Adams equally attractive. In Adams' earliest diary, he scratched the glowing words about Hannah (who he called "Orlinda"), "That Face, those Eyes."[3]

Shy John, however, procrastinated too much and fellow bachelor Bela Lincoln swooped in and married Hannah.[4]

In 1759, about the same time John had first met dazzling Hannah Quincy, he had also met the shy, fifteen-year old Abigail Smith. There reportedly had been no sparks of any kind between the two. In fact, John had found the very young Abigail lacking in "fondness" and "Tenderness."[5]

Pushing ahead just a few years, however, things were different. Hannah was engaged, and Mary Smith, Abigail's oldest sister, was being courted by another social circle bachelor, Richard Cranch. Now the twenty-seven year old John Adams had begun to take notice of the seventeen-year old Abigail Smith, and she of him. Abigail had also changed a lot. She had become poised and self-assured in her intelligence and wit. It showed.

John and Abigail began to see a lot of each other and their affection toward one another started growing more and more. In their early letters to each other, written while John was away on his legal riding circuit, they both referenced classical mythology—something they both were fond of. He would sign his letters "Lysander," who was a heroic Spartan admiral. To her, she was John's "Diana," the Roman goddess of the moon and hunting. In a February 1763 diary entry, John described Abigail (Diana) in a rapid and romantic bevy of Thesaurus words:

> Di. was a constant feast. Tender feeling, sensible, friendly. A friend. Not an imprudent, not an indelicate, not a disagreeable Word or Action. Prudent, modest, delicate, soft, sensible, obliging, active.[6]

3. "A Letter to Richard Cranch about Orlinda."

4. Ironically, Hannah Quincy Lincoln Storer (1736 - 1826) would go on to become an occasional pen pal to Abigail Adams.

5. "The Earliest Diary of John Adams," Introduction, Founders Online, National Archives, founders.archives.gov/documents/Adams/02-01-02-0001, accessed June 6, 2018 (original source: *The Adams Papers, Earliest Diary and Autobiography of John Adams, June 1753–April 1754, September 1758–January 1759, 1–42*).

6. The Diary of John Adams, "Braintree Feby. 1st. 1763. Tuesday.," Founders Online, National Archives, founders.archives.gov/documents/Adams/01-01-02-0008-0001-0001, accessed June 7, 2018 (original source: *The Adams Papers, Diary and Autobiography of John Adams, vol. 1, 1755–1770*, ed. L. H. Butterfield (Cambridge, MA: Harvard University Press, 1961), 233–235).

True, it was no "hot stuff" which sizzled the pages when he described Hannah. But maybe to Congregationalist John Adams, Abigail had so many admirable "sensible" qualities, that she would make a very agreeable consort—and more importantly a "tender . . . friend." There was never any hint that Abigail had felt differently about him—so many of her famous letters to John began with "My Dearest Friend." During their courting years, some of John's romantic letters would even start with "Miss Adorable" or "Ever Dear Diana." They became engaged.

Though the marriage date of October, 1764 had been chosen, John had one more duty he had to attend to before he could get married. Because his circuit law duties took him to so many areas and in contact with so many people—and now that he was getting married on top of it—Adams figured it was smart to get inoculated against smallpox.[7] He spent over forty days in isolation and recovery from April 6 through about May 10, 1764. He read and re-read Abigail's letters to him with "a joyful Heart,"[8] but reminded her of the disinfection treatment that his own letters to her required:

> I have one Request to make, which is that you would be very careful . . . Smoke all the Letters from me, very faithfully, before you, or any of the Family reads them. For, altho I shall never fail to smoke them myself before sealing, Yet I fear the Air of this House will be too much infected.[9]

JOHN TELLS ABIGAIL HER "FAULTS"

By May 7, John was successfully near the end of his smallpox isolation and observation period. With still so much time to think on his hands, he possibly overthought this next action. He had remembered that he'd made a promise to Abigail to give her a list of her faults and defects. Why? So that she could fix them. That gesture might not go over so well in today's world, but to John and Abigail it might've been another indication of becoming closer to each other, now with their wedding

---

7. John Adams was successfully inoculated against smallpox in Boston on April 13, 1764 by Dr. Joseph Warren.

8. John Adams to Abigail Smith, April 17, 1764, Founders Online, National Archives, founders.archives.gov/documents/Adams/04-01-02-0027, accessed June 9, 2018 (original source: *The Adams Papers, Adams Family Correspondence, vol. 1, December 1761–May 1776*, ed. Lyman H. Butterfield (Cambridge, MA: Harvard University Press, 1963), 32–35).

9. "John Adams to Abigail Smith, April 13, 1764," Founders Online, National Archives, founders.archives.gov/documents/Adams/04-01-02-0023, accessed June 4, 2018 (original source: *The Adams Papers, Adams Family Correspondence, vol. 1, December 1761–May 1776*, 28–29). Because germs, viruses and bacteria were still unknown, it was thought that applying smoke to paper could act as a disinfectant and it would be "purified."

just five months away. Maybe. Maybe it was also just John being his obnoxious self.

I promised you, Sometime agone, a Catalogue of your Faults, Imperfections, Defects, or whatever you please to call them. I feel at present, pretty much at Leisure, and in a very suitable Frame of Mind to perform my Promise. But I must caution you, before I proceed to recollect yourself, and instead of being vexed or fretted or thrown into a Passion, to resolve upon a Reformation—for this is my sincere Aim, in laying before you, this Picture of yourself.[10]

1. John told Abigail that she needs to learn to play cards better:

In the first Place, then, give me leave to say, you have been extreamly negligent, in attending so little to Cards. You have very litle Inclination, to that noble and elegant Diversion, and whenever you have taken an Hand you have held it but aukwardly and played it, with a very uncourtly, and indifferent, Air.[11]

2. She blushes at any little thing said:

Another Thing, which ought to be mentioned, and by all means amended, is, the Effect of a Country Life and Education, I mean, a certain Modesty, sensibility, Bashfulness, call it by which of these Names you will, that enkindles Blushes forsooth at every Violation of Decency, in Company, and lays a most insupportable Constraint on the freedom of Behaviour.[12]

3. She always refuses to learn how to sing:

In the Third Place, you could never yet be prevail'd on to learn to sing. This I take very soberly to be an Imperfection of the most moment of any. An Ear for Musick would be a source of much Pleasure, and a Voice and skill, would be a private solitary Amusement, of great Value when no other could be had.[13]

4. She hangs her head like a bent-over cattail with bad posture:

In the Fourth Place you very often hang your Head like a Bulrush. You do not sit, erected as you ought, by which Means, it happens that you appear too short for a Beauty . . .

10. "John Adams to Abigail Smith, May 7, 1764," Founders Online, National Archives, founders.archives.gov/documents/Adams/04-01-02-0035, accessed June 9, 2018 (original source: *The Adams Papers, Adams Family Correspondence, vol. 1, December 1761–May 1776*, 44–46.
11. Ibid.
12. Ibid.
13. Ibid.

but then John kidded with Abigail, writing that her posture was from a result of her reading and thinking too much!

> This Fault is the Effect and Consequence of another, still more inexcusable in a Lady. I mean an Habit of Reading, Writing and Thinking. But both the Cause and the Effect ought to be repented and amended as soon as possible.[14]

5. She sits with her legs crossed (also caused by thinking too much):

> Another Fault, which seems to have been obstinately persisted in, after frequent Remonstrances, Advices and Admonitions of your Friends, is that of sitting with the Leggs across. This ruins the figure and the Air, this injures the Health. And springs I fear from the former source vizt. too much Thinking.[15]

6. She walks "pigeon-toed":

> A sixth Imperfection is that of Walking, with the Toes bending inward. This Imperfection is commonly called Parrot-toed, I think, I know not for what Reason. But it gives an Idea, the reverse of a bold and noble Air, the Reverse of the stately strut . . . .[16]

Adams ended the letter before he committed the worst "Fault"— "that of tedious and excessive Length." Besides, he'd listed all of Abigail's "Spotts" that he could think of. He added that they were not in any particular order: "Have not regarded Order, but have painted them as they arose in my Memory."[17] Super.

ABIGAIL RESPONDS!

It's unclear when John's "list of faults" letter, dated May 7 from Boston, reached Abigail in Weymouth. But because her rapid reply is dated May 9, you can bet she whipped out a pen and paper pretty quickly after reading his letter.

Abigail wrote that she would continue with some of her faults listed until she knew for certain that John considered them a big deal. And that she would certainly continue to be modest and blush:

> I thank you for your Catalogue, but must confess I was so hardned as to read over most of my Faults with as much pleasure, as an other person would have read their perfections. And Lysander must excuse me if I still persist in some of them, at least till I am convinced that an alteration would contribute to his happiness. Especially may I avoid

14. Ibid.
15. Ibid.
16. Ibid.
17. Ibid.

that Freedom of Behaviour which according to the plan given, consists in Voilations of Decency, and which would render me unfit to Herd even with the Brutes. And permit me to tell you Sir, nor disdain to be a learner, that there is such a thing as Modesty without either Hypocricy or Formality.[18]

As for "singing," she advised him to give up on it and don't bring it up again:

> As to a neglect of Singing, that I acknowledg to be a Fault which if posible shall not be complaind of a second time, nor should you have had occasion for it now, if I had not a voice harsh as the screech of a peacock.[19]

She agreed to start standing up straight:

> The Capotal fault shall be rectified, tho not with any hopes of being lookd upon as a Beauty, to appear agreeable in the Eyes of Lysander, has been for Years past, and still is the height of my ambition.

As for sitting cross-legged, she said she thought it was no big deal, but if it made him happy, then she would stop. And she told him to stop thinking about women's legs:

> The 5th fault, will endeavour to amend of it, but you know I think that a gentleman has no business to concern himself about the Leggs of a Lady, for my part I do not apprehend any bad effects from the practise, yet since you desire it, and that you may not for the future trouble Yourself so much about it, will reform.[20]

As for walking "pigeon-toed", she simply wrote one single sentence:

> The sixth and last can be cured only by a Dancing School.

Abigail's letter to John ended by saying "I . . . will not add to my faults" by writing "a tedious Letter." It was not signed as "Diana," but simply: "A Smith."[21] Hmmmmm . . . .
And they got married anyway.

18. "Abigail Smith to John Adams, May 9, 1764," Founders Online, National Archives, founders.archives.gov/documents/Adams/04-01-02-0037, accessed June 9, 2018 (original source: *The Adams Papers, Adams Family Correspondence, vol. 1, December 1761–May 1776*, 46–47).
19. Ibid.
20. Ibid.
21. Ibid

The Conspiracy to Destroy the *Gaspee*

JOHN CONCANNON

With but few exceptions,[1] it has usually been surmised by historians that the 1772 attack on the Royal Navy schooner *Gaspee* was a spontaneous response to the accidental grounding of the King's vessel, allowing its opportunistic destruction by angry Rhode Island colonists. But was this really such a serendipitous event? What is presented here is an examination of the evidence that the entrapment and subsequent destruction of the *Gaspee* had actually been planned well ahead of time.

The highlights of the Gaspee Affair are well known in Rhode Island history, but are rarely acknowledged outside of the state's own borders. On the afternoon of June 9, 1772, while chasing the packet sloop *Hannah* suspected of smuggling, HMS *Gaspee* ran aground at Namquid Point (since called Gaspee Point) just south of Pawtuxet Village in Warwick. That night, Rhode Island patriots led by Providence merchant John Brown assembled at Sabin's Tavern in Providence and from there rowed down the Providence River, attacked, set fire to, and destroyed the *Gaspee*, and wounded her commander.

The British ministry was quite obviously dismayed, considering this an act of treason. Despite a sizable reward having been offered, efforts by the Crown to learn the names of the culprits were unsuccessful. A royally-appointed commission of inquiry was charged with sending any suspects it identified across the Atlantic to England for trial. This bypassing of the established American continental legal system greatly

---

1. Arthur M Schlesinger, Sr. "Political Mobs and the American Revolution, 1765-1776," *Proceedings of the American Philosophical Society*, 90:4 (1955), 245.

alarmed public leaders who perceived it as a direct threat to their rights as British subjects, and created much disaffection towards the Crown.[2]

To assess further threats to their liberties, the Committees of Correspondence were re-established among colonial legislatures. This simple act of unification was among the first steps leading towards the First Continental Congress and, eventually, the Declaration of Independence. In fact, Thomas Jefferson *et al.* included in the Declaration of Independence at least three grievances against King George III that were directly attributable to the Gaspee Affair:[3]

> He has combined, with others, to subject us to a jurisdiction foreign to our Constitution, and unacknowledged by our laws; giving his assent to their acts of pretended legislation. . . . For depriving us, in many cases, of the benefit of trial by jury; For transporting us beyond the seas to be tried for pretended offenses.

The Gaspee Affair also played a very large role in the newspaper coverage which drove the spirit for independence in the years just prior to the Revolution. Accounts of the attack on the *Gaspee* and the subsequent commission of inquiry were front page news, not only within the colonies themselves, but across the Atlantic in Britain. The Gaspee Affair was also the subject of an influential pamphlet, *An Oration on the Beauties of Liberty*, written by Rev. John Allen of Boston. This rebellious reverend decried the actions of an unjust British government, and went so far as to seriously question the legitimacy of the King's rule over America. This sermon was often quoted by John Adams, James Otis, and other Revolutionary leaders, and was among the most published pamphlets during the pre-Revolutionary years.[4]

In general, conspiracy theorists do not fare well in historical circles. But I beg the reader to consider the following essential points:

1. John Brown and other prominent Rhode Island leaders had both the motive and unique tactical resources necessary to entrap and destroy the *Gaspee*.

---

2. Lawrence J. DeVaro, "The Gaspee Affair as Conspiracy," *Rhode Island History*, 32:4 (1973), 107-122. To clarify the subject matter, DeVaro's paper dealt with quite a different topic: fears amongst colonists that there was a conspiracy within British government to use the Gaspee Affair as pretext to further restrict American colonial rights and privileges. As an additional example of this angst among colonists, see some reactions found in John Adams's diary 19, 16 December 1772 to 18 December 1773.
3. Thomas Jefferson, *et al.* Declaration of Independence, July 1776. Many on-line examples give the text with commentary.
4. Steven Park, *The Burning of His Majesty's Schooner* Gaspee: *An Attack on Crown Rule before the Revolution* (Yardley, PA: Westholme, 2016), 77-98.

2. The boats that attacked the *Gaspee* did so in an obviously coordinated fashion from the docks of both Providence and Bristol-Warren, some fourteen miles apart.

3. The timing of the raid occurred during a precise, but narrow window providing tactical advantage.

4. At least some of this group of rebels, including John Brown, were members of the Sons of Liberty and were in direct communication with its leaders.

5. The ship pursued by the *Gaspee* had been previously carrying large sums of gold or cash, an irresistible enticement to follow it into a trap.

6. Loyalist spies had forewarned the Royal Navy that such an attack on the *Gaspee* was being actively planned.

BACKGROUND

Rhode Island and Providence Plantations was founded by religious dissenter Roger Williams et al. in 1636. The Charter granted by King Charles II of Great Britain gave the colony many unique rights, such as independent governance, judiciary, and freedoms of religion.[5] Over the ensuing 136 years to 1772, Rhode Island had become accustomed to functioning as a relatively independent society. However, the rocky land of Rhode Island did not sufficiently support crop or cattle farming to export for profit; its best natural asset was (and is) Narragansett Bay, and maritime trading had become an essential component of the economy. As a tip of the triangular trade, the tiny colony also heavily relied on imports of molasses to distill rum for export.[6] Within this sphere, prominent Rhode Island merchants such as John Brown had also become heavily dependent on the ability to continue their maritime trading and smuggling activities.

To help offset the costs of defending the American Colonies during the French and Indian War, the Crown levied (and later rescinded) a host of taxes on the Colonists: the Stamp Act, Townshend Acts and others, but import duties remained on such items as Sugar and Molasses. Customs regulations also dictated that all such imports be restricted to be within British controlled territory; trading with French or Spanish interests was forbidden. By 1764 the British started to become serious in enforcing these maritime trade laws, much to the resentment of American colonists.

---

5. The complete charter is presented on-line by the Rhode Island Secretary of State: sos.ri.gov/divisions/Civics-And-Education/charter-1663. It was still the governing document for the State of Rhode Island until 1843, after the Dorr Rebellion.
6. For more information about the Triangular Trade see Stanley Lemons, "Rhode Island and the Slave Trade," *Rhode Island History*, 60:4 (2002), 95-104.

Nick Bunker, writing from the British perspective in his book *An Empire on the Edge*, relates that, "Of all the American colonies, Rhode Island was the freest, the most radical, and the one least inclined to follow royal instructions. And so it was here that the countdown to war began."[7]

THE GASPEE

His Majesty's schooner *Gaspee* was representative of a class of relatively small and fast revenue ships that the Royal Navy purchased from various American shipbuilders to enforce maritime law and trade regulations along the East coast. After an extended stint patrolling the Chesapeake Bay area [8] she took up station in Newport in February 1772 and lost no time in making her presence known by stopping, searching, and seizing ships that were suspected of carrying illicit or untaxed goods. The schooner's commander, Lt. William Dudingston, and his crew were considered particularly heavy-handed in performing their duties, plundering Rhode Island ships and cargos, and stealing cattle and supplies from coastal communities up and down Narragansett Bay. The *Gaspee* stopped a sloop found to be carrying rum, the *Gaspee's* crew beat up the vessel's captain, and the captured vessel and cargo were sent up to Boston to be sold off as a customs prize. Local citizens were incensed, a lawsuit was initiated for illegal seizure, and a warrant was issued for Dudingston's arrest.[9]

NEW INSIGHTS ON THE TIMING OF THE ATTACK

John Brown of Providence had been amassing a fortune in the sea trade, ship-building, privateering, and distilling.[10] But with the recent arrival of British revenue enforcement ships creating a stranglehold to their free enterprise, he and others in the sea-mercantile circles were only too willing to take action. And as it turns out, he also had personal experience with just how to lure the *Gaspee* to its demise.

---

7. Nick Bunker, *An Empire on the Edge* (London: Random House, 2014), 49.

8. Davis Bevan to the *Providence Gazette*, July 15, 1772, in *The Bridge* (historical community newspaper of Pawtuxet Village), 42:1 (Spring 2015), 15.

9. Samuel W. Bryant, "Rhode Island Justice—1772 Vintage," *Rhode Island History*, 26:3, (1967), 65-71.

10. It must be noted that John Brown also took part in, and defended the detestable slave trade, however his own business ventures at the time were usually more indirectly related, *e.g.*, distillery operations. As stated in a *Providence Journal* editorial of October 11, 2017, p.A14, "Vandals attack Columbus," "Any fair study, of course, would look at historical figures in the context of their times, rather than entirely divorced from the world in which they lived."

According to Moses Brown's diary,[11] Moses and his older brother John Brown were grounded near Namquid Point while they were on a sloop bound for Philadelphia on June 8, 1760:

> at half after 7 PM, Capt Douglas at the helm, myself and passengers below, run aground on the sunken rocks of off the rocks there lay, the passengers gone ashore to patuxet till half after 3 morning of the 9th

The fact that John Brown had the experience of having run aground near Namquid Point certainly gave him time to ponder his fate, observe the actions of the tide and currents, and familiarize himself with the treacherous area during the exact same conditions that would prevail precisely twelve years later.

Note that the attack on the *Gaspee* did not occur immediately after the ship's arrival in Narragansett Bay in January; Rhode Island citizens had four to five months to plan an appropriate response. The attack was likely not some sudden defensive reaction by colonists; and in fact, we know that the attack on the *Gaspee* occurred during what would be the best possible tactical circumstances.

The sandbar on which the *Gaspee* grounded at about 3 PM was obscured by the high tide that was just starting to recede. This would effectively trap the schooner for at least the twelve hours until at least the next high tide which would not occur until around 3 AM the following morning. This left enough time for Rhode Island Colonists to assemble the attack force which followed.

A most important piece of evidence is that the timing of the tides suitable to attract and ground the *Gaspee* were also perfect to provide the cover of darkness for the ensuing skirmish.[12] John Brown and Abra-

---

11. Moses Brown. "Diary. Journal of voyage to Philadelphia, 1760." Moses Brown's papers (Misc. MSS. I, 8). SS, Series II: Subject Files, Box 3, folder 62, Rhode Island Historical Society Library. I am indebted to the late *Gaspee* historical researcher Leonard Bucklin, Esq. for rediscovering this passage.

12. For more information on this tactical planning of the attack on the *Gaspee*, and to confirm the astronomical data likely used, one can consult any of a variety of sources for Pawtuxet Cove (Latitude +41.7617, Longitude -71.3883) which is just north of Gaspee Point.

Tuesday, June 9, 1772 to Wednesday, June 10, 1772 Local Standard Time

Date/Day	High Tide/Ht.	Low Tide/Ht.	Moonset	Moon Phase
06/09/1772	2:16 PM 5.1 ft.	8:03 PM 0.6 ft	12:47 AM	Waxing gibbous 63%
06/10/1772	2:39 AM 4.5 ft.	8:07 AM 0.2 ft		

Here, we consulted the Tide Graph app (www.tidegraph.com) and confirmed this tide data with the NOAA (tidesandcurrents.noaa.gov). Moon data was confirmed using data from US Naval Observatory Astronomical Applications Department (aa.usno.navy.mil/). All three sources make available such astronomical data even at times in centuries long past. Bryan Aamot of Brainware, LLC, developer of the TideGraph, confirmed that the

ham Whipple, who together led the raid, attacked at about 12:45 AM on June 10, which is exactly the time of the setting of the moon, thus providing the cover of darkness. Of course, this timing would also ensure that most of the crew of the *Gaspee* was sound asleep as the longboats approached. The *Gaspee* grounded on a Tuesday afternoon and attacked the following night, times not interfering with those who would object to violence on the Sabbath. Even more conveniently, it was scheduled as a militia training day with plenty of young men nearby the docks area of Providence. Some businesses had closed early, and other meetings were cancelled.[13]

For the necessary tide and moon predictions, John Brown had at hand his brother Joseph Brown, a well-respected natural philosopher (the word "scientist" was not coined until 1834) who could have competently provided the information necessary to plan such an attack. Joseph had engineered the Hope Furnace ironworks and other factories for the Brown family enterprise, and was a leading architect of the city, whose works included the First Baptist Church, the Market House, and mansions for himself and his brother. Most pointedly, Joseph Brown had been an integral part of the small group of Rhode Island men who took exacting astronomical measurements of the transit of Venus across the Sun in 1769.[14]

app does not present Eastern Daylight Savings Time in data before EDT was first enacted in 1918, and is therefore correct for 1772 (personal e-mail to the author). Slight adjustments must be made in that the concept of time zones was not in use until 1888, something necessitated by the advent of relatively fast rail trains requiring a standard time reference. The apparent local time (Local Solar Time) then in common use in Rhode Island in 1772 would have been approximately four minutes later than the calculated times and has been adjusted in the table above. It is noteworthy that the burning of the *Gaspee* is one of the very few incidents in American history that can be analyzed using such data as presented here.

13. The logbook of the St. John's Masonic Lodge in Providence contained an entry to the effect that the meeting that night of June 9, 1772 had been cancelled due to "pressing business" in Providence. Unfortunately, the records were severely damaged, perhaps by the Great Gale of 1815 or other calamity after the lodge moved to what is now the Market House in central Providence. Personal communication to the author (2017) by David C. Lavery, Right Worshipful Grand Historian, Masonic Grand Lodge of Rhode Island, *et al.*

14. Benjamin West, *An Account of the Observation of Venus Upon the Sun, the Third Day of June, 1769, at Providence, in New-England. With some Account of the Use of those Observations* (Providence, John Carter Press, 1769).

The data for the tides and moon confirm later testimony given about the raid.[15] Witnesses also stated that the *Gaspee* was set afire some three hours after the attack had commenced, or just before dawn. According to our astronomical sources (see endnotes) the "crack of dawn" or civil twilight began at 3:36 AM, with sunrise scheduled at 4:10 AM. There was no Daylight Savings Time in the eighteenth century, so this sunrise would have been equivalent to a more familiar 5:10 AM EDT we would be experiencing in modern times.

Detailed weather data recorded by the noted Rhode Island Rev. Ezra Stiles has been recently uncovered from archival files at the National Oceanic and Atmospheric Administration center by Adam Blumenthal of Brown University.[16] Near the time of the attack on June 9, 1772 winds were from the southeast, the weather was fair, and the temperature was a somewhat tolerable 44 degrees. Some variance may be assumed in that Stiles was usually recording observations in Newport, closer to the ocean, and was using a Benjamin Franklin thermometer of unknown calibration. But since the *Hannah* (the boat which lured the *Gaspee* aground) had just returned from New York, it brought back predictions of this fair weather that would typically follow a ship coming from the southwest. These were all favorable conditions in which to conduct the attack.

Given the capabilities of the men who planned the raid it is not surprising that it occurred within such a perfectly-timed scenario. And as noted before, John Brown had the personal experience of having run aground on Namquid Point, knew the area well, and had the logistical assets to assemble the raiding parties. His brother Joseph Brown had the astronomical wherewithal to provide the data necessary in planning the attack. Abraham Whipple's brilliance as a tactical commander was

15. Ephraim Bowen, in his account of the incident, stated that when the *Gaspee* ran aground around 3 PM, the tide was ebbing (progressing from high tide to low tide) and that John Brown rightly concluded that the ship would remain aground until at least well after mid-night. Ephraim Bowen, *An Account of the Capture and Burning of the British Schooner "GASPEE,"* broadside (Providence: B. Cranston & Co, 1839). See corrected version at gaspee.org/Bowen.html. As to the moonlight present, Rhode Island Deputy Governor Darius Sessions testified that while the moon had shone very brightly at 9 PM, his later deposition of the *Gaspee* crewmen affirmed that by the time of the initial attack at around 12:45 AM the moon had just set and it was dark. Samuel W. Bryant, "HMS *Gaspee* —The Court Martial," *Rhode Island History*, 23:3, (1966), 65-72.

16. Adam Blumenthal, personal e-mail to the author, March 2017. Mr. Blumenthal is the Virtual Reality Artist in Residence at the Granoff Center of the Creative Arts at Brown University. He is currently developing a Virtual Reality experience on the Gaspee Affair.

later proven, even more so, when during the Revolution he captured over ten British prize ships at once by posing as a fellow British ship escorting the hapless convoy, but then proceeded to secretively take over their commands one by one.[17]

So as it turns out, the timing of the tides and moon were perfect for the purpose of the attack which destroyed the *Gaspee*. An afternoon high tide followed by little or no moonlight in the early morning hours would have been in conjunction on less than seven percent of the dates from May through July, 1772. Granted that most experienced boat captains of the time would have been able to predict tides and moonset days ahead of time, but the precision of the window for the trap and subsequent attack on the *Gaspee* points to high-grade intelligence for not only the tides and moon far in advance, but also the location, day of the week, absence of a pilot, weather predictions, and baiting the chase. It was indeed a complex plan. One can certainly suspect that the day, time, and course of the *Hannah* when she left the docks of Newport for Providence were deliberately chosen well ahead of time for just the purpose for which she became famous—the destruction of the *Gaspee*.

THE CHASE

D. K. Abbass, of the Rhode Island Marine Archaeology Project uncovered an interesting reason why Dudingston may have been so hot to give chase to the *Hannah*:

> . . . in the month before the *Gaspee* chased the *Hannah* up the river, the *Hannah* had at least twice been carrying large amounts of cash, not just rum and other local merchandise. It is possible that Dudingston knew about the cash, and that could have been incentive enough for him to risk crossing those shallows.[18]

Of course, it is also quite probable that this information was leaked to Dudingston. As an officer in the Royal Navy he was also charged with enforcing maritime trade laws, and would have been seeking a hefty cut of whatever could be claimed as a customs enforcement prize.

---

17. Sally Wilson, "Who was Commodore Whipple?" in *Revolutionary Portraits: People, Places and Events from Rhode Island's Historic Past*, collected by the Rhode Island Short Story Club (Providence: Rhode Island Bicentennial Foundation, 1976), 6-15. See also Sheldon S. Cohen, *Commodore Abraham Whipple of the Continental Navy* (Gainesville: University Press of Florida, 2010), 98-104.

18. D. K. Abbass, "What's the *Gaspee* and What's Not, What's Passé and What's Hot, and Why the Public Should Care," paper presented at the 50th Anniversary Gaspee Days Maritime History Symposium, May 29, 2015.

In either event, the British ship was apparently all too easy to lure. Nautical custom at the time was for civilian boats to lower their flags in deference when passing by a vessel of the Royal Navy. The haughty nature of the *Gaspee*'s commander demanded its observance, and when the *Hannah* did not lower its flag as it passed, the chase was on.

Unlike native Rhode Island mariners, Lieutenant Dudingston had little, if any, familiarity with the waters in upper Narragansett Bay. Per standard practice, the *Gaspee* for its first few months in Rhode Island had taken on a harbor pilot knowledgeable of the local hazards involved in navigation, but we have no record of Dudingston's ship having previously traveled further up the Bay into the Providence River which ultimately trapped him. It is curious that the pilot, one Sylvanius Daggett, was not on board at the time of the *Gaspee*'s demise; he had been transferred six weeks earlier to HMS *Beaver* which was sailing Rhode Island coastal waters for the same purposes as the *Gaspee*. Daggett's transfer off of the *Gaspee* is an item of intelligence that could be easily confirmed by John Brown and his associates who had ships in the Newport area. In fact, some local inhabitants later caught up with Daggett shortly after the attack, and according to the *Providence Gazette* of June 13, 1772:

> We hear that one Daggett, belonging to the Vineyard, who had served the aforementioned schooner, as a pilot, but at the time of her being destroyed, was on board the *Beaver* sloop of war, on going ashore a few days since, at Narragansett, to a sheep-shearing, was seized by the company, who cut off his hair, and performed to him the operation of shearing, in such a manner, that his ears and nose were in imminent danger.

On the other hand, the *Hannah*'s Capt. Benjamin Lindsey had over the nine years of experience sailing passenger and cargo vessels between Newport and Providence, and had become very well acquainted with the waters of Narragansett Bay. He had been at times employed by John Brown and would have undoubtedly been involved in the planning to trap the *Gaspee*. Coastal transport packets such as the *Hannah* required the ability to get close-in to land in shallow waters and were appropriately designed with a shallow draft (how deeply the ship or boat sits into the water). In contrast, the two-masted *Gaspee* had a multitude of responsibilities such as patrolling the rich fishing grounds of the Grand Banks, requiring stability in rough, open waters, and thus a much deeper keel and draft.

As the chase arrived at Namquid Point, the *Hannah* easily skidded over the submerged sandbar. Captain Lindsey then turned slightly into the cove just beyond the Point and feigned to furl his sails, as if confused. Dudingston and the *Gaspee* were suckered into following, hellbent on catching their prey, and ran hard aground. The schooner would be stuck for at least the next twelve hours, long enough to set the stage for the attack that would ensue.

After parting shots were exchanged (it has been reported that the crew of the *Hannah* mooned that of the *Gaspee*),[19] Lindsey sailed back to Providence, arriving later that afternoon and docking as usual at Fenner's Wharf, directly opposite Sabin's Tavern, wherein the people met, plotted, and departed on their subsequent mission to attack the *Gaspee*. If not actually in the employ of John Brown, Lindsey must have had a close working relationship, for he immediately reported the plight of the *Gaspee* directly to him. Brown then set off his plan to attract others who would join in destroying the British ship; he was not wanting for volunteers.

By the call of a drummer sent out to proclaim the news, John Brown was able to quickly assemble a party of at least sixty-four men from the immediate Providence dock areas to join in the attack, an attack which could have resulted in them all being hanged if caught. Later testimony tells that many of these men were dressed in well-tailored clothing which suggested their belonging to the merchant class. It is also noteworthy that an experienced sea captain was placed in charge of each of the eight attacking longboats. This tactical force was too impressive to have been haphazardly recruited.

Word of the plans must also have been quickly sent fourteen miles south to the seafaring town of Bristol. Whether traveling by horse or by boat, the messenger would have spent at least an hour in transit. There, fellow merchant Capt. Simeon Potter was also able to muster enough men for at least one other longboat to join in the attack, providing valuable situational intelligence as they rowed up the bay past the stranded schooner, and later meeting up with the attacking boats from Providence.[20] It is very doubtful that a boat could be arranged, crewed, and imbedded into the raid in such a short time without considerable preplanning.

Unlike the genteel style of clothing worn by the crews from Providence, oral traditions indicate that the folks from the Bristol and nearby

---

19. "The Destruction of the *Gaspee*," *Saturday Evening Post*, August 22, 1829, VIII: 421. This is a fine example of the gentility of early nineteenth century style prose: "*Hannah's* crew shouted with exultation, and some few gave a parting salutation, with their faces to the opposite point of the compass, from those with whom they were parting company."
20. Revolutionary War Pension File, #S21404, for Ezra Ormsbee, submitted August 24, 1833.

Warren dockside area dressed as Narragansett Indians.[21] Along the way from Bristol, Captain Potter pressed into the raid one Aaron Briggs, an "indentured servant" (slave) from Prudence Island.[22] Why bother? Briggs happened to be of mixed Narragansett Indian and African American blood (at the time referred to as Mustee), and a perfect candidate to further the Bristol crew's ruse disguised as Indians. This is also the likely reason that the teenaged Briggs was deliberately seated next to the wounded Lt. Dudingston when the he was rowed ashore after the attack.

THE SONS OF LIBERTY

Revolutionary furor had been brewing in the American colonies since before the Stamp Acts in 1764, and no less so in Rhode Island, where the profitable mercantile shipping business had become particularly sensitive to British trade and taxation laws. The Sons of Liberty were noted for acts of violent intimidation, such as the tarring and feathering of tax collectors,[23] however in general they were well-controlled in their mob activities by leadership from men of means and property. Many early members were newspaper publishers, booksellers, and lawyers who had a vested interest in avoiding the Stamp Act that increased the price on their products. But the enthusiasm of the group seems to have been based more on principles of preserving colonial rights than on protecting economic interests, though during that time the two concepts were very much intertwined.

After repeal of the Stamp Act, the Sons of Liberty held large, celebratory reunions, and members gradually adopted elements of Revolutionary fervor. The concept took hold in urban centers within all thirteen colonies, and branches of the Sons of Liberty did indeed plant

21. Wilfred H. Munro, *The History of Bristol, RI—The Story of Mount Hope Lands* (Providence, 1860). See excerpted Gaspee Song at www.gaspee.org/Song.html. Note that the lyrics can be best sung to the music of *Yankee Doodle*, a common tune for derisive lyrics, even before the Revolution.

22. William R. Staples, *The Documentary History of the Destruction of the* Gaspee (Providence: Knowles, Rose & Anthony, 1845). See further discussion at Carolyn Fluehr-Lobban, "Aaron Briggs, African-American Patriot in the Gaspee Affair—His Complex Struggle for Freedom," *The Bridge* (historical community newspaper of Pawtuxet Village), 38:1 (Spring 2011), 1.

23. The Sons of Liberty have been long victims of identity theft. Even during the Revolution some imitation groups sprung up under the guise of Sons of Liberty as scams to steal money from people. A recent internet search confirms that the term "Sons of Liberty" is in the public domain. Besides the new Sons of Liberty brewery and distillery within Rhode Island, several web sites usurp the name in various forms—usually right wing or religious fundamentalist groups, particularly those with an anti-taxation theme. None can be traced legitimately to the original Sons of Liberty.

Liberty Trees in both Providence[24] and Newport;[25] John Brown is known to have been a member.[26]

As they continued their leadership in the immediate pre-Revolutionary years, publishers slanted news coverage in ways that favored the cause of independence. Men like Samuel Adams used the Sons of Liberty as cover to incite further rebellion against the British, annually commemorated the Boston Massacre,[27] and helped incite the Boston Tea Party, albeit some eighteen months after the burning of the *Gaspee*.

A mere five weeks after the attack (July 18, 1772) at least one London newspaper reflected British anxiety about this resurgence of the Sons of Liberty and the destruction the *Gaspee*:[28]

> The conduct of Rhode Islanders, on the foregoing occasion, it is thought, will be productive of much disturbance in America. If our government resents it with the spirit they ought we shall have fresh exclamations from the sons of liberty beyond the Atlantic; and if they do not, the colonies are immediately discharged from their dependence upon England.

Whatever the economic incentives John Brown and his compatriots harbored for ridding Narragansett Bay of the *Gaspee*, these leaders of Rhode Island society most likely held similarly principled distain for the increasingly oppressive control by British colonial policy. Arthur M. Schlesinger, Sr.[29] noted that an

> Outstanding example of premeditated lawlessness was the burning of the British revenue schooner Gaspee near Providence, Rhode Island, at midnight of June 9, 1772. John Brown, one of the town's leading merchants, not only organized the destruction ahead of time but personally took part in it.

24. Edward Field, ed., "Events Preceding the Outbreak of the Revolution," *Manual of the Rhode Island Society of the Sons of the American Revolution, 1893-1899* (Central Falls, RI: Freeman & Sons, 1900), 163.
25. "Original Deed of the Newport (RI) Liberty Tree," *The Historical Magazine, and Notes and Queries Concerning the Antiquities, History and Biography of America*, IV: 2 (Morrisania, NY, Henry B. Dawson, 1868), 91.
26. David S. Lovejoy, *Rhode Island Politics and the American Revolution, 1760- 1776* (Providence: Brown University Press, 1969), 120-121.
27. *American Military History Podcast*, Episode 02: "Boston Massacre Fallout, Gaspee Affair, and the Boston Tea Party", Jul 15, 2015, /www.youtube.com/watch?v=3Ew7WwZfU-0&t=627s.
28. As republished news from London in the *Virginia Gazette*, October 15, 1772, page 1, column 1.
29. Schlesinger, "Political Mobs and the American Revolution", 245.

We also know that Deputy Governor Darius Sessions, Chief Justice Stephen Hopkins, former Chief Justice John Cole, and Moses Brown all sought urgent advice from Bostonian Samuel Adams shortly after the British announced their investigatory response to the destruction of the *Gaspee*.[30] But why should these prominent, self-directed men from Rhode Island bother at all to ask advice from a rabble-rouser in neighboring Massachusetts? It is very likely because he was the pre-eminent leader within the Sons of Liberty and quite possibly involved in any plans to disrupt British control within nearby colonies. He and other leaders of the independence movement were known to be looking for ways to incite their fellow colonists against the British, and the *Gaspee* represented the continued taxation and oppression by the Crown against Americans.

In his letters of reply to Sessions, Adams seemed to be familiar with events, and did not express any misgivings about the incident. Of the men who corresponded with Adams, it can be shown that Darius Sessions went on to deliberately obstruct the royally-appointed commission of inquiry into the destruction of the *Gaspee*.[31] Chief Justice Hopkins later declared that Rhode Island courts would not cooperate with the Gaspee investigatory commission by refusing to hand over any citizen so-indicted to the British Admiralty.[32] John Cole was a lawyer present at the Sabin Tavern during the planning of the attack, may well have participated in it, and later perjured himself before the Gaspee commission by denying any knowledge of such events.[33] As previously discussed, Moses Brown's two brothers, John and Joseph, are figured to have led in planning the attack. It can be reasonably extrapolated that all of these same gentlemen could have been involved in the plans well ahead of time, and were probably in correspondence with

30. Darius Sessions *et al.* to Samuel Adams, December 25, 1772, in S. A. Wells, *Samuel Adams and the American Revolution*, manuscript in the Lenox Library, Lenox, MA, Vol. I., 363-365 and 370-371.
31. Richard M. Deasy, Introduction to the 1990 republication of William R. Staples *Documentary History of the Destruction of the* Gaspee (Providence: RI Publications Society, 1990), xxix. It should be noted that Staple's work was originally serialized in 1845 editions of the *Providence Journal*. For the sake of clarity, all references to Staple's *Destruction of the* Gaspee herein apply to the more easily found, and more complete 1990 republication.
32. This according to Ezra Stiles in his diary entry for January 20, 1773 and his letter to Elihu Spencer of February 16, 1773, in *The Literary Diary of Ezra Stiles*, ed. Franklin Bowditch Dexter, 3 vols. (New York: Charles Scribner's Sons. 1901), 1:337, 349.
33. "Chief Justice John Cole (1715-1777)", *Gaspee Virtual Archives*, gaspee.org/John-ColeEsq.htm.

Samuel Adams and men of like ilk well before the actual raid on the *Gaspee*.[34] Historian John C. Miller wrote:[35]

> It was well known that the Sons of Liberty regarded the Gaspee affair as a test case. . . . Certainly, the failure of the British government to punish the scuttlers of the Gaspee was a direct encouragement to Bostonians to stage the Tea Party.

Finally, as to motives for the attack, it was not likely some sudden ill thought out act of desperation to protect their molasses and rum smuggling. John Brown, Abraham Whipple, and others on the team undoubtedly foresaw that the British would react to any attack by filling Narragansett Bay with yet more ships to stranglehold their enterprises. Rather, the Sons of Liberty quite likely directed the attack as a strategic challenge to British authority in the colonies. The cited correspondence between the leading men in Rhode Island and Sam Adams give credence to such a "conspiracy theory."

LOCAL INTELLIGENCE

It was men like John Brown from the ranks of the sea-faring culture of Rhode Island who were most interested in removing the obnoxious vessel plying the waters of Narragansett Bay. By March, Brown and his compatriots prevailed upon Deputy Governor Darius Sessions, seated in Providence, to present their complaints to Gov. Joseph Wanton, then seated in the colonial capital of Newport.[36] This led to a series of heated letters between Governor Wanton and Lieutenant Dudingston, along with his superior officer, Adm. John Montagu, Commander of the Royal Navy for the northeast American coast. It is during this correspondence that Admiral Montagu let slip to Governor Wanton some interesting naval intelligence:[37]

34. We also have some "hard" evidence that the Sons of Liberty were directly involved in the raid on the *Gaspee*. The historical marker c. 1891 for the original site of the Sabin Tavern reads as follows:

SONS OF LIBERTY—

UPON THIS CORNER STOOD THE SABIN TAVERN IN WHICH ON THE EVENING OF JUNE 9TH 1772 THE PARTY MET AND ORGANIZED TO DESTROY H.R.M. SCHOONER GASPEE IN THE DESTRUCTION OF WHICH WAS SHED THE FIRST BLOOD IN THE AMERICAN REVOLUTION

Many elder statesmen alive at the time of the demolition of the Sabin Tavern undoubtedly knew some of men who participated in the raid; the last survivor was Col. Ephraim Bowen who died in 1841. It therefore seems logical that the plaque truly acknowledges the Sons of Liberty as having had a hand in the plot to destroy the *Gaspee*.

35. John C. Miller, *Origins of the American Revolution* (Boston: Little, Brown and Company, 1943), 327, 328.

36. Staples, *The Documentary History of the Destruction of the* Gaspee, 3.

37. *Ibid*, 6.

BOSTON, 6th April, 1772

... I am also informed, the people of Newport talk of fitting out an armed vessel to rescue any vessel the King's schooner may take carrying on an illicit trade. Let them be cautious what they do; for as sure as they attempt it, and any of them are taken, I will hang them as pirates.

Note also that Admiral Montagu does not mention here either the *Beaver*, a larger and more heavily armed brig, or the *Swan*, an armed sloop, as being the target of the Colonists' plot. Both ships were also patrolling the waters around Newport at the time for the same reasons. He mentions only the "King's schooner," which applies only to the *Gaspee*. Governor Wanton was perturbed at the contemptuous attitude these British officials had for the Colony of Rhode Island, and replied in kind to Montagu:[38]

RHODE ISLAND, May 8, 1772

... The information you have received "that the people of Newport talked of fitting out an armed vessel to rescue any vessel the King's schooner might take carrying on an illicit trade," you may be assured is without foundation, and a scandalous imposition, for upon inquiring into this matter, I cannot find that any such design was ever made, or so much as talked of, and, therefore, I hope you will not hang any of his Majesty's subjects belonging to his colony upon such false information.

Whatever the leanings of Governor Wanton, it's obvious that he would have little direct information about any such plot. He presided in Newport, some thirty miles south of Providence where the actual plotting would later be made to rid Rhode Island of the *Gaspee*. The citizens of Providence, on the other hand, were more concerned with ensuring the freedoms of its maritime trade (and smuggling), on which so much of its burgeoning economy depended.

There is yet more evidence that a plot had been afoot to destroy the *Gaspee* in the letter from Newport tax collector Charles Dudley to Admiral Montagu written a month after the attack. In his letter Dudley correctly predicted that the Rhode Island government would interfere with any investigation.[39]

I shall first of all premise that the Attack upon the *Gaspee* was not the effect of sudden Passion & forethought: her local circumstances at the time she was burnt did not raise the first emotion to that enormous act, it had been long determined she should be destroyed . . . Evidence

38. *Ibid*, 7.
39. *Ibid*, 132.

of respectable men will not be wanting to prove that this insult on His Majesty's Crown & Dignity was begun in the most public & open manner, nor will you want good Testimony to shew that the intention was spoke of many days before the Event. If Admiral Montagu will interest himself in promoting an inquiry into these things: not under the influence of a Governor & Company of Rhode Island but under the high Authority of a British Senate.

CONCLUSION

Given the preponderance of evidence presented, it is most likely that the burning of the *Gaspee* was part of a well-planned and executed trap conceived by John Brown, Abraham Whipple, and numerous others several weeks beforehand. The significance of this act cannot be underestimated, for rather than the attack on the *Gaspee* being simply a footnote in history, it was in fact a conspiracy by colonists to strike America's "First Blow for Freedom."[40]

The Gaspee Affair contributed directly to the unification movement of all the colonies, which, when formally united, became the United States of America. One can forever argue the point of which colonial fracas against the British was the earliest. But as to the first shot, it depends on when you define the "start" of the Revolution. We're not talking here of formal armed Revolution we will happily cede that to Lexington and Concord. We're talking instead about the ideological revolution for independence from Great Britain, and idea nourished by British attempts to subvert the liberties long cherished by American colonists. John Adams said, "The Revolution was effected before the War commenced. The Revolution was in the minds and hearts of the people."[41]

40. Trademark of the Gaspee Days Committee. "First Blow for Freedom" was embodied on Gaspee commemorative teacups sold in Providence around the time of the 1875-1876 American Centennial. But sadly, Rhode Island had completely forgotten to acknowledge the earlier 1872 centennial of the burning of the *Gaspee*. *Chicago Tribune*, April 23, 1875, p4, col. 5.
41. John Adams to Hezekiah Niles, February 13, 1818. Adams Papers, *Founders Online*, National Archives.

The "Parson's Cause:" Thomas Jefferson's Teacher, Patrick Henry, and Religious Freedom

✿ JOHN GRADY ✿

As Tidewater lands played out, exhausted from repeated tobacco plantings, or were encumbered by inheritance, the established church moved with young planters like Peter Jefferson into the Piedmont. One hundred thirty miles from the colonial capital Williamsburg and "planted close under the southwest mountains," James Maury preached the gospel of the Church of England in the sprawling Fredericksville Parish. He was a graduate of the College of William and Mary, a tutor for a time in Williamsburg, and was sent for further ecclesiastical study in Great Britain on the recommendation of the politically powerful (when it came to Anglican prerogatives in Virginia) James Blair. Blair was the Bishop of London's commissary—agent of the church's interests—in the colony.[1]

---

1. Ann Maury, *Memoirs of a Huguenot Family, Translated and Compiled from the Original Autobiography of the Rev. James Fontaine and Other Family Manuscripts, Comprising an Original Journal of Travels in Virginia, New York, etc., in 1715 and 1716* (New York: George P. Putnam, 1853; 2nd ed., 1872). James Fontaine, *A Tale of the Huguenots; or, Memoirs of a French Refugee Family*, trans. and comp. Ann Maury (New York: John S. Taylor, 1838); reprinted in a collection of Maury material as *Memoirs of a Huguenot Family* (Baltimore: Genealogical, 1973), 271-87; Virginius Dabney, *Virginia: The New Dominion* (Garden City, N.Y.: Doubleday, 1971), 73–77; Carl Bridenbaugh, *Seat of Empire: The Political Role of Eighteenth Century Williamsburg* (Williamsburg, VA.: Colonial Williamsburg Foundation, 1963), 27; John Hammond Moore, *Albemarle: Jefferson's County, 1727–1976* (Charlottesville: Univ. Press of Virginia for the Albemarle County Historical Society, 1976), 8; David Hackett Fischer and James C. Kelly, *Bound Away: Virginia and the Western Movement* (Charlottesville: Univ. Press of Virginia, 2000), 98–103; Henry Mayer, *A Son of Thunder: Patrick Henry and the American Revolution* (New York: Grove, 1991), 19–21; D. W. Meinig, *The Shaping of America: Atlantic America, 1492–1800* (New Haven, CT: Yale Uni-

Maury found the reaches of Virginia vexing service in the work of the Lord. The traveling over the primitive roads and traces of the Piedmont and through the slippery mountain passes "to baptize & marry & bury" took its toll. He lamented that his "Intervals of Leisure & Repose are as short, as they are rare."[2]

To supplement his income under laws covering the church, James Maury founded a school, just as his Huguenot refugee grandfather in Dublin had done. He enrolled his own son; other students included Peter Jefferson's son Thomas, who became one of the younger Maury's closest boyhood friends, Dabney Carr, later Jefferson's brother-in-law, John Walker, who would join Jefferson at William and Mary, and James Madison, a cousin of the president with the same name and decades later the first Anglican bishop of Virginia.[3]

"In a log house below the Southwest Mountains," Jefferson and other students "received at an impressionable age personal instruction from a sound scholar who was aware of the niceties of language and the beauties of literature." Jefferson, who spent two years living with the Maurys before enrolling at William and Mary College, recalled the reverend as "a correct classical scholar" who impressed upon him the value of literature and the study of nature. What Jefferson didn't write was how Maury influenced his thinking on the proper place for the church and the state. It wouldn't be in the clergyman's favor. The same could be said about his classmate James Madison.[4]

James Maury was a cleric, educator, and pathfinder in faith and knowledge, but he also was very much a man of his time and place. Like his neighbors and in-laws, he was a land speculator. Like his parishioners, he invested his family's financial future. All had been bitten by the "grab, grab, grab" reality of the colony's land policy, forming themselves into the Loyal (Land) Company in 1749. It was a gamble—on securing for themselves and posterity an even bigger future; buying

versity Press, 1983), 1:154; Clifford Dowdey, *The Virginia Dynasties* (New York: Little, Brown, 1969), 309; Fairfax Harrison, *Landmarks of Old Prince William*, 2 vols. (Richmond: privately printed, 1924), 1:133, 166, 233; Bishop William Meade, *Old Churches, Ministers, and Families of Virginia* (Philadelphia: J. B. Lippincott, 1861), 1:315; Genealogical Account, *Virginia. Magazine* 11 (1901): 289–304; Richard L. Maury, *The Huguenots in Virginia* (Richmond: Huguenot Society of America, n.d.), 113.

2. Letters of Rev. James Maury quoted in Fontaine, *Tale*, and specifically on 379.

3. Ibid.

4. Letters of Rev. James Maury as quoted in Fontaine, *Tale*, 379; Dowdey, *Dynasties*, 309; Thomas Jefferson Randolph, ed., *Memoir, Correspondence, and Miscellanies from the Papers of Thomas Jefferson* (Charlottesville, Va.: F. Carr, 1829), 1:1.

and selling far distant forests, water rights to creeks, runs, and rivers they had never seen on the western side of the mountains they had rarely if ever crossed.[5]

Although he was proficient in Greek and Latin, Maury belittled the teaching of "dead languages." He wrote that most of his charges "ought to be instructed as soon as possible in the most necessary branches of useful, practical knowledge" on running their holdings. These boys needed the skills and the discipline to record their future transactions down to the Daybook penny: the number, gender, age, and health of their slaves; livestock births and sales; dates of harrowing, planting, and harvesting—with volumes counted; and weather on all days, changes noted in the course of a day—sunny dawn, mild; sleet in the afternoon.[6]

Being a pastor and an educator in a county with frontier tinges, James Maury exerted influence over the colony's most ambitious men. By being a speculator as well, he shaped a vision of what new lands could be and he could rhapsodize about the possibilities—a salesman of earthly reward.[7]

In the 1760s, Maury's income and prospects for prosperity suffered two major setbacks, the first of which was in the forefront of most Virginians' concerns. The 1763 Treaty of Paris that ended the French and Indian War was of no help financially to Great Britain's oldest North American colony and men like Maury. What followed soon after was an abomination, an unforgiveable betrayal. A Royal Proclamation issued in October 1763 barred expansion west of the Appalachians, including the Loyal Company's 800,000 acres that lay in that now-forbidden territory. It was an outrage. Virginians, like Maury in Albemarle and George Washington in Fairfax, felt stabbed in the back. Westward expansion was the very reason they had gone to war, march-

---

5. Douglas Southall Freeman, *George Washington, A Biography* (New York: Scribner, 1948), 1:6 (on "grab, grab, grab").

6. James Maury to Robert Jackson, July 17, 1762, Albemarle County (Virginia) Historical Society Records; Dumas Malone, *Jefferson: The Virginian* (Boston: Little, Brown, 1948), 42–45; Maury, *Memoirs*, 386–88.

7. His grandson, Matthew Fontaine Maury, made turning that vision into reality his life's work in charting the world's oceans for the Navy. Cong. Globe, 32nd Cong., 2d Sess., appendix 238-39 (statement of Mr. Dodge on Railroad to the Pacific, citing Matthew Fontaine Maury's quoting his grandfather on value of western exploration); "Loyal Company Grant, July 12, 1749," *Exploring the West from Monticello: A Perspective in Maps from Columbus to Lewis and Clark*; An Exhibition of Maps and Navigational Instruments on View in the Tracy W. McGregor Room, Alderman Library, Univ. of Virginia, July 10 to Sept. 26, 1995, www2.lib.virginia.edu/exhibits/lewis_clark/exploring/ch3-16.html.

ing alongside Gen. Edward Braddock from Alexandria into the Ohio wilderness.[8]

The French and Indian War had left Virginia planters in greater debt than usual. Adding to their burden were poor tobacco harvests in 1755 and 1758 caused by drought. To ease their plight, the colonial government passed emergency acts allowing debts, such as those owed to the established church, to be paid in currency or tobacco notes and setting the price of a pound of tobacco at the artificially low level of two pence. Tobacco prices underwrote the value of Virginia's currency. The market price was about six pence. Planters naturally paid the church with the two-pence notes, keeping the difference for themselves.[9]

The Anglican clergy at first acquiesced, considering wartime necessity and the hardship of disastrous harvests. They were outraged, however, as the "emergency" acts, signed into law by Lt. Gov. Francis Fauquier, turned into the norm. They demanded their sixteen thousand pounds of tobacco, as guaranteed by statute. Thirty-five of the seventy Anglican priests in Virginia gathered in a convention to demand their due. To them, the legislature was daring to put itself ahead of Parliament and the king.

Because the 1758 law did not have a clause saying when the emergency act was to start—upon royal confirmation or on the day it was passed—the clergymen sent their case to the Board of Trade for a decision. There the Rev. John Camm, then in charge of William and Mary in Virginia and supported by the bishop of London and the archbishop of Canterbury, won a ruling invalidating the colony's law, but not from its inception. This provided maneuver space for more arguments later in counties across Virginia.

Matters didn't end there. Fauquier, a man who generally leaned toward the colonists' interests over the Board of Trade's ignorance of Virginia reality, became outraged when politically-ambitious Camm, accompanied by several witnesses, showed him a copy of the ruling. The meeting deteriorated quickly. Fauquier accused the Camm of breaking the seals of an official document intended for him alone. Lieutenant Governor Fauquier very likely was infuriated by Reverend Camm's pretense of civil power by taking the question to London in

---

8. Dr. Thomas Walker, *Journal of an Exploration in the Spring of the Year 1750* (Boston: Little, Brown and Company, 1888, 7-34; William Goetzmann, *New Lands, New Men: America and the Second Great Age of Discovery* (New York: Viking Penguin, 1987), 144; Fischer and Kelly, *Bound*, 152–53.

9. Ibid.

the first place. It reeked of James Blair's plotting and behind-the-scenes maneuvering in Williamsburg and London to remove royal officials he despised. Whether Camm was entitled to peek, or succumbed to his curiosity over what was written versus what he heard and remembered in the weeks of ocean-traveling, is not recorded.[10]

Although Fauquier let the relief act lapse, he left reimbursement to the courts, expecting they would rule that the clergy had no grounds for action, because the law had lapsed.[11]

Watching this all unfold in the usually quiet capital was Thomas Jefferson, fresh out of James Maury's tutelage and home. He was enrolled at the college, and was a regular invitee to the governor's palace through his friendship with the scholarly George Wythe, his own interesting companionship in serious conversation, and his proficiency with the violin.[12]

Jefferson was witnessing the first act in a drama that came to be known as the "Parson's Cause." This colonial legal struggle lead eventually to de-establishing of churches as part of government in Virginia and, many years later, to barring Congress from restricting "the free exercise of religion." The outcome of the case had another important impact on what became the drive for independence in Virginia, asserting the colonies' rights to determine what laws best fit their needs, not a far away Parliament in which they had no representation.

As a clergyman of the established church—in effect an employee of the government—Maury, with a large family to feed, believed like Reverend Camm that the burgesses had cheated him. Irrespective of his school and its little income, or his possible revenue from belonging to the Loyal Company, Maury wanted his base pay. Since the first cases by the clergy foundered in York and King William counties, he sued the collector of the parish levies for the difference between the two pence paid under the emergency act and the six pence market price of tobacco. His attorney, Peter Lyons, thought Maury's chances better if he filed in Hanover County, rather than Louisa County where the collector lived, served on the county court, and was a burgess—member of the body that had drafted and passed the "two-pence law." Lyons, born in Ireland and barely over thirty years old, also would be playing

10. Arthur P. Middleton, *Anglican Virginia: The Established Church of the Old Dominion 1607-1786* (Williamsburg: Colonial Williamsburg Foundation Library Research Report Series–0006, 1990), 182-84; notes 8,10.
11. Ibid.
12. Malone, *Jefferson*, 53, 73-4, also 44n19.

on his home court in the case before a judge who had strong familial bonds to church-state status quo.[13]

When the suit was filed, the Rev. Patrick Henry, the vicar of St. Paul's in Hanover County, took a proprietary interest in the case. In the small world of Piedmont society, the Henry brothers were church and state in Hanover. Back in the mid-1740s the interests of both intersected. The brothers had felt duty-bound to contain the "religious Phrenzy" of revivalists, their itinerant and usually unlicensed preachers, and the doings inside their meeting houses. For all that effort to hold back the trembling of the Great Awakening, they couldn't rein in John Henry's wife Sarah Winston Syme Henry. She was enraptured with the evangelists' message, particularly that of Samuel Davies. Instead of heading to one of Hanover's two Anglican parishes on the Sabbath, she loaded their son Patrick into a wagon and set off for Davies' Presbyterian services where the sermons were a heady brew of classical allusions in biblical reference.[14]

The Rev. Patrick Henry's position in the county was obvious by his long education and ordination. Although his brother John, also born in Scotland, was well educated at King' College, he took "a traditional shortcut on the road to wealth and power" in Virginia by marrying above his station.[15] By 1763, John Henry, a former teacher and a recognized surveyor, was a judge, a powerful man in handling local affairs. He was also a colonel in the militia; and, with his clergyman brother, an associate of key players in the Governor's Council.[16]

In November 1763, Maury's attorney Peter Lyons carried the first round when Presiding Judge Henry ruled the law invalid and ordered

13. William Wirt, *Sketches of the Life and Character of Patrick Henry* (Philadelphia: James Webster, 1817), 24; Mayer, *Son*, 26–31, 34, 35, 59–66; Arthur Scott Pearson, "The Constitutional Aspects of the Parson's Cause," *Political Science Quarterly* (New York) 31 (1916): 558–77; Dabney, *Virginia*, 120–21; William Wirt Henry, ed., *Patrick Henry: Life, Correspondence, and Speeches* (New York: Charles Scribner's Sons, 1891), 38, 41; Genealogical Account, *Virginia Magazine* 27 (1919): 375–76; John H. Gwathmey, *Twelve Virginia Counties Where the Western Migration Began* (Baltimore: Geneaological Publishing Co., 1997 reprint), 155.
14. His wife Sarah Winston came from a prospering colonial family when she married Col. John Syme, then a vestryman in her future brother-in-law's church. With his own fortunes and her dowry, Syme had an expansive view of his future, buying large tracts in Hanover, Goochland, and King Williams counties, and muscling his way into the House of Burgesses as one of the first members from Hanover admitted to that body. But they were ambitions cut short. He died in 1729. Middleton, *Anglican*, 182–84.
15. Same as notes 13 and 14. The quotes on Henry's address to the jury and Lyons' objections come from Wirt's account of Henry's life and the Reverend Maury's recollections.
16. Ibid.

a jury to be selected to determine the amount owed to Maury. For the first time, a colonial court had ruled in favor of the clergy. Earthly prayers answered, in part, Maury, Camm, and the others eagerly awaited the denouement—the damages. The collector's attorney then resigned, and Judge Henry's son Patrick took over the case. His uncle cautioned young Henry against "saying hard things of the clergy" at the session. The Rev. Patrick Henry knew his nephew well. As an adolescent, the young man had paid scant attention to academics, fumbled his way into young manhood trying this in planting, failing that in storekeeping, moving on, and finally becoming an attorney more by the patronage of those who saw his raw genius rather than by his real knowledge of law. Young Patrick Henry seemed most comfortable with the rough hunters, the men that hung around the county's taverns—loud talk, loud music with Patrick himself playing the violin. He certainly had a glib tongue—the mixture of known references and practiced allusions, delivered with passion, imbibed from his mother's religious persistence. The second act in the Parson's Cause drama had been reached.[17]

Court days always brought crowds to enjoy the spectacle even in the most rural courthouses, but the numbers milling about the single-story brick courthouse were larger than usual. On the December day of the trial to determine damages, men of property excused themselves when the sheriff tried to press them into jury duty. "Hence he went among the vulgar herd" for jurymen, enlisting tradesmen, deists, followers of evangelical preachers, and disgruntled Hanover County planters. Looking them over, lawyer Henry pronounced the jury "honest men." His opponent, Lyons, having practiced in this court for almost ten years, knew the panel as well; but his feelings about their competency, their biases, or their prejudices are not known.

Once the veniremen were picked, there was a scramble for space inside. There were no seats in the courtroom so flesh pressed hard against flesh. As many as twenty of the colony's Anglican clergymen were inside the court that day. Those in clerical robes and the men of property who could not squeeze into the small chamber battled with the vulgar herd to hold spots near the doorway to hear what was said.[18]

For a corpulent man who went about in measured stride, Lyons moved swiftly this day by calling two tobacco dealers to establish the price of leaf in the late spring of 1759. These experts in tobacco's value set the price. Since the court already had upheld the old law from Par-

17. Ibid.
18. Ibid.

liament, the damages—the clergy's salaries—were to be commensurate. As he finished, he admonished the jury to remember the clergy's good deeds in the community when deciding how much was owed this man. He then rested Maury's case.[19]

The "honest men" or "vulgar herd" were now primed for the "hard things."

Lawyer Henry declared, "The Act of 1758 had every characteristic of a good law." Drawing upon the oratorical skills he learned from evangelical preachers and passion that later impressed the college student Jefferson with its power, he said, "A King by disallowing acts of this salutary nature, from being the father of his people, degenerated into a tyrant and forfeits all right his subjects' obedience."[20]

Disbelieving-what-he-just-heard, Lyons shouted across the courtroom: "The gentleman had spoken treason." Although there were murmurs in the courtroom seconding Lyons, the court itself did not rule against Henry, and counsel tried several times to have the bench reprimand the defendant's lawyer.[21]

That didn't happen. Not pausing in his argument, Henry raced with his oratorical wind.

Taking the course the Reverend Henry feared he would, the twenty-seven-year-old, self-taught lawyer shot back for an hour that the clergy's challenge to Virginia's law made them "enemies of the community." The clergy had put themselves on a pedestal and needed to be knocked off it. Henry said Maury and all the Anglican clergy "deserved to be punished by signal severity" as "rapacious harpies." How malign was their intent? Instead of the "good deeds" that Lyons laid before the jury, Henry said the villains would "snatch from the hearth of their honest parishioner his last hoe-cake, from the widow and her orphan child their last milch cow! The last bed, nay, the last blanket from the lying-in woman!"[22]

If that were not enough, the lawyer wanted to leave this warning with the jurors, one so stark it kept clanging like the tocsin—a clear warning heard far beyond the tiny Hanover courthouse, given to those men wearing clerical robes, sitting in Parliament in their finery, wandering officiously through Whitehall, or sitting regally on a throne in Westminster:

19. Ibid.
20. Ibid.
21. Ibid.
22. Ibid.

Not to have the temerity, for the future, to dispute the validity of such laws, authenticated by the only authority, which, in his conception, could give force to laws for the government of this Colony, authority of a legal representative of a Council, and of a kind and benevolent and patriot Governor.[23]

Henry had the jury exactly where he wanted them. He had turned their anger over the levy into a way through the legal thickets of London boards and kingsmen on the Thames. To the jurymen it was as visible as "chopt trees" trails, hacked out through the entangling vines and underbrush of his father's ruling.

"We know best how to care for ourselves" was the intent of the final message, and the court let it stand. Why his father, the Judge John Henry, did not step in and remonstrate the jury is unknown, another secret lost in time.

Out for only five minutes, the jury awarded Maury one penny in damages. The insulting verdict stunned the clergymen. Lyons was on his feet offering motions to set aside the decision, but to no avail. Judge John Henry had lost control of his courtroom. He had a runaway jury marching to his son's drumbeat. The only recourse open to Maury was to take the case to the General Court in Williamsburg, far away from the boisterous crowd that now hoisted Patrick Henry on their shoulders and marched in glee toward the nearby tavern owned by his father-in-law, John Shelton.[24]

The third act in the Parson's Cause case was concluded.

The verdict affected James Maury instantly. Further frustrated by the Royal Proclamation's barring over-the-mountain white migration (and certainly land sales), his ever-expanding family had even less to go around than before. There also now showed a darker side to this brilliant man's legacy: self-righteousness. To his ordered mind, he had been cheated, a feeling shared by his fellow clergymen. Everything he had done in this matter had been lawful, proper. When the case ended up in Williamsburg on appeal before men who had been instrumental in writing the colonial law, they turned deaf ears to the clergy's prayers. Camm and all the Anglican clergy had been knocked down a peg or two.[25]

---

23. Ibid.
24. Ibid.
25. John Grady, *Matthew Fontaine Maury, Father of Oceanography, A Biography, 1806-1873* (Jefferson, NC: McFarland, 2015), 14; same as notes 13 and 14.

In 1769, the impoverished James Maury died, and his oldest son, Matthew, Jefferson's and Madison's classmate, took over his church and school. The primogeniture and entail traditions, if no longer law, were as strong in the Piedmont as they were in the Tidewater and Great Britain. There was little for the younger Maury sons but to keep faith in God and try their luck in planting.[26]

The "Parson's Cause" story didn't end in a royal governor's council before the Revolution. There were two more acts that needed to play out—to draw the sharpest of lines between what was the state's and what was the church's. The discontents on both sides—Why should a good Baptist pay anything to a church he finds popish? Where is the stipend guaranteed by law?—smoldered like tidal marsh fires as bonfires of Revolution were set and roared.

In the mid-1770s Patrick Henry was sent to the House of Burgesses by the grateful planters of Hanover after the Parson's Cause case. He was more fiery than ever, from damning the Stamp Act on the floor of the General Assembly upon arrival in the capital to declaiming more treason against Parliament and King a decade later in a Richmond Anglican Church.

With him in the assembly then was Thomas Jefferson, no longer in awe of Henry's power as a speaker, making a name for himself as a thoughtful and graceful writer on all matters political—collected as *A Summary View of the Rights of British America*. In Williamsburg, he socialized with James Madison, now an Anglican clergyman himself, but a different breed than Maury and certainly different from Blair or Camm.[27]

Madison, who cast aside a career in law, was teaching at the college after being ordained in Great Britain in 1775; but unlike Camm, William and Mary's president, a bitter ender on the elevated place of the church in a civil society, and a wealthy Loyalist to his death, Madison went the other way. He even organized a militia company of William and Mary students for the Revolutionary cause.[28]

By 1776, the Virginia revolutionary convention, already on its set course for independence, dumped the reference to praying for the well-being of the king, queen, and royal family from the *Book of Common Prayer*. In the attendees' minds, revision of a prayer book was firmly its business. That was small potatoes compared to what followed from Madison's pen. The Reverend Madison wrote shortly thereafter that

26. Ibid.
27. Malone, *Jefferson*, 181-90.
28. Middleton, *Anglican*, 196-98.

the establishment of any particular church was "in incompatible with the Freedom of a Republic." All "but two or three" of the one-hundred parishes—likely their vestries speaking, ignoring the rectors—agreed with the idea of dis-establishing.[29]

He had taken a sledgehammer to Blair's and Camm's pedestal.

The convention act of 1776 suspended the colonial law fixing the rector's stipend and did not require non-members to contribute to it. But the convention did require all to pay tithes for the support of the poor and the sick in the parish.[30]

Although a decade had passed to reach that stage from the jury's decision in Hanover, another nine years would have to pass before Jefferson's dormant bill became Virginia's Statute for Religious Freedom; and it would not be the first such law in the new republic.

The names of the players in this final drama on religious freedom were familiar—Jefferson, Henry, but now there were two James Madisons, clergyman and lawmaker, on the stage.[31]

29. Ibid., 192-94.
30. Ibid.
31. Middleton, *Anglican,* 201-02.

Creating American Nationalists: Presbyterians and the War for Independence

🙢 WILLIAM HARRISON TAYLOR 🙠

There was no turning back after the morning of April nineteenth.[1] When the militiamen under Captain John Parker defended themselves against the British regulars at Lexington, they signaled a transition in the imperial crisis. What was still primarily a war of words before the sun broke the horizon that morning in 1775 had intensified into an armed conflict by the falling of that evening's shadows. Meeting in Philadelphia shortly after this bellwether moment, the ruling body of the Presbyterian church, the Synod of New York and Philadelphia, wrestled alongside their fellow colonists with the repercussions. In the course of their annual meeting the synod decided to write a pastoral letter to the congregations under their care and throughout the colonies.[2]

This letter set out four things very clearly. First, God was still sovereign in all things, and that "affliction springeth not out of the dust," meaning, in other words, it was time to examine themselves and repent. Second, the synod insisted that they were still, and should be, loyal British subjects who hoped for reconciliation and peace. "Let it appear," they wrote, "that you only desire the preservation and security of those

1. This article is adapted from William Harrison Taylor, *Unity in Christ and Country: American Presbyterians in the Revolutionary Era, 1758–1801*, copyright 2017 University of Alabama Press.
2. John Witherspoon is given credit for penning this letter by Dr. John Rodgers in *The works of the Rev. John Witherspoon, D.D. L.L.D. late president of the college, at Princeton New-Jersey. To which is prefixed an account of the author's life, in a sermon occasioned by his death, by the Rev. Dr. John Rodgers, of New York. In three volumes.* (Philadelphia: Woodward, 1800): 3:599–605.

rights which belong to you as freemen and Britons, and that reconciliation upon these terms is your most ardent desire." Third, they affirmed that the elusive theory of justifiable rebellion was well within reach. If "the British ministry shall continue to enforce their claims by violence," then Presbyterians should fight, alongside the rest of the colonists.[3] Fourth, the synod noted that while the conflict lasted its members needed to maintain colonial unity by both supporting the Continental Congress and promoting "a spirit of candour, charity, and mutual esteem ... towards those of different religious denominations."[4] Wearing their orthodoxy and loyalty on their sleeves, the Presbyterians demonstrated that they saw no separation of the spiritual and the secular and that they would strive in this time of crisis to build and preserve unions within and for these blended realms.

It would be a mistake, however, to see these union efforts by the Presbyterians in May 1775 as occurring in a vacuum. Seventeen years earlier the Presbyterians had embarked on a mission that made union building a priority for the church. This effort of 1758 was prompted by the schism that had rent the church since 1741. The reunion of 1758 was not intended to be a private affair. The Presbyterians had very publicly split and so they decided to very publicly reunite. In this spirit, they published an account that combined their reunion efforts as well as four promises for the colonial reading world. They first promised to "study the Things that make for Peace;" second, to lead exemplary lives, both in word and deed; third, to ensure that their doctrines were orthodox and evangelical; and fourth, to commend "ourselves to every Man's Conscience in the Sight of God." There is no doubt that these efforts were first intended to heal the divisions within the church but this should not obscure the Presbyterians' intentions towards their fellow colonists in other churches. The synod made this point clearly when it wrote that the ultimate "Design of our Union is the Advancement of the Mediator's Kingdom."[5]

Thus, 1758 was the year the Presbyterians formally began an effort to heal the various divisions within the Body of Christ. This was no small undertaking, even if the initial scope was limited to colonial North America. Still, the church did find some success, as can be seen

3. General Assembly, *Records of the Presbyterian Church in the United States of America, 1706–1788* (Philadelphia: Presbyterian Board of Publication, 1904), 466, 467.
4. General Assembly, *Records of the Presbyterian Church in the United States of America, 1706–1788*, 468.
5. Synod of New York and Philadelphia, *The plan of union between the Synods of New-York and Philadelphia. Agreed upon May 29th, 1758* (Philadelphia: W. Dunlap, 1758), 13.

in their coordinated mission work with the Congregationalists among the Native Americans—including the ordination of the first Native American minister, Samson Occom—and their cooperative efforts with the Anglicans in Virginia to create an orderly and peaceful co-existence among the growing number of Protestant churches in the colony. Yet, for all of their notable success in the years that followed, the Presbyterians were still a long way from achieving their goal when British Prime Minister George Grenville introduced the Stamp Act resolutions, which helped spark the American Revolution. As the British Constitutional Crisis developed over the real and perceived challenges to colonial religious and civil liberties, some Presbyterians saw unions with other Christians as an ideal way not only to protect their liberties but also to strengthen the kingdom of Christ. As is evident in the synod's pastoral letter in the wake of Lexington and Concord, this blending of spiritual and temporal objectives would continue throughout the crisis, all the while altering their original cooperative vision established in 1758.

When Presbyterians throughout the colonies responded to the synod's four-fold charge in May 1775, most embraced rather than rejected the ruling body's petition. They joined with their fellow Americans and served as soldiers, chaplains, congressmen, and home support. One example is found in the minister and congregation of Philadelphia's Third Presbyterian Church, often simply referred to as the "Pine Street" church.[6] Third Presbyterian's reputation as the "Church of the Patriots" was well earned and a March 1776 worship service led by Rev. George Duffield—future chaplain to the Continental Congress—illustrates this point well. While Duffield supported the synod's four points in his sermon he also touched on a new idea that was becoming increasingly popular—God had chosen America for a special purpose; it was to be a safe haven for liberty. Duffield reassured his congregation that although through their violent measures the British leadership was actively opposing this plan, God would not be thwarted.[7] "Can it be supposed," he asked, "that God who made man free . . . should forbid freedom, already exiled from Asia and Africa, and under sentence of banishment from Europe—that he should FORBID her to erect her ban-

6. The Third Presbyterian Church, or Pine Street, still stands today but it goes by the name "Old Pine."
7. Quoted in Hughes Oliphant Gibbons, *A History of Old Pine Street: Being the record of an hundred and forty years in the life of a Colonial Church* (Philadelphia: The John C. Winston Company, 1905), 64.
8. Gibbons, *A History of Old Pine Street*, 64-65.

ners HERE, and constrain her to abandon the earth?"[8] No, he said, America was to be the new standard-bearer for liberty and would continue as such "until herself shall play the tyrant, forget her destiny, disgrace her freedom, and provoke her God." Giving their approval of the minister and the message, as one church historian has noted, the congregation let fly with shouts of "To arms! to arms!"[9]

The number of Presbyterians like Duffield borrowing the Puritan's elect nation ideology increased following the Declaration of Independence. In their various capacities as ministers and laymen, Jacob Green, William McKay Tennent, John Murray, and Abraham Keteltas, to name but a few, drew on the idea.[10] Yes, Great Britain had once been the defender of civil and religious liberty in the world, but they had let that mantle slip. Were Americans worthy, then God would bless them with that honor and "this land of liberty will be glorious on many accounts: Population will abundantly increase, agriculture will be promoted, trade will flourish, religion unrestrained by human laws, will have free course to run and prevail, and America [will] be an asylum for all noble spirits and sons of liberty from all parts of the world."[11] In this view America had tremendous potential, but as the Presbyterians warned, this glorious future was dependent on Americans humbling themselves through repentance before a holy God. To be sure there were some notable Presbyterian loyalists who resisted the break with the empire, such as William Smith, Jr and William Allen, but on the whole, the Presbyterians were remarkable for rallying around the cause

9. Ibid., 65; Third Presbyterian Church of Philadelphia alone, it is currently estimated, sent six hundred and seventy-two men into battle, with at least thirty-five serving as commissioned officers. This tally is the work of Old Pine Presbyterian's church historian, Ron Shaffer.

10. See: Jacob Green, *Observations, on the reconciliation of Great-Britain and the colonies. By a friend of American liberty* (New York: John Holt, 1776); Abraham Keteltas, *God arising and pleading his people's cause; or The American war in favor of liberty, against the measures and arms of Great Britain, shewn to be the cause of God: in a sermon preached October 5th, 1777 at an evening lecture, in the Presbyterian church in Newbury-Port* (Newbury, MA: John Mycall, 1777); John Murray, *Nehemiah, or The struggle for liberty never in vain, when managed with virtue and perseverance. A discourse delivered at the Presbyterian Church in Newbury-Port, Nov. 4th, 1779. Being the day appointed by government to be observed as a day of solemn fasting and prayer throughout the state of Massachusetts-Bay. Published in compliance with the request of some hearers* (Newbury, MA: John Mycall, 1779); the William McKay Tennent sermon is quoted at length in Joel Tyler Headley, *The Forgotten Heroes of Liberty: Chaplains and Clergy of the American Revolution* (Birmingham, AL: Solid Ground Christian Books, 2005), 376-380.

11. Green, *Observations*, 19.

of an independent America that God had set apart for a special purpose.[12]

While the American colonists were not strangers to war, the scope and scale of the Revolutionary War was unprecedented in the history of the British North American colonies. The realities of war's death and devastation raised difficulties for Presbyterians looking forward to the glorious state they believed God meant for them. The American cause, they still believed, was holy, yes, but something had to be wrong for them to suffer as they had. While many Americans endured devastating losses, a number of Presbyterians believed that the British were singling them out for special punishment as both their institutions and ministers frequently found themselves targeted. For example, following the battle of Long Island at the end of August 1776, the minister of the Presbyterian Church there, Ebenezer Prime, fled for safety. Although Prime escaped capture, his church did not. The British destroyed the minister's library and they repurposed the sanctuary as a depot and barracks. The redcoats leveled the church cemetery to create a common and the gravestones were used to construct the troops' ovens.[13] Following the Battle of Princeton in January 1777, Benjamin Rush described to Richard Henry Lee the destruction of one of the most important Presbyterian assets and a bastion of revolutionary sentiment, the College of New Jersey. Rush wrote, "Princeton is indeed a deserted village. You would think it had been desolated with the plague and an earthquake as well as with the calamities of war. The College and church are heaps of ruin. All the inhabitants have been plundered."[14] A similar fate befell George Duffield's Pine Street congrega-

---

12. Perhaps equally telling were Loyalist accounts of the colonial-wide support of the Presbyterians. For instance, Charles Inglis, Anglican loyalist and rector of Trinity Church in New York City, commented to a friend, "I do not know one of them, nor have I been able, after strict inquiry, to hear of any, who did not, by preaching and every effort in their power, promote all the measures of the Congress, however extravagant." For more see: William Warren Sweet, *The Story of Religion in America* (New York: Harper & Brothers Publishers, 1939), 258-259; and Randall Balmer and John R. Fitzmier, *The Presbyterians* (Westport, CT: Praeger, 1994), 37. On Presbyterian Loyalists see: Joseph S. Tiedemann, "Presbyterians and the American Revolution in the Middle Colonies," *Church History*, 74 (2005), 339-343.

13. Headley, *Forgotten Heroes of Liberty*, 108-109.

14. Benjamin Rush to Richard Henry Lee, January 1777, in L. H. Butterfield, ed, *Letters of Benjamin Rush*, Volume I: 1761-1792 (Princeton, NJ: Princeton University Press, 1951), 126. For more on the significance of the College of New Jersey and its president John Witherspoon to the Patriot cause see: Gideon Mailer, *John Witherspoon's American Revolution* (Chapel Hill: University of North Carolina Press, 2017), especially pages 217-284.

tion when the British took possession of Philadelphia in September 1777. The church was stripped for firewood and the graveyard excavated and repurposed for dead Hessian soldiers.[15] In August 1779 the *New Hampshire Gazette* only confirmed what many Presbyterians feared when it noted that the British "manifest peculiar malice against the Presbyterian churches, having, during this month, burnt three in New York State, and two in Connecticut. What, Britons! Because we won't worship your idol King, will you prevent us from worshipping the 'King of kings' Heaven forbid!"[16]

Although the destruction of property incensed the Presbyterians, reports of attacks on Presbyterian ministers and their families upset Presbyterians even more. At the meeting of the 1777 synod, the New Brunswick Presbytery told how "the Rev. Mr. John Rosborough was barbarously murdered by the enemy at Trenton on January second."[17] According to the story, Rosborough was captured by Hessians while he was looking for his horse. Once it was discovered that he was a Presbyterian minister, he was stabbed repeatedly and left to die.[18] There was also the fate of the "Fighting Parson" James Caldwell, who, as the stories circulating within the Patriot ranks claimed, was also singled out for particular punishment by the British. Accordingly, the British continuously persecuted him through a series of events that ultimately culminated in his death: In January 1780 his church in Elizabethtown, New Jersey was burned; six months later while the Reverend Caldwell was away from home, his wife and children were shot dead while they prayed and his house subsequently burned; in November 1781, a distraught but loyal James Caldwell was assassinated while he was under a flag of truce.[19] While what the Presbyterians suffered, both real and perceived, by hands of the British army only confirmed their need to separate from and resist the empire, they saw something else in their troubles as well. As the minister Jacob Green put it: "Though our con-

15. Following the British victory at the Battle of Brandywine, the army occupied Philadelphia from September 26, 1777 to June 18, 1778.
16. James Smylie, "Presbyterians and the American Revolution: A Documentary Account," *Journal of Presbyterian History* 52, no. 4 (Winter 1974): 412.
17. General Assembly, *Records of the Presbyterian Church, 1706-1788*, 477.
18. Headley, *Forgotten Heroes of Liberty*, 158-162.
19. Headley, *Forgotten Heroes of Liberty*, 224-230; Smylie, ed, "Presbyterians and the American Revolution," 408; Maude Glascow, *The Scotch-Irish in Northern Ireland and in the American Colonies* (New York: G. P. Putnam's Sons, 1936), 274; and J. J. Boudinot, ed, *The Life, Public Services, Addresses, and Letters of Elias Boudinot*, Volume 1 (Capo Press, New York, 1971), 188.

tention with Great Britain is so glorious, yet we have reason to be humbled and abased before God ... for the many sins, the many vices that prevail among us."[20]

Despite the efforts of Presbyterians to unite for the preservation of America's future as the bastion for spiritual and civil liberties, they suffered. Church members persuaded themselves that these hardships, like those of their revolutionary brethren, were the result of unrepented sin. In this spirit, the 1777 synod pleaded with their "congregations, to spend the last Thursday of every month ... in fervent prayer to God, that he would be pleased to pour out his Spirit on the inhabitants of our land, and prepare us for deliverance from the chastenings he hath righteously inflicted upon us for our sins."[21] Repentance and devotion to the law of God were the only safeguards for the proposed nation that the Presbyterians had helped imagine. The synod would repeat the call for repentance throughout the war. There were many sins to choose from—slacking church attendance, discipline and youth education were perennial standbys—but during the war two sins stood out: slavery and the divided Christian Church. Together, the prominent role of these very public sins indicated how the Presbyterian's new view of America was influencing their faith. Leaders in the church were not prioritizing sins that were confined, in many ways, to individual churches, but rather preference was given to American sins. The Presbyterian embrace of America as God's chosen land meant they had to engage the national sins that threatened the very potential of the country.

Slavery was seen as a threat not just because it was sinful, but also because it encouraged a great host of sins that crept throughout the land. As the intermittent Presbyterian Benjamin Rush put it, slavery was a "Hydra sin, and includes in it every violation of the precepts of the Law and the Gospel." These sins corrupted both masters and slaves, and all Americans who came into contact with slavery's spread. For Rush they were nothing less than "National crimes," and those, he reminded his readers, "require national punishments."[22] Echoing these

20. James Smylie, "Presbyterians and the American Revolution," 451.
21. General Assembly, *Records of the Presbyterian Church, 1706-1788*, 478.
22. Benjamin Rush, *An Address to the Inhabitants of the British Settlements in America, upon Slave-Keeping* (Philadelphia: Dunlap, 1773), 30. In many ways Benjamin Rush embodied the spirit of Christian unity discussed here. In 1787 he ended his membership with First Presbyterian Church in Philadelphia, but he would still regularly attend Presbyterian services. He also frequented Episcopal churches even after his brief formal relationship with that church ended in 1789. For a short while, Rush even attended a Universalist Baptist Church. However, that relationship seems to be largely due to his friend and minister Elhanan Winchester, as Rush never joined the church; after the minister died in 1797 his

ideas in 1778 Jacob Green told his congregation, "Can it be believed that a people contending for liberty should, at the same time, be promoting and supporting slavery? ... I cannot but think, and must declare my sentiments, that the encouraging and supporting of negro slavery is a crying sin in our land." All Americans needed to repent this sin, Green argued, or they would continue to "groan under the afflicting hand of God, till we reform in this matter."[23] According to New Jersey chaplain James Francis Armstrong, American slavery was far "worse than Egyptian bondage" and it had left on the hands of the colonists the "tortured blood of the sons and daughters of Adam." Like many of his fellow Presbyterians, he was not surprised God had visited them with war; rather he was surprised by God's mercy. "Good heaven!" he cried, "Where sleepeth the lightning and the thunderbolt?" "National calamites," he concluded alongside Rush, Green and numerous others, could only be remedied by popular repentance and "the exercise of virtue and religion."[24] The Presbyterians who targeted the institution of slavery saw it in national terms, because if God had set America apart, then that meant the sins it committed as a nation would demand all Americans to repent or suffer divine retribution.[25]

In addition to the sin of slavery, the Presbyterians also turned their attention to the divided Christian Church. From the beginning of the Revolutionary War the Presbyterians had been determined to maintain colonial unity as the synod had implored, by both supporting the Con-

visits ceased. Even if Rush was formally detached from churches, he maintained cordial relationships with Christians across the denominational spectrum. And Rush had an intimate relationship throughout his life with the Presbyterian Church, as he regularly attended its services and saw all of his children baptized by Presbyterian ministers. See Robert Abzug, *Cosmos Crumbling: American Reform and the Religious Imagination* (New York: Oxford University Press, 1994), 11–29; and Donald J. D'Elia, "Benjamin Rush: Philosopher of the American Revolution," *Transactions of the American Philosophical Society* 64, no. 5 (Philadelphia, PA, 1974).

23. James Smylie, "Presbyterians and the American Revolution," 451 and 453.
24. James Francis Armstrong, "Righteousness Exalteth A Nation," in *Light to My Path: Sermons by the Rev. James F. Armstrong Revolutionary Chaplain*, ed. Marian B. McLeod (Trenton, NJ: First Presbyterian Church, 1976), 17 and 18.
25. Other notable Presbyterians, including George Bryan, Elias Boudinot, David Rice, Ebenezer Hazard, William Livingston, John Murray and Daniel Roberdeau, who were influential in both Church and society opposed the "sin" of slavery in addition to men discussed in this article. For more information see Trinterud, *The Forming of an American Tradition*, 272-74; Douglas R. Egerton, *Death or Liberty: African Americans and Revolutionary America* (New York: Oxford University Press, 2009), 99–101; Gary B. Nash, *Unknown American Revolution: The Unruly Birth of Democracy and the Struggle to Create America* (New York: Viking, 2005), 322–23; and Arthur Zilversmit, *First Emancipation: The Abolition of Slavery in the North* (Chicago: University of Chicago Press, 1967), 128–29.

tinental Congress and by promoting "a spirit of candour, charity, and mutual esteem ... towards those of different religious denominations."[26] Success depended on cooperation, and as is evident, Presbyterians were cooperative. It was an ironic twist then as the war waned, that leaders in the Church, upon re-examining the nature of their unions, found those unions troubling.

The primary problem was that while Presbyterians were working with other Christians on these cooperative ventures, they had become too preoccupied with political liberties at the expense of Christ's kingdom. What would happen when the main threat to temporal civil and religious liberties was removed? Would the unions among Christians fracture and the old colonial hostilities resume? Samuel Stanhope Smith believed this to be a strong possibility, and in his home of Virginia he foresaw a terrible struggle between Protestants over education. The denomination that "enjoys the preeminence in these will insensibly gain upon the others, and soon acquire the government of the state" he wrote to an equally concerned Thomas Jefferson.[27] "It is time to heal these divisions," he continued, for "if they were united under one denomination their efforts, instead of being divided and opposed, would concentrate on one object, and concur in advancing the same important enterprise."[28] Ministers such as John Ewing raised another concern regarding the unions. He pointed out that a "well regulated Zeal for civil Liberty is a noble & generous Passion" and that "endeavours to promote & establish civil and religious Liberty are very commendable." However, Ewing cautiously added, "amidst all ye vigorous Efforts for Liberty in ye World ... how negligent and careless are Men in securing spiritual Liberty."[29] Spiritual liberty—the most important liberty, the minister commented—was in danger of being supplanted by concerns over civil liberty. The work of Christians, whether individually or in concert across denominational lines, was to primarily emphasize "spiritual Liberty" available through Christ. While the Presbyterians maintained support for the securing of civil and religious freedom, leaders like John Ewing and Samuel Stanhope Smith began calling for a renewed emphasis on strengthening the body of Christ.

Heeding the calls for repentance and renewal within the church, the synod met in May 1783 to address the situation. With peace finally within reach, the ruling body took the opportunity to publicly reclaim

26. General Assembly, *Records of the Presbyterian Church, 1706-1788*, 468.
27. Samuel Stanhope Smith to Thomas Jefferson, March 1779, in *The Papers of Thomas Jefferson*, ed. Julian P. Boyd (Princeton, NJ: Princeton University Press, 1950), 2:247.
28. Samuel Stanhope Smith to Thomas Jefferson, March 1779 in ibid., 248.
29. Smylie, "Presbyterians and the American Revolution," 478.

their cooperative goals of 1758. Included in this published statement was a formal Presbyterian position on religious freedom, which was intended to dispel rumors that the denomination planned, as the American Anglican Church lay in shambles, to make an Old World power play for a privileged position within the new governments. What many in the Presbyterian Church had begun to fear—that temporal concerns had overwhelmed the eternal goals—was a growing perception outside of the church as well. Their efforts during the war to help shape and lead the American cause were now being portrayed as the first stages of a master plan. Whether the fears were justified did not matter to the synod because the simple fact that they existed indicated a failure of the church. After all, among the promises the Presbyterians made in 1758 were those to "study the Things that make for Peace," and to commend "ourselves to every Man's Conscience in the Sight of God."[30] With their intentions in question, the 1783 synod wrote, "That they ever have, and still do renounce and abhor the principles of intolerance; and ... believe that every peaceable member of civil society ought to be protected in the full and free exercise of their religion."[31] In other words, they hoped to counteract this problem by publicly supporting religious freedom in the new American states.

The synod's recommitment in 1783 to the goals of 1758 saw the Presbyterians begin their most productive era of Christian cooperation to that point. The Presbyterians began negotiating terms of union with like-minded denominations, such as the Dutch Reformed Church, the Associate Reformed Church, and the New England Congregationalists. This spirit would continue well into the nineteenth century creating many of the voluntary societies that formed the backbone of the Second Great Awakening. But it would be a mistake to see the 1783 recommitment to the cooperative goals of 1758 as just an ecclesiastical affair. The Presbyterian Church had transformed as a result of its experiences during the war. This was perhaps most evident in the way they had embraced the whole of America as their vehicle for uniting and strengthening the "Redeemer's Kingdom." Presbyterians had become American nationalists, and while this did not necessarily mean they were wholly or even initially in favor of a strong central government—both adamant Federalist and Anti-Federalist were found within the pews—when the new Constitution was ratified the church's ruling

30. Synod, *The plan of union*, 13.
31. General Assembly, *Records of the Presbyterian Church, 1706–1788*, 499.

body fully welcomed and supported the new government.[32] Presbyterians had come to see America's success as vital to the success of their mission to strengthen the kingdom of Christ. In this way, the Presbyterian Church helped form the vanguard of the nationalist movement while continuing its cooperative efforts with other Christians.

The War for American Independence was a significant turning point for the Presbyterian Church. As the church re-imagined America's role in God's plan, they came to wrestle with national sins that threatened that future, specifically slavery and the continued division in Christ's kingdom. Repenting these sins, they knew, was the only real safeguard for both American independence and the country's new transformative role in the world. Although slavery would, by the war's end, take a back seat to spiritual schism, it was not forgotten and would be addressed specifically in 1787. Independence meant that the process of rebuilding lay ahead and the Presbyterian leadership was primarily concerned with uniting Christians for this purpose. However, when the Presbyterians restored Christian unity to its place of priority, it was not as it had been before the war. A nationalist spirit had been joined to their cooperative hopes and it was expected that this interdenominational nationalism would help to transform the newly independent states into an idyllic Christian republic that would benefit and expand the kingdom of Christ. This future, as they told themselves countless times during the war, depended on whether Americans held true to their Christian calling. If they could, as George Duffield told his Pine Street congregation in 1783, America would remain the land where: "God erected a banner of civil and religious liberty: And prepared an asylum for the poor and oppressed from every part of the earth ... Here shall the religion of Jesus; not that, falsely so called, which consists in empty modes and forms; and spends its unhallowed zeal in party names and distinctions, and traducing and reviling each other; but the pure and undefiled religion of our blessed Redeemer: here shall it reign in triumph, over all opposition."[33]

32. Prominent Federalists included Benjamin Rush, James Wilson, John Witherspoon, Samuel Stanhope Smith, and David Ramsay. Prominent anti-Federalist Presbyterians were George Bryan, Robert Whitehill, and William Findley. For more on religious divisions over the Constitution, see Owen S. Ireland, *Religion, Ethnicity, and Politics: Ratifying the Constitution in Pennsylvania* (University Park: Penn State University Press, 1995); Stephen A. Marini, "Religion, Politics, and Ratification" in *Religion in a Revolutionary Age*, 184–217; Miller, *The Revolutionary College*, 128–38; and Gordon S. Wood, *The Radicalism of the American Revolution* (New York: Vintage Books, 1993), 255. Marini sees at the heart of this disagreement a persistent Old/New Light contest. Howard Miller contends (and Gordon Wood agrees) that the disagreement was based on the fears of western settlers regarding an eastern centralized aristocracy.
33. Smylie, "Presbyterians and the American Revolution," 458–59.

Franklin's Secret Efforts to Bring about Reconciliation

✻ BOB RUPPERT ✻

Benjamin Franklin made two missions to London prior to the Revolution; the first from 1757 to 1762, the second from 1764 to 1775. In the final four months of his second mission he became involved in three efforts to secure a peaceful solution to the constitutional divergence that was growing between England and her American colonies. Because the efforts involved many of the same people, overlapped in time, and involved back-channel meetings, their stories need to be told simultaneously.

NOVEMBER 29, 1774

Caroline Howe, the sister of Rear-Admiral Lord Richard Howe, invites Benjamin Franklin to join her for a game of chess, "fancying she could beat me." He claimed being "long out of practice," but agreed to "wait upon the Lady."[1]

DECEMBER 1

David Barclay, a Quaker, merchant and banker, visits Franklin to discuss "the meeting of [London] Merchants [and their] Petition to Parliament." When they were finished, Barclay "spoke of the dangerous Situation of American Affairs and asked Franklin based upon his Knowledge of both Countries" if he thought something could be done to bring about a reconciliation. Franklin said, "I thought an Accommodation impracticable unless both sides wish'd it, and by what I could judge from the Proceedings of the Ministry, I did not believe they had the least Disposition towards it. . . . To which Barclay

---

1. Benjamin Franklin to William Franklin: Journal of Negotiations in London, March 22, 1775, in William B. Willcox, ed., *The Papers of Benjamin Franklin* (New Haven and London: Yale University Press, 1978), 21:540b (Journal of Negotiations).

responded you judg'd too hardly of the Ministers; he was persuaded they were not all [of] that Temper, and he fancy'd they would be very glad to get out of their present Embarrassment on any Terms. . . . He wished therefore that I would think of the Matter, and he would call again."[2]

DECEMBER 2

Franklin and Caroline Howe play chess for the first time.[3]

DECEMBER 3

Barclay and Dr. John Fothergill, physician to both Franklin and Lord Dartmouth, invite Franklin to meet the next day "to confer on American affairs . . . neither of us [are] insensible, that the Affair is of that Magnitude as should almost deter private persons from meddling with it . . . we are respectively such wellwishers to the cause, that nothing in our power ought to be left undone."[4]

DECEMBER 4

Franklin and Caroline Howe play chess for the second time. In the course of conversation she asks, "And what is to be done with this Dispute between Britain and the Colonies? I hope we are not to have a Civil War . . . Quarrelling can be of Service to neither but is Ruin to Both . . . I have often said that I wished the government would employ you to settle the dispute, I am sure nobody could do it as well."[5]

Franklin, Barclay and Fothergill meet. Fothergill was disappointed that Franklin came to the meeting having "not put Pen to Paper;" he had hoped that Franklin had "form'd some Plan for Consideration," but he hadn't. The reason Franklin gave was, "I thought of the Proceedings against the Colonies, the more satisfy'd I was, that there did not exist the least Disposition in the Ministry to an Accommodation [and] that therefore all Plans must be useless." Fothergill told Franklin if he "would draw a Plan which we three . . . should judge reasonable, it might be made use of . . . since he believ'd that either himself or D. Barclay, could get it communicated to some of the most moderate among the Ministers, who would consider it with Attention." Franklin agreed and promised to meet with them the next day and have "something for their Consideration."[6] In their own way,

2. Ibid.
3. Ibid.
4. Willcox, ed., *The Papers of Benjamin Franklin*, 21:360.
5. Journal of Negotiations.
6. Ibid.

Barclay and Fothegill were making the same request of Franklin that Ms. Howe had earlier in the day.

DECEMBER 6

Barclay, Fothergill and Franklin meet again. Franklin presents "Hints for Conversation upon the Subject of Terms that might probably produce a Durable Union between Great Britain and the Colonies;" each is discussed at length:

1. The Tea destroyed be paid for.
2. The Tea-Duty Act be repealed and all the duties received be repaid into the treasuries of the several colonies from which they had been collected.
3. The Acts of Navigation be re-enacted.
4. A Naval officer appointed by the Crown reside in each colony, to see that the Acts are observed.
5. All acts that restrain manufactures in the colonies be reconsidered. All Duties arising from the acts for regulating trade ... be for public use ... The collectors and custom-house officers be appointed by each governor, and not sent from England.
6. No requisitions be made from the colonies in time of peace.
7. No troops to enter and quarter in any colony without the consent of its legislature.
8. In time of war, the requisition made by the King with the consent of Parliament be based upon one quarter of the land rate charged in England.
9. Castle William will be restored to the Massachusetts colony.
10. The Massachusetts and Quebec Acts be repealed and a free government be granted to Canada.
11. All judges be appointed during "Good Behavior," with equal permanent salaries, paid out of the colonial revenues.
12. Governors be supported by the colonial assemblies.
13. If Britain gives up her monopoly of commerce, requisitions be given in times of peace as well as war.
14. The Act of Henry VIII stating trials for treason must be held in England to disowned by Parliament.
15. American Admiralty Courts can only exercise in the colonies the powers they exercise in England.
16. All powers of internal legislation in the colonies be disowned by Parliament.[7]

7. "Franklin's 'Hints' or Terms for a Durable Union," Willcox, ed., *The Papers of Benjamin Franklin*, 21:365-368.

DECEMBER 8

Barclay picks up a "fair copy" (an updated version) of the "Hints" based upon their discussion on the 6th.[8]

DECEMBER 12

Barclay delivers one copy to Thomas Villiers, Lord Hyde, a former diplomat and advisor to Lord North.

DECEMBER 13

Lord Hyde, after reading the "Hints" studiously, recommends modifications;[9] Barclay spends the next couple of weeks making them.

DECEMBER 12-15

Fothergill delivers a copy of the "Hints" to William Legge, Lord Dartmouth, and shows them to Sir Fletcher Norton, Speaker of the House of Commons.[10]

DECEMBER 17

The Petition of Rights and Grievances adopted by the First Continental Congress arrives in London. It asserted the colonists' loyalty to the King but not to Parliament and their Coercive Acts, and outlined the colonists' objections and related grievances. It concluded,

> To these grievous acts and measures, Americans cannot submit, but in hopes that their fellow subjects in Great Britain will, on a revision of them, restore us to that state, in which both countries found happiness and prosperity, we have for the present, only resolved to pursue the following peaceable measures: 1) To enter into a non-importation, non-consumption, and non-exportation Association; 2) To prepare an address to the people of Great Britain and a memorial to the inhabitants of America; and 3) to prepare a loyal address to his Majesty, agreeable to resolutions already entered into.[11]

DECEMBER 18

Barclay writes to Franklin;

> I am of the Opinion that it will be advisable to let a little time elapse before any other Steps are pursued, more especially when its consider'd, that at the approaching Season, many People go out of Town and will

8. David Barclay to Franklin, December 8, 1774," ibid., 21:372c.
9. Kingston Fox, *Dr. John Fothergill and his Friends* (New York and London: MacMillan & Co., 1919), Appendix, 329.
10. Ibid.
11. avalon.law.yale.edu/18th_century/resolves.asp.

not return until the commencement of the New Year . . . our Superiors will have some time for Reflection, and perhaps may contemplate on the propriety of the Hints in their possession.[12]

DECEMBER 21

Franklin and other colonial agents present *The Petition of Rights and Grievances* to Lord Dartmouth; "after a day's Perusal, [Dartmouth] told us it was a decent and proper Petition, and cheerfully undertook to present it to his Majesty." Three days later, Dartmouth "assur'd us, [the King] was pleased to receive it very graciously, and to promise to lay it before his two Houses of Parliament."[13]

DECEMBER 25

Franklin visits Caroline Howe. Shortly after his arrival, Ms. Howe mentions that her brother, Lord Howe, wished to meet him. "Will you give me leave to send for him?" Franklin soon was exchanging plaseantries with him. Lord Howe tells Franklin that his motive for wishing to meet was the "situation of our Affairs with America." He said, "no one he was persuaded understood [the situation] better than myself . . . no man could do more towards reconciling our Differences than I could if I would undertake it . . . He was desirous of doing what Good he could therefore had wish'd for an opportunity of obtaining my Sentiments on the Means of Reconciling our Differences." Franklin agreed to share his ideas with Howe if he could "rely on his keeping perfectly secret." Before departing the two men decided for the future that "as his being seen at my House or me at his might be thought some Speculation, it was concluded to be best to meet at his sister's."[14]

DECEMBER 26

Franklin meets with William Pitt, Lord Chatham, to discuss his "Hints;" "I mentioned to him . . . that no accommodation could properly be proposed and entered into by the Americans, while the bayonet was at their breasts; that, to have any agreement binding, all force must be withdrawn. His Lordship seemed to think these sentiments had something in them that was Reasonable."[15]

---

12. Barclay to Franklin, December 18, 1774, Willcox, ed., *The Papers of Benjamin Franklin*, 21:390a.

13. Arthur Lee to Richard Henry Lee, December 22 and 24, 1774," in Peter Force, ed., *American Archives*, Fourth Series, Containing a Documentary History of the English Colonies in North America (Washington DC: M. St. Clair Clarke and Peter Force, 1837), I:1058-64.

14. Journal of Negotiations.

15. Ibid.

DECEMBER 27

Franklin meets with Charles Pratt, Lord Camden. "He seemed anxious that the Americans should continue to act with the same temper, coolness, and wisdom, with which they had hitherto proceeded in most of their public assemblies, in which case he did not doubt they would succeed in establishing their rights and obtain a solid and durable agreement with the mother country."[16]

DECEMBER 28

Franklin meets with Lord Howe. "He could now assure me that there was a most sincere disposition in Lord North and Lord Dartmouth to accommodate the differences with America, and to listen favorably to any proposition that might have a probable tendency to answer that salutary purpose . . ." Howe showed a copy of the "Hints" and asked if Franklin knew anything about it; "I [made] no difficulty in owning to him, that I had been consulted on the subject, and had drawn up that paper. He said, he was sorry to find that the sentiments expressed in it were mine, as it gave him less hopes of promoting the wished for reconciliation . . . I promised to draw some sketch of a plan, . . . though I much doubted, I said, whether it would be thought preferable to that he had in his hand." He asked Franklin's opinion "on the dispatching of a commissioner to resolve misunderstandings and, with the help of leading Americans, seek means of reconciliation." Franklin responded that the right man might be "of great use." Howe thought it might be improper to have the plan seen in Franklin's handwriting; therefore, it would be better to send it to Ms. Howe, who would copy it and send the copy to be communicated to the ministry.[17]

DECEMBER 29–31

Franklin's "Sketch" is delivered to Caroline Howe who copies it and forwards the copy to her brother. It contains five articles:
    1. Repeal all of the laws requested in the petition from Congress
    2. Remove all troops to Quebec or the Floridas
    3. Grievances in the Petition left to the magnanimity and justice of the King and Parliament be removed
    4. The Continental Congress "be authorized by Government" and "a person of weight and dignity to be appointed to preside on behalf of the Crown."
    5. "Let requisitions be made to the Congress of such points as Government wishes to obtain for its future Security, for Aid, for

16. Journal of Negotiations.
17. Ibid.

the Advantage of general Commerce, and for reparation" for the destroyed tea.[18]

Even though these five were more general than his "Hints," Franklin made no substantive changes to his conditions.

JANUARY 2, 1775

Lord Howe informs his sister that he received the Sketch but notes "that the desired accommodation, threatens to be attended with much greater difficulty than I had flattered myself."[19]

Barclay delivers his modifications of the "Hints" to Franklin. There were four changes: condition 2 omitted "be turned over to the provincial treasuries;" 3 omitted "the statute defining Admiralty jurisdiction be re-enacted;" 10 omitted "required consent of the provincial legislature;" and 17 omitted "Parliament renounced its right to legislate on internal colonial affairs."[20] The last demand was omitted even though it was the initial reason for the conflict.

JANUARY 3

Barclay picks-up Franklin's comments on the accommodations.

Fothergill writes to John Pemberton, another Quaker who lives in Philadelphia; "They will pursue, in one shape or other, the same destructive plan - that no abatement of any consequence will be made, no material alterations or concessions . . . of course if you are as resolute as we seem unhappily to be firm, dissolution must follow." [21]

JANUARY 4

Lord Dartmouth issues a circular letter to all of the colonial governors:

> Certain Persons, styling themselves delegates of his Majesty's colonies in America, having presumed, without his Majesty's authority or consent, to assemble together at Philadelphia, in the months of September and October last; and having thought fit, among other unwarrantable proceedings, to resolve that it will be necessary that another Congress should be held in this place, on the 10th of May next, unless redress for certain pretended grievances be obtained before that time, and to recommend that all the colonies in North America should choose delegates to attend such Congress. I am commanded by the

---

18. Franklin's Proposal to Lord Howe for Resolving the Crisis, December, 28 and 31, 1774, Willcox, ed., *The Papers of Benjamin Franklin*, 21:408.

19. Lord Howe to Caroline Howe, January 2, 1775, ibid., 21:436a.

20. Barclay to Franklin, January 2, 1775, ibid., 21:435.

21. Isaac Sharpless, *Quakers in the Revolution* (Honolulu. HI: University press of the Pacific, 2002), 113.

King to signify to you his Majesty's pleasure, that you do use your utmost endeavours to prevent such appointment of deputies within the colony under your government; and that you do exhort all persons to desist from such unwarrantable proceedings.[22]

JANUARY 7

Caroline Howe shows Franklin a letter she just received from her brother that asks him two questions: "first, would his constituents approve his agreeing to pay for the tea, on the condition that they were promised redress of their grievances when their assembly petitioned for it [and] second, did he still hold to the proposition that he had taken in his "Hints" on aids or requisitions?"[23] Franklin responds, "The people of America conceiving that Parliament has no Right to tax them, and that therefore all that has been extorted from them by the Operation of the Duty Acts, with the Assistance of an armed Force, *preceding* the Destruction of the Tea, is so much Injury, which ought in order of time to be first repair'd, before a Demand on the Tea can be justly made of them."[24]

JANUARY 19

Lord Howe meets with Franklin. "He thought I had Powers or Instructions from the Congress to make Concessions on Occasion that would be more satisfactory. I disclaim'd the having any . . . We talk'd over all the Particulars in my Paper . . . and [I] finally said that if what I had proposed would not do, I should be glad to hear what would do: I wish'd to see some Propositions from the Ministers themselves. His Lordp. was not, he said, as yet fully acquainted with their Sentiments, but should learn more in a few Days."[25]

Lord Chatham wishes Franklin to come to Parliament the next day when he will present a motion that he believes Franklin will be interested in.

JANUARY 20

Lord Chatham presents his Motion on the floor:

> . . . in order to open the Way towards a happy Settlement of the dangerous Troubles in America, by beginning to allay Ferments and soften

22. Circular Letter from Earl of Dartmouth to the American Governors, January 4, 1775, in William Legge, *Documenting the American South,"* The Colonial and State Records (Chapel Hill, NC: University of North Carolina Library, 2004), 9:1108.
23. Caroline Howe to Franklin, January 7, 1775," Willcox, ed., *The Papers of Benjamin Franklin*, 21:444a.
24. Replies to Questions from Lord Howe, January 7, 1775, ibid., 21:444b.
25. Journal of Negotiations.

Animosities there; and above all, for preventing . . . any sudden and fatal catastrophe at Boston, now suffering under the daily Irritation of an Army before their Eyes, posted in their Town, it may graciously please his Majesty that immediate Orders may be dispatched to General Gage for removing his Majesty's Forces from the Town of Boston, as soon as the Rigour of the Season and other Circumstances indispensable to the Safety and Accommodation of the said Troops may render the same principle.[26]

JANUARY 21

Franklin receives the original paper from which Lord Chatham read his motion.[27]

JANUARY 23

The Petition from the merchants, traders, and others concerned in the North American commerce is laid before the House of Commons. [28]

JANUARY 27

Franklin meets with Lord Chatham who "acquainted me in a long Conversation with the Outlines of his Plan." He said he "communicated it only to Lord Camden whose Advice he much rely'd on, particularly the Law . . . that he would as soon as he could get it transcrib'd put it into my Hands for my Opinion and Advice, but should show it to no other Person before he presented it to the House; and he requested me to make no mention of it, otherwise Parts might be misunderstood and blown upon, beforehand, and others perhaps adopted and produc'd by Ministers as their own.[29]

JANUARY 29

Lord Chatham brings Franklin his plan transcribed in the form of an Act of Parliament. "He thought the Errors of Ministers in American Affairs, had been often owing to their not obtaining the best Information: that therefore tho' he had considered the Business thoroughly in all its Parts, he was not so confident of his own Judgment, but that he came to set it right by mine, as Men set their Watches by a Regulator."[30]

---

26. Francis Wharton, ed., *The Revolutionary Diplomatic Correspondence of the United States* (Washington DC: G.P.O., 1889), 38.

27. Lord Stanhope to Franklin, January 21, 1775," Willcox, ed., *The Papers of Benjamin Franklin*, 21:454a.

28. Petition of Merchants, January 23, 1775, *Dartmouth Manuscripts* (Stafford, England: William Salt Library), 261-2.

29. Ibid.

30. Ibid.

JANUARY 31

Franklin brings Lord Chatham his *Notes for a Conversation*. Even though their conversation lasts nearly four hours, Franklin later claimed "there was not time to go thro half my Memorandums." In the end, "the Addition of a single Word only was made at my Instance - 'Constitutions' after Charters."[31]

FEBRUARY 1

Franklin goes Parliament to hear Lord Chatham present his plan entitled *A Provisional Act for Settling the Troubles of America and for Asserting the Supreme Legislative Authority and Superintending Power of Great Britain Over the Colonies.* When Lord Chatham was finished, Lord Dartmouth rose and said a "Matter of such Weight and Magnitude requir'[d] much consideration and so [he] was willing to let it lye upon the Table". Lords Sandwich, Hillsborough, and Gower immediately condemned the plan as did several other Lords. Lord Chatham had his supporters, the Duke of Richmond, Lord Camden and Lord Shelburne, but their voices were not enough. After a number of opinions on both sides were aired, Lord Dartmouth rose and said after hearing so many against the proposal he decided to change his position. The Plan was rejected by a vote of sixty-one to thirty-two.[32]
   Franklin was dumbfounded:

> To hear so many of the *Hereditary* Legislators declaiming so vehe-
> mently against, not Adopting merely, but even the *Consideration* of a
> Proposal so important in its Nature, offered by a Person of so weighty
> a Character . . . gave me an exceeding mean Opinion of their Abilities,
> and made their Claim of Sovereignty over three Millions of virtuous
> sensible People in America, seem the greatest of Absurdities, since they
> appear'd to have scarce Discretion enough to govern a Herd of Swine.[33]

FEBRUARY 4

Franklin meets with Barclay and Fothergill to review a document entitled *Remarks*. Its authorship is uncertain, but Lord Hyde is thought to be the most likely candidate. The *Remarks* were responses to the

31. 'Franklin's Notes for a Conversation with Lord Chatham, January 31, 1775, Willcox, ed., *The Papers of Benjamin Franklin*, 21:459a; Journal of Negotiations.
32. "Chatham's Speech in Support of his Provisional Act," in William Cobbett. *The Parliamentary History of England* (London:1813), 18:203; William Taylor and John Henry Pringle, eds., *Correspondence of William Pitt, Earl of Chatham* (London: John Murray, 1840), Appendix, 4:533-36; Cobbett. *The Parliamentary History of England*, 18:217-18.
33. Journal of Negotiations.

Franklin's "Hints" and Barclay's accommodations. Many of the terms were found acceptable by the author, but acknowledgment of the Supremacy of Parliament remained. Barclay mentions that when he went to see Lord Hyde he found Lord Howe, Hyde's neighbor, with him and was told "You may speak any thing before Lord Howe, that you have to say to me, for he is Friend in whom I confide."[34]

Lord Hyde wrote to Lord Dartmouth. He was aware that in mid-January the Cabinet had rejected the idea of a Peace Commission, but Franklin recently had supported the commission and if he would sponsor it in the cabinet, Hyde said he had the man to lead it: Lord Howe.[35]

FEBRUARY 5

Franklin informs Charles Thomson, Secretary of the Continental Congress, that 149 American papers, of which the *Petition* from the Continental Congress was but one, were laid before the House of Commons by Lord North on January 19 and before the House of Lords on January 20. The Commons referred them to a Committee of the Whole, the Lords laid them on the table. As to Lord Chatham's bill, it

> was treated with as much Contempt as they could have shown to a Ballad offered by a drunken Porter . . . And this is the Government whose supreme Authority we are to have [or] our Throats cut if we do not acknowledge . . . It is thought by our Friends that Lord Chatham's Plan, if it had been enacted, would have prevented present Mischief, and might have been the foundation of a lasting good Agreement.[36]

Lord Hyde writes to Barclay,

> Your letter my good friend, raises surprize & concern: The Light I saw is obscured, great hopes are baffled. The rubbs you mention are not to be smoothed by an arbitrary hand, they should be first mollifyed by submission. I felt & saw so much zeal for Conciliatory measures that I craved your's & the worthy Doctor's assistance in order to render it general . . . I will still wish that it may not be lost.[37]

34. Remarks on Hints, February 4, 1775, Willcox, ed., *The Papers of Benjamin Franklin*, 21:383a; ibid., 21:540b.
35. Ira D. Gruber, *The Howe Brothers and the American Revolution* (Chapel Hill, NC: University of North Carolina Press, 1972), 55.
36. Franklin to Charles Thomson, February 5, 1775," Willcox, ed., *The Papers of Benjamin Franklin*, 21:475-9.
37. Lord Hyde to Barclay, February 5, 1775," in Fox, *Dr. John Fothergill and his Friends*, Appendix A, 397-8.

FEBRUARY 6

Fothergill writes to Lord Dartmouth,

> I wish it had been in my power to have informed My Noble Friend that our negotiation had been successful; But it is not. Our difficultys arose from the American acts . . . As a concession to pay a tax was the sine qua non on this side, so a rescinding of those acts, or rather repealing then, in the term of reconciliation on the other . . . The party we confer'd with, would have no objection to meet the Noble Lords who were pleased to intimate that our endeavours to promote a reconciliation would not be unacceptable, and to consider the whole affair with the utmost candour and privacy.[38]

FEBRUARY 13 OR 14

Barclay meets with Franklin. He informs Franklin that he had recently met and discussed the "Hints" with accommodations with Lord Hyde and "he thought himself now fully possess'd of what would do in this Business." He asks that they meet with Fothergill on the 16th.[39]

FEBRUARY 16

Barclay presents presents his softened Plan of Reconciliation to Franklin and Fothergill. It is different from the modified "Hints" in that two more conditions are omitted: 6, "the Collectors and Customhouse Officers to be appointed by each Governor, and not sent from England" and 8, "no troops to enter and quarter in any colony without the consent of its legislature." A discussion of the omissions takes up the rest of the evening.[40]

FEBRUARY 17

Franklin, Barclay and Fothergill continue the meeting from the previous night. Franklin presents his comments regarding the plan. Barclay and Fothergill "being of Opinion, that the Repeal of none of the Massachusetts Acts could be obtain'd by my Engaging to pay for the Tea, the Boston Port excepted, and I insisting on a Repeal of all, otherwise declining to make the Offer, that Measure was deferr'd for the present and I pocketed my Drafts. They concluded however to report my Sentiments, and see if any farther Concession could be obtained."[41]

38. John Fothergill to Lord Dartmouth, February 6, 1775, Willcox, ed., *The Papers of Benjamin Franklin*, 21:479a.

39. Journal of Negotiations in London.

40. Barclay's Plan of Reconciliation, February 16, 1775, Willcox, ed., *The Papers of Benjamin Franklin*, 21:491b; *Dr. John Fothergill and his Friends*, Appendix A, 398-400.

41. Journal of Negotiations.

FEBRUARY 18

Franklin meets with Lord Howe who tells him

> He was to be sent Commissioner, for settling the Differences in America; adding . . . that sensible of his own Unacquaintedness with the Business, and of my Knowledge and Abilities, he could not think of undertaking it without me, but with me he should do it most readily . . . That he was very sensible if he [should be so happy] as to effect any thing valuable [it] must be wholly owing to the Advice and Assistance [I should afford] him; that he should therefore make no Scruple of giving me upon all occasions the full honour of it . . . and what he now wish'd was to be authoriz'd by me to say, that I consented to accompany him.

Franklin responded, "I shall deem it a great Honour to be in any shape join'd with your Lordship in so good a Work . . . He then said he wish'd I would discourse with Lord Hyde upon the Business, and ask'd If I had any Objection to meet his Lordship. I answer'd none, not the least."[42]

FEBRUARY 20

Lord North presents his Resolution on Conciliation in the House of Commons. He and his Cabinet had been discussing it since January 21.[43]

> It is the Opinion of [the Ministry], that when the Governor, Council and Assembly or General Court ... shall propose to make Provision according to their respective Conditions, Circumstances and situations, for contributing their Proportion to the common Defence . . . raised under the Authority of the General Court, or General Assembly . . . and Disposable by Parliament; and shall engage to make Provision also for the Support of the Civil Government, and the Administration of Justice in such Province or Colony; it will be proper, if such Proposal shall be approved by his Majesty in Parliament and for so long as such Provision shall be made accordingly, to forbear in respect of such Province or Colony, to levy any Duties, Tax or Assessment, or to impose any further Duty, Tax or Assessment, except only such Duties as it may be expedient to impose for the Regulation of Commerce.[44]

---

42. Ibid.
43. Cabinet Meeting, January 21, 1775, *Dartmouth Manuscripts*, 1093.
44. Force, *American Archives*, 1:1598.

His Resolution surprised many of his supporters outside of the cabinet while his opponents in Parliament saw it as "insincere and insufficient." Lord Dartmouth attached all of his hopes for reconciliation on the resolution—he believed once the Supremacy of Parliament was acknowledged, the specifics of reconciliation could be discussed. Only a gross misunderstanding of colonial grievances and the rise of colonial unity can explain why so much hope was placed upon the resolution. Lord Howe writes to Franklin, "Not having had a convenient opportunity to talk with Lord Hyde until this morning . . . [he] apprehends, that on the present American contest, your principles and his, or rather those of Parliament, are as yet so wide from each other, that a meeting merely to discuss them might give you unnecessary trouble."[45] Franklin writes back, "Having nothing to offer on the American Business in Addition to what Lord Hyde is already acquainted with from the Papers that have passed, it seems most respectful not to give his Lordship the Trouble of a Visit."[46]

FEBRUARY 27

Lord North's Resolution was approved by a vote of 274 to 88, unfortunately, it never had a chance of being accepted in the colonies because by the time it reached there, the events of Lexington and Concord were unfolding.

FEBRUARY 28

Franklin tells Caroline Howe that he has not heard from her brother for better than a week. "I suppos'd it owing to his finding what he had propos'd to me was not likely to take place; and I wish'd her to Desire him, if that was the Case, to let me know it by a Line, that I might be at liberty to take other Measures." When Caroline Howe informed her brother of Franklin's request, he met with him later in the day.[47] Lord Howe was concerned about what Franklin meant by "take other measures."

> He said my last Paper of Remarks by Mr. Barclay, wherein I made the Indemnification of Boston for the Injury of Stopping its Port, a Condition of my engaging to pay for the Tea, a Condition impossible to be compl'd with, had discourag'd farther Proceeding on that idea. Having a Copy of that Paper in my Pocket, I show'd his Lordship, that I had propos'd no such Condition . . . nor any other than the repeal of

45. Lord Howe to Franklin, February 20, 1775," Willcox, ed., *The Papers of Benjamin Franklin*, 21:501a.
46. Franklin to Lord Howe, February 20, 1775, ibid., 21:502a.
47. Caroline Howe to Franklin, February 28, 1775," ibid., 21:514a.

all the Massachusetts Acts. That what follow'd relating to the Indemnification was only expressing my private Opinion that it would be just ... as I now explain'd myself it appear'd I had been much misapprehended; and he wished, of all things I would still see Lord Hyde ... [I said] I would wait upon Lord Hyde: I knew him to be an early Riser, and would be with him at 8 the next Morning; which Lord Howe undertook to acquaint him with.[48]

MARCH I

Franklin meets with Lord Hyde for the last time.

He had hoped that Lord North's Motion would have been satisfactory; and ask'd what could be objected to it. I repl'd the Terms of it were that we should grant Money till Parliament had agreed we had given enough, without having the least share in judging of the Propriety of the Measures for which it was to be granted ... that these Grants were also to be made under the Threat of exercising a claimed Right of Taxing us at Pleasure, and compelling such Taxes by an armed Force ... the Proposition was similar to ... a Highway-man who presents his Pistol and Hat at a Coach-Window, demanding no specific Sum, but if you will give all your Money or what he is pleas'd to think sufficient, he will civilly omit putting his own Hand into your Pockets.[49]

MARCH 4

Caroline Howe writes to Franklin that her brother "begs to have the pleasure of meeting him once more before he goes."[50]

MARCH 7

Lord Howe meets with Franklin for the last time.

He began by saying, that I had been a better Prophet than himself, in foreseeing that my Interview with Lord Hyde would be of no great Use: and then said, that he hoped I would excuse the Trouble he had given me, as his Intentions had been good both towards me and the Publick; he was sorry that at present there was no Appearance of Things going into the Train he had wished ... [but] if he should chance to be sent thither on that important Business, he hop'd he might still expect my Assistance. I assur'd him of my Readiness at all times of co-operating with him.[51]

48. Journal of Negotiations.
49. Ibid.
50. "From Caroline Howe to Benjamin Franklin, 4 March 1775," Willcox, ed., *The Papers of Benjamin Franklin*, 21:515a.
51. Journal of Negotiations.

MARCH 13

Franklin writes to Charles Thomson,

> The Petition of the Congress has lain upon the Table of both
> Houses ever since it was sent down to them among the Papers that ac-
> company'd it from above, and has had no particular Notice taken of it;
> [Chatham's] Petition to be heard in support of it, having been . . . re-
> jected with Scorn in the Commons; which must the future Congress
> that nothing is to be expected here from that Mode of Application . . .
> Our only Safety is in the firmest Union, and keeping strict Faith with
> each other.[52]

MARCH 17

Barclay and Fothergill meet with Franklin at his home. "They desired
me to assure their Friends [in the colonies] from them, that it was now
their fix'd Opinion, that nothing could secure the Privileges of America,
but a firm sober Adherence to the Terms of the Association made at
the Congress, and that the Salvation of English Liberty depended now
on the Perseverance and Virtue of America."[53]

MARCH 18

Barclay writes to James Pemberton of Philadelphia,

> We had an Intimation given by a noble person that if we had any
> Thing to offer more likely to produce the desired end (conciliating
> Measures) than the Hints which we had lately given, then was the pe-
> riod, before it was too late; declaring at the same time, that he had noth-
> ing particular to propose. This produced a Meeting, and a fair
> discussion of the Articles contained in the Hints, and a declaration,
> that we were determined to do nothing without Dr. Franklin, who had
> been instrumental in framing those Hints . . . after several Conferances
> enabled us to produce a paper entituled a Plan which we had some rea-
> son to believe was not disapproved by the Noble Lord who acted as a
> Mediator . . . At the same time a person of high rank (and equal repu-
> tation in your Continent) was by both sides agreed to be the most
> proper person to be sent from hence to effect this business; and our
> plan was, for Dr. Franklin to go at the same time, with the Ollive
> Branch. From this Period we could never make any Advancement nor

---

52. Franklin to Thomson, March 13, 1775," Willcox, ed., *The Papers of Benjamin Franklin*,
21:475-79.
53. Journal of Negotiations.

obtain any Concession . . . How far you will be allur'd thereby, or any other of the present Plans intended to Devide, time must shew.[54]

MARCH 18

Franklin spent the afternoon with Edmund Burke, member of the House of Commons who sympathized with the colonists' plight. Along with Lord Chatham, Burke pleaded in Parliament for understanding of and compromise with the American colonies. Franklin told him that the affection the colonies had for England was gone forever, that he lamented the separation which he feared was inevitable between England and her colonies, and that peace was lost because of an inability to compromise.

MARCH 19

Franklin had been in England for ten years. In the final four months, he did everything in his power to bring about some form of reconciliation. He spent his last day in London with his friend Joseph Priestley. They discussed the major topics in the London newspapers. Fearing that war now seemed inevitable, Franklin at times had to stop reading because of the tears in his eyes.[55]

Fothergill wrote to Franklin. He asked him when he got back to Philadelphia to gather some of their common friends and "acquaint them with D.B.'s and our united endeavours, and the effects. They will stun at least, if not convince the most courtly, that nothing very favourable is intended . . . farewel, and befriend this infant, growing empire with the utmost exertion of thy abilitys, and no less philanthropy, both which are beyond my powers to express."[56]

MARCH 20

Franklin sets out from London for Portsmouth.

MARCH 21

Franklin boards a ship in Portsmouth for Philadelphia.

MARCH 22

In a speech in the House of Commons, Edmund Burke presents *On Conciliation with the Colonies*. He begins by stating "The proposition is peace. Not peace through the medium of war, not peace to be hunted

---

54. Barclay to James Pemberton: Extract, March 18, 1775," Willcox, ed., *The Papers of Benjamin Franklin*, 21:531.
55. J.T. Rutt, ed., *The Life and Correspondence of Joseph Priestley* (1817; New York: Thoemmes Press, 1999), 1:227.
56. Fothergill to Franklin, March 19, 1775," Willcox, ed., *The Papers of Benjamin Franklin*, 21:537.

through the labyrinth of intricate and endless negotiations, not peace to arise out of universal discord . . . it is simple peace, sought in its natural course and in its ordinary haunts. It is peace sought in the spirit of peace, and laid in principles purely pacific. I propose, by removing the ground of the difference and by restoring the former unsuspecting confidence of the colonies in the mother country subsidies in Parliament."[57]

Even in his absence, Franklin was attempting one final time to bring about peace.

---

57. "Burke's Speech *On Conciliation with the Colonies*, March 22, 1775,"in Cobbett. *The Parliamentary History of England* 18:478-538.

The Route is by Way of Winnisimmet: Chelsea and the Refugees

❀❧ KATIE TURNER GETTY ❧❀

It was August 1775 and Belcher Noyes, worried about his son Nathaniel, was writing to him from Boston for a third time. "My dear son: Have received no letter from you since May 27, which I duly answered 3d June . . . I wrote you May 25, both of which I hope came safe to your hands."[1]

To his great anxiety, sixty-five year old Belcher Noyes found himself trapped in Boston that summer, frantically penning unanswered letters to his adult son, and surrounded by thousands of seething British troops and distressed townspeople. Boston and the Massachusetts countryside roiled with unrest. Patriot forces had locked up thousands of British troops on the Boston peninsula after the Battles of Lexington and Concord. Forming a ring around the town, militia and minute men managed to contain the British in Boston and prevent further forays into the country. Those men had since been organized into the Continental Army and were laying siege to Boston.

Rumors swirled that the destruction of Boston was nigh and dysentery wracked the town. People were desperate to escape. Belcher wrote to his son. "Provisions scarce and bad; no fuel nor money . . . Last week there was a notification posted up, that all those who were desirous to leave the Town, to give in their names to James Urquhart, Town-Major; and in two days time upwards of two thousand entered their names, and passes are now granted . . . The route is by way of Winnisimit."[2]

---

1. Letter from Boston, Peter Force, ed., *American Archives,* Documents of the American Revolutionary Period, 1774-1776, Ser. 4, 3:31, Digital Collections and Collaborative Projects, University Libraries, Northern Illinois University, amarch.lib.niu.edu/islandora/object/niu-amarch%3A80554, accessed December 12, 2017.
2. Ibid.

If places could have memories, then Winnisimmet's would be a long one. By the time of the Siege of Boston in 1775, Winnisimmet Ferry had already been in continuous operation for 144 years. For almost two centuries the ferry had served as a hub of humanity, spiriting passengers, horses and goods back and forth between Boston's North End and the coastal town of Chelsea, just to the northeast across Boston Harbor. Once in Chelsea, the fishing villages of Lynn, Salem, Marblehead and the entire Massachusetts north shore lay beyond.

At least as late as 1749, four boats comprised Winnisimmet Ferry—two row boats and two sailboats. At any given moment, two boats would be plying the waters of Boston Harbor, and "when any one of the said boats shall land at either shoar, the other boat on the same side shall immediately put off."[3] From April 1 to November 1, the ferry operated from sunrise to 9 p.m. and during the icy, dark winter months, it operated from 8:00 a.m. to 8:00 p.m. The ferrymen were responsible for remaining constantly "at or near each boat to keep them from grounding and attend on the passengers."[4]

Belcher Noyes must have given his letter to someone he knew who planned to leave Boston by crossing the harbor to Winnisimmet. "Several have gone off, by which means I have an opportunity of writing you. I have it in my mind to go to Mr. Little's, at Newbury, in case I can accomplish it," he informed his son. "On receipt of this, endeavor to write me your mind. Mr. Welles, the mason, lives at Chelsea, by which means a letter may be conveyed; be cautious what you write."[5]

Since April, the Boston Selectmen had been negotiating with British General Gage to allow Bostonians to escape the privations of the occupied town and flee to the countryside, but the process proved to be erratic and unpredictable. People attempting to leave encountered various oppressive and inconsistent policies. "All merchandise was forbid; after a while all provisions were forbid; and now all merchandise, provisions, and medicine. Guards are appointed to examine all trunks, boxes, beds, and every thing else to be carried out; these have proceeded such extremities, as to take from the poor people a single loaf of bread, and half pound of chocolate; so that no one is allowed to carry out a mouthful of provisions."[6]

3. *The Acts and Resolves, Public and Private, of the Province of the Massachusetts Bay*, Vol. 3 (Boston: Albert J. Wright, 1878), 466, books.google.com/books?id=RApHAQAAIAAJ &pg=PA1#v=onepage&q&f=false.
4. Ibid.
5. Letter from Boston, Peter Force.
6. Extract of a Letter to a Gentleman in Philadelphia, *American Archives*, , Ser. 4, 2:666, Digital Collections, Northern Illinois University, amarch.lib.niu.edu/islandora/object/niu-amarch%3A94412, accessed January 13, 2018.

Detail from "A plan of the town and harbour of Boston" by J. DeCosta, 1775. "Winisimit" is top center with a ferry boat illustrated in the river.

As Boston was a peninsula connected to the mainland by a narrow neck, any refugees who successfully wrested permission from General Gage to leave could only lawfully pass out of the town by way of the land route to Roxbury or the Winnisimmet Ferry to Chelsea.

Chelsea lay northeast of Boston; its expansive salt marshes and beachy shore running alongside Boston Harbor and the mouth of the Mystic River. The distant parts of Chelsea called Pulling Point and Point Shirley were situated on a peninsula further east, fronting the Atlantic Ocean. The Winnisimmet area of Chelsea was closest to Boston; Charlestown and Breed's Hill lay within direct eyeshot to the west and the Boston Harbor islands of Noddle's and Hog practically within wading distance.

The proximity of Chelsea to the thousands of British soldiers occupying Boston distressed the inhabitants of the coastal community. British men o' war loaded with troops could easily land upon their beaches—likely in less than half an hour.[7] In May 1775, the people of Chelsea and the neighboring town of Malden petitioned the Committee of Safety for protection and requested detachments from the Provincial Army to guard their towns.[8]

The army was unable to spare any men for such duty. But on May 3, 1775, the provincial congress voted that "two companies be raised in the towns of Chelsea and Malden for the defence of the sea coast of said towns."[9] The next month, those companies were joined to Col. Samuel Gerrish's Regiment.[10] Later that summer, Colonel Gerrish would be court-martialed and cashiered.[11] Lt. Col. Loammi Baldwin, of Woburn, was chosen to be Gerrish's successor in command of the regiment.

That summer, Lt. Col. Loammi Baldwin wrote to Gen. George Washington almost every day from Chelsea—which had become the furthest extremity of the left wing of the Continental Army. He and his men provided intelligence to General Washington by monitoring the movement of ships in the harbor and handling the boatloads of

7. *Journals of the House of Representatives of Massachusetts 1775–1776*, Massachusetts Historical Society (Boston: 1983), 78, Hathitrust Digital Library, babel.hathitrust.org/cgi/pt?id=mdp.35112104247293;view=1up;seq=11 accessed December 11, 2017.
8. Ibid.
9. *The Journals of Each Provincial Congress of Massachusetts in 1774 and 1775* (Boston: Dutton and Wentworth, 1838), 533, books.google.com/books?id=iFVMkRsFQh4C&pg=PP1#v=onepage&q&f=false.
10. Ibid, 401.
11. General Orders, August 19, 1775, *Founders Online*, National Archives, founders.archives.gov/documents/Washington/03-01-02-0225, accessed December 2, 2017.

refugees who fled Boston and disembarked at Winnisimmet Ferry.

Due to General Gage's unpredictability in issuing passes to the individuals and families desperate to leave Boston, the exodus had been sporadic and irregular. But in late July, the soldiers stationed at Chelsea were surprised by the arrival of a boat full of refugees.

On July 29, 1775, Baldwin notified General Washington of a boat unexpectedly landing at Winnisimmet. "We wase all allarm'd by the approach of a Boat to Winnisimmit Ferry & by a Signal Soon found them to be friends who Landed with their Houshold good . . . I would Beg your Excelency would Send me Some Assistence as the Boats are to Continue passing (*That is if we can believe General Gage*) and Somthing may Escape for want of Proper assistenc that may turn to our disadvantage."[12]

Expecting at any moment that General Gage might permit more people to leave Boston, Lieutenant Colonel Baldwin requested assistance from General Washington in managing the flow of refugees. He also sought assurance that he and his men were not inadvertently letting smallpox sufferers or potential malefactors through the lines.

After receiving Lieutenant Colonel Baldwin's request for help, General Washington immediately informed the provincial congress that Bostonians were arriving unexpectedly at Winnisimmet Ferry. In response, about fifty of its members convened in an emergency Sabbath-Day session. "Apprehensive that the people of the country may be exposed to take the small-pox; the said inhabitants of Boston being suffered indiscriminately to resort into the country," the congress dispatched a committee to Chelsea.[13]

The committee's duty was to "inspect the state and characters of such inhabitants of Boston . . . and be empowered and ordered to do and direct every thing that they shall find absolutely necessary for the safety of the Country, and the immediate relief of any helpless and indigent persons."[14]

Meanwhile, Lieutenant Colonel Baldwin attempted to contain the refugees in Chelsea and prevent possible communication of smallpox to the army. "Should be glad to know in what manner I am to proceed, with the People that come out of Boston, in order to pr[e]vent there

12. Lt. Col. Loammi Baldwin to Gen. George Washington, July 29, 1775, *Founders Online*, National Archives, founders.archives.gov/documents/Washington/03-01-02-0120, accessed November 22, 2017.

13. Committee to Repair to Chelsea, *American Archives*, Ser. 4, 3:292, Digital Collections, Northern Illinois University, amarch.lib.niu.edu/islandora/object/niu-amarch%3A92506, accessed December 22, 2017.

14. Ibid., 293.

going into Camp . . . There are People now waiting to know your Excellency's Answer that want to proceed into the Country . . . I am now obliged to let them go about among the neighbor for Suport as they Brought nothing of that nature with them."[15]

Lieutenant Colonel Baldwin soon received news that the provincial congress would provide assistance in caring for "the poor people Sent to Chelsea from Boston."[16]

Some of these "poor people" who arrived at Chelsea from Boston via Winnisimmet Ferry were mothers with their children. Among dozens of women (and some couples) with children who landed that month were Ellen Morgen with four children, Elesebeth Sinkler with four children, Anna Green with four children, and Mary Robards and two children.[17] On August 17, Ebenezer Higgins arrived with his and wife and four children, Huldah Bassett and four children, and Elisebeth Hopkins and six children.[18]

Upon arriving in Chelsea, the committee learned from the refugees they encountered that General Gage was not presently allowing any Bostonians to leave the town, nor was it known when the next group of refugees would be permitted out.[19] In light of this uncertainty and unable to remain away from their legislative duties for long, the committee decided to return to Watertown. They instructed the Committee of Correspondence of Chelsea to handle the refugees on their behalf. "If you suspect they or their effects are infected with the small-pox, that you see that they be cleansed; and all such persons as are so infirm that they cannot be removed, that you provide for them at the publick expense until they can be removed . . ."[20] Only about a week would pass, however, before General Washington would send word to the provincial congress requesting that a permanent committee be sent to Chelsea to help manage the refugees.

During the first week of August, boats filled with refugees started arriving from Boston at unpredictable intervals. Still concerned about the possibility of smallpox being transmitted to the army or letting po-

15. Baldwin to Washington, July 31, 1775, *Founders Online*, National Archives, accessed November 2, 2017.
16. Ibid., fn 2.
17. Baldwin's Regiment, Vol. 60, 985, Muster Rolls of the Revolutionary War, Massachusetts State Archives, Boston, Massachusetts.
18. Ibid., 974.
19. Peter Force, ed., *American Archives: A Documentary History of the English Colonies in North America*, Ser. 4, Vol. 3 (Washington: M. St. Clair Clarke and Peter Force, 1840), 293, books.google.com/books?id=WmpAAAAAcAAJ&pg=PP1#v=onepage&q&f=false.
20. Ibid.

tentially treacherous people through the lines, General Washington again contacted the provincial congress. In asking for additional assistance in managing the flow of people, he explained "Business multiplies so fast, and we are so much Strangers to the Characters, and Conduct of many, that I would wish to put it on some more proper Footing: especially as it takes Several Field Officers every day from their Duty."[21] The next day, the congress formed a permanent committee to provide "constant attendance at the place where the People coming out of Boston to Chelsea shall land."[22]

As summer turned to fall, the committee along with the men of Baldwin's Regiment continued to manage the refugees. The committee provided shelter for the refugees and tried to prevent the spread of smallpox by "smoking, cleansing, airing, and detaining Persons or Effects . . . to prevent a communication of the distemper to the army or inhabitants of this Colony."[23] Teams of horses were hired to relocate the refugees to other Massachusetts towns.

As refugees from Boston continued landing at Winnisimmet, Baldwin's men collected letters they carried and submitted them to General Washington to be scanned for intelligence-gathering purposes. "I have taken the names of all the Passeng[ers] and Stopd the Letters which I now Send for y[our] Inspection & Beg your Excellency would Send them Back to me again as soon as possable as the Bairers are Some of them in waighting and others are to call again tomorrow for theirs— Please to Keep the Inclosd Letters in there Respective covers."[24]

One of these letters was the one written by concerned father Belcher Noyes, to his son Nathaniel. This particular letter caught the eye of General Washington. In it, Belcher recounted distress and hardships faced by those trapped in Boston. "[There is] some conjecture the destruction of this Town is intended," and many townspeople feared that, if they did escape, the British might "plunder and demolish the Town" after they left. The refugees were prohibited from carrying with them "plate of any kind nor more money than five pounds sterling."[25] Passes, too, were denied to men without special permission.[26]

21. Washington to James Otis, Sr., August 5, 1775, *Founders Online*, National Archives, founders.archives.gov/documents/Washington/03-01-02-0158, accessed January 5, 2018.
22. Ibid. fn 2.
23. Peter Force, ed., *American Archives: A Documentary History*, 1516.
24. Baldwin to Washington, July 31, 1775, *Founders Online*, National Archives, founders.archives.gov/documents/Washington/03-01-02-0120, accessed November 2, 2017.
25. Letter from Boston, Peter Force.
26. Ibid.

General Washington, noting with interest Belcher's description of Boston's sufferings, forwarded it to John Hancock for his perusal. "As the Writer is a Person of some Note in Boston, & it contains some Advices of Importance not mentioned by others, I thought proper to forward it as I received it ... . General Gage has at length liberated the People of Boston, who land in Numbers at Chelsea every Day, the Terms on which the Passes are granted as to Money Effects & Provisions correspond with Mr Noyes's Letter."[27]

His concerns about smallpox and treacherous individuals crossing the lines still unappeased, in early October General Washington wrote to the provincial congress suggesting that the Winnisimmet ferry be shut down.

Agreeing with the General and likewise frustrated by General Gage's refusal to permit the Bostonians out with any regularity, the congress decided:

> Whereas this Court has reason to apprehend that the Small-Pox prevails in the Town of Boston, whereby great danger is apprehended of spreading that distemper through the country, by the Ferry at Chelsea, being open for the transportation of the Poor and other inhabitants of the Town of Boston into the country; and whereas General Gage does not comply with the just expectations of this Court, that the said inhabitants, with their effects, should come out indiscriminately, but perverts the communication to purposes that may prove dangerous to the community.
>
> Therefore, Resolved, That the Committee appointed to attend at Chelsea be ordered to retire, and give no further attendance, and that no boats pass and repass that ferry, from and to Boston; and whenever it shall appear to this Court that General Gage is disposed to comply with his engagement for a general liberation of the inhabitants of Boston and their effects, this Court will be ready to receive and make suitable provision for said inhabitants.[28]

On October 22, Lt. Col. Loammi Baldwin received orders that "no more Boats come over to Winnisimet ... If you have not already apprized the Boatmen of this Order you are to do it the first opportunity

27. Washington to John Hancock, August 4-5, 1775, Founders Online, National Archives, founders.archives.gov/documents/Washington/03-01-02-0150, accessed December 12, 2017.

28. Report on the Communication, *American Archives*, Ser. 4, 3:1454, Digital Collections, Northern Illinois University, amarch.lib.niu.edu/islandora/object/niu-amarch%3A90944, accessed December 28, 2017.

& in Case they persist after being warned to the Contrary you are to fire upon them."[29]

Despite that order, about one week later a boat carrying thirty-two people including many children arrived. Among the passengers were Anna Laurence and four children, Samuel Greenleaf, his wife and three children, Mary Wilson and child, Hannah Hughes and child, and "a Woman with 6 children."[30] A note under the passenger list reads, "According to orders I have forbid the boat coming out again."[31]

As for concerned father Belcher Noyes—he did succeed in getting out of Boston, but for him, the route was not, in fact, by way of Winnisimmet. In late November, 1775, he boarded the British transport ship *Symmetry* bound for Chelsea—or so he thought. But instead of sailing to Winnisimmet, the ship landed its passengers at "Point Shirley a Marooned Place," a long, narrow, beachy and windswept part of Chelsea situated across Boston Harbor.[32] Scarcely inhabited and with the crashing Atlantic pounding its eastern shore, Point Shirley was so isolated that it had historically been the site of a smallpox hospital.[33]

The Bostonians aboard the ship were ordered to immediately disembark, "no one suffered to Stay on board some of us were unwilling to go on Shore but were forc'd to go on Shore in the Dark this was cruel Treatment as some were laying dangerously ill, two dyed the next day, and one Woman [died] in two days occasioned by a fall in going on shore."[34]

Hiring a team of horses to carry his possessions, Belcher set out walking. Within the next few days, enduring bad roads, cold, and unexpected snow, he made the thirty-five mile journey northward to the home of Colonel Little in Newbury, Massachusetts. Both Belcher Noyes and his son Nathaniel eventually made it back to Boston and lived long enough to see not only the end of the siege, but the end of the revolution. Belcher died in 1791 at the age of eighty-two.

29. Washington to the Massachusetts General Court, October 6, 1775, fn 2, *Founders Online*, National Archives, founders.archives.gov/documents/Washington/03-02-02-0108, accessed December 30, 2017.

30. Baldwin's Regt, 958-959, Massachusetts State Archives.

31. Ibid., 958.

32. Belcher Noyes Diaries, 1775-1776, Octavo Vols "N," Manuscript Collections, American Antiquarian Society, Worcester, Massachusetts.

33. Mellen Chamberlain, *A Documentary History of Chelsea* (Boston: Printed for the Massachusetts Historical Society, 1908), 405, books.google.com/books?id=BQwpAAAAYAAJ &pg=PR3#v=onepage&q&f=false

34. Belcher Noyes Diaries, 1775-1776, American Antiquarian Society.

In March 1776, the British evacuated Boston and the siege ended. No longer trying to escape, Bostonians started pouring back into the town, anxious to reunite with loved ones and piece together whatever was left of their homes and livelihoods before the siege.

Winnisimmet Ferry operated for the next 142 years, long-outliving the refugees who boarded the boats with their children and the ferry-men who rowed them. In the end, the Winnisimmet ferry spanned four centuries, its last passenger from Boston disembarking in Chelsea in 1917.

The General, the Corporal, and the Anecdote: Jacob Francis and Israel Putnam

J. L. BELL

On August 18, 1832, a seventy-eight-year-old New Jersey man named Jacob Francis went before Hunterdon County officials and described his military service in the Revolutionary War. His affidavit became the core of his application for a federal government pension available to surviving veterans.[1]

According to Francis, he had joined the Continental Army besieging Boston in the fall of 1775 and served through the following year; he also had several shorter stints with the forces of his home state of New Jersey.[2] In his application Francis told of a passing encounter with Gen. Israel Putnam of Connecticut. That story and the ways in which it was publicly retold over the next century and a half help to reveal how American culture remembered and misremembered the Revolution.

Here is the anecdote Jacob Francis related, broken into paragraphs for easier reading:

> I recollect General Putnam more particularly from a circumstance that occurred when the Troops were engaged in throwing up a breastwork at Leachmore's-point across the river, opposite Boston, between that & Cambridge,

1. In the database of Revolutionary War pensions available through Fold3.com, Jacob Francis's application is filed under Massachusetts because he first enlisted in that state, even though he was born, later served, and settled in New Jersey. For this article Francis's anecdote about Putnam was transcribed directly from his application, not from the published version.

2. See Larry Kidder, "The American Revolution of Jacob Francis," *Journal of the American Revolution*, March 6, 2018.

the men were at work digging, about 500 men on the fatigue at once, I was at work among them, they were divided into small squads of 8 or 10 together, & a non commissioned officer to oversee them.

General Putnam came Riding along in uniform as an officer to look at the Work. They had dug up a pretty large stone which lay on the side of the ditch. The General spoke to the corporal who was standing looking at the men at work & said to him "my lad throw that stone up on the middle of the breastwork,"

the Corporal touching his hat with his hand said to the General "Sir I am a Corporal."

"O." (said the General) "I ask your pardon sir," and immediately got off his horse and took up the stone and threw it up on the breastwork himself. & then mounted his horse & rode on, giving directions, &c.

This is a great story. It's pithy, it has a nice twist with an unspoken moral lesson, and it reveals the general's character. This story fits with what other sources tell us about Israel Putnam. It shows the physical strength that led him to attack a wolf in her own den.[3] It confirms the lack of pretension that mustermaster general Stephen Moylan captured in late 1775 when he described "old PUT mounted on the large mortar [captured from an enemy ship] . . . with a bottle of rum in his hand, standing parson to christen" the big-mouthed artillery piece with the name of "Congress."[4]

As Francis applied for a pension, the value of his story lay in proving how he remembered vivid details of his military service in Massachusetts. He specified that the event happened at Lechmere Point. Indeed, troops under Putnam's command were busy fortifying that part of eastern Cambridge in late 1775 and early 1776.

Francis didn't need to tell this story to entertain or impress the bureaucrats who approved Revolutionary War pensions. In fact, if those officials had concluded that the man's anecdotes were too good to be true, then they might have denied him financial support in his old age. He therefore had little reason to make up a tale like this. Jacob Francis's pension was approved, and his recollections were filed away in Washington, D.C., with the rest of his paperwork.

3. Putnam's encounter with the wolf was well known during the Revolution and earned grudging respect even from the Loyalist Peter Oliver. *Peter Oliver's Origin and Progress of the American Rebellion: A Tory View*, Douglass Adair and John A. Schutz, editors (San Marino, CA: Huntington Library, 1961), 122-3.
4. Stephen Moylan to Joseph Reed, December 5, 1775, as printed in William B. Reed, *The Life and Correspondence of Joseph Reed* (Philadelphia: Lindsay & Blakiston, 1847), 1:133.

Only seven years later, a different version of the same story appeared in American newspapers. The earliest examples I've found were in the October 22, 1839, issue of *The North American*, published in Philadelphia, and the October 23 issue of the *Norwich Courier* in Connecticut. There was almost certainly an older source that both those newspapers drew from, but neither offered any indication of where. In this period, it was common for printers to pick up material without credit from other newspapers, magazines, or books. As electronic newspaper databases grow larger, an earlier printing will probably surface.

Here is the 1839 version of the anecdote, curious punctuation and all:

> THE CORPORAL.—During the American revolution, an officer not habited in the military costume, was passing by where a small company of soldiers were at work, making some repairs upon a small redoubt. The commander of the little squad was giving orders to those who were under him, relative to a stick of timber, which they were endeavouring to raise to the top of the works. The timber went up hard, and on this account the voice of the little great man was often heard in his regular vociferations of "Heave away! There she goes! Heave ho!" etc. The officer before spoken of stopped his horse when arrived at the place, and seeing the timber sometimes scarcely move, asked the commander why he did not take hold and render a little aid. The latter appeared to be somewhat astonished, turning to the officer with the pomp of an Emperor, said, "Sir, I am a corporal!["] 'You are not though, are you?' said the officer; 'I was not aware of it.' And taking off his hat and bowing, 'I ask your pardon, Mr. corporal." Upon this he dismounted his elegant steed, flung the bridle over the post, and lifted till the sweat stood in drops on his forehead. When the timber was elevated to its proper station, turning to the man clothed in brief authority, "Mr. Corporal," said he, "when you have another such job, and have not men enough, send to your Commander-in-chief, and I will come and help you a second time." The corporal was thunderstruck! It was Washington.

The core of this story is obviously the same that Jacob Francis had told in 1832, but many details are changed. Most important, the general is now George Washington instead of Israel Putnam. The task the soldiers are struggling with is different: lifting a log instead of a boulder. The specific place and time have disappeared entirely, rendering the tale difficult to confirm and impossible to refute. The general has more to say to the corporal, and the narrator more to say to readers, turning a subtle anecdote into a ham-handed moral lesson. Yet the lines "Sir, I am a corporal!" and "I beg/ask your pardon, sir" appear in both Francis's anecdote and in the newspaper version, strongly suggesting that they shared a common source—either an earlier telling of the tale or an actual event.

Washington was of course a more celebrated general than Putnam, and the attractive force of celebrity probably altered the anecdote to be about him. However, the behavior it describes does not fit the commander-in-chief. Washington was physically powerful like Putnam, but he strongly emphasized hierarchy, discipline, and proper military appearance. He valued the distinction between officers and ordinary soldiers. He would not have labored alongside enlisted men, no matter if Americans in the middle of the nineteenth century liked to imagine him doing so.

Many other American newspapers reprinted that tall tale about Washington and the corporal into the 1840s. *The Rural Repository* magazine ran the story in 1850, and it continued to pop up in publications through the end of the century. At some point Henry Alexander Ogden illustrated it for a magazine or textbook. Today blogs retell the tale of General Washington surprising the self-important corporal.[5]

That wasn't the only version of the story passed along in nineteenth-century America, however. Another finally saw print in 1883 in Alexander M. Gow's book *The Primer of Politeness*. In this variation, the conglomerations of quotation marks testify to how the author wanted to assure readers that he was directly quoting from a reliable source:

Washington at Dorchester.
An anecdote of Washington, told by the Rev. Simeon Locke, who died in 1831, aged eighty-three years, is thus related. Mr. Locke, who

5. Examples of the wide range of publications that reprinted or retold the 1839 story include the *Cyclopaedia of Moral and Religious Anecdotes* (1853); *A Nation's Manhood; or, Stories of Washington and the American War of Independence*, by the British author Mrs. E. Burrows (1861) with an illustration; *Encyclopedia of Wit and Wisdom*, compiled by Henry Hupfeld (1897); *Modern Eloquence*, edited by Thomas B. Reed (1900); *Modern English: A Practical English Grammar with Exercises in Composition*, by Henry P. Emerson and Ida C. Bender (1909); the November 1917 issue of *St. Nicholas*; the July 1966 issue of *Boys' Life*; the 2000 edition of *Bartlett's Book of Anecdotes*; and *A Story Is Told: Inspiring Stories and Illustrations from "Our Daily Bread,"* compiled by Dave Brannon (2010).

was a respected clergyman of Hollis, Maine, was a frequent visitor, about fifty years ago, at a friend's house in Kennebunkport. "When I was a boy," writes Mr. Andrew Walker, the narrator, "I have heard him more than once relate the following anecdote, and I recollect it as distinctly as if told yesterday. He said,—

"'I was a soldier in the army of the Revolution, and was detailed, with others, to build the breastworks on Dorchester Heights. A day or two after the works were begun, General Washington rode into the enclosure. I was a sentinel. Near me was a wheelbarrow and shovel; not far off was an idle soldier.

""'Why do you not work with the others?" asked Washington, addressing the soldier.

""'I am a corporal, sir," he replied.

"'The general immediately dismounted, and marched to the barrow, shovelled it full of sand, wheeled it to the breastworks, dumped his load, and returned the empty barrow to its place. Without uttering a word, he mounted his horse and rode away.'"

False pride he despised, and he was always ready to rebuke it.[6]

Again we have General Washington doing physical work that the corporal doesn't deign to do—but now that work is moving sand with a wheelbarrow. Again, we have the line, "I am a corporal, sir." And again, the story comes with an overt moral lesson.

Some details of this story check out. The Rev. Simon Locke—sometimes called Simeon—was indeed a minister in Hollis, Maine. He died on September 6, 1831, though he was actually only seventy-eight years old at the time (reported as seventy-nine, but a few days short of that age).[7]

Locke had indeed been a Revolutionary War soldier. We have no account of his service in his own words, but his widow Lydia filed for a pension after his death, and that application preserves stories that she

<hr/>

6. Alexander M. Gow, *The Primer of Politeness: A Help to School and Home Government* (Philadelphia: Lippincott, 1883), 149. This version of the tale about Washington was not reprinted nearly as widely as the earlier one. It did appear, with Locke's name attached, in the September 1907 issue of *The Children's Friend*, a magazine published by the Latter-day Saints church. Notably, the same magazine ran forms of the 1839 anecdote in its issues for February 1908 and December 1918.

7. Locke's obituary appeared in the *Eastern Argus* newspaper of Portland for September 16, 1831. His birthdate and other vital information are stated in Arthur H. Locke, *A History and Genealogy of Captain John Locke (1627-1696) of Portsmouth and Rye, N.H., and His Descendants* (Concord, N.H.: Rumford Press, [1916?]), 72-3.

and her neighbors had heard him tell.[8] Cutting through the haze of
secondhand accounts, it is clear that Locke served during the siege of
Boston for a few months in 1775 and 1776. His second stint was in a
New Hampshire militia company led by Capt. John Drew, which was
raised to bolster the Continental forces in December 1775. Though
those militia troops were called "six weeks' men," many stayed to the
end of the siege in March 1776.

However, no one in those pension records recalled Locke claiming
to have helped to build "the breastworks on Dorchester Heights" that
March. The New Hampshire men were stationed at Winter Hill on
the opposite wing of the American lines. Instead, Locke's survivors said
he was in the first company to take possession of the fort that the
British troops left behind on Bunker's Hill when they evacuated in
March 1776. His widow and a man who boarded with them even
recalled that Locke had come home with "a china punch bowl & a
china plate taken from the British camp."

Locke thus served closer to the area overseen by General Putnam
than he would have if he were part of the Continental contingent that
fortified Dorchester heights. That makes it plausible that he brought
home the same story about Putnam as Jacob Francis and retold it as an
old man in Maine. Andrew Walker could indeed have heard that story
from Locke as a boy and decades later remembered it (perhaps under
the influence of the widely published version) as involving a more
famous general and a more famous fortification.

The apparently independent transmission in New Jersey and Maine
of the story about a corporal and a general during the siege of Boston
suggests that the incident really did happen. Francis claimed to have
seen the event himself. The boy who heard Locke's version came away
believing that minister had seen it as well. Both veterans probably
shared the story multiple times, both privately and at celebrations of
the American Revolution.

8. The Revolutionary War pensions database available through Fold3.com contains files
on two different men from New Hampshire named Simon Locke, and correspondence
shows federal bureaucrats have sometimes conflated those veterans' service records. (That
mix-up in turn confused the genealogist Arthur H. Locke.) The Rev. Simon Locke died
in 1831 and left a widow named Lydia, who collected her pension until 1851. The other
Simon Locke, from Seabrook, served later in the war, was still alive in 1832, and had a
wife named Mary.

It seems likely that such oral recountings inspired the version of the tale published in 1839. But that version was "improved" with the general recast as Washington, new dialogue added, and details that tied the incident to the siege of Boston stripped away. Identifying the first appearance of that version might indicate whether the writer might have heard the tale from Jacob Francis, Simon Locke, or another veteran. But even without that original context it's clear that writer wasn't so interested in preserving exact historical details as in giving nineteenth-century Americans an entertaining and instructional tale.

The 1839 version erased Putnam, the less famous general. It also erased Francis, Locke, and the other individual soldiers on the scene. (Though Francis was African-American, there are no black soldiers in the illustrations, just as there were none in most other visual depictions of Washington's army made in the nineteenth and early twentieth centuries.) Ultimately that publication actually made the incident itself seem more dubious. When we view that 1839 version with any knowledge of Washington's orders and even a small dose of healthy skepticism, it looks like nothing more than an entertaining legend. In effect, the fictionalized version overwrote the actual incident.

In 1980 John C. Dann of the William L. Clements Library in Ann Arbor, Michigan, published a collection of autobiographies and recollections from the Revolutionary War pension files. That book, *The Revolution Remembered: Eyewitness Accounts of the War for Independence*, included a transcript of Jacob Francis's recollections alongside other soldiers, bringing his story of General Putnam and the corporal into print for the first time.[9] Since then, that anecdote has been reprinted in many histories—the story is hard to resist, especially now that it comes with documentation from a first-hand source.[10] That publication has thus not only resurrected Francis from obscurity, but it also gave us back the oldest, most reliable version of a delightful anecdote.

---

9. John C. Dann, *The Revolution Remembered: Eyewitness Accounts of the War for Independence* (Chicago: University of Chicago Press, 1980), 392-3.

10. Examples of recent authors quoting Jacob Francis's story about Putnam include Henry Wiencek in *An Imperfect God: George Washington, His Slaves, and the Creation of America* (2003); Thomas Ayres in *That's Not in My American History Book* (2004); Harry M. Ward in *George Washington's Enforcers: Policing the Continental Army* (2006); and the team behind the textbook *The Enduring Vision: A History of the American People* (2008).

The Death and Resurrection of Major John André

JOHN KNIGHT

John André's body hung in silence for thirty minutes before being taken down. It was placed carefully in a simple open coffin crudely painted black. The guard detail then withdrew and the "country people" of the villages around Tappan respectfully filed past his corpse. It was estimated upwards of 2,000 viewed his execution, a remarkable number given the speed with which he had been tried and condemned.[1] Many noted his face had quickly mortified; his handsome features already black, his neck swollen and distorted. He was buried without ceremony or marker in an unusually shallow grave just over three feet deep.[2] It was so shallow that decades later at his exhumation his skull was reported to have been embalmed by the fibrous roots of a peach tree planted "by some kind woman's hand to mark the grave."[3] It was an ignominious fate for one the British army's best-loved and most talented officers.

Five days later the men who had captured André, John Paulding, David Williams, and Isaac Van Wart were commended by Washington himself as "having prevented in all probability our suffering one of the severest strokes that could have been meditated against us." He went on to recommend that "the public will do well to make them a handsome gratuity."[4] Both Congress and New York State readily complied.

1. "Never since has Tappan had an assemblage of equal size. Many hundreds, if not thousands were present." Quoted in W. Abbatt, *The crisis of the revolution: being the story of Arnold and André, now for the first time collected from all sources, and illustrated with views of all places identified with it* (New York: W. Abbatt 1899).
2. W. Sargent, *The life and career of Major John André, adjutant-general of the British army in America* (Boston: Ticknor and Fields, 1861), 398.
3. Ibid., 410.
4. Washington to the President of Congress, October 7, 1780, *Writings of George Washington. Vol. 20*, text.virginia.edu/washington/fitzpatrick/.

Left, a German engraving from 1784 depicting John André being taken into custody by John Paulding, Isaac Van Wart, and David Williams, near Tarrytown, New York. Right, "The unfortunate death of Major André . . . , Octr. 2, 1780, who was found within the American lines in the character of a spy," from Barnard's *New, Comprehensive History of England*, c. 1783.

Each was awarded a farm, a sizable lifetime pension, and, unusually for common soldiers, a repoussé silver medal inscribed "Fidelity" and "Amor Patriæ Vincit." The men were lauded throughout the thirteen colonies as "Peasant Patriots."[5]

And that should have been the end of the story. Death by hanging of a treacherous enemy spy, and an enduring tribute to the patriotism of three virtuous Americans. Except history does not always follow a predictable and impartial path.

On the morning of his execution, John André shaved and cast aside the dusty civilian clothing he had been wearing since his fateful meeting with Benedict Arnold just nine days earlier. He now wore an immaculate dress uniform sent up from New York, a "brilliant scarlet trimmed with the most beautiful green."[6] As he looked in his glass he

5. H. J. Raymond, *An oration pronounced before the young men of Westchester County, on the completion of a monument, erected by them to the captors of Major André, at Tarrytown, Oct. 7, 1853* (New York: S. T. Callahan, 1853), 92.
6. Sargent, *The life and career of Major John André*, 397.

may have brooded briefly on the irony of this imposing martial reflection. For there is little doubt that had he worn his regimentals during his dealings with Arnold (as his commanding officer Sir Henry Clinton had ordered him to do) he would not now be facing execution as a spy.

André did not know it, but his uniform was not the only thing that had crossed the Hudson from British New York. Promises, appeals, even threats flashed from Clinton to Washington in the desperate hope that André could be saved. His army colleagues, mortified at his capture, offered to lead "forlorn hope" missions to rescue him from his prison in Tappan. Lt. Col. John Graves Simcoe pleaded to lead a hand-picked troop on what would have been a suicidal mission.[7] But Clinton refused all, naively putting his faith in the power of diplomacy. It was to no avail. A Court martial of fourteen senior officers headed by Maj. Gen. Nathaniel Greene unanimously condemned André and sentenced him to the most shameful death any officer could contemplate. A common hanging.[8]

The esteem André was held in at all levels of the army could be gauged from the shock that lay like a shroud over New York in the weeks following his execution. Whole regiments dyed their cockades and plumes black.[9] Ominous threats of retaliation and vengeance were proclaimed in print and on parade ground, and Clinton was urged to take advantage of the universal anger and lead his army out of his New York bastion and confront Washington's army head-on. All this for a man of humble birth who a few years previous had been entirely unknown.

John André seems to have been one of those rare characters, a man with the ability to enthrall both sexes in equal measure. He undoubtedly possessed an effortless capacity to charm anyone who made his acquaintance. Musical, artistic, and fluent in several languages, his "renaissance" veneer hid a fiercely ambitious nature allied to a keen intellect. His dashing good looks were commented on by male and female alike and in an army where privilege and money too often bought undeserved rank, André was the personification of a new breed of British officer: the ones who had raised themselves purely on merit.

7. John Graves Simcoe, *Simcoe's military journal: a history of the operations of a partisan corps, called the Queen's Rangers, commanded by Lieut. Col. J.G. Simcoe, during the war of the American* Revolution ; *now first published, with a memoir of the author and other additions* (New York: Bartlett & Welford.1844), 292.

8. *Proceedings Oo a Board of General Officers, Held by Order of His Excellency General Washington, Commander in Chief of the Army of the United States of America: Respecting Major* André, *Adjutant General to the British Army, Sept. 29, 1780* .(Philadelphia: Francis Bailey, 1780).

9. Simcoe, *Simcoe's military journal*, 152.

It was all the more remarkable then that as adjutant general in Sir Henry Clinton's army his handling of the Benedict Arnold negotiations bordered on the farcical and inept. Instead of their secret meeting being the catalyst for a significant blow at Washington's army, the scheme ended as an amateurish and deadly failure. Overly complicated and often unnecessary parlaying between André and Arnold was convoluted further by a British high command seemingly unsure of what they actually wanted to achieve from his treachery. Eventually, the delayed meeting on the banks of the Hudson between "Gustavus" and "Anderson" settled little that couldn't have been attained without them meeting face to face. André left dressed in the civilian attire that condemned him, concealing plans in his stockings that were already militarily irrelevant, before accidentally stumbling upon a trio of dubious partisans and proceeding to talk himself into capture.

Though there has been much debate about the severity of the sentence passed upon André, there is little doubt that in accordance with the rules of eighteenth century warfare he was guilty of espionage. The board of inquiry determined that he was "under a feigned name and in a disguised habit" and there is no disputing this.[10] Indeed, André himself seemed more concerned about the nature of his execution than the justice of his sentence. He spent his final days pleading to be shot rather than suffer the disgrace of the gallows.[11] On the day of his execution, he was clearly unaware that Washington had denied his request. André's only sign of emotion came when he realized he was to suffer a common hanging, and he blanched briefly at the foot of the gibbet, startled that this should be the crude method of his demise.[12]

Importantly for André's posthumous resurrection, his last words were probably not reported accurately. His servant Peter Laune recounted that André said, "As I suffer in the defence of my country, I must consider this hour as the most glorious of my life. Remember, that I die as becomes a British Officer while the manner of my death must reflect disgrace on your Commander." This version appeared in British newspapers within a month of his execution.[13] American eyewitness accounts, however, while agreeing that André uttered the first phrase (though they differ on the exact wording) always stop at the

10. *Proceedings of Board of General Officers.*
11. Ibid. André wrote to Washington, "Sympathy towards a soldier will surely induce your Excellency and a military tribunal to adopt the mode of my death to the feelings of a man of honour ... I shall experience the operation of these feelings in your breast, by being informed that I am not to die on a gibbet" Washington did not reply.
12. Sargent, *The life and career of Major John André*, 394.
13. *Evening Post*, November 14, 1780.

condemnation of Washington.[14] Even today this last line is rarely seen
in accounts of André's execution. It was important for Americans that
no stain should attach itself to the memory of Washington. Although
it can never be proven whether André actually uttered this denuncia-
tion, the important point is that its very possibility was denied by
American historians. The nineteenth century writer Winthrop Sargent
who published the most authentic narrative of André's life dismissed
out of hand Laune's version stating it was "distorted from the truth by
political bias. . .André's dying words are given in palpable error," though
he gives no reason for this conclusion other than that the Valet must
have been "bewildered and grief-stricken."[15] The result was that André
was allowed to die as a gentleman, his patriotism and loyalty applauded
by those of his class on both sides of the Atlantic. It is doubtful he
would have been granted the same memorial if his condemnation of
Washington had been more widely circulated.

The beatification of John André started almost immediately after
his death. Elegies were printed in England within months of his execution. The writer Anna Seward reflected the British mood in her 1781
" Monody on Major André," dedicating it "to his murdered saint . . .
who fell a martyr to the cause of his king and country with the firm
intrepidly of a Roman and the resignation of a Christian Hero."[16] By
the late Regency, André's name had become a byword for fidelity, his
death a symbol of the stoicism Britain expected from its officer class.
He had championed a system of monarchical government that by the
first part of the nineteenth century was tottering throughout continental Europe. It was not surprising therefore that George III, the Prince
Regent, and the Duke of York all went to extraordinary lengths to promote the memory of André and to pay particular homage to his gallows
declaration. "As I suffer in the defence of my Country, I must consider
this hour as the most glorious of my life—Remember that I die as becomes a British Officer."

In 1821, John André was exhumed with great reverence and ceremony in New York. Initially, the British consul James Buchanan feared
a public backlash in removing André's body and planned a clandestine

14. James Thacher was a Continental Army surgeon. His memoir quotes, "I pray you to
bear me witness that I meet my fate like a brave man." Eli Jacobs was chosen to guard
André on the day of his execution. His pension application quotes André's final words as,
"Bear me witness that I bear my fate like a brave man."
15. Sargent, *The life and career of Major John André*, 400.
16. Anna Seward, *Monody on Major André. (Author of the elegy on Capt. Cook); To which are
added, letters addressed to her by Major André, in the year 1769* (London: J. Dodsley, 1780), 1
(dedication).

THE UNFORTUNATE MAJOR ANDRÉ.

"The Unfortunate Major André," an undated print showing a merciful angel lifting André's protrait toward the heavens. (*New York Public Library*)

transfer of his remains. This proved to be impractical, but much to his surprise, his expectations of public abuse were largely unfounded. Though he had been apprised to expect universal and perhaps even violent opposition, on his arrival at Tappan opinion was symbolically divided between those "of a lower caste" who believed the exhumation "a disgrace to the memory of George Washington" and the local clergy and gentry who were supportive and aided in the exhumation. Importantly this show of support by many "respectable" and prominent residents in a such a close-knit community as Tappan dampened all violent objections to Buchanan's plan. In the end, the consul placated the protesters through the traditional British expediency by simply taking them to the local inn and buying them all a drink. "The bones were then carefully uplifted and placed in a costly sarcophagus of mahogany, richly decorated with gold . . . ladies sent garlands to decorate the bier..and six young women of New York united in a poetical address that accompanied the myrtle tree they sent with the body to England."[17]

His remains were then transported across the Atlantic and entombed in that most scared of Britain's resting places, Westminster

17. Sargent, *The life and career of Major John André*, 409-411.

Abbey. The sarcophagus, inscribed "universally beloved and esteemed by the Army in which he served, and lamented even by his foes," now lay alongside medieval kings, Renaissance statesmen, and Georgian poets.[18]

Like André, Paulding, Williams, and Van Wart became hostage to political forces beyond their control—though in their case it produced a far less laudatory outcome.

In 1817, John Paulding petitioned the House of Representatives for an increase in his pension. Startlingly it was opposed by one the Revolution's greatest heroes, Benjamin Tallmadge. Worse, not only did Tallmadge seek to deny the captors an increase, he openly cast aspersions on both their loyalty and motivation. His motion passed with a large majority and by default André's resurrection from dishonourable criminal to venerated martyr was complete. But was this remarkable reversal of reputation justified; or was it evidence that even in this new and supposedly meritocratic republic, class played as large a part in honoring virtue and commemorating patriotism as it ever did in aristocratic Britain?

By 1817, American politics had changed dramatically from the Revolution. The Jeffersonian versus Hamiltonian debate about who should rule the new republic was in full flow. Federalists believed that the United States should be governed by the "best people." "Those who own the country," wrote Federalist John Jay bluntly, "ought to govern it."[19] Theirs was to be an America run by an educated, wealthy elite; men with "breeding" like Benjamin Tallmadge. Or indeed, John André.

In contrast, agrarian democracy was the goal of Thomas Jefferson's Republicanism. Jefferson believed that it was the humble farmer—owning his own land, tilling it with his own hands, and at one with nature—who formed the bedrock of American democracy. He wrote, "cultivators of the earth are the most valuable citizens. They are the most vigorous, the most independent, the most virtuous, and they are tied to their country and wedded to its liberty and interests by the most lasting bonds."[20] Though they were far from this ideal, Paulding, Williams, and Van Wart were lauded by Republicans as if they were its

---

18. 3,300 people have been buried or commemorated at Westminster Abbey, many of them among the most significant in the nation's history. See www.westminster-abbey.org/about-the-abbey/history/famous-people-organisations.

19. Attributed to John Jay; in Frank Monaghan, *John Jay*, chapter 15, p. 323 (1935). According to Monaghan, this "was one of his favorite maxims." Unverified in the writings of Jay, although the essence of this is expressed in several passages.

20. Thomas Jefferson to John Jay, August 23, 1785, *The Letters of Thomas Jefferson*, avalon.law.yale.edu/18th_century/let32.asp.

The monument of John André at Westminster Abbey with Britannia and the British Lion weeping on top and a tableau of André's capture on the side.

very embodiment. All three, not coincidentally, became partisan Jeffersonian Republicans.

Washington's army recruited heavily from America's artisan and farming classes. It was undoubtedly a propaganda coup that Paulding, Williams, and VanWart were all "farmers." It was significant that initially each was honored not just as a selfless adherent to the Continental cause but also as an incorruptible representative of his class. Within weeks all three men were officially honored for their morality and "simple" patriotism, with much being made of their refusal to accept the bribes offered to them by André.

Interestingly, in light of the later attitude of Federalists like Tallmadge, Alexander Hamilton himself had originally said of the three, "posterity will repeat with reverence the names of Van Wart, Williams and Paulding."[21] But this attitude, at first seemingly universal, gradually declined alongside the practical need for a Continental army composed of yeoman farmers. By 1817, a mercantile, peaceful America had different priorities and more contemporary heroes.

21. Alexander Hamilton, *The official and other papers of the late Major-General Alexander Hamilton* (New York and London: Wiley & Putnam, 1842), 473.

The "facts" of the encounter between André and his captors became political football for decades. As the military significance of André's capture diminished with each passing year, a romantic but politically potent myth began to flourish. That of the gallant, educated, and honourable officer robbed by three lower-class illiterate thieves leading to his regrettable execution.

André in conversation with Tallmadge—who as Washington's adjutant general spent much of his last hours with the major—referred to them as mere brigands. He solemnly asserted that they first ripped up the housings of his saddle and the cape of his coat in search of money, but finding none said, "He may have it [money] in his boots."[22] Tallmadge seems to have been almost in thrall to André and was sickened by his death. He clearly accepted André's opinion of his captors without question. In 1817, opposing Paulding's petition, he described them as "of that class of person who passed between both armies," and insinuated that had he come across them on the day would have arrested them as soon as André.[23] His use of the word "class" to describe the three is especially relevant. Though officially described as "yeoman," all were certainly on the economic periphery of that relatively affluent class. Williams and Van Wart were illiterate.

Tallmadge's accusations were backed up by other former Continental officers. Joshua King, a lieutenant in Sheldon's regiment, had been among the first to converse with André concerning the circumstances of his capture. His opinion was particularly damning. He scornfully concluded, "the truth is to the *impudence* of the men and not the *patriotism* of any one is to be attributed the capture of Major André."[24] An "anonymous" officer of the Massachusetts line who walked beside André in the funeral cortege was even more incriminating. In a report of the events by the *New York Courier*, he made a particularly specific attack: "It was an opinion too prevalent to admit of any doubt, that these men were of that description of persons usually called 'cow-boys,' or those who, without being considered as belonging to either party, made it a business to pillage from both. He has frequently heard it expressed at that time by several officers, who were personally acquainted with all these men, and who could not have been mistaken in their gen-

22. Benson J. Lossing, *The pictorial field-book of the revolution; or, illustrations, by pen and pencil, of the history, biography, scenery, relics, and traditions of the war for independence* (New York: Harper & Bros., 1850), 206.
23. Henry Phelps Johnson, *Memoir of Col. Benjamin Tallmadge* (New York: Gillis Press 1904), 135-137.
24. Samuel Blachley Webb, *Correspondence and journals of Samuel Blachley Webb*. (New York: Wickersham Press, 1893), 294.

eral characters."[25] Abruptly, it was now the captors, not André, who required vindication for their actions that day.

Political opponents of Tallmadge and the Federalist party sprung to the defense of the injured party, but it was significant that they came to champion the class they represented as much as the individuals themselves. *The New York Courier* editorialized its objections as "Col. Tallmadge has endeavoured to tear the fairest leaf from our history, and to deprive the yeomenry of our country of a theme in which they gloried."[26]

This is not to say there was not considerable embroidering of the facts on the part of adherents to Paulding, Williams, and Van Wart. As the years went by the capture became more idealized. Paulding's supposed acclamation, "No by God if you give us ten thousand guineas you should not stir a step! We are Americans and above corruption. Go with us you must" when André offered him money for his escape seems especially melodramatic and unlikely.[27]

Ultimately the real issue was not whether these men were Loyalist "cowboys," Patriot "skinners," or self-serving banditti. What is remarkable is that within their lifetime they had gone from vaunted heroes of the Revolution to disreputable opportunists on no other evidence than the testimony of an enemy spy. That André's evidence was not questioned for its credibility and given such a prominent voice showed just how much American society had changed since the Revolution.

The result of this political ferment on both sides of the Atlantic was that all four men came to be misrepresented in similar ways but for opposite reasons. As far as Britain's aristocracy was concerned André's reputation had to be salvaged. For America's elite, that of his captors needed to be diminished: André embodied the European model of a gentleman to which they aspired. For them this was not yet the age of the "common man." Britain's goal was achieved with success. The latter less so.

Ironically, André is better known today in America than his captors, whose lives though commemorated in lofty marble throughout New York are largely a historical footnote.[28] In contrast, in a quiet suburb in Tappan, a small blasted, stump of a monument sits in commemoration

25. E. Benson, *Vindication of the Captors of Major André* (New York: Kirk & Mercein, 1817), 25.
26. *New York Courier*, February 18, 1817.
27. *Connecticut Courant*, November, 1827, 358.
28. John Paulding Memorial at Patriots Park, Tarrytown, NY. The Issac Van Wart grave obelisk at the Elmsford Reformed Church and Cemetery David Williams Monument Old Stone Fort, 145 Fort Rd, Schoharie, NY.

to John André. Once known as "Treason Hill" it now goes under the name "Andre Hill," and with the name change, the resurrection of John André seems complete.

The Connecticut Captivity of William Franklin, Loyalist

LOUIS ARTHUR NORTON

War, an odious invention of man, attempts to portray the enemy as subhuman, unworthy of normal sympathy. Civilized societies respected the sanctity of human life; but enemy prisoners were a byproduct of conflict and open to abuse via military policies designed to debase and dehumanize. Historically, prisoner-of-war internment facilities were harsher than those used for civilian populations.

Although it was generally agreed that prisoners of war possessed basic rights to be treated humanely and then to be released at the end of hostilities, the application of these rights frequently was not carried out and progressed to grievances and disputes. Inhumane and cruel treatment in unsanitary environments produced disease, as well as emotional and physical trauma. Atrocities committed by empowered men against helpless weakened prisoners resulted in callous indifference to human suffering, filth, uncontrolled disease and inhumane conditions; obnoxious stenches, vermin infestations, rotten food, polluted water and despicable living situations; of waiting for someone to die to gain their space closer to better ventilation avoiding bodies of the retching or recently dead to gain access to an overflowing "necessary bucket" in the dark.[1]

Toward the beginning of the American Revolutionary War, George Washington issued orders known as the Laws of War regarding captives or prisoners of war. On September 14, 1775, Washington wrote to Col. Benedict Arnold stating that: "Should any American soldier be so base and infamous as to injure any [prisoner] . . . I do most earnestly enjoin you to bring him to such severe and exemplary punishment as the enor-

1. Thomas Dring, *Recollections of Life on the Prison Ship Jersey.* Edward Swain, ed. (Yardley, PA: Westholme Publishing), 2010.

mity of the crime may require."[2] Washington became appalled at the treatment of American captives, particularly those who were extradited to Canada. They were taunted, abused and subjected to starvation often resulting in wretched deaths. He wrote, "The inhuman treatment of the whole, and murder of part, of our people, after surrender and capitulation was . . . a flagrant violation of faith, which ought to be held sacred by all civilized nations, and was founded in the most savage barbarity. It highly deserved the severest reprobation."[3]

In spite of Washington's order, Americans at the local level incarcerated some prisoners in a dank copper mine known as Old Newgate Prison in what was then Simsbury (now East Granby), Connecticut.[4] This grim facility largely housed Loyalists who did not support independence and a few prisoners of war. Loyalists (Tories) were often treated more like common criminals than POWs, depending on the state or township. The members of each colony intensely debated whether Loyalists should be treated as enemy soldiers or treasonous citizens.[5] Some thought that the Tories presented an even greater danger to the revolutionary cause than soldiers because of their potential for sedition, real or imagined.

A poignant example of ill treatment of Loyalists by the Rebel government is that of William Franklin.[6] During his early life William Franklin was a frontiersman, soldier, a captain in the Pennsylvania militia, and aide-decamp to his father. He ventured into the Ohio Valley where Indians and whites waged an expansionist war. At this time William and his father Benjamin Franklin had shared interests that included Franklin's inventions and provincial politics. William's parental influence helped get him appointed as Philadelphia's postmaster and comptroller of the North American postal system. In 1758, at age of

2. *The writings of George Washington: Being his correspondence, addresses, messages, and other papers, official and private,* Jared Sparks, ed. (Salt Lake City, UT: Benchmark Books, 1847), 90.
3. Washington to the president of Congress, July 15, 1776, in *The Papers of George Washington*, Revolutionary War Series, vol. 5, *16 June 1776–12 August 1776*, ed. Philander D. Chase, ed. (Charlottesville: University Press of Virginia, 1993), 325.
4. Old Newgate prison was variously known as "Hell" and other damning epithets such as "the catacomb of Loyalty," "Inferno," and by some "the prison of the Inquisition," "Sepulcher," and "the living tomb."
5. Charles H. Metzger, *The Prisoner in the American Revolution* (Chicago, IL: Loyola University Press, 1962), 31-63.
6. William Franklin, born in 1760, was the illegitimate child of Benjamin Franklin. His mother has never been determined, but he may have been born from an illicit encounter with a prostitute or Franklin's later common-law wife, Deborah. William was raised by Ben and Deborah whom he called mother.

twenty-one, he elected to pursue a legal career and became a lawyer. King George III appointed Franklin as Royal Governor of New Jersey in 1762.

During the 1770s, when the colonies political opinions became divided between loyalties to the king or open rebellion, William remained loyal to the Crown. Benjamin visited his son in New Jersey to inform him that the Americans were uniting behind George Washington against the British. The elder Franklin assured William that he would be welcome to join the armed rebellion and would likely be offered a generalship in Washington's new Continental Army. William Franklin affirmed his loyalty to the king and felt that the majority of Americans would not support the Revolution. Thus his actions put father and son at odds. As the war with Britain gained momentum, the animosity between them grew.

In January 1776 the Continental Congress ordered the disarming of all potential threats to the patriotic cause. The provincial Congress ordered all royal governors removed. On July 15, 1776, the provincial congress of New Jersey declared that William Franklin was a "virulent enemy to this country, and a person that may prove dangerous."[7] Franklin was to be arrested, but the congress suggested that he be handled "with all the delicacy and tenderness which the nature of the business can possibly admit."[8] He was sent to Connecticut and consigned to the authority of Gov. John Trumbull. Franklin, however, made a defiant speech at his subsequent June 21 trial that a judge described as "every way worthy of his exalted birth," referring to his illegitimate origin rather than his well-known paternity.[9]

On July 4, 1776 Franklin was led to a small outbuilding of the Connecticut War Office and became an official prisoner of the Rebel government. He was confined first to a rented room in the house of an unnamed officer in Wallingford, Connecticut. Then, as a parolee, he was sent to the Connecticut River town of Middletown and the home of Jehosaphat Starr. The obstinate governor-in-exile refused to be a compliant prisoner. Instead he gathered intelligence and passed it on to Loyalists. This was used by Connecticut Tories to protect their property as royal pardons issued by the authority of a colonial governor appointed by the king.

7. Walter Isaacson, *The First American: The Life and Times of Benjamin Franklin* (New York, NY: Simon and Schuster, 2003), 525.
8. Sheila Skemp, *William Franklin: Son of a Patriot, Servant of a King* (New York, NY: Oxford University Press, 1990), 308.
9. Ibid.

Because of abusing his parole while in Wallingford, Franklin was sent to the "Litchfield Gaol" in May 1777. This notorious facility was crowded with Loyalists, many of whom were condemned to death. On May 2, 1777, an armed escort took Franklin to Litchfield's jail, considered only a slightly better fate than Simsbury's Old New-Gate prison.

Litchfield, in a hilly rugged inland region of Connecticut, was far from any navigable river, presumably to deter potential rescuers.[10] The jail was an unpleasant place. At the time, rehabilitation was not the purpose of a jail, thus prisoners were made to suffer in horrid accommodations. Author Willard Randall described the Litchfield jail as "a long squat log building of two stories, almost obscured when [William Franklin] first saw it by a huge Elm tree."[11] The elm tree served as a whipping post and nearby was a sturdy gallows.

Up on Franklin's arrival, Sheriff Lynde Lord had the prisoner incarcerated in a second floor cell for the condemned. "The smell hit him first, then the darkness," Randall wrote. "There was only a small window with bars, the floor was covered with straw long since matted with the wastes of earlier prisoners. There was no chair to sit on, no bed to lie on, no toilet facilities."[12] Franklin was ordered to speak with no one except the sheriff.

Franklin subsequently wrote, "They hurried me away about 40 Miles to Litchfield, where I was thrown into a most noisome filthy Room of I believe, the very worst Gaol in America."[13] Shortly after his arrival, he was placed in a solitary confinement cell that contained a straw mat on the floor and nothing else – no bed, no seat, no toilet facility. In September, he wrote a complaint to Governor Trumbull stating,

> I feel myself in a sensible Decline and am already so much reduced in Size, and become so weak and relax'd, as to render it extremely improbable that I shall ever recover my health and Strength again . . . I suffer so much in being thus, as it were, buried alive, having no one to

10. Peter C. Vermilyea, *Hidden History of Litchfield County* (Charleston, SC: The History Press, 2014), says that the jail was on East Street, but a map in the Litchfield Historical Society, depicted in the same book, shows the location as Meeting House Street.
11. Willard Sterne Randall, *A Little Revenge-Benjamin Franklin & His Son* (Boston, MA: Little, Brown and Company, 1984), 446. Only one reference to the colonial jail appears in Alain Campbell White, *The History of the Town of Litchfield, Connecticut, 1720-1920* (Litchfield, CT: Litchfield Historical Society, 1920).
12. Randall, *A Little Revenge*, 446.
13. William Franklin to Lord George Germain, November 10, 1778, in Vermilyea, *Hidden History of Litchfield County*.

speak to Day or Night, and for the want of Air and Exercise, that I should deem it a Favour to be immediately taken out and shot - a speedy or sudden Death being, in my opinion every Way more eligible than such a miserably lingering though equally sure one as I seem at present doom'd to.[14]

In a subsequent writing Franklin described his surroundings:

In this Dungeon, for I can call it no other, it having often been appropriated to condemn'd Criminals, I was closely confined for about eight Months, overrun and molested with the many kinds of Vermin, debarred of Pen, Ink, and Paper and of all Conversation with every Person, except now and then, a few Words with the Sheriff, Gaoler, or Centries. In short I was in a manner excluded human Society, having little more connexion with Mankind than if I had been buried alive. My Victuals was generally pok'd thro' a Hole in the Door, and my servants but seldom permitted to come into the Room, and then only for a few Minutes in the Presence of the Goaler and the Guard.[15]

Franklin also sent a plea to General Washington, requesting to visit his ailing wife, Elizabeth Downes, in New York. Washington replied that only the Continental Congress could grant a furlough order. Washington passed the request to Congress, but they refused. Franklin's wife died while he was imprisoned. His general health had declined as a result of his ordeal in solitary confinement, perhaps abetted by malnutrition.[16] On December 31, 1777, William Franklin was released from the Litchfield Gaol after serving eight months. He was still a prisoner, but kept more humanely in the East Windsor house of Capt. Ebenezer Grant. The poor conditions in his confinement in Litchfield had taken their toll.

While William Franklin languished in prison, his father did not intervene. In the autumn of 1778, Franklin, whose health was now partly recovered, was exchanged for Delaware's Rebel governor, John McKinley, who was held by the British in New York. Franklin entered New York City on November 1, 1778, where he continued to work for the British during the war and remained loyal to the king throughout his life.

14. William Franklin to Jonathan Trumbull, September 15, 1777, Litchfield Gaol, in *Proceedings of the New Jersey Historical Society*, vol. III, no. 1, 1918, 47.
15. William Franklin to Lord George Germain, November 10, 1778.
16. Franklin remained in New York and fought against the Americans, but left for refuge in England in 1782. His motto, *Pro Rege & Patria*, amply demonstrated his devotion to the British crown and country.

While living in London in 1784, William received a letter from his father who was still pained by the rift between them, but unwilling to forgive. Benjamin Franklin felt pain in his old age, having been being deserted by his only son who took up arms against the revolutionary cause. He wrote that he attempted to understand William's position, but could not find a father's natural forgiveness.[17] When the elder Franklin died in 1790, he left nothing to his Tory son.

Surprisingly, William Franklin may have been a fortunate man. Capital punishment was the probable fate for Connecticut Loyalists found guilty of treason or spying. Moses Dunbar was briefly imprisoned under a charge of disloyalty for several weeks. He escaped, fled across Long Island Sound and enlisted in the British Army, receiving a commission as a captain. Dunbar subsequently returned to Connecticut and tried to recruit some other young men to enlist in the Royal Army. He was recognized as an escapee, arrested, and, when his royal commission as captain was found in his possession, was indicted for high treason. He was tried in a Hartford court, found guilty and then executed by hanging on January 23, 1777.[18] Two other Connecticut Tories, William Stone of Stamford and Robert Thomson of Newton, were convicted and hanged for the offenses of espionage, sedition and treason, as was Daniel Griswold later in the spring of 1777. On November 3, 1778 John Blair and David Farnsworth were similarly hanged for espionage and sedition.[19] On the cold morning of February 8, 1779, Edward Jones was convicted of espionage and put to death by a firing squad. Hostile attitudes of the Rebels toward Tories in some communities grew as the war progressed.

When the Treaty of Paris 1783 ended the conflict in 1783, many Tories (sometimes forcefully) immigrated to places of refuge such as Britain or Canada to escape the excoriation and humiliation they endured from their neighbors. The treatment of Loyalist captives of the Americans has little historical coverage, but evidence of William Franklin and others held in Connecticut suggests that their plight during the Revolutionary War was appalling.

17. Randall, *A Little Revenge*, 486.
18. J. Francis Ryan, *Plymouth Conn., 1776–1976* (Plymouth, CT: privately printed, 1976), chapter 17.
19. Daniel A. Hearn, *Legal Executions in New England* (Jefferson, NC: McFarland, 1999), table of victims of execution.

Norfolk, Virginia, Sacked by North Carolina and Virginia Troops

❦ PATRICK H. HANNUM ❦

If the headline of a January or February 1776 edition of any North American Tory newspaper read, "Norfolk, Virginia, Sacked by North Carolina and Virginia Troops," it would not have constituted propaganda. Loyalists in Tidewater Virginia, under the leadership of Lord Dunmore, Virginia's Royal Governor, were under siege by rebel Whig or Patriot troops from the colonies and future states of North Carolina and Virginia, under the military leadership of a North Carolinian, Robert Howe.[1] The actions of Howe, operating under both Convention and North Carolina authority, and William Woodford, the senior Virginian, and their troops proceeded with the approval and consent of the North Carolina and Virginia provisional governments.[2] The provisional Whig governments formed military units to protect their interests and challenge the military capabilities of the royal governors. Howe's soldiers, tasked with the destruction of Norfolk, the largest city in Virginia and the Chesapeake Bay region, performed their task with rigorous efficiency.[3]

1. Charles E. Bennett and Donald R Lennon, *A Quest for Glory: Major General Robert Howe and the American Revolution* (Chapel Hill, NC: University of North Carolina Press, 1991), 28; Robert Howe was appointed colonel of the 2nd North Carolina Regiment by the North Carolina Provincial Congress on September 1, 1775. The Continental Congress took both the 1st and 2nd North Carolina regiments into Continental service in late November 1775. When Howe assumed command of the combined North Carolina-Virginia forces he did so as a Continental officer.
2. Minutes of the Virginia Convention December 01, 1775, in William Laurence Saunders, *Colonial and State Records of North Carolina.* (Raleigh NC: P.M. Hale, 1886), 10:396, http://docsouth.unc.edu/csr/index.html/volumes/volume_10, accessed June 18, 2017.
3. James E. Heath, *Journal and Reports of the Commissioners Appointed by the Act of 1777, to ascertain the Losses occasioned to individuals by the burning of Norfolk and Portsmouth, in the year 1776* (Richmond, VA: House of Delegates, Auditor, Richmond: Virginia General Assembly, 1836).

The Whig's systematic and deliberate destruction of Norfolk denied the British a capable military base of operations in the southern Chesapeake Bay, and complicated future British military operations in the region. As a result, Virginia provided critical economic, manpower, military, and logistical support to the Whig or Patriot side in American Revolution largely unimpeded until 1779.[4] The destruction of Norfolk proved a crucial decision with far reaching strategic military consequences that sowed the seeds of the British defeat at Yorktown in October 1781.

THE IMPORTANCE OF NORFOLK IN RELATION TO THE CHESAPEAKE BAY

In 1775, Norfolk, Virginia was the largest city in Virginia and the largest costal city in North America between New York and Charleston, South Carolina. Norfolk had a population of approximately 6,250, the eighth largest city in America and twice the size of Savannah, Georgia.[5] Its location only a few miles from Williamsburg, the colonial capitol of Virginia, and near the entrance to the Chesapeake Bay amplified the city's strategic political, military, and economic value. As a trading and economic center, Norfolk represented the commercial interests of the ruling elite and therefore had a large Loyalist population with a substantial number of Scottish merchants, whose presence often irritated the planter-dominated Virginia society.[6] The Scottish merchant class tended to remain loyal to the British Crown based on the close ties between commercial and political interests in the mercantile system.[7] Controlling the mouth of the Chesapeake Bay facilitated access to over forty percent of the commerce from the thirteen colonies transiting to Great Britain.[8] Numerous rivers provided water access to the lower portions of Virginia. A large Loyalist-dominated port city, with the capability of hosting a British fleet, in a key strategic location posed a significant threat to the rebel governments of both Virginia and North Carolina and to the Continental Congress.[9]

4. Paul H. Smith, *Loyalists and Redcoats: A Study in British Revolutionary Policy* (New York: W. W. Norton & Company, 1964), 82-109; and John E. Selby, *The Revolution in Virginia, 1775-1783* (Charlottesville, VA: Colonial Williamsburg Foundation, 1988), 204-210.
5. Carl Bridenbaugh, *Cities in Revolt: Urban Life in America 1743-1776* (Oxford: Oxford University Press, 1955), 217.
6. Ernest McNeill Eller, ed., *Chesapeake Bay in the American Revolution* (Centerville, MD: Tidewater Publishers, 1981), 312; and Selby, *The Revolution in Virginia*, 205.
7. Bennett and Lennon, *A Quest for Glory*, 31.
8. Selby, *The Revolution in Virginia*, 26.
9. Worthington C. Ford, et al., ed., *Journals of the Continental Congress* (Washington, DC, 1904-37), December 2, 1775, 3:395-6, http://memory.loc.gov/cgi-bin/query/r?ammem/hlaw:@field(DOCID+@lit(jc00362)), accessed September 23, 2017.

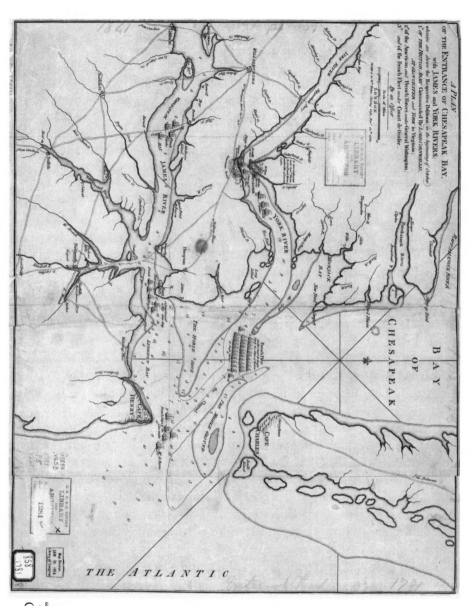

"A Plan of the Entrance of Chesapeak Bay," 1781.

VIRGINIA AND THE CHESAPEAKE BAY REGION

A shadow government formed in Virginia during 1774 supporting rebel interests; it led directly to provincial military forces challenging the authority of John Murray, Lord Dunmore, the Royal Virginia Governor. It was clear to Dunmore, in the spring of 1775, that the Chesapeake Bay would prove essential to maintaining control of Virginia. As part of his plan to defend the crown's interests in Virginia, Dunmore sought the support of the British North American Squadron under command of Adm. Samuel Graves. He requested British naval support and emphasized the value of maritime operations in the numerous tidal rivers that extended into Virginia from the Bay. These rivers provided water access via relatively deep and navigable channels that allowed powerful ocean-going warships of frigate class, possessing up to forty-four guns, access deep into the colony and throughout portions of Chesapeake Bay. His request emphasized the value of controlling Virginia's waterways and preventing contraband and illegal trade in arms and ammunition to supply the rebels. Dunmore believed a large man-of-war in Virginia waters, "would strike Awe over the whole Country."[10] Unfortunately for Dunmore, with all the British colonial governors under siege, Admiral Graves had a limited number of ships available and some that did arrive carried less cannon than originally designed to mount.[11] Graves reported that "His Majesty's Ship *Liverpool* and the *Kingsfisher*, *Otter*, *Tamer*, *Raven* and *Cruizer* Sloops are at Virginia, North Carolina, South Carolina and Georgia. The *St Lawrence* Schooner is at St Augustine."[12] The dispersal of British naval power throughout the southern colonies made it difficult to mass or concentrate available resources to support Lord Dunmore or any other distressed colonial governor. The size and scope of the rebellion facing the British military and civil leaders in 1775 exceeded their immediate ability to address. They failed to heed the warnings of those who understood the potential magnitude of the developing crisis.[13] The inability to hold the strategic Chesapeake Bay region early in the

10. Lord Dunmore to Samuel Graves, May 1, 1775, in William B. Clark, ed., *Naval Documents of the American Revolution* (Washington, DC: Naval History Division, Deptment of the Navy, 1964), 1:257-8, http://www.ibiblio.org/anrs/docs/E/E3/ndar_v01.pdf, accessed June 29, 2017.
11. Thomas Ludwell Lee to Richard Henry Lee, December 23, 1775, in Clark, *Naval Documents*, 3:219, http://www.ibiblio.org/anrs/docs/E/E3/ndar_v03.pdf, accessed July 4, 2017.
12. Vice Admiral Samuel Graves to Capt. Andrew Barkley, December 26, 1775, in Ibid., 3:256.
13. John Ferling, *Almost a Miracle: The American Victory in the War of Independence* (New York: Oxford University Press, 2007), 29.

Revolution would haunt the British in the future when they attempted to reestablish the King's authority there.

IMPORTANCE OF CHESAPEAKE BAY

During the colonial era, both the northern and southern portions of Chesapeake Bay contributed to the commercial importance of the region. By 1775, the northern portion so Chesapeake Bay produced significantly more food stuffs for export than the southern portion. Records from the Annapolis District for December 1774 through July 1775 reflect the sailing of 146 ships bound for overseas ports, primarily to Europe and the West Indies. Only six of these vessels carried tobacco; wheat had become king in the upper Chesapeake. Records from the southern portion of the bay, from the James River District for December 1774 to September 1775, reflect 64 overseas departures, sailing primarily to Scotland, all carrying tobacco. The actual number of shipments was likely much higher than reflected in the official records because smuggling was common.[14] The Continental Congress understood the importance of Chesapeake Bay commerce and took steps to interdict Loyalist trade as early as December 2, 1775.[15] The bay was critical because it provided access via water to Virginia, Maryland, Delaware, and Pennsylvania. At the time of the American Revolution these states collectively represented forty percent of the population of the new United States[16] and Virginia alone accounted for forty percent of the trade from the thirteen colonies with Great Britain.[17]

VIRGINIA'S REVOLUTIONARY ERA POPULATION

During the revolution, Virginia was the most populous state in the new nation. The population was disbursed and spread relatively evenly across the state resulting in no large cities other than Norfolk.[18] There was no formal census of the United States until 1790, but analysis derived from available records indicates Virginia had a white population of about 400,000 and a black slave population of about 200,000 at the

---

14. Eller, *Chesapeake Bay*, 14, 16.
15. Ford, *Journals of the Continental Congress*, December 2, 1775, 3:395-6, http://memory. loc.gov/cgi-bin/query/r?ammem/hlaw:@field(DOCID+@lit(jc00362)), accessed September 23, 2017.
16. Peter Smith, *American Population Before the Federal Census of 1790* (Glouchester, MA: Columbia University Press 1966), 8-8, 141; Robert K. Wright, *The Continental Army* (Washington, DC: Center for Military History 1983), 94.
17. Selby, *The Revolution in Virginia*, 26.
18. Smith, *American Population*, 141; Wright, *The Continental Army*, 94; Selby, *The Revolution in Virginia*, 23-27; and Emily J. Salmon and Edward D.C. Campbell, Jr., eds., *Hornbook of Virginia History*, (Richmond, VA: The Library of Virginia, 1994), 92.

beginning of the revolution, representing twenty percent of the population of the new United States.[19] The Continental Congress used the 400,000 number to assign recruiting quotas to Virginia for the Continental army in 1776.[20] The first American governor of Virginia, Patrick Henry, corroborated these contemporary population estimates in a letter dated January 14, 1779 addressed to Bernardo Galvez, Spanish Governor of Louisiana, when he stated Virginia's population was "six hundred thousand of all ages."[21]

The City of Norfolk had a population of 6,250 in 1775. After the destruction of Norfolk, the largest cities in Virginia were Fredericksburg and Alexandria, both with populations of about 3,000.[22] After Norfolk's destruction, the absence of a key population center required any occupying force to control broad expanses of territory, which subsequently necessitated a large occupying land force to control the population of Virginia. While a small raiding force could terrorize the population and destroy commerce, this type of force could not seize and hold terrain or control the population.

Virginia had a relatively well-developed county government structure when compared to other less politically mature states, which allowed for effective governance and communication with the citizenry.[23] The failure of the British government to quickly suppress the rebel force in Virginia allowed the rebels to control the local government structures resulting in those with strong Loyalist sentiments to moderate their enthusiasm and wait for strong and sustained British military presence before rising. The lack of initial Loyalist success in Virginia "convinced the weak-hearted to remain neutral, or acquiesce in support

19. Smith, *American Population*, 6-8, 141.
20. Wright, *The Continental Army*, 94.
21. Henry to Galvez, January 14, 1779, in Ian Saberton, ed., *Cornwallis Papers: The Campaigns of 1780 and 1781 in the Southern Theatre of the American Revolutionary War*, (Uckfield, England: The Naval & Military Press Ltd, 2010), 3:300.
22. Eller, *Chesapeake Bay*, 314-15.
23. J. T McAllister, *Virginia Militia in the Revolutionary War* (Hot Springs, VA: McAllister Publishing Co., 1913), introduction, http://lib.jrshelby.com/mcallister-harris.pdf, accessed July 4, 2017. "Of the present 69 counties of the former Eastern District, [present State of Virginia] 58 were already in existence at the outbreak of the Revolution in 1775." Virginia's government was much closer to the people of the sate when compared to a politically less mature state. For example, Pennsylvania consisted of only eleven counties in 1775, yet Pennsylvania possessed the third largest population of the original thirteen states behind Virginia and Massachusetts. Pennsylvania Historical and Museum Commission, *1681-1776: The Quaker Province*, Pennsylvania on the Eve of the Revolution, http://www.phmc.state.pa.us/portal/communities/pa-history/1681-1776.html, accessed August 20, 2017; Salmon and Campbell, *Hornbook*, 159.

of the rebels."[24] Dunmore's November 7, 1775 decree to free "all indented servants Negroes or others (appertaining to Rebels) . . . that are able and willing to bear Arms,"[25] also alienated many former loyal supporters of the King and his royal governor,[26] as well as raising fears of the committees of safety in other southern colonies.[27] Following the destruction of Norfolk, the absence of serious British military activity for three years allowed Virginia to become the breadbasket of the revolution. Virginia possessed a surge capacity to support the American war efforts and supplied between 3,000 and 6,200 troops to the Continental army throughout the war as well as Whig militia and critical economic, political, and military leadership contributions. The only other state to achieve this type of success in supplying manpower to the Continental army was Massachusetts.[28] The destruction of Norfolk and the lack of large population centers prevented British forces from rallying Loyalist support and controlling the state without a major commitment of forces.

HOWE AND NORTH CAROLINA'S INTEREST AND LINKAGE TO NORFOLK

The provisional government of North Carolina viewed the Tidewater region of Virginia as an avenue of approach into the Albemarle region of North Carolina. A Loyalist stronghold in the Norfolk area provided a base for future operations into northeast North Carolina, a region known for some Loyalist sentiment. As Lord Dunmore worked, during the summer and fall of 1775, to build a military capacity to challenge the rebel forces in the lower Chesapeake Bay, North Carolina repositioned forces north and activated militia units adjacent to Virginia in Edenton, Pasquotank, and Currituck Counties to reinforce the Virginians and challenge Dunmore's assembled forces. The Continental Congress ordered the two battalions of troops raised by North Carolina into Continental service on November 28, 1775. This positioned North

24. Eric Robson, *The American Revolution: In its Political and Military Aspects, 1763-1783* (New York: W.W. Norton & Company, 1966), 118.
25. H. S. Parsons, "Contemporary English Accounts of the Destruction of Norfolk in 1776," *The William and Mary Quarterly*, 13, no. 4 (1933): 219-224.
26. Committee to draw up a Declaration in answer to Lord Dunmore's Proclamation of November 7, December 8, 1775, in Peter Force ed., *American Archives, Documents of the American Revolutionary Period, 1774-1776* (Washington, DC: M. St. Clair Clarke and Peter Force, 1844), ser. 4, 4:79, http://amarch.lib.niu.edu/islandora/object/niu-amarch %3A87007, accessed June 27, 2017.
27. Minutes of the South Carolina Council of Safety, December 20, 1775, in Clark, *Naval Documents*, 3:190.
28. Selby, *The Revolution in Virginia*, 131.

Carolina Continental troops and North Carolina Militia, under the command of Robert Howe, to quickly respond to the military actions of Lord Dunmore in Tidewater Virginia.[29]

VIRGINIA MILITARY ACTIONS AND GREAT BRIDGE

After successfully repulsing a British assault on Hampton, Virginia, the state's provisional government repositioned Virginia's 2nd Regiment, under command of William Woodford, to the south side of the James River and ultimately to Great Bridge to prevent Dunmore's force from controlling that strategic location and advancing into the Albemarle region of North Carolina.[30] Norfolk was located strategically on the banks of the Elizabeth River in relation to Princess Anne, Norfolk and Nansemond Counties of Virginia and the Albemarle region of North Carolina. The Great Bridge provided the only land access from the north to the Albemarle region, east of the Great Dismal Swamp. Possession of Great Bridge controlled the north-south traffic between Virginia's Norfolk and Princess Anne Counties and North Carolina's Albemarle region.

Based on his success in defeating the Princess Anne County Militia in the skirmish at Kemps Landing on November 15, 1775, Dunmore felt confident his disciplined regulars, recently reinforced by a detachment of sixty men of the 14th Regiment from St. Augustine, East Florida,[31] and local militia could drive the rebel defenders from the south end of the Great Bridge, opening the road into North Carolina before the North Carolina troops could arrive to reinforce them. Dunmore underestimated the strength and determination of the entrenched enemy. Great Bridge was a British bloodbath. The elevated causeway over marshy terrain required the British regulars to advance on a narrow front that exposed them to direct frontal and flanking fire from the muskets and rifles of the defenders, which decimated the regulars leading the attack. Immediately after the battle, Col. William Woodford, the rebel commander, reported British casualties as, Captain Fordyce and twelve privates killed with Lieutenant Batut and seventeen privates

29. Minutes of the Virginia Convention December 1, 1775, in Saunders, *Colonial and State Records*, 10:341; Minutes of the Continental Congress [Extracts] November 24–26, 1775, in Saunders, *Colonial and State Records*, 10:338-339; Bennett and Lennon, *A Quest for Glory*, 29; and *Virginia Gazette* (Purdie), November 10, 1775, http://research.history. org/DigitalLibrary/va-gazettes/VGSinglePage.cfm?IssueIDNo=75.P.79, accessed June 30, 2017.
30. Selby, *The Revolution in Virginia*, 63.
31. Alexander Ross to Captain Stanton, October 4, 1775, in Force, *American Archives*, ser. 4, 4:335, http://amarch.lib.niu.edu/islandora/object/niu-amarch%3A91713, accessed July 1, 2017.

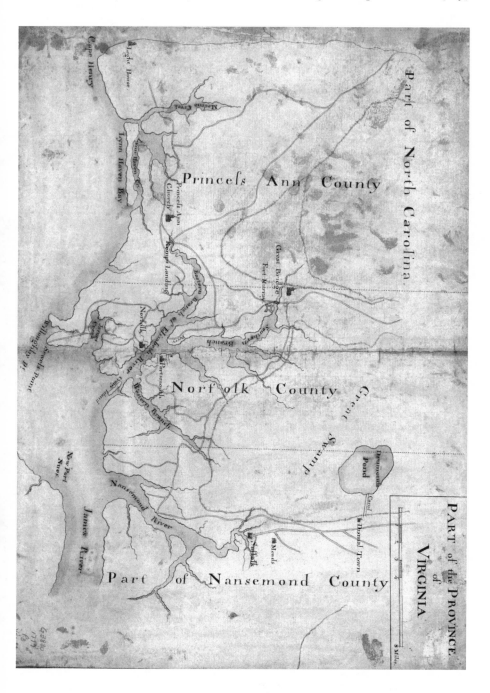

"A Part of the Province of Virginia," c. 1791.

wounded.[32] Another contemporary account reported Dunmore's force left thirty-one killed and wounded on the battlefield in the hands of the rebels.[33] The day after the battle, Woodford made a more detailed inspection the battlefield and indicated British losses were higher than first reported, but he provided no numbers. Reports circulated indicating as many as one hundred British casualties, but these were likely overstated. More recent estimates place the British casualties at sixty-one killed and wounded with one rebel wounded producing casualty figures more consistent with Woodford's initial reports and estimates.[34] Regardless of the numbers lost, regulars killed and wounded represented a sizable portion of Dunmore's regular troops, the backbone of his military capability.[35] The defeat of the regulars shattered the confidence of Dunmore's Loyalist forces, and emboldened the Virginia rebels who were subsequently reinforced by Howe's North Carolina Continentals just three days after Dunmore's assault failed to dislodge Woodford's troops.[36]

NORFOLK OCCUPATION AND HOWE'S ASSUMPTION TO COMMAND

After the resounding Great Bridge victory, the rebels possessed the initiative and proceeded north in pursuit of Dunmore's depleted and demoralized force. Dunmore was in trouble, and he knew it. With insufficient forces to hold the Loyalist-dominated city of Norfolk, Dunmore moved his command, the Virginia Royal Government, and desperate Loyalists aboard ships in the adjacent Elizabeth River. After discussions between Colonels Howe and Woodford, and with consent of Virginia's provisional government, on December 14, 1775, Howe assumed command of the combined North Carolina-Virginia military force as the senior Continental officer present.[37]

32. William Woodford to the President of the Virginia Revolutionary Convention, December 9, 1775, Revolutionary Government, Papers of the Fourth Virginia Convention, Record Group 2, Accession 30003, Library of Virginia, Richmond, VA; William Woodford to Edmund Pendleton, *Virginia Gazette* (Pinckney), December 13, 1775, http://research. history.org/DigitalLibrary/va-gazettes/VGSinglePage.cfm?IssueIDNo=75.Pi.61, accessed June 30, 2017.
33. Full account of the battle at the Great Bridge, in Force, *American Archives*, ser. 4, 4:228-9, http://amarch.lib.niu.edu/islandora/object/niu-amarch%3A105647, accessed 20 June 2017.
34. Mark M. Boatner, "Great Bridge Va.," *Encyclopedia of the American Revolution* (Mechanicsburg, PA: Stackpole Books, 1994), 447-448.
35. "Correspondant," *Virginia Gazette (Pinckney)*, December 13, 1775.
36. Bennett and Lennon, *A Quest for Glory*, 30.
37. Colonel Howe to the President of the Virginia Convention, 15 Dec 1775, in Force, *American Archives*, ser. 4, 4:278, accessed 1 July 2017; Colonel Woodford to Virginia Convention, 15 Dec 1775, vol. 4, 278-9, http://amarch.lib.niu.edu/islandora/object/niu-amarch%3A101159, accessed July 1, 2017.

The consolidated command facilitated unity of effort and command, and enabled Howe to effectively negotiate from a position of strength.[38] Conversely, Dunmore's troops and the Loyalist refugees struggled to subsist aboard cramped ships that floated, at times, only yards from the Norfolk waterfront. Just obtaining fresh water became difficult as the troops occupying Norfolk challenged all attempts to forage for food, water and other necessities. Dunmore made attempts to exchange prisoners and acquire supplies from the provision-rich Tidewater and Albemarle regions, but Howe resisted and began to assess his strategic options.[39]

ASSESSMENT OF THE SITUATION IN NORFOLK

Howe's combined North Carolina-Virginia force outnumbered Dunmore's military strength, yet neither side fielded the number of troops needed to occupy and effectively control Norfolk, Virginia's largest city. Both Howe and Dunmore estimated a requirement of 5,000 troops to hold Norfolk; Howe's entire force numbered 1,275 men on December 17, 1775.[40] The stalemate around Norfolk presented an unpleasant environment for both Dunmore's Loyalists aboard ship and Howe's men ashore. Whig Col. Scott described Norfolk as a horrible cold, damp, miserable place where men stood duty for forty-eight hours without relief.[41] Frustration aboard the British ships flared as the cramped quarters and limited provisions took their toll.[42] Howe refused to allow those aboard to go ashore or purchase food. The situation worsened as the rebels occupying Norfolk made their presence visible to those aboard ship. Waving and hollering devolved into obscene gesturing, then, the ultimate insult, firing on the British warships.[43] As early as

---

38. Chairman of the Joint Chiefs of Staff, *Joint Publication 1, Doctrine for the Armed Forces of the United States*, (Washington, D.C.: 2017). Howe understood the importance of dealing with the Royal Governor with a single military voice guided by the political leadership of North Carolina and Virginia.
39. Bennett and Lennon, *A Quest for Glory*, 30-1.
40. Louis Van L. Naisawald, "Robert Howe's Operations in Virginia 1775-1776," *The Virginia Magazine of History and Biography* 60, no. 3 (1952): 438; Return of the Forces under command of Colonel Howe, at Norfolk, December 17, 1775, in Force, *American Archives*, ser. 4, 4:278-9, http://amarch.lib.niu.edu/islandora/object/niu-amarch%3A95607, accessed July 1, 2017; Bennett and Lennon, *A Quest for Glory*, 30-32; and Selby, *The Revolution in Virginia*, 68.
41. Colonel Scott to Captain Southall, in Force, *American Archives*, ser. 4, 4:292, http://amarch.lib.niu.edu/islandora/object/niu-amarch%3A84260, accessed July 1, 2017; Naisawald, "Robert Howe's Operations," 438.
42. Minutes of the Virginia Convention, January 2, 1776, in Saunders, *Colonial and State Records*, 10:380-1.
43. Bennett and Lennon, *A Quest for Glory*, 31-2.

UNIT	STRENGTH
Virginia 2nd Regiment	350
Virginia Minute Battalion	165
Detachment of Virginia 1st Regiment	172
North Carolina 2nd Regiment	438
North Carolina Volunteers	150
Total	1275

Table 1. North Carolina & Virginia Troop Strength at Norfolk, December 1775.

December 14 the journal of HMS *Otter* reported shots fired at the warship by troops occupying Norfolk.[44] An ensign aboard the *Otter*, knowing that there were insufficient British forces to prevent the occupation of Norfolk by the rebels, went ashore under a flag of truce carrying a message from Dunmore demanding Colonel Howe stop firing on the British warships followed by the threat that, "if another shot was fired at the *Otter*, they must expect the town to be knocked about their ears."[45]

Capt. Matthew Squires, commanding the *Otter*, had previously witnessed the same type of rebel behavior he experienced along the waterfront at Norfolk. The ship's journal or log recorded a similar experience a few months earlier when the *Otter* supported General Howe's forces under siege by the rebels in Boston. An entry for Thursday, May 4, 1775 reads, "Off Castle William Island [Boston Harbor] at 11 the Rebels came down the Point & fired several times at the Ship & our boats as they passd on which we discharged some Musquets at them but they taking no notice of it we fired seven Swivels & dispersed them."[46] Captain Squires shared the view of his admiral when using force to suppress the rebels to modify their belligerent behavior. Upon learning of the events of April 19, 1775, at Lexington and Concord, Adm. Samuel Graves, the British North American squadron commander, recorded his thoughts on a course of action to punish the rebels, "It was indeed the Admirals opinion that we ought to act hostiley from this time forward by burning & laying waste the whole country, & his inclination and intentions were to strain every nerve for the

44. Journal of his Majesty's Sloop *Otter*, Matthew Squires Commanding, December, 14, 1775, in Clark, ed., *Naval Documents*, 3:197.
45. Letter from a Midshipman Onboard H.M. Sloop *Otter*, December, 14, 1775, in ibid., 3:103.
46. Journal of his Majesty's Sloop *Otter*, Matthew Squires Commanding, Thursday, May 4, 1775, in ibid., 1:278.

public Service" He also proposed, "the burning of Charles town and Roxbury, and the seizing of the Heights of Roxbury and Bunkers Hill."[47] No doubt, the opinions and intent of the Admiral Graves influenced the actions of the officers commanding his warships assigned to support the various royal governors as they attempted to regain control of their respective colonies.

Capt. Henry Bellew, in command of the twenty-eight-gun frigate HMS *Liverpool*, arrived in Virginia to support Lord Dunmore and his Loyalist followers on December 21 with 400 marines and the store ship *Maria*. Captain Bellew warned the rebels they would use force if parties were not permitted to come ashore to purchase supplies from the locals. By Christmas Day the situation continued deteriorating, and the rebels received timely reinforcements in the form of 180 men of a minute battalion to help with security responsibilities.[48] The arrival of these men, on Christmas Day, likely raised the spirits of the men who were standing duty for two days at a time without relief. On December 30, Captain Bellew issued an ominous warning: "As I hold it incompatible with the honour of my commission to suffer men, in arms against their Sovereign and the Laws, to appear before His Majesty's ships, I desire you will cause your sentinels, in the town of Norfolk to avoid being seen, that women and children may not feel the effects of their audacity; and it would not be imprudent if both were to leave the town."[49] Howe, however, remained impervious to the British attempts and held steadfast in his resistance to all British intimidation and threats.[50]

While Colonel Howe took a hard line on dealing with the British military leaders and Lord Dunmore aboard ship, he and Colonel Woodford were more understanding of the plight of more recent immigrants. A group of Scottish Highlanders, apparently bound for North Carolina, found themselves stranded in Norfolk during the rebel occupation. Woodford requested guidance from the Virginia Convention on how to deal with these individuals and received instructions from the Convention to "take the distressed Highlanders with their families under his protection, permit them to pass by land unmolested to Carolina and supply them with such provisions as they may be in immediate want of."[51]

47. Narrative of Vice Admiral Graves, Boston, April 19, 1775, in ibid., 1:193.
48. Robert Howe to Edmund Pendleton, in Saunders, *Colonial and State Records*, 10:365.
49. Henry Bellew to Howe, in ibid., 10:372.
50. Howe to Bellew, in ibid., 10:372.
51. Minutes of the Virginia Convention, December 14, 1775, in ibid., 10:346.

DESTRUCTION OF NORFOLK

The assembled British fleet unleashed a barrage of cannon fire on Norfolk and the rebels at about 3:00 p.m. on New Year's Day of 1776. In all, ships mounting an estimated one hundred naval cannons participated in the firing that continued through 2 a.m. on January 2. Dunmore also sent ashore landing parties to forage through the warehouses and burn houses and buildings near the waterfront, but the rebels repulsed most of these landing parties.[52] Firing a variety of ammunition into wooden structures, one would envision massive destruction near the waterfront followed by fires, fanned by winds off the water that consumed adjacent structures. Legend has it that Norfolk disappeared as Dunmore took out his frustrations on the only city capable of sustaining a substantial British military presence in the lower Chesapeake Bay. The facts are quite different, however, in terms of the amount of damage inflicted in this January 1, 1776 cannonade.

The bombardment provided an opportunity for the rebel troops to join in the destruction of the principally Loyalist city and the associated private property of its citizens. The Americans, Patriots from North Carolina and Virginia, not Lord Dunmore and his fleet, destroyed Norfolk to deny its use to the British. Howe realized the American rebels did not have sufficient forces to hold the city and prevent its use by the British in the future. The American Patriots finished what Lord Dunmore started and in doing so, destroyed the only large and capable military port in the southern Chesapeake Bay.

VIRGINIA'S FORMAL ASSESSMENT OF THE DESTRUCTION OF NORFOLK

In 1777, the State of Virginia appointed commissioners to examine the details of the destruction, with a mission to "ascertain the Losses occasioned to individuals by the burning of Norfolk and Portsmouth, in the year 1776." The committee, including Richard Kello, Joseph Prentis, Daniel Fisher and Robert Andrews, conducted the assessment of damages between September 8 and October 10, 1777. Other committee members conducted a similar assessment of the cities Portsmouth and Suffolk. The commissioners determined Dunmore's bombardment of the city only destroyed nineteen structures valued at 1,616 pounds sterling.[53] While the bombardment may have been a sight to behold, and terrorized those in the vicinity, it did not result in the destruction of Norfolk. The tables presented here show the losses attributed to the British forces and to the American or Patriot forces,

52. Parsons, "Contemporary English Accounts," 222.
53. Heath, *Journal and Reports*, 16.

indicating the losses in Norfolk only; the committee found the losses in Portsmouth and Suffolk were much less extensive.

THE IMPACT OF NORFOLK'S DESTRUCTION

The systematic and deliberate destruction of Norfolk was one of the more important and far-reaching strategic military decisions made by the southern provisional rebel governments early in the American Revolution. The provisional governments of North Carolina and Virginia understood the importance of denying the use of the most capable port city between New York and Charleston to the British. When the British returned to the Chesapeake Bay region in 1779 and again in 1780 and 1781, the lack of a capable port and port city resulted in Generals Alexander Leslie, Benedict Arnold and William Phillips ultimately establishing their base of operations in Portsmouth, Virginia. Portsmouth retained some infrastructure after the destruction of Norfolk but proved a poor location with low-lying terrain and an inadequate channel depth to support ships of the line.[54] This led the British to Yorktown, after considering other basing options,[55] where Lord Cornwallis eventually surrendered 8,000 British forces on October 19, 1781.

Had Norfolk remained a functional port city, the British could have used the location to rally and consolidate Loyalist support, build local Loyalist militia units and counter the rebel militia. This is exactly what Benedict Arnold tried to do in early 1781 when the British committed land forces to the region, but it was too little too late. Upon his arrival in Virginia in 1781, Lord Cornwallis made a similar analysis of the importance of controlling the Chesapeake Bay, the area's commerce and the population. He appropriately concluded that Virginia's navigable rivers made the state vulnerable to the mobility and sustainability of a land force with adequate maritime support. He stated in a letter to his superior, Gen. Henry Clinton, on August 20, 1781, "that if we have the force to accomplish it the reduction of the province would be of great advantage to England on account of the value of its trade to us, the blow that it would be to the rebels, and as it would contribute to the reduction and quiet of the Carolinas."[56]

The local population lived under rebel control for years and the raiding strategy implemented in 1779 proved to the locals that the British did not intend to remain in force and instead only punish those who

54. Clinton to Cornwallis, July 8, 1781, in Saberton, *Cornwallis Papers*, 5:140; and 3:3.
55. Clinton to Cornwallis, July 11, 1781, in ibid., 5:139; and Cornwallis to Graves, July 26, 1781, in ibid., 4: 41.
56. Cornwallis to Clinton, August 20, 1781, in ibid., 6:24.

DATE OF DESTRUCTION	NO. HOUSES	HOUSE VALUE*	PERSONAL PROPERTY VALUE*
November 30, 1775	32	1,948	180
January 1, 1776	19	1,616	1,305
January 21, 1776	3	114	
Totals	54	3,678	1,485

*Value in Pounds Sterling

Table 2. Losses in the City of Norfolk attributed to the British forces

DATE OF DESTRUCTION & RESPONSIBLE PARTY	NO. HOUSES	HOUSE VALUE*	PERSONAL PROPERTY VALUE*
State troops, Before January 15, 1776	863	110,807	8,085
Convention (Virginia government) ordered February 1776	416	49,663	2,707
Totals	1,279	160,470	10,792

*Value in Pounds Sterling

Table 3. Losses in the City of Norfolk attributed to the American forces

These tables reflect the findings of the commission that American Patriot or Rebel forces destroyed 1,279 of the 1,333 homes or structures, or ninety-six percent. The actions of British and Loyalist forces, under the command of the Royal Governor, Lord Dunmore, destroyed only 54 structures.

supported the Whig-controlled government. When General Leslie remained in the area for only a month during 1780, the locals again came under rebel control upon his departure. The local population viewed Benedict Arnold's arrival in late 1780 as one more temporary British occupation. Local, politically moderate leaders remained skeptical of British seriousness to remain in the region.[57] As the British attempted to regain control of Virginia in 1781, by committing large numbers of land forces, the true strategic value of Norfolk emerged.

The British occupation of the Tidewater region in 1780-1781 reignited an ugly phase of the local civil war that festered in the area as the British evacuated Portsmouth in favor of a base at Yorktown. Gen.

57. Johann Ewald, *Diary of the American War, A Hessian Journal,* Joseph P. Tustin ed. and trans. (New Haven: Yale University Press, 1979), 276-7.

Charles O'Hara, Lord Cornwallis's second in command and the man who formally surrendered the British forces at Yorktown, had the responsibility to close the base at Portsmouth. As he removed the remaining supplies and soldiers from Portsmouth he decided to bring numerous local Loyalists to Yorktown as well. He wrote to Lord Cornwallis at Yorktown, "It is unavoidable, I am brining you all the inhabitants of Princess Anne and Norfolk Counties. What an unfortunate scrap they are in!"[58]

Had the city of Norfolk remained functional and avoided complete destruction in 1776, the history of the revolution in the Chesapeake Bay would have been very different. Had the Royal Government possessed the capability to physically protect Norfolk, the loyal population would have remained in place, and with the infrastructure largely intact, provided a base for sustaining the British maritime and land forces. A base near the mouth of Chesapeake Bay would have allowed for more aggressive maritime patrolling and would have assisted in closing the bay as an effective shipping route. The decisive actions of Col. Robert Howe and the North Carolina and Virginia provisional governments in authorizing the destruction of Norfolk were bold and crucial. These men deliberately destroyed the second largest American city south of Philadelphia and the eighth largest city in North America. Had they waivered in this decision, the history of the war in the south would have been quite different.

Without a persistent British maritime and land presence in the lower Chesapeake Bay, the rebels just waited to act until the maritime and land forces departed the area. As one early twentieth century Virginia researcher and historian noted, the British navy "enabled them to dominate the sea, and the counties lying on navigable waters were thus kept in frequent alarm." But the, "British had no foothold on Virginia soil."[59] While there was no way for the Whig government of Virginia to prevent the more capable British navy from actively patrolling Chesapeake Bay with limited naval vessels, and prior to the commitment of significant numbers of British land forces during 1781, the rebels devised a method to help safeguard commerce and provide a warning to mariners of active British maritime or privateer presence in the bay. Virginia established a very simple system to alert vessels attempting to enter the Chesapeake Bay if British ships were on patrol there. If the bay was clear, officials hoisted a large red and white striped flag on a fifty-foot-high pole mounted on the sand dunes at Cape

58. O'Hara to Cornwallis, August 15, 1781, in Saberton, ed., *Cornwallis Papers*, 6:51.
59. McAllister, *Virginia Militia*, 1.

Henry. At night, a lantern served as a signal. When the British navy or privateers closed the lower Chesapeake Bay to shipping, cargo traveled by wagon to South Quay, a port that could handle ships up to 200 tons, located southwest of Franklin, Virginia, in Southampton County. South Quay, located along the Blackwater River, allows access into the Chowan River reaching into the Albemarle Sound in North Carolina, at Edenton. This route provided access to the Atlantic Ocean through the Outer Banks at Ocracoke Inlet. This route into southeastern North Carolina validated North Carolina's concerns expressed early in the revolution that the two regions, Tidewater Virginia and Albemarle North Carolina, were accessible to forces occupying Norfolk. The destruction of Norfolk served both the States of North Carolina and Virginia preventing the British from retaining control of the region.[60] One may correctly conclude that the seeds of the British defeat at Yorktown in October 1781 took root with the destruction of Norfolk in early 1776.

60. Eller, *Chesapeake Bay*, 310-20.

Finding Edward Wigglesworth's Lost Diary

C.E. PIPPENGER

Col. Edward Wigglesworth took part in some of the most consequential actions of the American Revolution, but, like so many such men, we know little about him. Happily, Wigglesworth left a diary which was once presumed lost, but has now has been found. The manuscript provides more details concerning Wigglesworth's extraordinary military career.*

A BRIEF HISTORY OF THE WIGGLESWORTH DIARY

Wigglesworth was born January 4, 1742 and grew up in Newburyport, Massachusetts. After graduating from Harvard in 1761, he worked for the mercantile business of Jackson and Terry, which was based in Newburyport. During his employment he served as a ship captain in the Caribbean trade.

On June 24, 1776, at age thirty-four, he was commissioned a colonel by the "Council of the Massachusetts Bay in New England" and placed in command of a Militia Battalion (6th Continental Regiment of Massachusetts). His battalion was ordered to Fort Ticonderoga, which was then in the midst of furiously preparing for a British assault up Lake Champlain. Ticonderoga and Crown Point were being reinforced, and a new stronghold, Mount Independence, was under construction across the lake from Fort Ticonderoga. In Skenesborough (now Whitehall)

*The author gratefully acknowledges his co-author James L Nelson. A special thanks to the following for their assistance and guidance essential to bringing this document to publication: Art Cohn, Emeritus Director Lake Champlain Maritime Museum; Ernie Haas, Richard Hibbert, James K. Martin; Ms. Nichole Russell, Public Services Manager, Special Collections Department, Library University of Glasgow; Ms. Callie Raspuzzi, Registrar Archives, Bennington Museum; Ms. Elizabeth Fuller, Rosenbach Museum and Library, Philadelphia; Don N. Hagist and the *Journal of the American Revolution* staff.

Patriots were hurriedly building a fleet to counter British movement on the lake.

Colonel Wigglesworth was an experienced mariner, a skill set much needed but rarely found in that northern theater. General Gates appointed Wigglesworth third in command of the American fleet, then under the command of Benedict Arnold, himself a former merchant captain.[1] Wigglesworth joined the fleet on September 9, 1776, and participated in the Battle of Valcour Island, October 11-13, 1776. After the near complete destruction of the American fleet, he escaped to Fort Ticonderoga and resumed command of his battalion, which was disbanded November 30, 1776. In January 1777, Wigglesworth was appointed colonel of the 13th Massachusetts Regiment. He served in several battles and was present at Valley Forge. Like many other officers he exhausted his financial reserves and resigned from the army in 1779. He returned to Newburyport and ultimately was appointed tax collector for the port. He held this post for many years prior to his death on December 8, 1826.

The Diary of Colonel Edward Wigglesworth was first described by Mrs. E. Vale Smith (Blake), who published portions of the manuscript in her *History of Newburyport* in 1854. In a biographical sketch of Colonel Wigglesworth, she quoted excerpts from his diary and summarized other diary segments. Following Smith's publication, for the next seventy-eight years, the diary was presumed lost. It apparently stayed in the hands of the Wigglesworth family heirs, however, until 1932.

In that year the Wigglesworth diary was offered for sale in an auction by Stan. V. Henkels, Jr., a Philadelphia literary and art auctioneer.[2] A portion of the diary containing Wigglesworth's description of the Battle of Valcour Island was printed in the sale catalogue (No. 1464, sale date May 17, 1932). There were twelve Wigglesworth items for sale in this catalog, including Gen. Horatio Gates's appointment of Wigglesworth as third in command of the American fleet.

After the Henkel's auction, the diary again disappeared and was presumed to be either in the hands of a private collector or lost. In fact, it had been purchased from the auction by a wealthy Vermont resident, Hall Park McCullough, a Wall Street lawyer, philanthropist, and one of the founders of Bennington College. McCullough, throughout his life, was a collector of early Vermont memorabilia. He paid $230 for

1. Mrs. E. Vale Smith (Blake), *History of Newburyport; From the Earliest Settlement of the Country to the Present Time with a Biographical Appendix* (Newburyport, 1854), 357-359.
2. Stan. V. Henkels, Jr., Catalogue No. 1464, sale date May 17, 1932.

the Diary.[3] At his death in 1966, McCullough's collection was divided between The University of Vermont and the Bennington Museum and Library. The Bennington Collection was not cataloged until an archivist began examining it around 2000. The Wigglesworth diary was cataloged in 2009 and listed online in late 2017.[4] The registrar confirmed there are no other Wigglesworth documents in the collection.

In March 2018 the author found the online listing and visited the library. Richard Hibbert photographed the entire diary and the author transcribed it from the photographs. (Prior to the author's request, no one had asked to see the Diary.) The Museum's registrar clarified the history of the diary during the years it was thought to be lost, and told the author they also held a typewritten transcription made by Mr. McCullough.[5] In comparing the McCullough transcription to the author's there were only minor differences. Having the advantage of PDF magnification, discrepancies were resolved by the author.

The University of Vermont portion of McCullough's collection was cataloged, and a description published as the Hall Park McCullough Collection in 1998.[6] It is housed in the Special Collections Department of the Bailey Howe Library, Burlington, Vermont. The collection at the University of Vermont contains no documents related to the Battle of Valcour Island.

The complete diary is paper bound, thirty-four pages including front and back covers. The narrative describing the Battle of Valcour Island and events through December 1776 is fourteen pages. The remainder of the bound document consists of Wigglesworth's expenses traveling between Newburyport and Fort Ticonderoga, officers' signatures acknowledging receipt to pay their troops, etc. While the various receipts are of interest to Revolutionary war scholars they are not relevant to Wigglesworth's narrative. The only exception is an itemized list of his personal possessions and their value which were lost when the *Royal Savage* was burned by the British on October 11, 1776.

Here, published for the first time, is the complete text of the diary, and the list of items from the *Royal Savage*. The diary is on pages 5

3. Personal Communication from Ms. Elizabeth Fuller, Rosenbach Museum and Library, Philadelphia, Pennsylvania per American Book Prices Current, 1932.

4. Edward Wigglesworth Diary, 1776-1777, Bennington Museum, Bennington, Vermont, Catalog Number 2012.14, bennington.pastperfectonline.com/archive/35DE0164-32EE-463B-90DB-454513270615.

5. Hall Park McCullough transcription of the Wigglesworth Diary 1776-1777, Diary of Colonel Edward Wigglesworth, September 1776-March 1777, Bennington Museum, Bennington, Vermont, 2009, 163.440.

6. Robert Maguire and Kevin Graffagnino, *Hall Park McCullough: Americana Collector 1872-1966* (University of Vermont, 1988).

thru 19 of the bound book, describing the Battle of Valcour Island and events until Wigglesworth's Battalion was disbanded in December 1776.

THE WIGGLESWORTH DIARY

Cumberland Bay Lake Champlain – Fryday Octr 11th 1776. at 9 ^{0}clock mor^g were alarmed by the Guard Boats y^t the Enemy's fleet were in sight coming down. the wind at N^o at 1/2 past nine the Genl Arnold order'd me into the Yaul to go to wind^d to observe thier motions I returned at 10. & inform'd him they were round the Island of Valcour. in half an hour they began to fire upon the Royal Savage who had gone to Land. for at my return: the three galleys and two schooners were under sail stand^g across the Lake between the Island & Main the Royal Savage had the misfortune to run aShore by missing Stays. The Genl then ordered the Galleys & Gondolas to form the Line which they did quite across from ye Island to the main-the Enemy came on with 1. Ship 18. 12 pound^r two schooners of 16 guns each 1. Bomb and a floating battery of 22. Brass 12 and 24 pounde^r. ~~when their ensued a most terrible fire without~~ & 18. flat bottom'd boats carrying each 1.18 & 24/ pound^r besides howitz^r when their ensued a most terrible fire without the least intermission till 1/2 past five PM. when the Enemy drew off. our fleet rec'd considerable damaged. & we had about 50 killd & wound^d which we carried on board the Hospital Sloop. who did not engage_ _. _. _ _____

Upon Consultation with Genrls. Arnold and Waterbury. I was order'd to get under way. as soon as twas dark. & show a Light aStern for the Gondolas. in order to retreat up the Lake as far as possible it being calm. we row'd but cleared the enemy without being discovered–at 12 ^{0}clock the wind breezed up at S^O in the morning
on Saturday 12th. I found my Self up with Schulers Island. at 10. came to anchor under Ligonier Point to wait for the fleet & stop our leaks & secure our M$^{n.}$ mast which was shot in too– & at sunset the Hospital Sloop and the Revenge Schooner. were abreast of us. & the other two Galleys about 2 Leg^s. to Leeward. at 12 night Capt Summer of the Boston Gondola came by. & at 1 Capt Simmons in the Phila^d.[7] came up and inform'd me that the Enemy had pursued us & taken 1. gondola viz. Capt. Grimes. & that Capt. Ulmore[7] had quitted his D^o & sunk her. & taken his boat[8]–I immediately got underway. & stood up along

---

7. This section clearly names Captain Simmons as commanding the *Philadelphia* and Captain Ulmore as commanding the sunk gondola which was the *Spitfire*.
8. It is plausible (but without collaborating evidence) that the comment "& taken in his boat" meant Simmons took Ulmore's crew onto the *Providence*.

Shore but the wind com^g. to the Southw^d. I was obliged to stand over to the Eastw^d.

in the morning on Sunday 13th. the Hospital Sloop and the Revenge were ahead. & the two galleys in the Rear & the rest of the Gondolas rowing up in shore. & the Enemys fleet in chase of us the wind deying away. They came up with us fast wind fresh W. at N^o. at 9 ^{o}Clock Genl Arnold sent his Boat on board to desire me to l^y by for the fleet. which I did by stretching across the Lake at 10. AM the Enemy began to fire upon the two galleys. in the rear. about. against Split-Rock. I soon discovered that the Washington. Galley. In which was Genl. a Waterbury had struck & that Genl. Arnold was engaged with the Ship & two Schooners. & that he could not get clear. I thought it my duty to make Sail & endeavor to save the Trumbull Galley if possible. About 1 ^{o}clock Genl Arnold run his galley ashore with 4 other Gondola's & blew all up. we the doublemann'd our oars & made all the Sail we could. which by throwing over our Ballast we got off clear. with 1. Gondola. the Revenge & Hospital Sloop. which were we sav d. as the Lee Cutter was missing we suppos'd her taken. which with 1. Gondola and the Washington were all the Enemy got Possession of–. I came to anchor at Cr Point took in some Provisions in for Col^o Hartley as he was preparing to leave that Place. & arrived at Tyconderoga at Sunset. went aShore waited on Gates & inform'd him of our Affairs & that I believed Genl. Arnold would be in the morning. which he accordingly was.

Monday 14th. Employed in putting the Galley in the best State of Defence. Genl Waterbury–arriv'd with all his People. disch^d on Parole–.

Tuesday 15th employed as before. sent Guard Boats down the Lake. to give Intelligence of the Coming of the Enemy.

Wednesday 16th. Wind still at S^o. & very warm. expect the Enemy the first fair Wind

Thursday 17th. Wind at N.E. rainy W^r look for the Enemy every minute, keep the guard boats at 3 mile Point. to look out. & make Signals

Fryday 18th Wind N. E. small Breeze & rainy W^r. the Boats made no Discoveries. the Boats were order'd to carry a flagg to distinguish y^m from any other boats–

Saturday, 19th. Wind NW. fine pleasa^t Weather after the Rain. expect the Enemy every minute–

Sunday 20th. wind at S.W. fine W^r understand the Enemy are preparing to come as soon as possible

Monday. 21st wind at N. N.W. fresh Breeze. If the Enemy don't take advantage of this wind–shall think they are not ready. past 3 ^{o}clock no Vessels in sight.– at 4. the guard boat came in fired an Alarm. & said there were 12 Canoes at dark sent a boat to Putnam's Point return'd. said she saw a number of Lights. expect the Enemy <u>before morning: but they did not come</u>

Tuesday 22nd Wind NW. fine pleasant W^r but cool–went up to see Col^o Breur & Carleton. Return'd at Sunset immediately rec'd the news that the Indians had scalp'd aman just beyond the Bridge. & took 2 Prisoners–

Wednesday–23^d wind SSW. fresh Breeze nothing material happen'd to the Guard Boats Blew very hard till 12 ^oclock. night–

Thursday. 24th. wind W. small Breeze & very warm for the Season.– Sent a Boat down the Lake in ye Night as far as 5-mile Point discover'd some Canoes. rowing down the Lake. returned

Fryday. 25th. wind. W. still continues remarkable warm & pleasant–sent Letters home by Mr. Whitridge of Danvers, by whom I inclos'd 20 Dollars to my wife, which he promis'd to deliver at Major (Illegible) at Danvers. for the Sum of 3/-

Saturday 26th Wind SW & rainy W^r laid a boom across from the Jersey Battery. hauled the Galley's down to cover Boom

Sunday 27th. Wind SE the Boats discovered nothing down Lake At 4 PM the Enemy's Boats to the number of 4 or 5 appeared in sight but upon 3 or 4 Boats of ours rowing down they made off.

Monday 28th. Wind N^o Fresh Breese expect the Enemy every minute joyn'd the Reg^t. & manned the Lines at our Alarm Post at Dawning– at 9AM alarm'd by our Gaud Boats coming in, soon after 4-5 of the Enemy's Boat came in sight, one of them came so nigh our Batteries fir'd a few shot upon which she returned__

The Army under Arms all Day nothing happened at Night

Tuesday 29th. Wind at NW. & quality complet'd Bridge across Lake from Fort Ty^a to Independence M^t nothing remarkable during that Night

Wednesday 30th. Wind SW clear W^r nothing material to Day

Thursday 31st. Wind W. reiny cloudy W^r Latter part clear. A party went to 3 mile Point & brought a Quanity of Hay,Oats &_____

Fryday Novr 1st. Wind W. pretty cool_ nothing remarkable down the Lake Col^o Daton's Reg^t. arrived from Fort Stanwick & Part of 2 or 3 Reg^{ts.} of Militia from N. Hampsure & the Grants__

Saturday Novr 2nd. Wind SW. fresh Breeze Snow Squalls. The Committee arrived from Massachusitts State__

Sunday 3^d Wind. S.W. pleas^t W^r the Committee arrived from Watertown

Monday 4th There is a Repot that the Enemy have left. C. Point–

Monday 4th Wind S[o] pleas[t] W[r] tis confirmed the Enemy have left Crown Point–rec'd her Letter fr my Wife. & one from M[r] Jackson & one from M[r] Tracy–

Tuesday. 5th W. SE. pleas[t] W[r] nothing remarkable. happen'd–

Wednesday. 6th Calm. & warm W. Nothing material—

Thursday. 7th Wind SW. D[r] Weather rec'd Orders to prepare to go to S[t]. Johns a flag of Truce–set out at 5 [O]clock with Lieut Evans and a frenchman Prisoners lodg'd at CPoint

Fryday. 8th. Wind N[o] row'd all Day & incamp'd 3 mile below Split Rock–

Saturday. 9th Wind N. thick hazy w[r] between Valcour & the Main saw the Ship & Schooner & Gondola went on board the Ship to deliver our Prisoners: but were detain'd Prisoners ourselves–

Sunday 10[th.] Wind still at N[o]

Monday. 11th D[O] wind–

Tuesday 12th. D[o]—

Wednesday 13th Wind came to y[e] west[d]. got underway. in comp[y] with all the fleet–came to off Point aux Rochie[9] at 2 o'clock

Thursday–14th weighe'd in y[e] Morn[g] came too Riverine laCole[10] at 5 [O]Clock PM–

Friday 15th at 10 [O]C weigh'd and run a Ground about a mile from Riverine laCole _____

Saturday–16th Wind. Westw[d]. cold Squally W[r]. just informed that I'm to be sent back immediately–

Sunday 17[th.] Wind N[o] arrived at Tycond[a]. 8 [O]Clock morning in 16 Hours from Isle aux Noix[11]–

Monday 18th Wind. Westw[d]. pleas[t] set in company with Gen[ls] Gates–Arnold. and Brickett. for Fort George. on our way to Albany. Left Reg[t]. to follow under Comm[d]. of Col[o] Roberts. & Major Rogers. arrived at Fort George 1. [O]Clock. night–

Tuesday 19th. fine pleasant W[r] Set out at 10 o'clock on foot arriv'd at Fort Edward. at sunset lodged at D[r] Smith's–

9. Probably Point aux Roche on the Western New York shore north of Cumberland Head. The British fleet often rendezvoused there.

10. Probably the Lacolle River in Canada which empties into the Richelieu River about five miles north of the present U. S.–Canadian border.

11. Wigglesworth does not state whether he was returned to Fort Ticonderoga by one of the schooners (*Maria* or *Carlton*) or the *Inflexible*. Sixteen hours from Isle aux Noix to Fort Ticonderoga is a rapid passage.

Wednesday. 20th. pleas^t W^r din'd– McNeil's, Saratoga–lodg'd at Bemis Stillwater–

Thursday 21st Fine pleast and warm morning arrived at Albany at Night. lodg'd at M^{rs}. Hilton's near the City Hall–

Friday 22nd Wind Westw^d cloudy & cool–Mr Hitchcock and the Doct^r. set out for home. Genl Brikett & Col Poor arriv'd. Bought a horse at 50 Dolls.

Saturday 23^d Wind Northw^d cloudy

Sunday 24th. Calm & warm Rainy W^r Col Poor's & De'Hass's Reg^{ts} march'd to their respective homes. –

Monday 28th Wind at SW. fresh cloudy prepare to set out for Newberry to Day– to morrow–. At 12°clock head the disagrrable news that the Enemy had landed on the Jersey shore–which determined me to wait for the Reg^t

Tuesday 26th W.N.W. pleasant weather Col^o. Greaton's Reg^t arriv'd from Tycond^a

Wednesday 27. Peterson came to town nothing remarkable

Thursday 28. fine pleas^t. morning paid Cap^{ts}. Fairfield & Pillsbury. 1000D Dollars cash for recruiting money.

Friday 29th Col^o arrived with– part of the Reg^t. Greaton's imbarked for New York–

Saturday 30th. Rainy cloudy W^r paid off the Reg^t—

Sunday, 1st. Decemb^r Wind Westw^d Expect orders to send Reg^t. home but they went without Leave–Express arriv'd informing that the Enemy we(re) marching towards Brunswick

Monday the 2^d Wind Westw^d pleas^t W^r. Col^{os} Brewer & Carleton arrived

Tuesday 3^d. Wind. N^o. Cloudy the Generals sail'd for the York Army G. Brickett went over the Ferry

Wednesday. 4th Cress'd the Ferry at 10 ½ Clock– left Brewer & Carleton Prentice &c at the Ferry din d at (Scudock?) Millers– lodged at Sharp's Noble Town–

Thursday 5th Fine pleas^t W^r. being very much fatigued lodged at Tryingham Chadwicks– waiting for company till 9 ^{o}clock

Friday the 6th Wind Westw^d fine pleas^t W^r. lod'g at Emenson's at the foot of Westfield mountain–

Saturday 7 fine pleas^t W^r. lod'd' at Palmer Scott's–

Sunday 8th Cloudy W^r first part prov'd a fine Day lod'g'd Jone's at Worcester–Monday–9th Wind W. NW. pretty cold Squally W^r

Sunday– 10th

Acc. of Sundry Articles lost on board Royal Savage arm'd Schooner in
the Engagement with the Enemy on Lake Champlain 11th. Oct. 1776[12]

---

1. Suit of Regimental Cloth^{g.}
 Super f. Broad Cloth. . . . £10, , 10–
9. Shirts new (Shirts xout) @24 10, , 16–
6. Hankerchiefs @ 6/ . . . . 1, , 16–
2. Broad Cloth Jackets @ 26/ ^{each} . 2, ,–
1. Linnen Vest and Breeches @ . . 1, ,–
2. Pr. Knit Breeches @ 24/ each... 2, , 8–
3. Blankets @ 12/ . . . . 1, ,16–
Jones's military Guide @ , ,12–
7. Pr. Jersey knit worsted hose. 3, ,10
1. P new shoes @ 12/ . . . . . . , ,12
Cash 12 Dollars . . . . 3, ,12

£ 38, , 12, ,–
1. Silver spoon @ 15 15

£ 39, . 7
1. Pr. Double Bar.^{ll.} Pistols . . . . 4, ,16, ,–
1. (D?) Vest and Breeches , , , , , 1, , 8–

£ 45, ,11–
1. Great Coat . . . . 3, ,10.

49, , 1

The discovery of the entire Wigglesworth diary is significant not only
for its historical value; but because it also resolves some major issues
and controversy surrounding the previously published diary extracts.
The first controversy surrounds the events on Saturday, October 12.
Mrs. Smith did not publish the entire diary entries from that day. For
that date she states, "In the morning on Saturday, 12th, I found myself
up with Schuters Island. At 10 came to anchor under Ligonier Point
to wait for the fleet & stop our leaks & sew our Mn. mast which was
shot in two." The Henkel's catalog did publish the day's full entry. In
the Henkel's version it states that Captain Simmons in the gondola

---

12. Page 32 of the manuscript; this page is written upside-down from the diary.

Philadelphia at Schuyler Island conversed with Colonel Wigglesworth on the *Trumbull* at about 1 A.M. It has always been known that Captain Simmons commanded the gondola *Providence* not the *Philadelphia*, which was sunk at Valcour Island. It had been assumed a typist incorrectly transcribed the word *Philadelphia*. That is not true; in the original diary Wigglesworth clearly abbreviates *Philadelphia* and not *Providence*. Since he was extremely busy between the 11th and 13th of October, it is highly probable Wigglesworth wrote his account after the battle, and forgot Simmons commanded the *Providence* and not the *Philadelphia*. In his October 11 entry, Wigglesworth wrote the phrase "when their ensued a most terrible fire without" and then crossed it out and then inserted the same exact phrase in the following line, supporting the idea that the diary was written some days after the fact (the Henkel's transcription does not include Wigglesworth's crossed out phrase). Although there may be other explanations, this appears the most logical. The second also surrounds Saturday, October 12. The Henkel's transcription states "At 12 night Capt. Summer of the Boston gondola came by & 1 Capt. Simmons in the Philad. came up & informed me the Eney had pursued us & had taken 1 gondola, viz., Capt. Grimes & that Capt. Moore had quitted his D. & sunk her & taken his Boat." Unfortunately, the typist making the transcription made a severe error in typing "Capt. Moore." Valcour scholars have always been confused by this statement because no one named Captain Moore was ever associated with command of any vessel in Arnold's fleet. For many years the scholars have searched in vain for an additional reference. Wigglesworth's diary clearly states that Captain Ulmore sank his gondola. Captain Ulmore was Captain of the *Spitfire* which sank in Lake Champlain and still lies in perfect condition on the bottom today.

While these are the two most important controversies resolved by the diary there are other minor points which are also resolved. For example, the Journal of Bayze Wells states that Wigglesworth joined the fleet on September 9, 1776. The Wigglesworth diary in a separate entry states that Wigglesworth joined the fleet on September 6. The difference is probably accounted for by the time it took Wigglesworth to sail to Arnold's fleet.

Sadly, Wigglesworth never explained why he was taken prisoner by the British. The answer to that question can only be pure speculation.

William Taylor: Loyalist Refugee in East Florida

❧ GEORGE KOTLIK ☙

During the War for American Independence, displaced Loyalists from the southern colonies sought refuge in East Florida. Due to a large influx of refugees, the towns of Hillsborough and St. Johns, both towns built in Northern Florida, were erected; the former was built at the modern day Old Town Fernandina on Amelia Island.[1] Refugees like Louis Lowry,[2] Michael Wernel,[3] and James Gordon[4] are among those Loyalists who found temporary refuge in East Florida during the war.

In his book, *Conservatism in Early America*, Leonard Woods Larabee discusses the motives for loyalism during the Revolutionary period. The types of Loyalists he discusses include pessimists who had no confidence in rebel victory, procrastinators who believed independence would come someday but not in the 1770s and 1780s, neutralists who were forced to take a side, individuals who felt it was morally wrong to move against the Crown, people who were well established in their jobs, people who disliked violence, people who had ties to Britain through family or business contacts, people who were afraid of anarchy,[5] people who liked order,[6] individuals persuaded by "Influential Men,"[7] minority

1. Bland and Associates. "Appendix A: Historic Context and References," Historic Properties Resurvey, City of Fernandina Beach, Nassau County, FL, 5-6.
2. Louis Lowry record, Florida History Online, www.unf.edu/floridahistoryonline/Plantations/plantations/Louis_Lowry.htm.
3. Michael Wernel record, Florida History Online, www.unf.edu/floridahistoryonline/Plantations/plantations/Michael_Wernel.htm.
4. James Gordon Surveyor's Map, Florida History Online, www.unf.edu/floridahistory online/Plantations/plantations/James_Gordon.htm.
5. Leonard Woods Larabee, *Conservatism in Early American History* (New York: New York University Press, 1948), 164-165.
6. N.E.H. Hull, Peter C. Hoffer, Steven L. Allen, "Choosing Sides: a Quantitative Study of the Personality Determinants of Loyalist and Revolutionary Political Affiliation in New York," *The Journal of American History*, 65(2) (1978) 352.
7. Ibid., 347, 354, 365.

groups who felt threatened by the American majority,[8] slaves who were promised freedom by Britain, and businessmen whose interests were tied to those of the Crown.[9]

It is evident that Loyalist community numbers spanned peoples who came from every distinct social class in North America. Their reasons behind Loyalty to the Crown varied by the individual. One Loyalist settler on the East Florida backcountry was William Taylor. Patriot raiders dislocated Taylor, along with many other settlers, who were then forced to find refuge in undeveloped or underdeveloped British lands commissioned to them by the Crown. A letter that he wrote offers a new perspective on loyalist motives during the war, showing that certain loyalist sentiments stemmed out of an obligation to an individual's employer rather than loyalty to a political cause.

According to Florida History Online, the William Taylor letter was a part of a collection of documents titled Treasury 77, Papers of the East Florida Claims Commission. The papers in this collection were not widely available until recently when these documents were digitized and made accessible through the Internet.

Taylor wrote from the safety of a British plantation known as Cecilton Plantation. Under the heirs of Lord Egmont, Taylor found refuge as a Loyalist after his frontier settlement on the St. Johns River had been raided by rebels from the north. He wrote to his employer, William Chapman,[10]

> [Your instructions to me were to] ship out to St. Marys [River] to lead fifty slaves, likewise that you expected a house in Liverpool would consign to us a cargo of slaves, but I hope both you and they have laid aside your plan of so doing. You are unacquainted with the present alarming situation of affairs in the province. About 60 [rebels] from Georgia under Capt. Mack Encamped on the north side of St. Mary's about a mile above our place in order to [claim] cattle being drove out of that province into this and likewise [intent] on driving a stock of 200 head out of this province into Georgia, in which they succeeded. Mr. Clark from Augustine came to our place and intended to stay with us all night, the rebel party having intelligence of his being there and that

8. Bruce G. Wilson, "Loyalists," The Canadian Encyclopedia, www.thecanadianencyclo pedia.com/en/article/loyalists/.

9. Shannon Duffy, "Loyalists," *Mount Vernon Digital Encyclopedia*, www.mountvernon.org/digital-encyclopedia/article/loyalists/.

10. William Taylor to William Chapman, May, 1776, Florida History Online, www.unf.edu/floridahistoryonline/Plantations/plantations/Refugee_Plight_William_Taylor.htm.

he was come out to drive off cattle, about midnight a party of them consisting of 12 men and a sergeant armed with rifles broke open our door and fetched Mr. Clark and carried him off. The night following thirty of them crossed the river and proceeded toward the lower settlement and returned the next day with Mr. [Martin] Jollie and two or three more prisoners. The same day a company of [British] soldiers consisting of 60 men commanded by Captain Graham arrived at our place sent out for the protection of our settlers; the instant they arrived a Negro brought us an account of his having seen the Rebels about a mile distant [at] the old Ferry. Capt. Graham shot across the river at them and they likewise shot back but did no damage, but it gave them opportunity to escape in confusion. So Captain Graham decided to take his men to the lower part of the river as they were not strong enough for [the rebels].

As we were to be left to ourselves, the rest of the settlers being carried off and we in hourly expectation of sharing the same fate and in danger of losing our Negroes I resolved to quit the place which we did that night with all our Negroes and what effects we could carry in our boats and proceeded down towards Amelia Island where we arrived late. Two or three days after we got to Amelia, I engaged an old man to go to take care of our plantation and sent him with four of the worst of our Negroes to assist him in taking care of the crops. Three of these Negroes have since been carried off by the Rebels, the one they left being lame and not able to travel with them. They likewise plundered and destroyed all the buildings on the plantation. I stayed some time at Amelia expecting Graham's party would be reinforced with a sufficient number to protect us; that not being done and the Rebels making daily incursions into this Province. I thought it best to endeavor to get a piece of lumber land on the south side of the St. Johns River to employ our Negroes upon until we could venture to go back to our own place. I could not find any contiguous to rent but have purchased a tract of 400 acres for £60 Sterling pleasantly situated about a mile below the Cowford. Mr. Jollie, who some time ago made his escape from Savannah, has taken half of it and as he had the same number of hands as we have and his people having been in the lumber way at St. Marys, I thought it best to go into partnership with him in exporting lumber, to which he consented. We have been here about two months, have got half our houses built for ourselves and Negroes, [and] two large saw mills and about 12,000 feet of lumber.

This letter helps illustrate the dangers loyalists faced on the frontier, particularly in the face of renegade rebel groups keen on dislodging any British presence that posed a threat to the Revolution.

To the list established by Larabee and other scholars of reasons why loyalists decided against social, economic, and political upheaval in the North American colonies during the American Revolution, we can add the "Careerist," characterizing those who were loyal to Great Britain out of obligation to Loyalist/Pro-British employers and not the Crown itself. Although their heritage ties to the mother country did not alienate them from the British cause, heritage did not motivate them either.

Taylor's letter illustrates this perspective in many ways. First, it is interesting to note that Taylor never spoke ill of those who caused his displacement and distress. He always refers to them simply as "rebels."[11] Other Tory accounts of the time period use more colorful words to describe the American Patriots. For example, in a letter to her brother, Loyalist Ann Hulton describes the colonials most disdainfully: "These Sons of Violence, after attacking houses, breaking windows, beating, stoning and bruising several gentlemen belonging to the Customs, the Collector mortally, and burning his boat."[12] Derogatory terms, like Sons of Violence, used to denote the Patriots and their cause is common in Loyalist writings. These terms, however, are absent in William Taylor's letter. It could be argued that this is because Taylor's letter is a professional letter to an employer, in which derogatory language would not have been appropriate. This reasoning can be counteracted by recognizing that the environment of East Florida during Patriot raids throughout the backcountry, raids that particularly affected William Taylor and his employer's business ventures in the region, merited negative sentiment in the form of insults geared towards the belligerent rebel groups. The fact that the settlement had to be relocated and the business venture paused from further development due to war-time activities would have been reason enough for derogatory remarks by a writer who was a personal victim of the war.

The Careerist is one who remained on the side of Britain throughout the war, but who's loyalty to the Crown was out of obligation to his employer. This person, most likely a man as in Taylor's case, was an ambitious individual whose employer was a Loyalist throughout the war. Due to his financial aspirations for the future mixed with a need to make a living, the careerist aligned with the

11. William Taylor to William Chapman, May, 1776, Florida History Online, www.unf.edu/floridahistoryonline/Plantations/plantations/Refugee_Plight_William_Taylor.htm.
12. Ann Hulton to Henry Hulton, June 30, 1768, Alpha History, http://alphahistory.com/americanrevolution/letters-female-loyalist-1768/.

Crown for purposes of employment, not out of political affiliation as one might assume in a very political war.

During his time on the frontier, Taylor experienced life-threatening moments that would have influenced many in his position to rethink their political affiliation. These dangers took the form of breaking and entering, threat of abduction, and death.[13]

> A few days after we left Amelia with our Negroes a party of the Rebels to the number of 100 came to St. Marys by water in a flat [along with] a schooner and the flat had one 18-pounder mounted on the hull and two or three swivels [guns]. An armed [British] schooner commanded by Lieutenant Grant was to protect the river, [but as he could see them coming it caused] him to weigh his anchor [and go] out to sea. Captain Graham being then at Amelia with his party being [threatened] followed his example and retreated . . . The Rebels plundered Lord Egmont's plantation and other plantations on St. Marys River and have since plundered all the plantations between St. Marys and St. Johns . A few days ago one of their scouting parties carried off 15 prisoners from the Cowford amongst which was a Sergeant and six men who included a Capt. and four seamen who belong to vessels in this river and some other gentlemen. We have had frequent alarms . . . [seven lines illegible].

The mere fact that Taylor worked in a war zone without abandoning his duties in the face of danger shows loyalty not to the Crown, but to the employer who provided Taylor with a way to make a living. Without his job he would be out of work in a frontier colony where work must have been scarce, particularly in a period where slaves took much of available manual labor in the colonies. Examples of these "Careerist Loyalists" are most likely more prevalent in government careers, but there were also private careers such as William Taylor's. Political loyalties take a back seat when compared to individual loyalties pertaining to wage relationships, in the face of practicality with regards to survival, eating and maintaining a roof over one's head.

Taylor's letter offers a fresh perspective on Loyalist motives during the American Revolution. It indicates that some Loyalists chose to side with the Crown out of obligation to employer interests rather than personal affiliations. In his letter, Taylor had plenty of opportunities to express his Toryness by insulting the rebels, but instead he chose a

13. William Taylor to William Chapman, May, 1776.

neutral tone. He also chose to remain in the backcountry to settle the affairs of his employer despite the danger his involvement in this part of the world imposed on him. Whether his reasons for staying on were out of loyalty to his employer or lack of job prospects in the region, it is arguable Taylor faced destitution if he did not remain on the job assigned to him. In essence, due to the nature of his environment and need for work to maintain his well-being, Taylor is among those who were labelled Loyalists during the war, not due to political sentiments, but out of a mixed need to survive in the wilderness and out of obligation to his employer for causes that could have been reputation-oriented for future employment.

Revisiting the Prayer at Valley Forge

⚘ BLAKE MCGREADY ⚘

When George Washington died in 1799, partisan infighting and international crises threatened the survival of the American experiment. Many Americans believed in Washington's unique ability to unite the country, and his death exacerbated national uncertainties. Enter Mason Locke Weems, whose contributions to Washington mythmaking dwarf those of any individual then or since. As national yearning for Washington increased after his passing, Weems authored *The Life of George Washington*, capitalizing on the current cultural and financial opportunity. While future scholars would devote volumes to Washington's life, Weems required a mere two hundred and forty-four pages to communicate his essential stories. He did not write a historical biography. Rather, Weems celebrated Washington's most admired virtues through a series of instructive lessons. Many of the tales he included, such as the fabled cherry tree episode, are fiction. Weems thrived in the space between evangelist and huckster, between historian and fabulist.[1]

One of the book's most famous excerpts remains Washington's prayer during the 1777-1778 Valley Forge winter encampment, which Weems wrote as an allegorical defense of revolutionary-era values. Weems repeatedly referred to his source for the story, Isaac Potts, as "Friend Potts" to highlight his religious affiliation with the Society of Friends, or Quakers. According to Weems, Potts passed through the woods and spied "the commander in chief of the American armies on his knees at prayer." He observed Washington until the general con-

---

1. Phillip Levy, *George Washington Written Upon the Land: Nature, Myth, Memory, and Landscape* (West Virginia University Press, 2015), 136-39; François Furstenberg, *In the Name of the Father: Washington's Legacy, Slavery, and the Making of a Nation* (New York: The Penguin Press, 2006), 145; Michael Kammen, *A Season of Youth: The American Revolution and the Historical Imagination* (New York: Oxford University Press, 1978), 41, 251.

cluded his devotions, at which point Potts returned home to report the encounter to his wife. He reminded her of his Quaker vow to pacifism, declaring, "I always thought that the sword and the gospel were utterly inconsistent. But George Washington has this day convinced me of my mistake." The General's reverence converted Potts to the American cause, now certain that "Washington will yet prevail" and "work out a great salvation for America." Weems designed the prayer legend to remind his audience that national obligations superseded religious differences.[2]

2. Mason Locke Weems, *The Life of George Washington: With Curious Anecdotes, Equally Honorable to Himself and Exemplary to his Young Countrymen* (Philadelphia: Lippincott, 1817; Internet Archive edition, archive.org/details/lifeofgeorge washweem), 198-199. This essay does not interrogate the "accuracy" of the prayer in an attempt to focus on the context in which Mason Locke Weems first crafted the story. However, understanding the debate about its veracity might be of value to situate the legend in changing times. Mason Weems's source for the prayer story was Isaac Potts, who owned the millhouse that General Washington, his military staff, and domestics occupied during the Valley Forge encampment. However, Isaac Potts spent the winter of 1777-1778 around Pottstown, Pennsylvania, not Valley Forge. Potts may have visited his properties at Valley Forge during the winter, and could have witnessed the scene as described by Weems. However, Weems then misidentified Potts's wife as Sarah Evans (his second wife) when he would have reported any such prayer to Martha Boulton (his first wife). Most significantly, there is no contemporary evidence that the prayer took place. Likewise, there is no evidence Isaac Potts abandoned his pacifism to support the Patriot war effort. See Daniel A. Graham, *Isaac Potts (1750-1803) of Montgomery County, Pennsylvania and the Valley Forge "Washington at Prayer" Legend: A Biographical Sketch*, (2000), Historical Society of Pennsylvania Collections, 3-7, 9.

Debating the accuracy of the prayer legend, too, has a long past. In the mid-nineteenth century a Valley Forge local named Henry Woodman published a series of letters in the *Doylestown Intelligencer*, one of which expressed skepticism about the truth of the prayer legend. Considering the amount of hearsay, Woodman was "not prepared to say" whether the story was true. See Henry Woodman, *The History of Valley Forge: With a Biography of the Author and the Author's Father who was a Soldier with Washington at Valley Forge during the Winters of 1777 and 1778*, ed. the Woodman Family (Oaks, Pennsylvania: John U. Francis, Sr., 1922); Hathitrust edition, catalog.hathitrust.org/record/100556090, accessed May 8, 2018, 65; Lorett Treese, *Valley Forge: The Making and Remaking of a National Symbol* (University Park: The Pennsylvania State University Press, 1995), 12-13.

The first concerted attempts to debunk the prayer legend can be found in the early decades of the twentieth century, when the newspapers such as *The Washington Post* (1877-1922) and *The New York Times* ran articles questioning the history of the legend. In 1926, in his book on Washington iconography, William E. Woodward called the image "grotesque." According to Valley Forge historian Lorret Treese, Valley Forge Park commissioners rejected a statue of the prayer in 1918, citing the opinion of the chief of the manuscript division of the Library of Congress who wrote "the prayer story ... cheapens Valley Forge, and tends to destroy the atmosphere of the place when mere tradition is monumented with all the solemnity of established fact." See "Unveiling of Tablet: "Washington

Thus, published in 1804, the prayer at Valley Forge entered the lexicon. Fresh memories of the revolutionary civil war, the loss of the nation's foremost leader, and intensifying political discord all meant the story resonated with Weems's readers. And yet, that lesson of national unity, intended to bind Americans of differing religious backgrounds together, has been overlooked or ignored in many interpretations of the prayer story. More recently in the twentieth century, politicians and religious leaders have used the tableau to celebrate Washington as a pious patriot. Such interpretations often disregard the tale's dubious origins and forget that as times have changed so has the meaning of the prayer myth. Those that neglect changing contexts can misread the prayer's valuable lessons. If we think beyond the prayer's ubiquitous reproductions, and into the revolutionary times in which its characters lived, we can rediscover precepts of one of the country's most enduring parables.[3]

at Prayer" Now at New York Subtreasury," *The Washington Post*, February 23, 1907, ProQuest Historical Newspapers, 5; "To Issue Valley Forge Stamp Of Washington at Prayer" *New York Times*, May 4, 1928; ProQuest Historical Newspapers, 2; "Doubts Washington Kneeling In Prayer at Valley Forge", *New York Times*, October 28, 1932, *ProQuest Historical Newspapers*, 42; William E. Woodward, *George Washington: The Image and the Man* (New York: Boni and Liveright, 1926); Internet Archive edition, archive.org/details/ george-washington009269mbp, accessed June 7, 2018, 342-43; Treese, *Valley Forge: The Making and Remaking*, 168-69.

Mid-twentieth scholars added to the skepticism. In 1968, for instance, Thomas Bailey thought the story no better than a propaganda piece intended to "indoctrinate" American children. Thomas A. Bailey, "The Mythmakers of American History," *Journal of American History* 55, no. 1 (June 1968): 5-21; Marshall W. Fishwick, *American Heroes: Myth and Reality* (Washington: Public Affairs Press, 1954), Hathitrust edition, catalog.hathitrust. org/Record/000331181, accessed June 3, 2018, 53.

More recent historians as well have not shied away from confronting the factual accuracy of the prayer legend. See Jon Fea, *Was America Founded as a Christian Nation?: A Historical Introduction*, revised edition (Louisville: Westminster John Knox Press, 2011, revised 2016), 171-72; Mary V. Thompson, *"In the Hands of a Good Providence": Religion in the Life of George Washington* (Charlottesville: University of Virginia Press, 2008), 91; Karal Ann Marling, *George Washington Slept Here: Colonial Revivals and American Culture 1876-1986* (Cambridge: Harvard University Press, 1988), 1-2; Edward G. Lengel, *Inventing George Washington: America's Founder in Myth and Memory* (New York: HaperCollins Publishers, 2011), 83-9.

3. Recent historians have differed about the date in which the prayer at Valley Forge first appeared in print. In 1929, Emily Ellsworth Ford Skeel finished her brother Paul Leicester Ford's endeavor to gather the papers of Mason Locke Weems thereto known. Their collective research compilation remains the most thorough work on Weems, and they dated the first appearance of the story to March 12, 1804 as an article in the *Washington Federalist*. See *Mason Locke Weems His Works and Ways in Three Volumes: A Bibliography left Unfinished by Paul Leicester Ford*, ed. Emily Ellsworth Ford Skeel, vol. 1 (New York: 1929), vii, 31.

George Washington's respect for religious tolerance helped inspire Weems's famous legend. Washington repeatedly defended religious cooperation in both writings and practice (although the courage and effectiveness of these stances varied throughout his course of public life). Mount Vernon Research Historian Mary V. Thompson argues that Washington customarily practiced as an Anglican Christian who maintained latitudinarian sentiments. Eighteenth-century latitudinarians "stressed" that Christians must transcend "doctrinal differences" which historically divided Protestant denominations. Thompson situated Washington among a group of believers who preached harmony and abhorred zealotry. By inspiring the Quaker Isaac Potts to join in common cause, Weems captured that spirit of religious cooperation and national unity. Washington hoped that his infant nation, which had been midwifed by prevailing Enlightenment values, would create a society that respected religious pluralism. In 1792 he wrote,

> Of all the animosities which have existed among mankind those which are caused by a difference of sentiment in Religion appear to be the most inveterate and distressing and ought most to be deprecated. I was in hopes that the enlightened & liberal policy which has marked the present age would at least have reconciled Christians of every denomination so far that we should never again see their religious disputes carried to such a pitch as to endanger the peace of Society.

The prayer captured that spirit, showcasing an ecumenical Washington converting political dissenters to his national cause. That Weems chose a Quaker as his convert was not a mistake.[4]

Weems's audience could recall the role Quakers played in the struggle for independence. Bound by pacifist doctrine, cultural and economic connections to the Crown, or a combination of these and other factors,

---

4. Enlightenment values with respect to religious tolerance varied widely over the course of that era. Prominent enlightenment thinkers such Thomas Hobbes, John Locke, or Jean Jacques Rousseau maintained different ideas about religious tolerance, religious cooperation, and religious liberty. The specific values that motivated founders like Washington, Thomas Jefferson, or James Madison, however, were a set of radically secular precepts grounded in the idea that a nation that proselytizes least governs best. For Washington, and many of the founders ensconced in the New World, the tragic histories of Old World religious wars were cautionary tales about the dangers of religious coercion. These ideas encouraged the Constitution's framers to build walls between the church and the state, such as the prohibition on religious tests for public office or the first amendment ("Congress shall make no law respecting the establishment of religion"). Moreover, Washington's support for religious tolerance radiated through his letters to Jewish congregations, treaties

many Quaker families remained neutral in the conflict. The "if-you're-not-with-us-you-must-be-against-us" mentality meant the revolutionaries harbored little sympathy for neutrals and dissenters. As war consumed southeast Pennsylvania from 1777 to 1778, frequent encounters between revolutionaries and Quakers did not improve these bitter relationships. To celebrate the first anniversary of the Declaration of Independence, for example, maddened Patriots smashed windows of Philadelphia Quakers leaving a trail of broken glass to honor the progress of liberty. Continental soldiers forcibly converted tranquil, sunlit meetinghouses into dark, musty hospitals and jails for wounded soldiers and prisoners. And at gunpoint, revolutionaries pressed unwilling Quakers into military activities in service of the American war effort. During the Valley Forge encampment of the prayer legend, area Quakers who dared refuse aid to the Continental Army only triggered more scorn and suspicion.[5]

Distrust bred suppression. In 1777, even the latitudinarian Washington moved swiftly to curtail Quaker speech and assembly, cautioning his officers that "the unfriendly Quakers and others notoriously disaffected to the cause of American Liberty do not escape your vigilance." Throughout the Valley Forge encampment, Washington's struggles with the Society of Friends multiplied. That spring, he ordered the Pennsylvania militia to intercept Quakers travelling to Philadelphia and even permitted soldiers to seize Quaker horses, concerned that the Friends were scheming with "the most pernicious tendency." Hostile revolutionaries under order from the commander in chief interrupted the free passage of area Friends, long accustomed to selling their crops in Philadelphia and practicing their pacifist creed. Weems envisioned the prayer as an overture to reluctant Quakers, and yet the General's

---

with Muslim nations, and his regular attendance in varied Christian houses of worship. See Jill Lepore, *These Truths: A History of the United States* (New York: W.W. Norton and Co., 2018), 52-4; Noah Feldman, *The Three Lives of James Madison: Genius, Partisan, President* (New York: Random House, 2017), 9-14; Thompson, *"In the Hands of a Good Providence,"* 4-5, 165-66; George Washington to Edward Newenham, October 20, 1792, *Founders Online*, National Archives, founders.archives.gov/documents/Washington/05-11-02-0132; original source: *The Papers of George Washington*, Presidential Series, vol. 11, *16 August 1792–15 January 1793*, ed. Christine Sternberg Patrick (Charlottesville: University of Virginia Press, 2002), 246–247; Ron Chernow, *Washington: A Life* (New York: Penguin Books, 2010), 132, 569, 611.

5. Thomas J. McGuire, *The Philadelphia Campaign Volume I: Brandywine and the Fall of Philadelphia* (Mechanicsburg: Stackpole Books, 2006), 67-8, 266-67.

actions during that fateful winter are a more akin to a heart-hardened Pharaoh than a righteous deliverer.[6]

Other Continentals echoed Washington's frustrations with the Pennsylvania Friends. Nathanael Greene, himself a practicing member of the Society of Friends in his home state of Rhode Island, had no patience for these Pennsylvania cousins who shirked their service to the revolution. "The villinous Quakers are employd upon every quarter to serve the enemy," he told his wife, "Some of them are confind and more deserve it." James Varnum, Greene's fellow Rhode Islander who occupied the home of a Quaker family for months during the Valley Forge encampment, compared southeastern Pennsylvania to a "heathenish land" and a "Tory labyrinth." Officers' attitudes also prevailed among the rank and file. Valley Forge historians have argued that Quakers became "particular targets" for the "generalized scorn" that prevailed among the troops. From 1777 to 1778, no religious group suffered as much persecution at the hands of the Patriot war effort as Pennsylvania's Quakers. They endured widespread abuses and disparagements that lingered in the memory of Weems's readership.[7]

Quaker repression was not merely a product of Washington's army but also of the Continental Congress and their arbitrary applications of justice. In late August 1777, as the Crown Forces threatened Philadelphia, a fearful congress moved to jail dissidents they believed might harbor British sympathies. On the 28th they approved resolves recommending that individual states should be granted the right to "apprehend and secure all persons . . . who have . . . evidenced a disposition inimical to the cause of America." These resolves mentioned only one group of Patriot enemies: "the people called Quakers." By the end of the month forty-one individuals in Pennsylvania, mostly Friends, had been arrested. State officials later imprisoned twenty-six of them

6. "Powers to Officers to Collect Clothing, etc.," *The Writings of George Washington from the Original Manuscript Sources*, ed. John Fitzpatrick, vol. 9, August 1, 1777 - November 3, 1777 (Washington: 1934); Hathitrust edition, catalog.hathitrust.org/Record/000366819, accessed June 10, 2018, 318; Washington to John Lacey, Jr., March 20 1778, *Washington Writings* 11: 114; Joseph Ellis, *American Creation: Triumphs and Tragedies at the Founding of the Republic* (New York: Vintage Books, 2007), 75.
7. Nathanael Greene to Catherine Greene, September 14, 1777, *The Papers of Nathanael Greene*, eds. Richard K. Showman, Robert E. McCarthy, and Margaret Cobb, vol. 2 1 January 1777- 16 October 1778 (Chapel Hill: University of North Carolina Press, 1980), 163; James Varnum to Nathan Miller, March 7, 1778, John Reed Collection, Valley Forge National Historical Park Archives; Wayne K. Bodle and Jacqueline Thibaut, *The Valley Forge Historical Research* Project, vol. 1, *The Vortex of Small Fortunes: The Continental Army at Valley Forge, 1778-1778* (Valley Forge: United States Department of the Interior National Park Service, 1980), 158.

without a hearing. By the time the ordeal ended eight months later, twenty-two had been exiled to Staunton, Virginia as "enemies" of the cause. Congress's refusal to tolerate any doubts about their righteousness encouraged these acts of rank-bigotry. Weems and his readers shared knowledge of these kinds of episodes, informing the way those audiences understood the prayer legend.[8]

Revolutionaries had considered Quakers duplicitous, irredeemable obstacles to American independence, "wolves in sheep's cloathing." But when Isaac Potts declared his allegiance to the Patriot camp, Weems argued even the "deceitful" Quaker could learn the error of their ways. The story also praised Washington's ability to reach across denominational boundaries and unite Americans as much as it praised his personal piety. In the context of the early republic, moreover, with sectional and political strife threatening the young nation's future, that message of religious tolerance was perhaps more meaningful to readers. Nineteenth-century retellings of the prayer story suggest that this lesson of national unity long resonated. Decades later, hardly a printed version of the prayer legend excluded the anecdote of the pacifist Quaker turned patriot. Some writers, such as Benson Lossing, altered Potts's pre-prayer political identity by claiming Potts was not merely a neutral Quaker but rather an avowed Tory, strengthening Washington's claim to unifier-in-chief even further.[9]

8. *Journals of the Continental Congress*, vol. 8 (Washington, D.C.: Government Printing Office, 1907), Hathitrust edition, catalog.hathitrust.org/Record/00677112, accessed August 28, 2018, 694-95; *Letters of the Delegates to Congress*, Paul Smith, ed., vol. 7 (Washington, D.C.: Library of Congress, 1981), Hathitrust edition, catalog.hathitrust.org/Record/000 143048, accessed August 24, 2018, 572-74; Alan Taylor, *American Revolutions: A Continental History, 1750-1804* (New York: W.W. Norton & Company, 2016), 216.
9. John Lansing to Richard Varick, April 10, 1777, digital image, Richard Varick Papers, 1743-1871 (bulk 1775-1830), Series I: Correspondence, 1775-1830, Subseries I: Letters received, nyhs_rvp_b-02_f-17_038-02.jpg 29009, New-York Historical Society; for versions of the prayer legend in which Potts is described as a Tory, see Benson J. Lossing, *Life of Washington: A Biography Personal, Military, and Political*, vol. 2 of 3 (New York: Virtue and Company, 1860), Google Books, books.google.com/books/about/Life_of_Washington.html?id= Q2oLAQAAIAAJ, accessed May 8, 2018, 602-03; E.C. McGuire, *Religious Opinions and Character of Washington* (New York: Harper and Bros., 1836), Hathi Trust edition, catalog.hathitrust.org/Record/000366318, accessed June 3, 2018, 158-160; Theodore W. J. Wylie, *Washington a Christian: A Discourse Preached Feb. 23, 1862, in the First Reformed Presbyterian Church, Philadelphia, by the Pastor* (Philadelphia: William S. and Alfred Martien, 1862), Hathitrust edition, catalog.hathitrust.org/Record/009609559, accessed June 3, 2018, 28-29.

"The Prayer at Valley Forge," engraving by John McCrae, ca. 1889, based on the 1866 painting by Henry Brueckner. Isaac Potts, a Quaker, and source of the story of Washington praying at Valley Forge, is shown behind a nearby tree at the left.

Later images of Washington at prayer also depict Potts observing Washington's devotions. Lambert Sachs's *George Washington at Prayer at Valley Forge* (1854) includes a curious Quaker looking on, as does the most famous nineteenth-century rendition, Henry Brueckner's *The Prayer at Valley Forge* (1866). In Brueckner's interpretation, despite the icy wind and snow, Potts watched Washington from behind a gnarled, leafless tree. Artists, writers, orators, and storytellers deliberately included Potts in their retellings, an enduring symbol of the deep divisions of the revolutionary civil war. In other words, nineteenth-century prayer interpretations repeatedly reminded their audience that religious dissenters still belonged within the body politic. National obligations exceeded such narrow, domestic walls.[10]

More recently, however, the prayer has been exploited in the fight to render George Washington an evangelical leader. In the latter half

10. Mark Edward Thistlethwaite, "The Image of George Washington: Studies in Mid-Nineteenth Century History Painting," Phd. diss., University of Pennsylvania, 1977, 99-100; Although the Continental Army remained encamped at Valley Forge until June 19, 1778, over decades Americans began to associate Valley Forge with harsh winter conditions. Henry Brueckner was one of the first artists to set the scene as a snowscape, and also took the liberty of other additions that have become commonplace in prayer iconography, such as a horse tied to a tree, soldiers huddled around a campfire, and a hut.

"Washington at Valley Forge," a lithograph by Frederick Heppenheimer, c. 1853. Isaac Potts is not part of the illustration. The exclusion of Potts and his role in the story of the prayer allowed Washington's piety to stand alone.

of the nineteenth century artists began excluding Potts from the scene altogether, and few twentieth century references to the prayer referenced Potts's conversion, whether in print, artwork, or oratory. Rather, these traditionalist interpretations often cast the vignette as a celebration of Washington's prayerful leadership. In 1967, for instance, former Secretary of the Army and cold warrior Wilber M. Brucker, urging his country to stay the course in Vietnam, employed the prayer. "[Washington] didn't cringe during eight long years of warfare," he declared, "Instead of listening to impatient counsel of defeat, America should tighten its belt and resolutely turn again to the grim task of destroying Communist aggression." Perhaps no politician more effectively deployed the prayer to further their political goals than President Ronald Reagan. Extoling the values of religious conservatism, a pillar of the Reagan Revolution, the president called the tableau "the most sublime picture in American history." At the 1982 National Day of Prayer he preached, "That image personifies a people who know that it's not enough to depend on our own courage and goodness; we must also seek help from God, our Father and Preserver." Weems's legend encouraged his readership to shed their parochially pious sentiments for the national good. Since his time, however, subsequent cultural artificers with different priorities have re-suited the prayer story to meet their present, often political, needs. Such images of Washington often tell us more about the times in which they were created than the man himself.[11]

Traditionalists who recast the prayer legend as an example of Washington's evangelism have compromised Weems's original message in an effort to strengthen ahistorical connections between the founding of the United States and religious values. In the process, the tableau has become a part of American scripture that testifies to the destined progress of this one nation, under God. Not surprisingly, the parallels between the prayer at Valley Forge and the account of Jesus in Gethsemane or Moses at the burning bush inspired a host of comparisons. Ironically, while these scenes may appear *visually* appropriate, symbolically and culturally, Weems's original vignette is more akin to the Gospel of Luke. For much like the Good Samaritan, a righteous individual from a historically vilified group, Potts established that Quakers too could behave virtuously. And without the appropriate revolutionary context such lessons can be lost. The lesson of Potts's political awakening and bridging religious difference would have resonated throughout the nation Washington helped build, a nation purportedly committed to religious liberty for all.[12]

11. Ironically, Reagan's event for the 1982 National Day of Prayer (where he prominently referenced the prayer in his address) included a small, meaningful, though likely coincidental homage to the original moral of the Valley Forge legend. As he strode to the podium to deliver his speech, the President exchanged pleasantries with Protestant, Jewish, and Catholic faith leaders. Uniting these different religious figures behind the Presidential seal illustrated a form of religious diversity that Weems and Washington argued was an essential part of the national character. See "Remarks at a White House Ceremony in Observance of National Day of Prayer," May 6, 1982, www.reaganlibrary.gov/research/speeches/50682c, accessed March 18, 2018. Brucker quoted in Treese, *Valley Forge: The Making and Remaking*, 168-69. Reagan also used the image in his second inaugural address; see Ronald Reagan, "Second Inaugural Address," delivered January 21, 1985, *The Avalon Project at the Yale Law School: Documents in Law, History and Diplomacy* (New Haven: The Avalon Project, 1996), avalon.law.yale.edu/20th_century/reagan2.asp.
12. Marling, *George Washington Slept Here*, 5; Garry Wills, *Cincinnatus: George Washington and the Enlightenment* (Garden City, NY: Doubleday & Company Inc., 1984), 48-50.

The First Countries to Diplomatically Recognize the United States

JOHN L. SMITH, JR.

"Diplomacy is seduction in guise . . .", whispered Benjamin Franklin to his fellow commissioner John Adams. "One improves with practice."

Although the quote isn't real and was written into the script of the HBO/Playtone miniseries *John Adams*, the spirit of the words rang very true when it came to the infant "United American-States"[1] trying to find its place alongside the other countries of the late-eighteenth century. The world of America's Founders looked totally different than what we're used to today and really emphasizes how unique the concept of "The United States of America" was compared to other countries of that time. As you'll see, many of those other names began with "The Kingdom of . . ."

Before America could be inaugurated as its own country, it first had to be officially recognized as an independent and sovereign entity by, preferably, another powerful global force apart from Great Britain. That country had to be France, the archenemy of Britain and the only country that was roughly equal in military might to Britain, despite losing much to that same country in the French and Indian War.[2] Secretly since 1776, France had been supplying limited money and arms to the United States through a dummy company. But to *openly* show support, France would be risking another war with Britain. Nonetheless—in the private circles of Versailles, France smelled the possibility of a vengeance opportunity by using America for its own gain. Otherwise, quite obviously, King Louis XVI had no interest in supporting a revolutionary movement to throw off a ruling royal king—that would be bad for the monarchy business.

---

1. General Orders, May 5, 1778, The Papers of George Washington, *Revolutionary War Series, vol. 15*, Founders Online, National Archives, founders.archives.gov/documents/Washington/03-15-02-0039, accessed April 6, 2018.
2. The "French and Indian War" had the Euro-name of "The Seven Years' War."

So in a mutual, self-interested way, France and America both needed each other. France wanted revenge, and as well to possibly reclaim territories lost in the most recent war. America needed "foreign alliances"[3] from countries like France for financial loans, for naval support, for military arms of cannons, balls, muskets, powder, tents and clothes—and for *recognition of independence*. As John Adams clearly put it, "it was the Interest and Policy of France, to Support our Independency."[4] That important status would make it more likely for America to attract new loans and possibly other military assistance from other countries. But, throughout the War for American Independence, that important status of "independence" was the single stipulation that Britain refused to budge on.

In poker talk, no foreign country would show its hand until America could demonstrate that it could win a decisive battle. That point came with the two battles of Saratoga in fall 1777, which brought a crucial American win. That engagement opened the door for France to *openly* support the United States of America in men and materials—and for France to recognize America, not as a rebelling colony, but as an independent country.

And so, the first country to formally recognize the independence of The United States of America was:

I. THE KINGDOM OF FRANCE.

On February 6, 1778, American independence was formally recognized in a double treaty-signing ceremony in the Hôtel de Coislin in Paris. The American envoy signers were Silas Deane, Arthur Lee and (possibly our greatest diplomat ever) Benjamin Franklin.[5] Signing for France was Secretary of His Majesty's Council of State, Conrad Alexandre Gérard. The next month, March 1778, the first consular[6] post was established in Bordeaux, France, although no consul assumed the post until 1781[7]. Formal bilateral (two-way) diplomatic relations

3. John Adams to Edmund Jenings, July 18, 1780, The Adams Papers, *Papers of John Adams, vol. 10,* Founders Online, founders.archives.gov/documents/Adams/06-10-02-0005, accessed April 7, 2018.

4. Ibid.

5. Gordon S. Wood wrote, "He [Franklin] was the greatest diplomat America has ever had." In *Revolutionary Characters—What Made the Founders Different* (New York, Penguin Books, 2006), 86.

6. A consul, different from a minister-ambassador's duties of national representation, looked after American business needs abroad as well as the needs of Americans within that country's borders.

7. William Palfrey of Massachusetts had been appointed the first official consul to France on November 4, 1780, but Palfrey and his transport ship were lost at sea. Thomas Barclay of Pennsylvania was then appointed consul on October 2, 1781.

were established on August 6, 1778 when Gérard presented his credentials to the U.S. Continental Congress as "Minister-Plenipotentiary and Consul-General" from France. The following month, September 14, 1778, Benjamin Franklin was officially appointed by Congress "Minister Plenipotentiary from the United States of America at the Court of Versailles". On March 23, 1779 Franklin, in turn, presented his credentials to the French court. Franklin's credentials were accepted, thereby establishing the first diplomatic mission.

Establishing full, formal recognition and diplomatic relations was (and still is) like choreographed dance steps between two countries ... assuming the new country had met the basic requirements of a *want-to-be* country.[8] After that—there are usually four ordered diplomatic steps:

Formal recognition
Treaties of amity and/or commerce (or equivalent)
Diplomatic relations
Consular relations

But those steps can occur separately, concurrently with each other, or even out of order by decades—as are shown in this timeline of America's post-France diplomatic relations:

2. THE REPUBLIC OF THE UNITED NETHERLANDS

The Republic of the United Netherlands (also States General of the Netherlands) was the second country to recognize American independence on April 19, 1782. The same day, diplomatic relations were also established when the credentials of United States Minister-Plenipotentiary John Adams were accepted in The Hague. A United States legation[9] building (the first American "embassy" in Europe) was also opened in The Hague "situated upon the Canal called the Fleweele Burgwal" at "the Hôtel des Etats Unies de l'Amerique."[10] Adams then began negotiating loans from the new ally, a tiresome feat of "innumerable Vexations"[11] to which Adams wrote, "I can represent my Situation in this Affair of a Loan, by no other Figure than that of a Man in the

8. Having a defined territory, a permanent population, a government, and an ability to interact with other countries.
9. A "legation" could mean either a minister (who was below a "diplomatic ambassador") or an entire staff working for the minister; or the official residence/office of a legation.
10. John Adams to Robert R. Livingston, May 16, 1782, The Adams Papers, *Papers of John Adams, vol. 13*, Founders Online, founders.archives.gov/documents/Adams/06-13-02-0020 accessed April 26, 2018.
11. "1782 September 14. Saturday." The Adams Papers, *Diary and Autobiography of John Adams, vol. 3, Diary, 1782–1804; Autobiography, Part One to October 1776*, Founders Online, founders.archives.gov/documents/Adams/01-03-02-0001-0002-0001, accessed April 7, 2018.

midst of the Ocean negotiating for his Life among a School of Sharks."[12] (It should be noted, however, that the first minister to the Netherlands was Henry Laurens in 1779. The British captured Laurens en route to the Netherlands along with his draft of a treaty proposal, and they threw him into the Tower of London. Not appreciating the hostile gesture of American recognition from the Netherlands and an associated trade agreement, Great Britain declared war against that republic the next year).[13] American consular relations weren't established until 1798 when offices were opened in Amsterdam and Rotterdam.

3. THE KINGDOM OF SPAIN

The Kingdom of Spain finally entered the war as France's ally[14] on June 21, 1779. John Jay was sent to Madrid as Minister-Plenipotentiary just a few months after that event, but his credentials weren't recognized by the Spanish court for fear of retaliation by Britain. Jay spent two years in Spain vainly waiting for Spanish recognition of America. But Spain's King Charles III wouldn't take that step until he was almost sure that Britain and America would be signing a peace treaty recognizing American independence. In the international poker game of diplomacy, Spain held her cards closely, showing a cautious poker face: "Spain very naturally developed a policy of procrastination and delay . . . She leaned on France for protection."[15] One evening during a diplomatic reception in The Hague, John Adams recalled that he, "Fell into Conversation naturally with Don Joas Theolonico de Almeida, Envoy Extraordinary of Portugal. He said to me . . . 'Spain will be the most difficult to satisfy, of all the Powers. Her Pretensions will be the hardest for England to agree to.'"[16] (Spain was holding out to regain Gibraltar).

12. John Adams to Robert R. Livingston, May 16, 1782, The Adams Papers, *Papers of John Adams, vol. 13*, Founders Online, founders.archives.gov/documents/Adams/06-13-02-0020, accessed April 26, 2018. A treaty of amity and commerce was signed with the Netherlands on October 8, 1782.

13. In 1781, the Netherlands had planned to join Russian Empress Catherine the Great's "League of Armed Neutrality," a group of countries which had banded together to protect their neutral shipping interests from British incursions to its own blockades. But Britain declared war upon the Netherlands first, knocking that republic out of the "neutral" classification. The countries who successfully joined the League from 1780 to 1783 however, were Russia, Denmark, Sweden, Prussia, Austria, Portugal, the Ottoman Empire and Naples/Sicily (later "The Two Sicilies"). Spain was already at war with Britain, as was France.

14. However, *not* an ally of the United States.

15. Samuel Flagg Bemis, *A Diplomatic History of the United States*, Third Edition (New York, Henry Holt and Company, Inc., 1950), 13.

16. "1782 September 14. Saturday." The Adams Papers, *Diary and Autobiography of John Adams, vol. 3, Diary, 1782–1804; Autobiography, Part One to October 1776*, Founders Online, founders.archives.gov/documents/Adams/01-03-02-0001-0002-0001, accessed April 7, 2018.

Spain didn't recognize American independence until February 20, 1783, just seven months before Great Britain. Spain also established diplomatic relations the same day, receiving William Carmichael as U.S. "Chargé d'Affaires *ad interim*" to the Spanish court. The first American consulate opened on December 29, 1797 in Barcelona.

4. THE KINGDOM OF SWEDEN

The Kingdom of Sweden (which also ruled Finland) surprised everyone. In 1782, when the British-American terms of peace were still being hammered out, Swedish King Gustavus III directed his minister in Paris, Gustav Filip, Count Creutz, to make contact with Benjamin Franklin. He was to approach Franklin with the secret proposal for a treaty of amity and commerce between the two countries. The prospect that the King of Sweden wanted to negotiate a friendship treaty with America was only matched by the remarkable reason that fueled the King's desire—he was a huge fan of Benjamin Franklin! Ben wrote, "The Ambassador from Sweden to this Court, applied to me lately to know if I had Powers that would authorize my making a Treaty with his Master in behalf of the United States . . . the King had directed him to ask the Question, and had charged him to tell me, that he had so great an Esteem for me, that it would be a particular Satisfaction to him to have such a Transaction with me."[17] Congress was so enthusiastic with this prospect that it granted Franklin full negotiating powers for crafting the treaty's provisions. By early February 1783, Franklin and comte de Creutz had finalized much of the secret treaty. It was kept secret for two reasons: 1. Because Sweden was a member of Russian Empress Catherine the Great's "League of Armed Neutrality" (see footnote 13); and 2. So that Sweden could avoid British backlash until after the Anglo-American treaty was signed. The Swedish treaty was signed and sealed, but it was left undated until the diplomatic coast was clear. However, fellow commissioner John Adams (not knowing the secrecy of the treaty's nature), let the Swedish cat out of the bag when he wrote to the president of Congress, Thomas McKean, on Feb. 6, 1783 proclaiming the joyous news: "a Treaty of Commerce was Signed Yesterday with Sweeden, by the Sweedish Ambassador here and Dr Franklin."[18] Oops. Franklin and Creutz quickly wrapped up the

17. Benjamin Franklin to Robert R. Livingston, June 25, 1782, *The Papers of Benjamin Franklin, vol. 37, March 16 through August 15, 1782,* Founders Online, founders.archives. gov/documents/Franklin/01-37-02-0337, accessed April 10, 2018.
18. John Adams to Thomas McKean, February 6, 1783, The Adams Papers, *Papers of John Adams, vol. 14,* Founders Online, founders.archives.gov/documents/Adams/06-14-02-0156, accessed April 11, 2018.

treaty's tiny details, penned the advanced date of April 3, 1783 and dispatched copies off to their respective bosses. To this day, Sweden is still proud of the fact that it was the first neutral, non-warring country to recognize the United States and hoped that it would always be remembered for that. As Dr. Franklin reported to Congress, "The Ambassador added, that it was a pleasure to him to think, and he hop'd it would be remember'd, that Sweden was the first Power in Europe, which had voluntarily offer'd its Friendship to the United States, without being sollicited."[19]

5. THE KINGDOM OF GREAT BRITAIN

The Kingdom of Great Britain finally gave in and gave up with The Definitive Treaty of Peace Between the Kingdom of Great Britain and the United States of America, signed and sealed in the Parisian Hôtel d'York on September 3, 1783. Britain and America had actually begun secret negotiations for peace terms some time before the signing. His Brittanic Majesty's government was already looking to make America a valuable trading partner again and was *very* interested in separating America from its allies for the settling of peace terms. The American negotiators (Benjamin Franklin, John Adams, and John Jay) saw their poker-hand advantage in the British stance and leveraged it to gain the maximum for America in concessions. Those included enlarged boundaries for the country, fishing rights, and the handling of Loyalist property rights and prisoners of war. But the crown jewel in the British concessions would *have* to be—and *was*—Article 1 of the 10 article treaty: recognition of the "United States" as "free, sovereign and independent states."[20] The preamble of that same treaty even set the warm and fuzzy "forgive and forget" feeling that both sides wanted, that we should "forget all past misunderstandings and differences." King George III even accepted John Adams as the first "United States Minister to the Court of St. James's", thereby establishing diplomatic relations on June 1, 1785. And except for some future minor "misunderstandings and differences" like the War of 1812, and when Britain nearly recognized the Confederate States of America as an independent country, the diplomatic relationship between the two countries has been one of the longest and strongest of all world bonds.

19. Benjamin Franklin to Robert R. Livingston, June 25, 1782, *The Papers of Benjamin Franklin, vol. 37, March 16 through August 15, 1782*, Founders Online, founders.archives.gov/documents/Franklin/01-37-02-0337, accessed April 10, 2018.
20. The Definitive Treaty of Peace 1783, text of the treaty provided by Yale Law School's Avalon Project, avalon.law.yale.edu/18th_century/paris.asp, accessed April 10, 2018.

5A. THE PRINCIPALITY OF BRUNSWICK-LÜNEBURG

What we know today as "Germany" was, in the eighteenth century, "more than 300 independent kingdoms, duchys, principalities and free cities."[21] So it's interesting that one of the tiny dominions among them was one of the first to recognize American independence—until you realize that on the very same day The Kingdom of Great Britain finally recognized American independence, this principality (later known in 1814 as "The Kingdom of Hanover") did so as well, automatically. That's because King George III wore two hats, er, crowns. He was also the "Duke and prince-elector of Hanover." This goes way back in the line of English Hanoverian kings who came from this German region instead of (ironically) from England. Very complicated. Anyway, this Hanoverian principality also recognized the United States on September 3, 1783, with the signing of The Definitive Treaty of Peace Between the Kingdom of Great Britain and the United States of America.

6. THE PAPAL STATES

The country we know of as "Italy" didn't exist in the late-eighteenth century. Instead, it was a hodge-podge of little kingdoms and republics squeezed between France, Austria, and the Ottoman Empire. From 1775 to 1799, Pope Pius VI was the "temporal" (political and secular) ruler of the Papal States (also called The States of the Church), which was a swatch of Italian land in the central and northern areas of the Italian "boot," including Rome and San Marino. The Papal States also owned the two little southern enclaves of Pontecorvo and Benevento, embedded down inside the Kingdom of Sicily; back then, that kingdom took up the whole lower half of the Italian peninsula. To round out the patchwork nature of "Italy," the Papal States also included the isolated town of Comtat Venaissin, up near Avignon in modern day France! On December 15, 1784 Franklin, still in Paris, was approached by the "Papal Nuncio," the permanent diplomatic representative from the Pope to France, a Roman Catholic country. Franklin wrote of the encounter, "I send also a Copy of a Note I recd from the Pope's Nuncio. He is very civil on all Occasions and has mentioned the possibility of an advantageous Trade America might have with the Ecclesiastical State which he says has two good Ports, Civita Vecchia and [blank]."[22]

---

21. history.state.gov/countries/germany, accessed April 15, 2018.
22. The second port was Ancona; Benjamin Franklin to Elias Boudinot, September 13,1783, *The Papers of Benjamin Franklin, vol. 40, May 16 through September 15, 1783,* Founders Online, founders.archives.gov/documents/Franklin/01-40-02-0393, accessed April 13, 2018.

That simple, civil gesture signaled recognition of the "young republic of America"[23] and a bilateral[24] agreement by both America and Pope Pius VI and his Ecclesiastical States. Starting in 1797, American consuls to the Papal States were received with full honors as those of official diplomatic representatives, even though that step hadn't occurred yet. That event happened in 1848 when full bilateral diplomatic relations were established.

To round out the list, here are the next nation-states with the initial date of the first officially-recognized unilateral or bilateral diplomatic overture:

7. The Kingdom of Prussia—July 9, 1785[25]
8. The Sultanate of Morocco—June 23, 1786[26]
9. The Free and Hanseatic City of Hamburg—June 17, 1790[27]
10. The Kingdom of Portugal—May 13, 1791[28]
11. The Republic of Genoa—October 25, 1791[29]

23. history.state.gov/countries/papal-states, accessed April 12, 2018.
24. A bilateral agreement is a formal two-way contract, in this case, between two nations or city-states.
25. havalon.law.yale.edu/18th_century/prus1785.asp, accessed April 12, 2018. The Treaty of Amity and Commerce between the U. S. and Prussia was a four-signature process. In Paris, Franklin and Jefferson signed on July 9 and July 18, 1785 respectfully; then Adams in London signed on August 5, 1785. The treaty was then signed by the envoy for the King of Prussia at The Hague, the Netherlands on September 10, 1785. Adams then went to the Netherlands to officiate a mutual ratification exchange with Prussia on August 8, 1786.
26. According to State Department records, "Morocco recognized the United States on June 23, 1786, when a [bilateral] treaty of peace and friendship was signed by U.S. Minister Thomas Barclay and Sidi Muhammad, Sultan of Morocco, at Marrakech." However there are conflicting records that the treaty was re-signed on January 25, 1787, and at this time it was accompanied with an anti-piracy "tribute" protection payment. history.state.gov/countries/morocco , accessed April 21, 2018. "On 20 December 1777, Sultan Mohammed ben Abdallah commissionned the Dutch consul in Salé to write letters to the European merchants and consuls in Tangier, Salé, Larache and Mogador stating that vessels sailing under the American flag could enter Morocco's ports, alongside those of European countries with which Morocco had no diplomatic ties, such as Russia and Prussia, under the same conditions as those enjoyed by the nations that had treaty relations. Information about the Sultan's desire for friendly relations did not reach Benjamin Franklin, the American emissary to the Kingdom of France in Paris before April 1778 at the earliest." In some circles, it's reported that Morocco was the first country to officially recognize American independence, however ". . . that [unilateral] 'recognition' did not include the necessary treaty nor the exchange of ambassadors, only the admission of American ships." en.wikipedia.org/wiki/Morocco%E2%80%93United_States_relations#1777_%E2%80%93_1787, accessed April 21, 2018.
27. history.state.gov/countries/hanseatic-republics, accessed April 21, 2018.
28. history.state.gov/countries/portugal, accessed April 21, 2018.
29. history.state.gov/countries/genoa, accessed April 21, 2018.

12. The Kingdom of Denmark (also the United Kingdoms of Denmark-Norway—June 9, 1792[30]
13. The Free and Hanseatic City of Bremen—March 28, 1794[31]
14. The Grand Duchy of Tuscany—May 29, 1794[32]
15. The Barbary State of Tunis (also the Kingdom of Tunis)—March 28, 1795[33]
16. The Regency of Algiers—September 5, 1795[34]
17. The Kingdom of Naples—May 20, 1796[35]
18. The Bey and Subjects of Tripoli of Barbary (also the Kingdom of Tripoli)—November 4, 1796[36]
19. The Archduchy of Austria (also Trieste)—February 17, 1797[37]
20. The Kingdom of Sardinia (also the Kingdom of Piedmont-Sardinia)—September 29, 1802[38]
21. The Imperial Russian Empire—October 28, 1803[39]

30. history.state.gov/countries/denmark, accessed April 21, 2018.
31. history.state.gov/countries/hanseatic-republics, accessed April 21, 2018.
32. history.state.gov/countries/grand-duchy-tuscany, accessed April 21, 2018.
33. history.state.gov/countries/tunisia, accessed April 21, 2018.
34. history.state.gov/countries/algeria, accessed April 21, 2018. Article 22 of this Treaty of Peace and Amity requires that the United States pay "Consideration" to Algiers "annually the Value of twelve thousand Algerine Sequins" (or "$21,600") in order to "keep the Articles Contained in this Treaty Sacred and inviolable". avalon.law.yale.edu/18th_century /bar1795t.asp#b1, accessed April 21, 2018.
35. history.state.gov/countries/two-sicilies, accessed April 21, 2018.
36. history.state.gov/countries/libya, accessed April 21, 2018. As early as 1786 Jefferson and Adams, both in London, had attempted to negotiate a treaty to protect American shipping from Tripoli pirates. But it failed because "tributes" or "presents" could not be paid to the envoy of the sultan. Finally on November 4, 1796, a Treaty of Peace and Friendship was signed in Tripoli by Joel Barlow and Hassan Bashaw Dey. The treaty was in effect with the receipt by Jussuf Bashaw-Bey of "forty thousand Spanish dollars, thirteen watches of gold, silver & pinsbach, five rings, of which three of diamonds, one of saphire and one with a watch in it, One hundred & forty piques of cloth, and four caftans of brocade." The ending "Note" also stipulated that "On the arrival of a consul of the United States in Tripoli he is to deliver . . . twelve thousand Spanish dollars;" avalon.law.yale.edu/18th_century/bar 1796t.asp, accessed April 21, 2018.
37. history.state.gov/countries/austrian-empire, accessed April 21, 2018.
38. history.state.gov/countries/piedmont-sardinia, accessed April 21, 2018.
39. history.state.gov/countries/russia, accessed April 21, 2018. John Quincy Adams (along with Francis Dana, the American minister to Russia) had traveled to Russia in August 1781 to try to negotiate official American recognition. However Catherine the Great refused to accept Dana's credentials because of Russia's neutral status.

My sincere thanks to Dr. Sara E. Berndt, Historian, Policy Studies Division, Office of the Historian, U.S. Department of State for her kind assistance with this article.

Women on Trial: British Soldiers' Wives Tried by Court Martial

❦ DON N. HAGIST ❦

Wives of British soldiers were allowed to accompany their husbands overseas, much like spouses of military personnel often do today. Unlike modern militaries, however, wives of soldiers often lived in the barracks and encampments, and accompanied their husbands on campaigns. Although not under the contractual obligations of an enlistment, wives were fed by the army and subject to some of the same regulations as the soldiers. They could be put on trial for violations of military law, and a number of British army wives were tried by general court martial in America for an assortment of crimes.

In the National Archives of Great Britain are the proceedings of hundreds of general court martial trials, including several at which army wives were prosecuted. Five examples appear below, revealing a few vignettes in the lives of women whose lives would otherwise be almost completely unknown.

ISABELLA MCMAHAN, 43RD REGIMENT OF FOOT

When a knock came on the door in the middle of the night, Thomas McMahon did not want to answer it. The soldier in the 43rd Regiment lived in a house in Boston with his wife Isabella, an indulgence allowed by the army to married couples who were trustworthy and who could afford their own lodgings. It was December of 1775, and the city had been under siege for eight months. At the McMahan's door were three soldiers of the 59th Regiment, married men who had been to their house before to drink. Thomas McMahon finally opened the door, and seeing that the visitors had bundles asked where they had gotten them. One soldier said they had clothing and fabric that they'd found in a house abandoned by a man who had gone to the West Indies, and then asked if they could store them for a while at the house?

There were enough abandoned buildings in Boston, and enough animosity among British soldiers toward the Yankees who had started a
war, that McMahon allowed the men to store the goods in the cellar
in return for a share of them. Over the next day or so, Thomas and Isabella McMahon helped them parcel out the goods; Thomas retained
some cloth for a coat, Isabella kept six pairs of stockings and some cala-
manco for a petticoat. They sold some of the goods and divided the
proceeds with the soldiers who'd brought them. Then the provost martial came to search the house.

The provost martial was the senior military law enforcement officer;
he and his men were searching for goods stolen from a store, and they
knew where to look. The store was some distance away, but one of the
soldiers of the 59th Regiment had confessed to the theft and agreed to
testify against the others.

On December 13, 1775, two soldiers of the 59th Regiment were
tried by a general court martial and convicted for theft. Thomas and
Isabella McMahon were tried for "receiving Sundry stolen goods knowing them to be such" (it was not unusual to have two or more defen-
dants on trial at the same time if they faced charges for the same crime).
They were found guilty; he was sentenced to receive one thousand
lashes, a fairly typical punishment for this type of crime. She was sentenced "to receive one hundred lashes on her bare back at the Cart's
tail in different portions in the most conspicuous parts of the town, &
to be imprisoned for three months." The number of lashes was low
compared to sentences for soldiers, and the mode of giving them was
quite different. Whereas soldiers were usually lashed in front of their
regiments to set an example, Isabella McMahan was to be tied to the
back of a cart and lashed in front of townspeople, which would both
humiliate her and show that the army would not tolerate crimes against
the civilian population.[1]

As of yet, there is no record of whether the punishments were carried out or forgiven.

MARY JEFFRIES, BRIGADE OF GUARDS

The British army included three regiments of Foot Guards charged
with protecting the royal family and government institutions. After war
broke out in America, a composite brigade consisting of about 1000
men was formed of volunteers from each of the three Foot Guards regiments to serve in the war. The Brigade of Guards arrived in America

---

1. Trial of Thomas Owen and Henry Johnston, WO 71-82, 203 – 206; Trial of Thomas
and Isabella McMahon, WO 71-82, 207 – 210, The National Archives, Kew, Richmond,
Surrey, England (TNA).

in 1776 and participated in major campaigns throughout the war, including New York, Philadelphia, the Carolinas, and Virginia. One soldier in the brigade was John Jeffries, a private from the 1st Regiment of Foot Guards. While the brigade was wintering in Philadelphia in late 1777 and early 1778, Jeffries met a local woman, Mary Staiger. He dutifully applied to his colonel for permission to marry her but was disappointed when his request was not granted.

They married anyway in Philadelphia's Gloria Dei Church on April 9, 1778.[2] When the army left the city in early June, Mary accompanied her new husband. Not all women were officially allowed on the march and she may have been among those excluded, for John and Mary stayed at the rear of the company while the army was on the move. Each time the army halted, they "made their Hut" some distance away from the rest of the company. This behavior, uncharacteristic of the soldier who had in the past always kept up with his comrades, aroused the suspicion of Jeffries' sergeant, James Wilson. Rather than take any direct action such as ordering Jeffries to keep up and to bivouac with his company, Sergeant Wilson reported to the colonel his suspicion that the couple intended to desert. The officer directed Wilson "particularly to observe Jeffries."

The army arrived at Sandy Hook in New Jersey, and there waited to board ships for the final part of their journey to Staten Island. On the morning of July 3, in spite of his sergeant's close observation, John Jeffries was absent from the ten o'clock roll call. Following the usual protocol when a man was absent, a search was made for his spare shirts, stockings and shoes; when it was discovered that they were missing, a typical sign of desertion, search parties were sent out. They found Mary in a house a quarter mile behind the encampment at about two o'clock that afternoon with her own clothing packed up but none of her husband's. She said that she knew nothing of his whereabouts or intentions, but she was nonetheless confined on suspicion of having "advised and persuaded" him to desert. She sailed with the army to New York and awaited her trial.

She was brought before a general court martial in Brooklyn three weeks later. The court called her Mary Jeffries and a "follower of the army," but she used the terms "husband" or "wife" (in many other trials, wives are explicitly referred to as, for example, "Mrs. Lindon of the 22nd Regiment"). Sergeant Wilson, the sole witness, related the circumstances above and claimed that she spoke of returning to Philadel-

2. Park M'Farland, jr., *Marriage Records of Gloria Dei Church* (Philadelphia: M'Farland & Son, 1879), 75.

phia where her father lived. In her defense, Mary repeated that she knew nothing of her husband's desertion. She said not only that she had gone to the house in the rear of the encampment to wash her clothing, but that she had informed Sergeant Wilson of her intentions before doing so. While the sergeant claimed to have found her at the house with her clothing packed up, she said that another soldier had found her there while her clothes were hanging out to dry, and that she then packed them up and went herself to the sergeant. Responding to the claim that she would return to Philadelphia, Mary Jeffries explained that many soldiers' wives had heard they might not be allowed on the transports, and some decided that they would return to Philadelphia if they were so refused; she herself had planned to see her husband on board the ship before returning.

The court acquitted her, probably because Sergeant Wilson was the only witness against her and her explanations were reasonable enough. Although the sergeant testified that he had "heard since Jeffries's Desertion that he has been seen" in Philadelphia, we have no information on his actual fate, nor the life pursued by Mary Jeffries after the trial.[3]

ELEANOR WEBB, BRIGADE OF GUARDS

Another soldier from the Brigade of Guards who married an American woman was Edward Webb. The twenty-five-year-old soldier from Sedgley, Staffordshire, married Eleanor Deley on May 14, 1778, in Philadelphia's Gloria Dei Church.[4] Although the six-year army veteran had never learned to write, he had learned the trade of a nail maker before enlisting. An inch under six feet tall, with dark brown hair, grey eyes, and a dark complexion, he was a good specimen for a soldier. He took his new bride back to New York with the army. In October of 1779 they were living with their brigade in huts of boards or logs with thatched roofs, which were often built into the sides of hills. A dozen or so men and their wives might live in these one-room huts; they were cramped but cozy quarters for the cold season.

One night in late October, three soldiers of the Guards arrived at the door of the hut that Eleanor Webb shared with her husband and others. They asked for something to drink, and she obliged. Then they asked if they might leave a bundle there for a while, which she also allowed. They returned the next day to open the bundle and divvy up the contents, one soldier saying he'd found the bundle, containing an assortment of cloth and three pairs of women's stays, in the street. They

3. Trial of Mary Jeffries, WO 71/86, 174-176, TNA.
4. M'Farland, *Marriage Records of Gloria Dei Church*, 76.

gave Eleanor Webb a pair of stays, two pieces of calico cloth, and one piece of plain cloth. She hesitated to take them, saying she was afraid they were stolen, but the soldiers assured her they had been found. Some of the goods remained in the hut, and one of the soldiers took the remainder.

The next day more people arrived at the hut—a shopkeeper, a constable, and some men assisting them. They searched the hut and found some of the things from the bundle, which had indeed been stolen from the shopkeeper's shop. She had received a tip that they'd be found in the Webbs' hut. Other things had been found in the camp of a Hessian regiment, where soldiers and wives had bought them from a British soldier. A few days later the constable and his men returned, and this time they dug into the ground under Edward Webb's bed. They found more stolen goods. Edward and Eleanor Webb, and four other soldiers of the Brigade of Guards, were put under arrest.

Three soldiers were tried in early December for breaking into the shop and stealing an assortment of goods, the key witness being another participant in the crime who agreed to turn "King's evidence," that is, to testify on behalf of the prosecution in return for immunity. When that trial concluded, Edward and Eleanor Webb, along with one other soldier, were tried for "receiving and secreting of goods stolen" from the shopkeeper. The prosecution's testimony was straightforward, relating the events described above. Eleanor Webb testified honestly about her concern that the items had been stolen as well as the reassurance she'd been given that they were not. The court, however, did not accept this as an excuse. Plundering and the distribution of stolen goods had been a rampant problem in the British army in America, and many similar trials were held during the eighteen months that Mrs. Webb had been with the army. Edward and Eleanor Webb were found guilty; he was sentenced to receive five hundred lashes, while she was sentenced to be "drummed out of the lines with a rope around her neck."[5]

Having an American wife, and having been sentenced to lashes, Edward Webb had every reason to desert. But he didn't. He remained in the army until 1796, in the Foot Guards and then in a militia regiment, after which he received a pension. Twice he was called up from the pension rolls to serve in garrison corps, taking his final discharge in November of 1807. What became of his wife Eleanor, however, is unknown.[6]

5. Trial of William Grinsell, Edward Webb and Eleanor Webb, WO 71-91, 47 – 51, TNA.
6. Discharges of Edward Webb, WO 121/13/11, WO 121/116/36, WO 121/145/497, WO 121/156/113, TNA.

SOPHIA SINCLAIR, 76TH REGIMENT OF FOOT

The 76th Regiment was raised in Scotland in late 1777 and 1778, one of several regiments created for the duration of the American war and disbanded after hostilities ended. The regiment sailed for America in 1779. On board one of the transports, the *Kingston*, a soldier named Hugh Fraser was walking on the forecastle when Sophia Sinclair approached him and grabbed his collar. They apparently had some sort of joke between them that she was playing upon, but something went wrong. For reasons that remain a mystery, Fraser didn't take it lightly. He turned on Sophia, put his hands around her throat and shouted, "You will not do that, I am not afraid of you!" She struggled with him, apparently trying to free herself, but his arms were longer than hers. Her husband John sprang to her aid, punching Fraser once on the left side of the head and once in the stomach. Fraser collapsed immediately against the rigging, then fell to the deck without a sound and almost without movement. A crowd gathered; someone swore that Fraser was dead, and Sinclair, still agitated by the apparent assault on his wife, responded, "If he could he would give him more."

Hugh Fraser was, in fact, dead. The regimental surgeon was summoned from another transport, but by the time he arrived to examine Fraser, the lower part of his stomach had become discolored. It was nightfall, so the surgeon waited until the next morning to examine Fraser's body. By that time "the Putrefaction had so suddenly taken place, that he was prevented seeking further into it."

A few months later, in November, after the regiment arrived in New York and settled in, John and Sophia Sinclair were put on trial for murder. They were tried together, each witness testifying once. Although no one had seen exactly what began the scuffle, several people had seen John Sinclair strike Fraser, including one man who had been "looking over a Corporal's Shoulder who was reading" when the noise on deck caught his attention. Everyone agreed that Fraser had been in good health, that there had been no previous sign of animosity between him and Sophia Sinclair, and to have "seen people engage in a fiercer manner without such a fatal accident happening."

John Sinclair presented a brief written defense that read simply, "Honorable Gentlemen, The unhappy blow given to the deceased Hugh Fraser, was with no intent of taking his Life, I therefore leave myself to your mercy, and to the Character of the Gentlemen who appear in my behalf." Sophia testified that she had only taken hold of Fraser's collar, and that "what she did in the late unhappy affair was with no intention." Two officers testified to their good character, including one for whom John Sinclair had been a servant for a year before incident occurred; "he behaved himself honestly, and with Sobriety . . . he should not have parted with him, but for this late unhappy affair," and she "always behaved herself exceedingly well."

John and Sophia Sinclair were acquitted of murder. Incomplete surviving muster rolls make it impossible to trace their subsequent lives.[7]

ANN HENNESSEY, 52ND REGIMENT OF FOOT

When Boston was besieged by a nascent American army in 1775, the British garrison, in order to adopt a war footing, allocated a single barracks building for soldiers' wives rather than the usual mode of allowing them space in the barracks of each regiment.[8] Wives were not required to live in this barracks, however, if they could afford something on their own. Ann Hennessey of the 52nd Regiment rented a ground-floor apartment in an otherwise-vacant house in the city's north end. The house abutted another vacant house (which suggests something about conditions in the besieged city which many residents had abandoned), and there was a doorway adjoining the garrets of the two buildings.

In December of 1775, a widow named Ann Powers came to Hennessey's apartment to make a gown for her. She fell ill while there, and stayed for a few days to recover. During her convalescence, she discerned various aspects of Hennessey's routine, although, being bedridden, she heard more than she saw. Hennessey went upstairs from time to time, only briefly. Her husband John, a soldier in the 52nd Regiment, came to the house for meals, an indulgence allowed to responsible married soldiers. Once she heard her tell her husband something about things in the basement. And one morning a man came to buy tobacco from Hennessey; Powers heard them talking about things for sale, and the man saying he'd come back that evening with another man to make some purchases with Hennessey telling him, "don't fail."

Later that same day, Ann Hennessey came home from running errands and found two more men in the house: the owner of the house next door and a soldier employed by the provost martial. They had a search warrant, and proceeded to search the house for clothing, bedding and some other things that had gone missing from the adjoining house. They had to break into two upstairs rooms and a closet, since Hennessey had no keys to them. In the closet they found the missing bedding, so they took both women, Ann Hennessey and Anne Powers, to the jail. Once there, Powers suggested that there might be more things in the basement, and the remainder of the missing goods were in fact recovered from there.

7. Trial of John and Sophia Sinclair WO 71-91, 22 – 27, TNA.
8. General Orders, America, WO 36/1, TNA, entry for May 31, 1775.

John and Ann Hennessey were put on trial for theft. During the testimony, however, several things became clear: the garret door adjoining the two houses was not locked; neither the back entrance nor the outside basement entrance to the house where Hennessey lived had locks either. Anyone could have gotten in, and Hennessey had to prop the doors shut with chairs because she couldn't lock them. The homeowner told the court that Hennessey had a key that opened the closet, but the provost martial soldier explained that they had first broken the lock such that any key could have opened it. As to the conversations overheard by Powers, Hennessey explained that she had told her husband that she found things in the basement that hadn't been there before; that a soldier had come to buy tobacco from her (it was quite common for army wives to earn their living by selling consumables to soldiers), and when she explained that she had none, the soldier said he would return in the evening with a man who had some that she could purchase. Both John and Ann Hennessey denied having any knowledge of the stolen goods, other than Ann having found things in the basement.

Lacking any evidence that the Hennessey's had stolen the goods, Ann and John were acquitted. One would hope that the homeowner took better care to secure his house.[9]

9. Trial of John and Ann Hennessey, WO 71/82, 235-240, TNA.

A Curious "Trial" on the Frontier: Zeisberger, Heckewelder, et. al. vs. Great Britain

ERIC STERNER

For most of the American Revolution, a community of Lenape/ Delaware, Munsey, Mahican, and Mingo Indians who had adopted the Christian faith lived along the Tuscarawas River in present-day Ohio with their missionaries from the Moravian Church.[1] The most famous of these were David Zeisberger (1721-1808) and John Heckewelder (1743-1823), who documented their experiences and studies of the local Native Americans extensively over careers on the frontier that spanned some sixty years. In 1781, the British commander at Fort Detroit, Maj. Arent Schuyler De Peyster, summoned both men to Detroit where he conducted a quasi-trial to determine whether they were American agents. Their fates depended on his conclusion.

MISSIONARIES ON THE MOVE

Zeisberger was born on April 11, 1721 in Moravia. When he was five, his family fled religious persecution to join a small community of reform Catholics (Hussites) in Saxony. Finding that unsafe as well, they left for the British colony of Georgia in 1735. Young David remained behind to finish his education, joining a German sponsor in Holland, and then reunited with his parents in Georgia in 1738.[2] There, he assisted a German minister, Peter Boehler, who sought to establish a church in South Carolina, from where he would preach to the local slave community. Zeisberger's education benefitted from Boehler's close tutelage. But, when rumors of war between England and Spain reached

1. The Munsey were the Wolf division within the Lenape fold, but often referred to separately as their dialect differed from the Turtle and Turkey divisions.
2. Edmund De Schweinitz, *The Life and Times of David Zeisberger: The Western Pioneer and Apostle of the Indians* (Philadelphia: J.B. Lippincott & Co., 1871), 13-21.

the border between Spanish Florida and English Georgia in 1739, the Moravian community's unwillingness to involve itself in the conflict forced it to move again in 1740, this time to Pennsylvania. It eventually founded the town of Bethlehem.

Thus, by the age of nineteen, Zeisberger had experienced religious persecution on two continents, responding each time by relocating to remain true to his faith. As a young man, he moved among several Native American tribes (particularly the Mohawk and Delaware) assisting an elder pastor's missionary work, was imprisoned in New York under suspicion of being disloyal, and developed a special affinity for Indian languages.[3] In 1749, Zeisberger became an ordained minister, just shy of his twenty-eighth birthday. He spent the next two decades among Native Americans in present-day Pennsylvania and New York, seeking converts to the Christian faith.

John Heckewelder was born in Bedford, England on March 12, 1743. His parents too were Moravians exiled from their homeland, although they settled in England before moving on to New York in 1754, eventually making their way to the growing Moravian community in Bethlehem.[4] Heckewelder's poor command of German, the primary spoken language in Bethlehem, retarded the young boy's education and cast a melancholy shadow over his youth, which was dominated by work and absentee parents. Heckewelder recalled, "almost the only enjoyment I experienced during this period, and which tended in some degree to comfort my troubled mind, was the sight of so many Indians, who were frequently encamped near Bethlehem, and who at such times came into town for the purpose of trading."[5]

In 1762, Heckewelder crossed paths with Christian Frederick Post. The latter was something of a free-agent Moravian missionary, but had spent more time working as a messenger for the Pennsylvania government and Indian tribes scattered along the Ohio River, particularly the Delaware, Shawnee, and Mingo.[6] Having built a cabin on the Muskingum River, a tributary of the Ohio and the territory of the Ohio Lenape/Delaware tribe, Post asked the Moravian church for assistance

3. Ibid., 121-130.
4. Rev. Edward Rondthaler, B.H. Coates, MD, ed., *Life of John Heckewelder* (Philadelphia: Crissy & Markley, Printers, 1847), 29-33.
5. Ibid., 33.
6. Ibid., 35-36. Post kept a journal and his account of his work as an agent for the government of Pennsylvania during the French and Indian War makes interesting reading. See Christian Frederick Post, *An Enquiry into the Causes of the Alienation of the Delaware and Shawanese Indians from the British Interest, and into the Measures taken for Recovering their Friendship* (London: J. Wilkie, 1759). Post's journals went through several iterations and printings.

with his mission, preferably, John Heckewelder. Heckewelder apparently impressed the Delaware, who often asked him to join them and gave him the name "Piselatulpe," or Turtle.[7] Post was due to return to Pennsylvania but Heckewelder opted to stay among the Delaware. Frequently ill and malnourished, Heckewelder eventually heeded warnings from friendly Indians in the area and departed the Muskingum. (Missionaries were often suspected of being disguised surveyors after Indian lands).

Zeisberger and Heckewelder surely knew one another. They had extensive missionary service and Heckewelder spent much of the 1760s working as a messenger for the church moving between Bethlehem and the various mission towns where Zeisberger spent much of his time. In 1771, Zeisberger arrived in Bethlehem from his new station on Beaver Creek in western Pennsylvania and requested the Moravian Conference dispatch Heckewelder to the frontier as his assistant.[8] When the conference agreed, it established one of the most successful partnerships on the frontier. Together, they helped relocate Zeisberger's Beaver Creek mission and several other Moravian missions to the Tuscarawas River, not far from the site of Christian Post's first cabin.[9]

Initially, the Moravian mission on the Tuscarawas proved extraordinarily successful, growing into two distinct towns named New Schoenbrunn and Gnadenhutten, the former dominated by converts from the Lenape tribe and the latter by those of the Mahican with representatives from other tribes, including the Munsey and Mingo, sprinkled between both.[10] The towns prospered, despite frontier tensions caused by Dunmore's War (1774) between the Shawnee and Virginia and the eventual outbreak of war between the colonies and Great Britain (1775).

The American Revolution put the Moravian missions in a difficult place between American power at Pittsburgh and British power at Detroit. The British succeeded in enlisting the Iroquois Confederacy and

---

7. Rondthaler, *Life of John Heckewelder*, 48-50.

8. Ibid., 66.

9. George Henry Loskiel, Christian Ignatius La Trobe, trans., *History of the Mission of the United Brethren among the Indians in North America* (London: Brethren's Society for the Furtherance of the Gospel, 1794), Part III, Chapter IV. Loskiel's volume was written in three parts. John Heckewelder, *A Narrative of the Mission of the United Brethren among the Delaware and Mohegan Indians, from its Commencement in the Year 1740 to the Close of the Year 1808* (Philadelphia: McCarty and Davis, 1820), 112. Heckewelder is fond of run-on sentences and commas, which is reflected in the quoted text. Tuscarawas is the current name of a tributary of the Muskingum along which the Moravian towns were located. Eighteenth century writers often referred to it as the Muskingum itself.

10. Loskiel, *History of the Mission of the United Brethren among the Indians in North America*, Part III, Chapter V, 89-90.

the western nations around Detroit (most importantly the Wyandot, Huron, and Miami Tribes) in their cause. However, the Delaware, who afforded the missions a degree of protection and provided many converts, remained neutral. The situation could not last. The British and western tribes rebuffed Delaware peace efforts, while Americans recommended that they, particularly the missionaries, come under the protection of the Continental Congress at Pittsburgh. Of course, the Delaware were well aware of American mistreatment of Native Americans, the Delaware included, and opted to remain on the Muskingum.[11] The missionaries too decided to remain with their flocks, rather than abandon them or the Delaware. Nevertheless, the western tribes continued to pressure the Delaware to join their war effort against the Americans.

As the war on the frontier intensified, the pacifist Moravians were determined to remain neutral. Whereas today one might expect a neutral party between two warring societies to rebuff both sides, the Moravians had little choice but to appease both sides through cooperation and accommodation. They helped the Delaware correspond with a changing series of officials at Fort Pitt, sheltered American civilians passing through the area, supported Delaware efforts to remain neutral, and provided regular intelligence to military forces at Pittsburgh.[12] For example, in March 1779, Heckewelder relayed information to Gen. Lachlan McIntosh at Pittsburgh concerning deliberations among the Shawnee, Wyandot, and Huron regarding an attack on Fort Laurens, an American post on the Tuscarawas.[13] He similarly relayed information from the Shawnee about events between the Ohio River and Detroit that spring, going so far as to recommend sites for forts that would best advance the cause of Indian neutrality.[14] As late as 1781, Zeisberger was forwarding information about pending Indian raids on Fort Henry at Wheeling, West Virginia, something the Indians suspected as some of their captives admitted it.[15] The Wyandot, Huron, and British had

11. Heckewelder, *A Narrative of the Mission of the United Brethren*, 147.

12. Ibid., 155-160, 166.

13. Daniel Brodhead to George Washington, March 21, 1779, *Founders Online*, note 1, founders.archives.gov/?q=John%20Gibson%20Author%3A%22Brodhead%2C%20Daniel%22&s=1111311111&sa=&r=1&sr=, accessed May 2, 2018.

14. Brodhead to Washington, April 3, 1779, *Founders Online*, note 8, founders.archives.gov/?q=John%20Gibson%20Author%3A%22Brodhead%2C%20Daniel%22&s=11113111 11&sa=&r=2&sr=, accessed May 2, 2018. Heckewelder's chief concern appears to have been defending the behavior of the Delaware tribe to the Americans.

15. C.W. Butterfield, ed., "Introduction," in *Washington-Irvine Correspondence: The Official Letters Passed Between Washington and Brig.-Gen. William Irvine and Between Irvine and Others Concerning Military Affairs in the West from 1781 to 1783* (Madison, WI: David Atwood, 1882), 58-60.

sketchy information about Moravian relations with the Americans, but the tribes blamed persistent Delaware neutrality on the missionaries, which made them an object of enmity and frustration.

Moravian relations with the western tribes were equally frustrating to frontier settlers, although Continental officials and officers may have been more understanding. When tribal raiding parties passed through Moravian territory, the Moravians would feed them rather than see their crops and livestock despoiled.[16] Heckewelder was quite blunt:

> Providing food for so many warriors at a time, was a very disagreeable business for the inhabitants . . . yet it could not be avoided, especially with the more northern Indians, who were both noisy and mischievous, if not served with food. Upon the whole, the quickest way to get rid of all warriors, is to give them a meals victuals, which is all they want, and to refuse them would be folly, as then they would shoot cattle, and destroy the corn in the fields.[17]

Of course, this did nothing to endear the Moravians to the frontier towns and cabins that would be raided by the aforementioned warriors. Indeed, one party of "freebooter" Americans crossed the Ohio intent on destroying Delaware towns in October 1777 but were detected and destroyed by Wyandot warriors.[18] About this time, internal tensions split the Delaware. Those encamped on the Cuyahoga River, which empties into Lake Erie rather than the Ohio, and led by Hopocan, known as Captain Pipe among the Americans, resolved to join the Wyandot and Huron and wage war on the Americans.[19] Over time, most Delaware joined him. Those few who desired peace moved east and sought the limited and unreliable protection of Continental authorities at Fort Pitt.

SUMMONED TO DETROIT

The situation was untenable for both the British and western tribes, who saw an obstacle to their designs in the persistent presence of the missionaries. The British still sought to mobilize native power against the American frontier, while the Wyandot and their allies sought to build cohesion against the continued spread of American settlers. In the fall of 1781, the western tribes arrived on the Muskingum and

16. Loskiel, *History of the Mission of the United Brethren among the Indians in North America*, Part III, Chapter VII, 126-127.
17. Heckewelder, *A Narrative of the Mission of the United Brethren*, 162.
18. Ibid., 165; Loskiel, *History of the Mission of the United Brethren among the Indians in North America*, Part III, Chapter, VII, 129. Loskiel reports that the Indians were Huron.
19. Loskiel, *History of the Mission of the United Brethren among the Indians in North America*, Part III, Chapter VII, 129.

forced the Moravian communities to relocate west and join them on the Sandusky River. Conditions were deplorable. Nothing had been prepared and most of the planted areas had already been harvested. The Indians quickly built primitive shelters and frantically searched for food to last the winter.

The British officer in command at Fort Detroit, the New York-born Maj. Arent Schuyler De Peyster, was part of the reason for their exodus. De Peyster was born in New York in 1736 and entered the British 8th Regiment of Foot in 1755, serving in the French and Indian War under his uncle Peter Schuyler.[20] He was sent to command the British post at Mackinaw in 1774, remained loyal during the Revolution, was promoted to major in 1777 and assumed command at Detroit in 1779 after the capture of British Lt. Gov. Henry Hamilton.[21] He eventually became the regiment's colonel and after the war retired to Dumfries, Scotland. All throughout 1780, he was beset with Indian war parties seeking supplies and support for their raids on the American frontier, writing a colleague, "I am so hurried with war parties coming in from all quarters that I do not know which way to turn myself," and complaining to the lieutenant Governor that "Every thing is quiet here except the constant noise of the wardrum."[22]

That noise reflected British "success" in mobilizing the western tribes to wage war on the American frontier. With the Delaware split and larger numbers joining Captain Pipe in his war on the Americans, however, the Moravian outposts remained a thorn in the British side. De Peyster was likely aware that the missionaries had provided intelligence to the Americans. Simon Girty had been a messenger for the Americans in the early years, even participating in an inept campaign led by Brig. Gen. Edward Hand in 1778. Shortly after, Girty and several other Pittsburgh frontiersmen, including Matthew Elliott and Alexander McKee, fled the town, made their way through Ohio, and joined the British cause at Detroit. Their first stop in flight was

20. Mark Boatner III, *Encyclopedia of the American Revolution, 3rd ed.* (Mechanicsburg, PA: Stackpole Books, 1994), 328.

21. Silas Farmer, *The History of Detroit and Michigan or The Metropolis Illustrated: A Chronological Cyclopedia of the Past and Present* (Detroit: Silas Farmer & Co, 1884), 260; C.W. Butterfield, ed., *Washington-Irvine Correspondence: The Official Letters which Passed Between Washington and Brig.-Gn. William Irvine and Between Irvine and Others Concerning Military Affairs in the West 1781-1783* (Madison, WI: David Atwood, 1882), 416-417, note 2; Arent Schuyler De Peyster, J. Watts De Peyster, ed., *Miscellanies by an Officer* (Dumfries, Scotland: C. Munro, Printer, 1888). The edited version is based on an earlier version printed in 1813. Most of the book consists of various poems and stories written in verse for De Peyster's friends.

22. Quoted in Farmer, *The History of Detroit and Michigan*, 260.

Coshocton, where they joined Captain Pipe in arguing that the Americans simply wanted to seize Indian lands in Ohio.[23] Elliott would later turn up with a British officer's commission; McKee became an Indian agent; and, Girty led raids against the frontier settlements south and east of the Ohio River. All were well known among the Ohio tribes and had acted as go-betweens and messengers for decades. Girty's role as a scout and messenger for the Americans at Fort Pitt likely made him privy to some of the intelligence the missionaries had passed on. De Peyster needed to find out for himself what role the missionaries were playing on the frontier.

The Moravians had only arrived at abandoned villages on the Sandusky River a few days earlier when they received word on October 25, 1781 that De Peyster had ordered the missionaries to Detroit. Captain Pipe himself delivered the news. Exactly what that message said is open to interpretation. Zeisberger offered few specifics about the content, other than to say that the British commandant, De Peyster, wanted to see them in person. Furthermore, he indicated that the missionaries succeeded in entreating Indian leaders to leave two brothers behind with the women in their party.[24] Heckewelder's memoir, however, indicates that the message was delivered as a speech, quite possibly by Captain Pipe. In Heckewelder's version, the message was clearly addressed to the Indians along the Sandusky and indicated that De Peyster was concerned with two things when it came to the missionaries: 1) the "little birds," i.e., missionaries, "cannot sing so many lies in your ears," and 2) the "Virginians will sit in the dark, and hear nothing more about us, from which we expect to derive great advantages."[25] Clearly, De Peyster was concerned about both the missionaries arguments against war and their passing of intelligence to the Americans. The major further left it to the tribes along the Sandusky to decide how to care for the displaced Moravians. Zeisberger and Heckewelder's accounts disagree slightly over the attitude of the missionaries in receiving De Peyster's command. Zeisberger described a compliant group of missionaries that requested to leave two brothers behind; Heckewelder portrayed a more defiant group of missionaries who refused to go to Detroit unless they could leave two brothers behind.

In any case, Captain Pipe and a fellow chief, Wenginund, conveyed Zeisberger, Heckewelder, and their colleagues Senseman and Edwards

23. Edward Butts, *Simon Girty: Wilderness Warrior* (Toronto: Dundurn, 2011), 79.
24. Eugene Bliss, translator and editor, *Diary of David Zeisberger: A Moravian Missionary among the Indians of Ohio, Volume I* (Cincinnati: Robert Clarke & Co, 1885), 29.
25. Heckewelder, *A Narrative of the Mission of the United Brethren*, 284-285.

by a roundabout way to Detroit, where they arrived on Saturday, November 3.[26] Heckewelder described their entry:

> curiosity drew the inhabitants of the place into the street, to see what kind of people we were. The few clothes we had on our backs, and these tattered and torn, might have induced them to cast looks of contempt upon us, but we did not find this to be the case. We observed, that we were viewed with commiseration.[27]

Cold, hungry, and tired they were promptly brought before De Peyster and the first phase of their trial in Detroit commenced.

De Peyster confirmed they were the Moravian missionaries he had summoned and was perplexed by the fact that the missionaries had not brought their entire families with them, as he had ordered. The missionaries said they had expressly asked the chiefs along the Sandusky, again likely Captain Pipe, whether their wives had also been summoned and received a simple "no" in response.[28] Zeisberger did not discuss De Peyster's response, but the question suggests the major's real intent was to separate the missionaries from their flocks by giving them no excuse or reason to return to those Moravian Indians camped along the Sandusky. Of course, De Peyster could not admit that so bluntly, lest he be perceived as opposing the spread of Christianity. However, Captain Pipe's speech back on the Sandusky, allegedly composed by De Peyster, hinted at the purpose as it spoke of removing the missionaries so that the "little birds" could not "sing so many lies in your [the British allied tribes] ears."

De Peyster informed the missionaries that he had summoned them from the Sandusky River because he had heard they corresponded with the rebel government to the detriment of British authorities and interests at Detroit. He stated plainly that he had heard complaints to that effect, although he did not identify the source. Zeisberger evaded answering the specific question, telling De Peyster, "We did not doubt at all that much must have come to his ears about us, for this we could infer from the treatment we had to endure, but that he must have been wrongly ill informed about us, and we [were] accused of things of which, were they investigated, we should be found innocent."[29] Zeisberger, of course, had to evade a straightforward answer to such a direct

26. Bliss, *Diary of David Zeisberger*, 33; Heckewelder, *A Narrative of the Mission of the United Brethren*, 289.

27. Heckewelder, *A Narrative of the Mission of the United Brethren*, 289.

28. Bliss, *Diary of David Zeisberger*, 33.

29. Bliss, *Diary of David Zeisberger*, 33-34; Loskiel, *History of the Mission of the United Brethren among the Indians in North America*, Part III, Chapter IX, 165.

question, since the Moravian policy of appeasing both sides included providing intelligence to the Americans.

De Peyster next turned his attention to the Moravians' flock. How many had travelled with them to Detroit; how many remained on the Sandusky; had they ever gone to the war; were they harmful to the British government? Zeisberger responded to these questions more directly. Four had come with the missionaries to Detroit; three to four hundred remained on the Sandusky—the missionaries intended and needed to return to them as quickly as possible lest their life's purpose go to waste; and, the Moravian Indians would not be harmful as they were industrious and focused on peaceful pursuits.[30] Zeisberger did not record De Peyster's reaction in his diary, other than to note that the major listened carefully. His questions answered for the moment, De Peyster told the Moravians he did not have time to complete their discussion, dismissed them, and handed them over to a British Indian commissioner, who settled them at the home of a Frenchman, Mr. Tybout, and his family.[31]

Tybout took good care of his guests, providing them with ample shelter, food, and refreshment. Heckewelder recalled, "In other circumstances than we at the time were, we might have felt ourselves contented and happy; but, knowing that our families, were not only suffering from hunger and cold, but were also kept continually, (on our account) between hope and fear, and being so repeatedly told by the savages, that we never would be permitted to return to them again, added to which [the continuing arrival of more mouths to feed], produced great mental anxiety to us."[32] In such a state, Heckewelder and his colleagues, convinced they had done nothing inimical to British interests, were eager to complete their discussions with De Peyster and return to their flock on the Sandusky.

The missionaries passed Sunday the 4th quietly in Tybout's home, but received a number of visitors likely curious about their guests, or prisoners, depending on one's point of view. It became clear on Monday that De Peyster was not so eager to resume his interview with the missionaries as they were to see him. So, Zeisberger asked the commissary for pen and ink in order to write De Peyster a letter explaining themselves. Not surprisingly, the commissary immediately asked whether the missionaries intended to write notes to send far and wide, essentially implying that they were spies eager to communicate what they

30. Bliss, *Diary of David Zeisberger*, 34.
31. Ibid., 34; Heckewelder, *A Narrative of the Mission of the United Brethren*, 290.
32. Heckewelder, *A Narrative of the Mission of the United Brethren*, 290.

had learned.[33] The missionaries, of course, denied it and announced their desire to write De Peyster, but were denied paper and ink and then informed that De Peyster was waiting for the arrival of Captain Pipe, at which point he would agree to see the missionaries again.[34] On Tuesday, the Indians who had accompanied the missionaries also asked to see De Peyster and were similarly refused.

THE MISSIONARIES ON TRIAL

Finally, after repeated delays, Zeisberger, Heckewelder, and the other missionaries were conducted to a council house to face Captain Pipe as their chief accuser in front of De Peyster. They assumed seats on a bench off to the side. Not surprisingly, Captain Pipe was surrounded by other Indians allied with the British.[35] De Peyster sat in front of the Indians, accompanied by a few of his officers, and turned to Captain Pipe to start his speech.

The Indian began with a ceremonial function, rising from his seat and passing scalps that he and his fellow Indian leaders had amassed on their most recent raids on the Americans directly to De Peyster. Each chief made a brief speech affirming his recent involvement in the war. According to Zeisberger, Captain Pipe expressed some sense of uncertainty about his role. In all likelihood, Captain Pipe's expressions of doubt were insincere, intended more to remind De Peyster that Indian participation in the war was conditional and to lay the groundwork for getting greater support from the British in the future. Although the missionary let the speech pass without comment in his diary, he and his fellows silently questioned the appropriateness of having to make their case in a war council.[36]

When all the chiefs had presented scalps to De Peyster, Captain Pipe again took to his feet and addressed the major. He stated plainly that they had brought the "believing" Indians from the Muskingum River and the missionaries and a few leading Moravian Indians to Detroit, as ordered by De Peyster. The chief reminded De Peyster that the major had told him he would find it easier to speak with the missionaries than would Captain Pipe. According to Zeisberger, Captain Pipe then cautioned the British officer to "speak kindly" to the missionaries, as the Moravians were friends to the pro-British Indians. More personally, Captain Pipe claimed "I hold them dear and should not like to

33. Bliss, *Diary of David Zeisberger*, 35.
34. Ibid., 35.
35. Heckewelder, *A Narrative of the Mission of the United Brethren*, 290-291.
36. Bliss, *Diary of David Zeisberger*, 37.

see harm befall them."[37] He repeated this last assertion at least once. Heckewelder, however, did not mention such favorable comments from Captain Pipe – understandable, perhaps, since Heckewelder blamed many of the miseries inflicted on the Moravian community on that Indian. In truth, Captain Pipe was clearly attempting to shift responsibility for the situation onto De Peyster and the British.

For his part, the major was having none of it. Rather than taking the lead in accusing the missionaries of being spies, De Peyster turned the matter right back on Captain Pipe, reminding the Delaware chief that he himself had leveled the accusations of passing information to the Americans. According to Heckewelder, De Peyster said to Captain Pipe,

> You have for a long time lodged complaints with me, against certain white people among your nation, and whom you call teachers to the believing Indians, who, as you say are friends to the Americans, and keep up a continual correspondence with them, to the prejudice of your father's interest! You having so repeatedly accused these teachers, and desiring that I might remove them from among you; I at length commanded you to take them, together with the believing Indians, away from the Muskingum, and bring them into your country.[38]

He then put it to Captain Pipe to prove that his accusations were true since everyone was present to answer for himself.

Now it was Captain Pipe's turn to hedge with the major, just as Zeisberger had a few days earlier. The Indian conceded that some of what De Peyster said might be true, for Captain Pipe himself could not declare everything that had been said about the missionaries was a lie. He turned to the gathered chiefs looking for support, but finding none, moved on. In any event, the Indian argued that the truth of the matter was beside the point now that missionaries had been removed to Detroit.[39]

Naturally, De Peyster was not satisfied with this answer either. He repeated his demand that Captain Pipe demonstrate the truth of his accusations that the missionaries were passing information to the Americans to the detriment of British interests. Again, finding no support from the Indians gathered around, Captain Pipe conceded that the accusations might be true and then declared that the missionaries

---

37. Ibid., 37-38; Loskiel, *History of the Mission of the United Brethren among the Indians in North America*, Part III, Chapter IX, 167.

38. Heckewelder, *A Narrative of the Mission of the United Brethren*, 292.

39. Bliss, *Diary of David Zeisberger*, 38; Heckewelder, *A Narrative of the Mission of the United Brethren*, 292-293.

were innocent! "They have done nothing of themselves, what they have done, they were compelled to do!"[40] Indeed, Captain Pipe admitted that the missionaries had done things that the war parties passing through their country had forced them to do, likely meaning feeding those very parties raiding the Americans. Thus, he held them blameless for anything they might have done for the Americans, which the Americans similarly would have compelled them to do. Things could not be going better for the missionaries, who had yet to open their mouths in their own self-defense. The irony was that the missionaries were indeed guilty of the principal accusation that De Peyster attributed to Captain Pipe, namely, passing information to the Americans!

De Peyster, likely knowing this from Girty, Elliott, and McKee, could only have been frustrated. He announced to Captain Pipe that the Indian's temporizing could lead him to conclude that the missionaries were indeed guilty of the principal charge, passing information to the Americans. He then asked Captain Pipe what the western tribes wanted the British to do with the missionaries: send them home to their Indians, presumably meaning return them to their flock on the Sandusky, or keep them at Detroit. According to Zeisberger, the interpreter mistranslated this, but the missionaries remained silent about it rather than interject themselves into a trial that seemed to be going their way.[41] Captain Pipe eventually responded that the Delaware and Wyandot had promised the Moravian Indians that their pastors would be returned to them, so he preferred to see the missionaries returned to their congregants on the Sandusky. He had long hoped to separate the brethren from their congregations, which might then be more easily swayed to join the war, but he wanted the blame to fall on British shoulders. When De Peyster did not take the bait, Captain Pipe must have been crestfallen.

With that, De Peyster ended his interrogation of Captain Pipe and turned to the missionaries themselves. He first questioned whether they were ordained ministers and not simple free agents using proselytization as a cover for espionage work. The answer was of course that they were. The major determined who was in charge, confirming Zeisberger was the senior missionary. Then, he got to the heart of the matter, asking how long they had been "with the Indians." Zeisberger indicated that he had been with the Indians more than thirteen years. This was

40. Loskiel, *History of the Mission of the United Brethren among the Indians in North America*, Part III, Chapter IX, 167; Bliss, *Diary of David Zeisberger*, 38; Heckewelder, *A Narrative of the Mission of the United Brethren*, 293.
41. Bliss, *Diary of David Zeisberger*, 39.

more or less true. Heckewelder had indeed first stayed on the Muskingum with Christian Post in 1762, but did not stay. The missions were not formally established on the Tuscarawas until 1772, although Zeisberger had been their pastor before they relocated to the Tuscarawas. Zeisberger's diary suggests De Peyster was satisfied with the answer. In any event, it predated the war.

De Peyster then started his most critical line of questioning: why were they there? He started asking whether they had "gone among the Indians of [their] own accord, to teach them, or whether [they] had been sent." His main concern was determining how much control over their actions others had. In other words, were they spies working on behalf of a superior authority? Zeisberger admitted that the missionaries had been sent by their church to preach the gospel, that the church bishops resided in both Europe and America, that they were in fact ordained (which he had already indicated); and that their purpose was to preach the gospel. Then came the all-important question from De Peyster: "Did Congress know about this, or did you have permission from the same to go?"

Zeisberger was blunt: "We have not been with our Indians, without the knowledge and permission of Congress; it has put nothing in the way of our labor among the Indians, but also it has prescribed us no rules and given us no instructions in what way we should conduct ourselves."[42] This gave De Peyster nowhere to go. The missionaries were known to Congress, which would explain communications, but were not agents of Congress any more than they were agents of the British, even though they had supplied raiding parties headed to the frontier.

Rather than asking directly whether the Moravians had communicated intelligence of raids to the Americans, the major changed gears, expressing his own support for their spiritual work. What else could he do? If he had asked and the missionaries had confirmed that they were passing militarily-useful intelligence, De Peyster could only hang them as spies or keep them in Detroit, knowing full well that it would embarrass Captain Pipe, one of his biggest advocates for war who had already pledged to return the missionaries to their flocks. In other words, De Peyster chose not to ask a question he already knew the answer to, but did not want voiced publicly for fear it would force his hand. Instead, he announced he would leave them alone with regard to their spiritual work, but warned them they "should be on [their] guard, and not interfere in war-matters; for, if [they] did so, he would be forced to interfere in [their] affairs and make [them] halt, for he was a soldier."

42. Bliss, *Diary of David Zeisberger*, 40.

More importantly, he declared that they had been wrongly accused and "things were not as they had been represented to him."[43]

Just as New York officials had asked Zeisberger to take a loyalty oath over three decades earlier, De Peyster then asked if they would take "the" oath now, presumably to Great Britain. The missionaries declined and De Peyster let the matter drop. With that, De Peyster turned to the assembled Indians, reminded them that he would like to see the missionaries remain safe, and ended the council. The "trial" was over and could not have gone better for Zeisberger, Heckewelder, and their colleagues. Not only had the reigning British authority thrown a blanket of protection over them, he had discredited Captain Pipe's whispering campaign against them, announced them innocent of wrongs they had actually committed in British eyes, and would permit them to return to their flocks! The ersatz trial was over, the missionaries essentially found innocent.

In coming days, De Peyster and the missionaries at Detroit had a considerably warmer relationship. He treated them as true guests, recovered goods that had been stolen from them during their long and arduous trip from the Muskingum, provided supplies from the king's stores at the king's expense, and sent them on their way back to the Sandusky.[44] They arrived in a deep snow on November 22. More privations lay ahead. A rough winter, near starvation, and growing tensions with the local Wyandot eventually led De Peyster to summon the missionaries back to Detroit, not for trial, but for protection from western tribes mobilizing against the influence of Christianity. The major eventually found a relatively safe place for them to reassemble their communities north of Detroit among the Chippewa Indians, where by 1783 they had built yet another town and sought to live peacefully.[45] Their fate would be decided elsewhere.

43. Ibid., 40; Heckewelder, *A Narrative of the Mission of the United Brethren*, 294-295.

44. Bliss, *Diary of David Zeisberger*, 41-42; Heckewelder, *A Narrative of the Mission of the United Brethren*, 296-297; Loskiel, *History of the Mission of the United Brethren among the Indians in North America*, Part III, Chapter IX, 168.

45. Heckewelder, *A Narrative of the Mission of the United Brethren*, 348.

A Loyalist's Response to the Franco-American Alliance: Charles Inglis's "Papinian" Essays

JIM PIECUCH

At nine o'clock on the morning of May 6, 1778, Continental soldiers at Valley Forge emerged from their huts to hear their regimental chaplains announce the American alliance with France. This was followed by the troops forming in ranks for a review by General George Washington, the firing of muskets by Washington's guard, a thirteen-gun artillery salute, a *feu de joie* fired by the whole army, and shouts of "huzza" and "Long live the King of France."[1] This enthusiastic celebration of the new relationship with the French marked a complete reversal of American opinion: just fifteen years earlier, France had been a hated enemy. Loyalists were quick to seize upon this evident hypocrisy and use the alliance to validate their own allegiance to Britain while attempting to rekindle anti-French sentiment to undermine the revolutionary movement. Foremost in this effort was Charles Inglis in New York City, who in a series of essays compiled in the pamphlet *The Letters of Papinian*, used a host of arguments to persuade the revolutionaries that the alliance would prove disastrous. His work, however, had little impact, in part because his writings did not circulate widely outside British-controlled areas and also because most Americans were by then firmly committed to the cause of independence and willing to do whatever was necessary to achieve that goal.

Animosity toward France had been a hallmark of colonial identity for more than a century before the Revolution began. Hostility toward Britain's longtime enemy increased during the several colonial wars,

1. Charles Royster, *A Revolutionary People at War: The Continental Army and American Character, 1775-1783* (New York: W. W. Norton, 1979), 250-253.

reaching a peak in the period from 1744 to 1763 when the British and colonists engaged in two wars with France: King George's War, 1744-1748, and the French and Indian War, 1754-1763. Historian Nathan O. Hatch observed that "the conflict with France gripped New England society with an overriding intensity." To the colonists, New France posed more than a military threat; a French victory would, they believed, destroy their "religion and liberties." In contrast to Britain, with its safeguards for liberty and the Protestant religion, France was seen as an absolutist state where the people had no political rights under a tyrannical king, whose "Romish Antichristian" government also acted as an agent for promoting the false, even Satanic doctrines of Roman Catholicism with the goal "to subjugate God's elect."[2]

During the French and Indian War, "fighting the French became the cause of God" in New England. As the Reverend James Cogswell proclaimed when preaching to New England troops in 1757: "Fight for Liberty and against Slavery. Endeavour to stand the Guardians of the Religion and Liberties of *America*; to oppose Antichrist." Such views were not confined to New England. Similar sentiments were held by people throughout Britain's North American colonies. During the French and Indian War, "fighting the French became the cause of God."[3]

The Anglo-American victory over France and the expulsion of the French from the North American mainland was cause for colonial celebration, but distrust of the French and their Roman Catholic faith did not vanish. When Parliament passed the Quebec Act in 1774, the colonists considered it part of the Coercive Acts intended to punish Massachusetts for the "Tea Party," although the law was an entirely separate measure intended to reconcile French Canadians to the British regime by making accommodations for their political and religious institutions. American colonists feared that the lack of an elected legislature in Quebec and toleration of the Roman Catholic Church in the province represented the "popish" absolutism they had long detested.[4]

Given the prevalence of anti-French and anti-Catholic sentiment in the colonies, American leaders' courting of France, and even French Canadians, from the early days of the Revolution represented a complete shift in opinion by Congress. This policy, confirmed by the subsequent Franco-American alliance, could not help but confuse and

---

2. Nathan O. Hatch, *The Sacred Cause of Liberty: Republican Thought and the Millennium in Revolutionary New England* (New Haven, CT: Yale University Press, 1977), 36-39.
3. Hatch, *Sacred Cause*, 41, 43, 47.
4. "The Quebec Act," www.u-s-history.com/pages/h648.html, accessed August. 8, 2018.

perhaps anger some colonists whose hatred of France had become instilled in childhood. While revolutionary leaders might justify the change of attitude as necessary for the achievement of independence, not all Americans agreed, and for Loyalists in particular, the alliance proved that they had made the right decision in maintaining their allegiance to Britain, while the revolutionaries had thrown themselves into the arms of absolutist France where their cherished liberties and Protestant religion would soon be smothered.

One of the most prominent Loyalists to articulate these ideas, in part hoping to convince at least some Americans to return to the British fold, was Reverend Inglis. Born in Ireland in 1734, Inglis came to America in the early 1750s and settled in Pennsylvania, where he taught at an Anglican school in Lancaster. In 1758 he departed for England to be ordained, and upon his return he served in Dover, Delaware, under the auspices of the Society for the Propagation of the Gospel. He was appointed a minister at New York's Trinity Church in 1766, where he supported the controversial proposal to appoint an Anglican bishop for the American colonies. He backed the British government in its disputes with the colonies throughout the 1760s and early 1770s; in 1776, he argued against independence in *The True Interest of America Impartially Stated*, a reply to Thomas Paine's *Common Sense*. Inglis endured harassment until the British army occupied New York later that year, and he continued to advocate for Loyalism until the city was evacuated in 1783, whereupon he settled in Nova Scotia.[5]

Inglis's attack on the Franco-American alliance was undertaken in a series of newspaper essays later combined into a pamphlet, *The Letters of Papinian: In Which the Conduct, Present State and Prospects, of the American Congress, Are Examined*. Published in 1779, the nine essays, most signed with the pseudonym "Papinian" (a Roman judge and legal scholar), originated as a response to Congress's imprisonment of a British naval officer. Thus the first three "letters" were addressed to Henry Laurens, then president of the Continental Congress, the fourth, sixth, seventh, and eighth to Laurens's successor John Jay, and the fifth and ninth letters to the "People of North America." Over their course, the letters expanded from their initial focus on the captured officer to include criticism of Congress's refusal to honor the Saratoga Convention and return the prisoners to Britain as the agreement had specified, as well as into a lengthy critique of the alliance with France and the grave threat it posed to the revolutionaries.

5. Judith Fingard, "Charles Inglis," www.biographi.ca/en/bio/inglis_charles_5E.html, accessed August 8, 2018.

The incident that caused Inglis to begin writing was the capture and imprisonment of Royal Navy lieutenant Christopher Hele and his crew. In early October 1778, Hele left New York aboard the sloop *Hotham* carrying a final message to Congress from the Carlisle Peace Commission, which had attempted for months to negotiate an end to the war and return the colonies to the imperial fold. While sailing up the Delaware River, the *Hotham* was wrecked and Hele and his crew spent three days aboard the partly submerged vessel before they were seized by the revolutionaries. Two sailors died before the crew was captured, "and those who escaped with life, were confined by order of Congress in a miserable dungeon in Philadelphia." Because the British vessel was sailing under a flag of truce, the British Commissary for Navy Prisoners, James Dick, wrote to Congress on October 27 demanding the release of Hele and his crew. However, John Beatty, Commissary-General of Prisoners for Congress, refused in a reply of November 14. He cited an act of Congress exempting anyone carrying "seditious papers" from the protection of a flag of truce. His assertion was dubious, since the act had been passed on October 16, at least a week after the crew was captured, and it was something of a stretch to claim that a message to Congress from British peace commissioners should be considered "seditious."[6]

After focusing his attention on this issue and other examples of Congress's duplicity in his first three letters, Inglis turned his attention to France in the fourth essay. He blamed the influence of the French minister to the United States, Conrad-Alexandre Gerard, for Congress's rejection of the generous terms offered by the Carlisle Commission. "Mr. *Gerard* well knew," Inglis asserted, that permitting the Americans to reach an accommodation with Britain "was never the design or purpose of the French king." This was not surprising, in Inglis's opinion, because "for two centuries past, France hath been the common incendiary of Europe—the plague of every neighbouring state, by interfering and embroiling in their affairs, to serve her own ambitious purposes. She is now playing the same game in America that she has played a thousand times before in Europe." Inglis claimed that Congress had dithered in its dealings with the British commissioners until Gerard "at last bullied you into a compliance" with his wishes.[7]

6. Entry dated New York, November 20, 1778, in *The Remembrancer, or Impartial Repository of Public Events, for the Year 1778, and Beginning of 1779* (London: J. Almon, 1779), 177-178.

7. Charles Inglis, Letter IV in *The Letters of Papinian: In Which the Conduct, Present State and Prospects, of the American Congress Are Examined* (New York: Hugh Gaine, 1779), 40, 41.

Inglis reminded his readers of "the fury" of France's "Popish bigotry," mentioning the 1685 revocation of the Edict of Nantes that had granted toleration to French Protestants, alleging that this had been followed by the execution or banishment of "not less than a *million*" Protestants while others were "stript of all their property." In following Gerard's instructions, Inglis declared, members of Congress were "offering incense to, and throwing yourselves at the feet of, that insidious crown which has extinguished liberty, and extirpated the protestant religion in all its territories." Such behavior was disgraceful; worse, "its consequences are more serious and fatal to the American colonists," for Congress had placed them "in a state of vassalage to France."[8]

Next, Inglis remarked that Congress's acceptance of the French alliance was "a sure indication of weakness in you, however it may enable France to exert her strength." He cited the difficulties the revolutionaries faced in recruiting troops, shortages of military supplies, the nearly worthless Continental currency, and the large war debt the United States had accumulated. The result of these problems had been the solicitation of an "inglorious alliance with France, by which you lie at the mercy of that perfidious power." The longer the war continued, the worse America's problems would become, Inglis predicted, and dependence on France would grow. Eventually, the French would demand territory when Congress could not pay its debts to France, so that "the French King must in the end, according to your blessed schemes, be Lord Paramount and Proprietor of North-America. So that every American who is fighting against Britain," Inglis wrote, "may have the pleasure to reflect, that . . . he is extending the empire and glory of the *grand Monarque*."[9]

In his fifth letter, addressed "To the People of North-America," Inglis substituted the pseudonym "Clarendon" for "Papinian." The purpose of the change was to send a message to Americans who were familiar with the history of the English Civil War. Edward Hyde, Lord Clarendon, had originally supported Parliament in its revolt against King Charles I, but had switched sides and become a Royalist when he decided that Parliament had become too radical. Inglis wanted readers to know that there was a precedent, in the actions of an admired historical figure, for shifting one's allegiance. Inglis advised Americans that they had no opportunity "to avoid the yoke of despotism now, and probably the shackles of Popish superstition, and counting beads, unless you open your eyes, think and act for yourselves as free-men." He re-

8. Inglis, Letter IV, *Letters of Papinian*, 42-43.
9. Inglis, Letter IV, *Letters of Papinian*, 44-45.

stated his claim that Congress "had so entangled themselves with France, had MORTGAGED these Colonies so deeply to that insidious power," that they had rejected Britain's generous peace terms. Furthermore, "the Congress have so entwined themselves with France, that were even the British power set aside, they could not break loose from the former. If not dependent on Britain, the Colonies must be dependant on France; and were the Congress now to declare LOUIS XVI, sovereign and liege Lord of North-America, it would not shock or surprize me." France, insisted Inglis, was now actually an obstacle to American independence.[10]

In his seventh essay, addressed to John Jay, Inglis estimated the human and economic cost of the rebellion. "Now, for what has all this profuse waste of blood and treasure been made?" Inglis asked. He then provided the answer: "For the sake of a nominal independency, which established, would be more destructive to this continent, for ages to come, than even the present rebellion has been! For the sake of a ruinous alliance with France, the enemy of liberty and protestantism." Furthermore, Inglis remarked, neither the French nor the Americans had benefited from their collaboration. He pointed to "the disgraceful, wretched state of France." That nation had accomplished nothing in North America other than to send a fleet that, "after hovering a few months on this coast, without doing any thing," had sailed to the West Indies, where it had been "blocked up" at Martinique by the Royal Navy. Inglis went on to list other disasters that had befallen France since its entry into the war. "The French West-India trade is nearly ruined. The French fisheries at Newfoundland are annihilated— Pondicherry, the only place of consequence which France possessed in the East-Indies, is wrested from her, and her East-India company and trade totally ruined." Both the French merchant fleet and navy in Europe were confined to port by British naval blockade, driving French merchants into bankruptcy and leaving the government "without credit at home or abroad, and covered with indelible infamy, A just reward this of her perfidy!"[11] Inglis implied that an ally that could not protect its own national interests would not be able to accomplish much on behalf of the American revolutionaries.

The eighth letter, also addressed to Jay, accused Congress of corruption. "Some do not hesitate to aver that the Congress have been tampering with French gold," Inglis wrote without identifying the sources of the allegation. "Nothing else can account for their adherence to

10. Inglis, Letter V, *Letters of Papinian*, 50, 52, 54-55.
11. Inglis, Letter VII, *Letters of Papinian*, 84-85.

France, contrary to every dictate of reason and duty—every principle of protestantism and good policy, and to the manifest interest of America," he asserted. Turning yet again to the heavy debt Congress had incurred and the high taxes that would be required just to pay for current expenses, he wrote that Congress had attempted to downplay its financial difficulties, assuring Americans that "the conduct of one Monarch, the Friend and protector of the rights of mankind, has turned the scale so much" that victory was certain and any problems could be resolved after securing independence. "Considering the mischiefs you have brought on France," Inglis chided, "it is a pity to quarrel with you for affording her some kind and gracious words, since you can give her no more."[12]

Inglis followed by reiterating several points he had made in previous essays. He again noted the hypocrisy of Congress's claim to be leading the battle for liberty and the creation of a republic while attaching the United States to a despotic and "faithless" monarchy. He repeated that France had not been able to protect its own overseas trade or colonies, and that the country was suffering from such financial distress that no funds were left to support the Americans; in fact, the "King's palaces and gardens are going to ruins for want of money to repair them." Meanwhile, "Agents of France are soliciting loans" across Europe, with little to show for their efforts. Inglis declared that France did not form an alliance with the United States "from affection to you or to the rights of mankind, but to serve her own ambitious purposes." The French king's ultimate goal was to add America to his dominions, just as his predecessors had expanded their boundaries in Europe. "By duplicity, intrigue, perfidy and violence, France has gained more provinces in Europe than you had to bestow in America," Inglis observed, mentioning Burgundy, Alsace, and Corsica as examples, and adding that "she gained them without half a claim so plausible as you have given her to the *Thirteen United States*."[13]

Inglis drew on this material once more in his final essay, addressed to "The People of North-America." By this point his arguments had become repetitive. The French alliance endangered "the liberties of America" and Protestantism. The only new elements in the ninth letter were an expansion on the religious threat from France, with Inglis warning that the United States would soon be swarming with Catholic priests, rosaries, and other "Popish" religious items. A second fresh argument was that the clause in the treaty of alliance prohibiting either

12. Inglis, Letter VIII, *Letters of Papinian*, 94, 96-97.
13. Inglis, Letter VIII, *Letters of Papinian*, 97, 98-99.

nation from making a separate peace with Britain would result in Americans fighting and dying until France achieved its war aims.[14]

The opinions that Inglis espoused were shared by other Loyalists. An anonymous writer using the pseudonym "Britannicus" addressed an essay "To the Inhabitants of the Revolted Colonies in America" in April 1779 that used a somewhat different approach to denounce the French alliance. For several years, the writer stated, Americans had been "grossly deceived by the false, though confident assertions of your Congress," yet the revolutionaries' situation had steadily worsened. Now, "Britannicus" stated, Congress claimed that French aid would bring independence, but the alliance had not brought success. Instead, the French forces sent to America and their leader, the Comte d'Estaing, had "failed in every particular." Joint Franco-American operations in Rhode Island the previous year had ended in a fiasco, and d'Estaing "threw the whole blame of his failure upon the Americans" for not adequately supporting him. The comte had gone to the West Indies, where he was held in check by the British navy. "Britannicus" asked whether the king of France would incur the expense of sending additional forces given the large debts owed to his country by the United States, which had nothing to offer except its trade. The alliance was a poor arrangement for both sides, serving only to entangle Americans in "a connection with the most perfidious nation on earth." If France somehow did manage to triumph, the writer warned, "you may expect that she will send a fleet and army to take possession of this country for her *own emolument.*"[15]

Another loyalist writer, calling himself "Refugee," expressed his objections to the Franco-American alliance more concisely. He wrote in the *Royal American Gazette* that Congress's purposes in entering the alliance were "dethroning the king and treading under foot the British constitution and power in America, as well as introducing popery and republicanism, or an humble dependence (a slavish one) on France."[16]

A year after Inglis composed the "Papinian" essays, John Joachim Zubly, a Swiss-born Georgia Loyalist who had been ordained a minister in the German Reformed Church before moving to America in the mid-1740s, put forward his own criticism of the alliance. Writing as "Helvetius," Zubly published seven essays in Savannah's *Royal Georgia Gazette*. In the second, he echoed Inglis's claim that Congress had thrown Americans "into the arms of a power the most remarkable for

14. Inglis, Letter VIII, *Letters of Papinian*, 112-113, 115-117.
15. *Royal Gazette* (New York), April 21, 1779.
16. *Royal American Gazette* (New York), October 23, 1779.

despotism and oppression of any in Europe" and examined at greater length the story of how Corsica's fight, with French support, for independence from Genoa instead resulted in the French making "a conquest of [Corsica] for themselves." Zubly briefly denounced France in his fifth essay and did so at greater length in the sixth in language similar to that employed by Inglis. France was an "arbitrary perfidious power," some revolutionary leaders had "sold their country and dupes" to the French, and the deceived Americans would soon find themselves controlled by France, or perhaps even the Pope. Congress had "mortgaged" the United States to France and had no means to escape from that dangerous nation's clutches. A catalog of evils, duly described by Zubly, was certain to ensue.[17]

Undoubtedly some Americans shared these views. Perhaps the most notable was Benedict Arnold, who insisted that the alliance with France was inconsistent with Revolutionary principles and a major part of the reason he shifted his allegiance to Britain. He published an open letter "To the Inhabitants of America" in the New York Loyalist newspapers in October 1780 explaining his decision. Contrasting Congress's refusal to negotiate seriously with the Carlisle Commission with its embrace of France, Arnold termed these actions "a dangerous sacrifice of the great interests of this country to the partial views of a proud, antient and crafty foe." Like "Britannicus," Arnold insisted that France was unlikely to be able to defeat Britain: Americans had been "duped" to make them "serve a nation wanting both the will and the power to protect us and aiming at the destruction both of the mother country and the provinces." Arnold also raised a new objection: because the Articles of Confederation had not yet been officially adopted, Congress lacked the authority to enter into foreign alliances, and the people themselves had never granted that body such a power. Under these circumstances, Arnold wrote, Americans would be wise to support Great Britain rather "than to trust a monarchy too feeble to establish your independency, so perilous to its own dominions; the enemy of the Protestant Faith, and fraudulently avowing an affection for the liberties of mankind, while she holds her native sons in vassalage and chains."[18] In his subsequent proclamation urging officers and soldiers of the Continental Army to enlist in the British forces, Arnold appealed to those "who are determined to be no longer the tools and dupes of Congress, and of France."

17. John Joachim Zubly, "Helvetius" Essays, No. 2, No. 5, and No. 6, in Randall M. Miller, ed., "A Warm & Zealous Spirit": John J. Zubly and the American Revolution, a Selection of His Writings (Macon, GA: Mercer University Press, 1982), 179, 180, 190, 192-193.
18. Royal American Gazette (New York), October 10, 1780.

The former had "brought the colonies to the very brink of destruction," and as for France, he testified that he had personally witnessed members of Congress attending Roman Catholic Mass, "participating in the rites of a Church, against whose anti-christian corruptions your pious ancestors would have witnessed with their blood."[19] In Arnold's case, every statement cannot be taken at face value, although his hostility toward Catholicism was probably genuine.

The arguments laid out by Inglis and other Loyalists were potentially effective, tapping into longstanding animosity toward France and its Roman Catholic religion at a time when many Americans were weary of war and struggling with the consequent economic dislocations. However, the years of war had also fueled antipathy toward Britain and increased the desire of most Americans to achieve independence. Nevertheless, with widespread circulation *The Letters of Papinian* and similar writings may have convinced some wavering Americans to return to the British fold. Appeals to Protestant solidarity against "popery" might have helped win the allegiance of the numerous Presbyterians and other Dissenters in the South after British control was established in Georgia and South Carolina in 1780, but no organized effort to capitalize on anti-French sentiment was made in the South, and the "Papinian" essays do not appear to have been reprinted in the southern Loyalist press, leaving Zubly as a solitary voice crying in the wilderness. In the North, Loyalist pamphlets and newspapers did not circulate widely outside British lines, and anyone who attempted to distribute them risked the same punishment for carrying "seditious papers" that had caused Lieutenant Hele's imprisonment and inspired Inglis to begin writing his essays. Therefore Inglis and other critics of the Franco-American alliance were able to preach primarily to those already converted, and the British derived little benefit from a potentially valuable source of propaganda.

19. *Royal Gazette* (New York), November 1, 1780.

Grace Galloway—Abandoned Loyalist Wife

⚜ RICHARD WERTHER ⚜

Grace Galloway was living in a world of woe. The pressure had been building, and a little after ten p.m. on August 20, 1778, it came to a head. Knock, knock, knock came the persistent rapping on the door of her Philadelphia mansion at the corner of Market and Sixth Streets[1]. She informed the unwelcomed visitors that she was in possession of her own home and would remain in possession. Soon after, she heard the sounds of someone trying to pry open the kitchen door. She knew the invaders and what they wanted. Grace, along with several servants, held her breath and waited in the dark for nearly ten minutes as her adversaries worked to gain entry.[2] The group breaking and entering was led by none other than Charles Willson Peale, the famous artist, acting in the capacity of a commissioner in charge of confiscating Loyalist properties.

Where was the man of the house while all this was happening? He was in England with the couple's only daughter, Elizabeth (known as Betsy or Betsay). He probably wasn't somewhere kicked back and re-

---

1. There is some disagreement in the literature on whether this event took place at the Galloways' downtown mansion or at their Bucks County retreat, Trevose. Source documents (including the diary itself) are unclear, but most secondary sources indicated the former. Trevose still stands and is operated as a museum by the Historical Society of Bensalem Township. Consultation with staff there indicated that they also believe the eviction took place at the Philadelphia location. The Galloway home at the Philadelphia location no longer stands, and no renderings of it are available. The site is adjacent to George Washington's presidential home and was home to the original Wanamaker's department store, which opened there in 1861.

2. Grace Growden Galloway and Raymond C. Werner, "Grace Growden Galloway Diaries with Introduction and Notes," *The Pennsylvania Magazine of History and Biography*, Vol. 55, No. 1 (1931), 51, www.jstor.org/stable/20086760, accessed November 26, 2017. All diary quotations use original spelling, capitalization, and punctuation.

laxing with a cool drink, but he surely wasn't being terrorized or being forced from his home either. This turn of events, with the Loyalist husband gone from the scene and his wife remaining home to face the music, was not unusual during the Revolution. To modern sensibilities, this abandonment seems, at the very least, cowardly on the husband's part, and in the late eighteenth century, when women had very little in the way of legal rights or powers, it seems downright cruel. There were, however, complex considerations and pragmatic reasons that made such a move necessary, at least in the calculus of the Galloways. While the Galloways' case may not be the most representative of the Loyalist experience due to his political prominence and their (mostly her) significant wealth, it does illustrate much of what Loyalist women in similar situations faced.

Grace's treatment may have been harsher than that of most other abandoned loyalist wives. After all, her husband Joseph Galloway was not just any loyalist; he had long been a prominent Philadelphia politician and lawyer, and a delegate to the First Continental Congress. There he voted for the non-importation agreement, Congress's response to what they viewed as Britain's violations of their liberties. While in Congress Galloway had argued forcefully (and unsuccessfully) for reconciliation between the colonies and Great Britain. His proposal was heard, debated, and even voted on. All these details were stricken from the official records of Congress. The motion for his plan of reconciliation was defeated by the narrowest of margins, six states against to five in favor. He continued the reconciliation debate later in America, and continued to push it in England, all the while tweaking his plan through 1788.[3] Galloway was one of only two members of that First Continental Congress to "go loyalist," and certainly the highest profile one. All this combined to make him one of the most notorious traitors in the eyes of the patriots. Torturing Grace was the new state administration's way of "striking a blow against an absent enemy: her husband."[4]

Grace's own distinguished pedigree also made her a target. Grace Growden Galloway was born into privilege, the daughter of Lawrence Growden, a justice in Bucks County and eventually Second Justice of the Pennsylvania Supreme Court where he served for fifteen years.

---

3. Julian P. Boyd, *Joseph Galloway's Plans to Preserve the British Empire, 1774-1788* (Philadelphia: University of Pennsylvania Press, 1941), Appendix V.

4. Kacy Dowd Tillman, "Women Left Behind: Female Loyalism, Coverture, and Grace Growden Galloway's Empire of Self," in Mary McAleer Balkun and Susan C. Imbarrato, ed., *Women's Narratives of the Early Americas and the Formation of Empire* (New York: Palgrave MacMillan, 2016), 142.

Judge Growden died in 1770, and upon his death the value of his property was estimated at 113,478 pounds Sterling. Key components of his
holdings included Trevose, the crown jewel of their holdings (where
Grace lived earlier in 1778 before returning to their Philadelphia mansion to live with Joseph after the British ended their occupation of the
city), Belmont, King's Place, and Richland, a combined nearly 11,500
acres, plus various tracts associated with the Durham Iron Company.
Growden's will provided a two hundred pound per year stipend for his
widow, with the remainder of the estate split between his two daughters.[5] As a result, when Grace and Joseph were married in 1753, she
brought a substantial portfolio of assets into their union.

While on the surface their marriage appeared steady, there were clear
fissures in the foundation. Both had headstrong personalities. Grace
came from a privileged background and was used to having her way
while living in high style. She felt constrained by the institution of marriage, writing in her diary well before Joseph's departure, "Never get
tied to a man/for when once you are yoked/'Tis all a mere joke/of seeing
your freedom again,"[6] and even more glumly, "I am Dead/Dead to each
pleasing thought each Joy of Life/Turn'd to that heavy lifeless lump a
wife."[7] Even before becoming a Loyalist, Joseph was haughty, self-ab-
sorbed, and preoccupied with political matters. His personality and
fame made Grace feel overshadowed and limited.

To comprehend the position into which Grace was placed, it is important to understand what legal rights women had during this time
period. The unfortunate, though unsurprising, answer is: not many.
Since men controlled the legal system, when a woman married, her
identity was subordinate to that of her husband. As Sir William Blackstone, the famous British legal scholar put it:

> The husband and wife are one person in law . . . the very being or
> legal existence of the woman is suspended during the marriage, or at
> least is incorporated and consolidated into that of the husband; under
> whose wing, protection, and cover, she performs every thing; and is
> therefore called in our law-french a feme-covert.[8]

5. Elizabeth Evans, *Weathering The Storm: Women of the American Revolution* (New York:
Charles Scribner's & Sons, 1975), 185-186.
6. Carol Berkin, *Revolutionary Mothers: Women in the Struggle for America's Independence*
(New York: Alfred A. Knopf, 2005), 94.
7. *In The Words of Women* website, archive for Galloway, Grace Growden, inthewordsof-
women.com/?cat=426, accessed January 20, 2018.
8. Merril D. Smith, *Women's Roles in Eighteenth-Century America* (Santa Barbara, CA:
Greenwood, 2010), quoting Blackstone, 9.

This was more commonly referred to as "coverture." Covered (married) women could not own property, earn wages, or make contracts.[9] Any property they brought into the marriage was signed over to the husband and did not revert back to the wife until the husband died. If the husband absconded as a loyalist, the property would generally be attainted, eventually confiscated and, subsequently, sold by the state. Women had little legal standing to challenge such confiscations. What little wiggle room there was came in the form of prenuptial agreements where a woman or her male relatives would govern how much control the husband would have over property brought into the marriage. Because of the legal complexities involved, these were rare and generally confined to wealthier families.[10] Despite being one of those wealthier families, the Galloways had no such agreement, and even if they did it probably would have been superseded by the initiative to confiscate Loyalist properties. A husband's abandonment left the woman, particularly a woman such as Grace Galloway, to forge ahead for very first time to "exercise [her] own judgment on legal, economic, or political matters"[11] in her attempt to protect her (their) property.

So why was abandonment of their spouses a tactic used by so many Loyalists, especially the notorious and/or well to do ones?[12] One reason is that technically, under coverture, women were deemed incapable of taking political action separately from their husbands, and, therefore, they should not have to suffer for their husbands' political transgressions.[13] Unfortunately, this was not the reality of the situation. Despite the technical legalities of coverture, the politics of the husband were usually imputed to the wife. Certainly, in the case of a notorious loyalist such as Joseph Galloway, the patriot authorities were not about to permit legal technicalities to let his wife get away unpunished; indeed, with his departure to England, the only way they could get to him was through his wife. Though far less vocal in them, Grace also had Loyalist sympathies, rendering this point somewhat moot anyway.

In many cases, the Loyalist husband had already left home to serve in the British armed forces and was barred from returning. This was true of Galloway who was working for General Howe in New York and would have had a difficult time making his way back to Pennsylvania. There was also the very real threat of violence. Galloway had

9. Smith, *Women's Roles in Eighteenth-Century America*, 31.
10. Ibid., 32.
11. Carol Berkin, *First Generations, Women in Colonial America* (New York: Hill and Wang, 1997), 168.
12. Ibid., 166.
13. Tillman, "Women Left Behind," 143.

been threatened in the past, such as when a box containing a noose appeared on his front porch one morning, with a note that said, "hang yourself, or we shall do it for you"[14] Furthermore, the Loyalist husband felt that authorities would treat his wife more gently without his inflammatory presence. This logic did not work for Grace Galloway for many of the same reasons explained above. More subtle reasons for parting could include marital strife. While as described above there was friction in the Galloway union, their parting seems to have been amicable. Lastly, there may have been a measure of cowardice involved. It is apparent that the threats to Joseph were real and possibly these threats played a role in abandoning his wife and leaving her exposed to the possible baser depredations of the patriot mob. Luckily, Grace did not face this indignity.

The most important reason to leave the wife behind, and the reason that mattered most to the Galloway's, was to protect their property in the hope of recovering it as conditions changed and passions cooled. Trevose had already been stripped clean of anything not nailed down (though Betsy had reportedly buried the china in the barnyard), but they wanted to protect the structures and the land. For example, Grace noted in her diary how she took legal action to try to prevent the forests around Trevose and other tracts from being cut down for firewood.[15] Among the casualties of the Trevose looting was a trunk Galloway was storing for Benjamin Franklin containing the latter's papers detailing Franklin's years in Paris.[16] Their possessions in the Philadelphia had been left intact, and had been carefully inventoried by Peale.

Their decision for Joseph and daughter Betsy to leave for New York and eventually for England in late 1778 was obviously not one they took lightly, and though it seemed cruel at first blush, it was the best in a collection of bad options. It was fraught with its own set of risks. The Atlantic crossing was always dangerous, and even more so for a Loyalist of Galloway's stature should he be captured in flight by a Patriot cruiser. There were gut-wrenching emotions that come when leaving the place of one's birth and the many friendships one leaves behind, not knowing

14. Ernest H. Baldwin, "Joseph Galloway, the Loyalist Politician (concluded)," *Pennsylvania Magazine of History and Biography* Volume XXVI, 1902, No.4., 430, www.jstor.org/stable/20086051, accessed October 1, 2017.
15. Grace Growden Galloway and Raymond C. Werner, "Grace Growden Galloway Diaries with Introduction and Notes," *The Pennsylvania Magazine of History and Biography*, Vol. 58, No. 2 (1934), www.jstor.org/stable/20086864, accessed November 14, 2017. The diary entries of ten different days refer to the wood-cutting issue.
16. *The Magazine of American History with Notes and Queries Illustrated*, Volume VIX, January to July, 1883, 430.

whether they would ever return. From a political point of view, Joseph felt a sharp combination of disappointment and betrayal related to the failure of his efforts to save his native country from what he viewed as a grave mistake:

> I call this country ungrateful because I have attempted to save it from the distress it at present feels, and because it has not only rejected my endeavors but returned me evil for good. I feel for its misery . . . still deeper distress will attend it. Was it in my power, I would notwithstanding its severity to me preserve it against such destruction. But it is not for mortals to counteract the will of heaven.[17]

Despite their sometimes tempestuous marriage, Joseph and Grace Galloway obviously felt similarly acute emotions that would be expected between spouses at such a parting, though Grace, in the end, urged Joseph to leave as a pragmatic matter, fearing for his safety. In one letter she said, "I have such a relief of mind from your going out of the reach of your enemies that it takes all the pain of your leaving."[18]

We are able to understand what ensued from Grace's point of view by the diary she kept. She began her diary soon after Joseph's departure with Betsy for New York in June 1778 and continued, with a few minor breaks, until September 1779. The diary includes mundane details of daily life, such as the weather and who she had dinner with, but on a deeper level, she shared updates on the legal wrangling and, most poignantly, her evolving emotions as to her deteriorating situation and health. Many of Grace's letters to Betsy are also preserved, and they provide an acute window into the emotions of the mother-daughter relationship that was so central to Grace's decision to stay behind. All of this brings us back to the troubled scene which started this article.

Though he probably would rather have been in his studio painting portraits, Charles Willson Peale took his job as an agent for confiscated estates in Philadelphia seriously, and soon he confronted Grace Galloway face to face. She showed him the legal papers she had to support her presence. Peale quickly skimmed these and just as quickly dismissed them. He advised Grace that he had removed people from their homes before; boasting of having removed over forty people in one day, removing just these few would be no problem. In fact, according to

---

17. Patton Gardenier Galloway, *The Loyal Traitor—Joseph Galloway and the American Revolution* (Morrisville, NC: Lulu Press, 2016), 233. The quote here is from a letter Joseph wrote to his sister. I assume, though couldn't verify, that the author of this book is a descendant of Joseph Galloway.
18. Galloway, *The Loyal Traitor*, 234.

Grace's diary, he threatened that they would "throw her cloaths in ye street"[19] should she not come quietly. Peale went upstairs, brought down Grace's "Work bag and 2 bonnets,"[20] and the group sat in the entryway waiting for a chariot dispatched by a local Patriot general (most likely, ironically, Benedict Arnold). When it arrived and Peale took Grace's arm to lead her to the chariot that would take her away from her beloved home, she reiterated that she was not leaving her home on her own accord, declined Peale's assistance by pushing his arm away, and boarded the carriage on her own, bound for the home of a friend. Even for a woman with connections, and Grace had many, coverture proved to be no protection. If Joseph thought Grace's wealth and social standing would protect her, he was sadly mistaken. Not only did it not protect her, it likely made her a more of a target.

It may be a cliché that in adversity one discovers who one's true friends are, but Grace quickly found out she had far fewer friends than she thought. On August 16, 1778, she wrote, "as I have no friends, they [Joseph's friends] treat me as they please. So much for Mr. G['s] great friends he has not one that will go out of ye way to serve him. I am in hopes they will let me have my Estate but that will be on my own Account. No favor shewn JG or his Child: Nor has he a friend that will say one word in his favour."[21]

As it turned out, the Philadelphia Quaker community became Grace's friends and surrogate family support.[22] Their names dominate her diary, especially frequent dinner companion Debby Morris (with whom she lived after being evicted from the Philadelphia mansion) and later on another woman whose friendship she found very comforting, referred to only as "Neighbor Zanes" (first name likely Sarah). Even some Whigs (Patriots), such as John Dickinson, offered support and advice.[23] This woman of wealth slowly took to, and eventually came to even embrace, the simpler life that her diminished financial status dictated. Late in her diary, on August 2, 1779 she states "Sup[p]ed with Debby [Morris] & six country friends these honest Ignorant people are the happyest on earth I am pleased to see their ways."[24]

Early on, she was able to find an inner strength she did not know she possessed, and between periods of severe doubt and self-pity that

19. Galloway and Werner, "Grace Growden Galloway Diaries," 51.
20. Ibid., 52.
21. Ibid., 50.
22. Galloway, *The Loyal Traitor*, 243.
23. Ibid.
24. Galloway and Werner, "Grace Growden Galloway Diaries," 164.

strength shined through. At times it manifested as outright defiance, such as in her April 20, 1779 diary entry:

> I told them I was ye happyest woman in town for I had been strip[p]ed & Turn'd out of Doors yet I was still ye same & must be Joseph Galloways Wife & Lawrence Growdons daughter & that it was Not in their power to humble Me for I shou'd be Grace Growdon Galloway to ye last & as I had now suffer'd all that they can inflict Upon Me I shou'd now act as on a rock to look on ye wrack of others & see them tost by the Tempestuous billows while I was safe ashore"[25]

Joseph's standing with her gradually declined as her ordeal progressed. Earlier in her diary she wrote with affection about Joseph (called "JG" or "Mr. G" throughout the diary), but gradually this turned to disdain as her despair deepened. On August 10, 1779, upon receiving a letter from London she "was so Moved on My childs account that I cou'd Not forgive J G for [not] takeing More Care of his family."[26] A letter to Betsy turned into what one might call a "virtual divorce," stating she is "happy not to be with him . . . I want not to be kept so like a slave as he will always . . . preven[t] every wish of my heart."[27]

In the second half of the ordeal, she began to self-medicate, recording nearly every night taking an "Anodine" to cope with her depression and to help her sleep. This could represent a number of medications; a medical dictionary from the late 1800s defines Anodynes as "Medicines which relieve pain by lessening the excitability of nerves or of nerve-centres." They ranged from opium, morphine and cannabis to more benign substances.[28] It not known exactly what Grace was taking, but her nearly daily use of this substance is indicative of her mental slide.

In the latter months of her life, she became a virtual recluse. Daily diary entries almost always end with expressions like "very low spirited," "I am wretched," "Oh how we are fallen," "so distressed," etc. On Friday, November 13, 1778, she recorded the indignity of seeing the carriage she formerly owned drive by as she was forced to walk in a driving rain storm: "came on a storm & it rain'd very hard but I wou'd come home . . . I was so wett in My feet & pettycoats as if I had been dipp'd in water was so frighten'd . . . & as I was walking in the Rain My own

25. Ibid., 76.
26. Ibid., 167.
27. Tillman, "Women Left Behind," 149. This quotes a letter from Grace to Betsy dated November 23, 1778.
28. Richard Quain, M.D., ed., *A Dictionary of Medicine* (New York: D. Appleton and Company, 1883), 55.

Chariot Drove by I own that I then thought it hard but I Kept Up pretty well."[29]

Her deteriorating health, coupled with her building anger at her husband for putting her in this situation and her need to desperately cling to her daughter's inheritance, caused her to forgo any opportunity to travel to England to reunite with her husband and daughter again. Consequently, she never followed up on Joseph's entreaties for her to join them there.

Though her diary ends in September, 1779 she kept writing, maintaining a letter book in which she expressed her feelings in letters to her daughter. Due to the difficulty of smuggling correspondence out of Philadelphia, these letters were never sent. Instead, they represented an outlet for her feelings which she hoped someday Betsy, or even Joseph, would read.[30] In late 1781, in one of her last letters, she wrote, "It is now going on three years since I was left in this dreadful situation, and my health is now so impaired that I never hope to have it in my power to see my relations or native country more. Want of health and to save your inheritance alone detains me. If by it I save my child all will be right."[31] Never to see either her daughter or husband again, she died on February 6, 1782 in Philadelphia. She is buried in an unmarked grave at Byberry Quaker Friends Cemetery. Joseph, on the other hand, was awarded a pension of 500 pounds per year by the British Loyalist Commission, and outlived her by more than twenty years, dying in Watford, Hertfordshire, England, on August 29, 1803.[32]

As the laws of coverture dictated, Grace's share of the Growden estate was placed under the ownership of her husband when they married in 1753. Grace, likely unaware of these legalities when they married, found out after the property was confiscated that she had been left off the deed,[33] making the blow that much worse. Thus, the property Grace brought to the marriage, and desperately wished to pass on to Betsy, was effectively owned by her husband until his death, at which point it reverted to Grace who could then bequeath it to descendants. Even though her husband was an ocean away and unlikely to return, these rules held up that transfer for over twenty years.

Grace executed a will dated December 12, 1781, even though it was unclear whether she had any standing to do so. In it, she left some household items to Debby Morris and fifty pounds in specie plus cloth-

29. Galloway and Werner, "Grace Growden Galloway Diaries, 57.
30. Evans, *Weathering The Storm*, 237.
31. Ibid., 239.
32. Baldwin, "Joseph Galloway, the Loyalist Politician," 439.
33. Tillman, "Women Left Behind," 148.

ing, a bed and quilt to her long-time servant Nurse Jane Harrison, who had been there on that dark August evening when they were evicted. The remainder, including the property she thought and hoped would eventually revert to her, would be held in trust by a group of her Quaker friends for eventual distribution to Betsy.[34]

Trevose was purchased at auction in 1779 by Gen. James Wilkinson,[35] another noted scoundrel and alleged traitor and double-agent in the pay of the Spanish; Wilkinson swore allegiance to Spain in 1787, which led to Trevose being reacquired by Grace's trustees in 1789. The Philadelphia home was used for a time by a Spanish merchant[36] and was later the residence of the president of the supreme executive council of the state,[37] Galloway's political enemy Joseph Reed.

Betsy Galloway married William Roberts in England in 1793. They had one child, Grace Ann, before the marriage foundered and the couple went their separate ways. Betsy retained custody of Grace Ann, later remarried and had two sons. Included in this marriage was a post-nuptial agreement to ensure that Betsy's inheritance would not be further encumbered by William Roberts upon Joseph Galloway's death. This agreement, while not valid in England, was valid in Pennsylvania where the estate was being adjudicated. After much legal wrangling and many appeals, it took until 1806 before State Supreme Court of Pennsylvania ruled in that subsequent to his death, Joseph Galloway's treason vested in the state no right to his wife's assets.[38]

At last, the estate that her mother sacrificed so much to protect belonged to Betsy. She had returned to America in 1791 for a short time while the matter was still being contested, trying to push the case forward to conclusion. But, she was uncomfortable in the place where her father was unwelcome (Joseph having been officially banned from returning to America) and where her mother had suffered, so, after a short stay, she returned to England.[39] After the case was settled, some properties were sold while others, including Trevose, were held. Betsy died in 1815 at age forty-four, thus having little time to enjoy the benefits of the fortune she inherited. The remaining proceeds were inherited by Grace Ann, who lived until 1837, after which the property

34. I was provided with a copy of the original handwritten will by the Historical Society of Bensalem Township.
35. Per property ownership timeline provided by the Historical Society of Bensalem Township, copies obtained January 23, 2018.
36. Berkin, *Revolutionary Mothers*, 95.
37. Boyd, *Joseph Galloway's Plans*, 84.
38. Evans, *Weathering The Storm*, 244.
39. Galloway, *The Loyal Traitor*, 283.

passed on to her half-brother Robert Burton.[40] Today Trevose is a museum and historical site, open to the public.

The best epilogue to Grace Galloway's miserable experience comes in an excerpt from a poem called "The Deserted Wife" written by Elizabeth Graeme Fergusson, an eminent writer of the period who was herself a spouse left behind:

My Shatter'd fortunes I with calmness Bore
A Loss in Common but with thousands more
A Public Evil dire Effects of War
Yet on my Mind left an Indented Scar[41]

40. Per Historical Society of Bensalem Township ownership records, copies obtained January 23, 2018.
41. Rodney Mader, "Elizabeth Graeme Fergusson's 'The Deserted Wife'," *Pennsylvania Magazine of History and Biography*, Vol.CXXXV, No.2 (April 2011), 163-164.

Benedict Arnold's Masterplan for (British) Victory

❦ JOHN KNIGHT ❦

Even by Victorian standards Great Massingham, Norfolk, was a sleepy hamlet. Though it had been a settled community since Norman times, in 1880 it comprised little more than a few farms, an inn, and a handsome medieval church. Local humour had it that there were more ducks in the village pond than there were people. But it was here, in the parish rectory, that a remarkable document was unearthed. It was a manuscript that threw new light on its author but refuted too the commonly held belief that the American war was considered over with the surrender at Yorktown.

The owner of this document was the Right Rev. Edward Gladwin Arnold. Its author was his grandfather the notorious traitor, Benedict Arnold.

By 1880 there had been little attempt to re-evaluate the reputation of Arnold. To Americans, he remained the personification of betrayal. George Cannings Hill had recently published his influential biography on Arnold with the preface, "of true manhood, lofty purpose and persevering effort . . . Benedict Arnold offers no such example. On the contrary, his memory shall be detested as long as time shall help to keep it alive."[1] In Britain on the other hand, his name was all but forgotten, a dishonourable and embarrassing coda to a lost war.

It would have been easy then for this document to have been either destroyed or mislaid but fortunately for historians, the vicar doggedly preserved it, and in 1880 it was published as an appendix to a more sympathetic biography by congressman and distant relative Isaac N Arnold.[2]

1. George Canning Hill, *Benedict Arnold: A Biography* (Boston: E.O. Libby & Co., 1858), 14.
2. Issac N Arnold, *The Life of Benedict Arnold: His Patriotism and His Treason* (Chicago: Jansen, McClurg & Co., 1880).

The paper "Thoughts on the American War" comprised nine handwritten pages that were never intended for public view. They contained
remarkably prescient observations on the failure of the British cause in
America. Arnold being the man he was, they also presented his proposed remedies for those deficiencies. Though it was framed just
months after the capitulation at Yorktown, the work reasoned a plan
of action that in no part acknowledged defeat as inevitable.

Written at the behest of the George III, it was well received by both
the sovereign and his ministry. As such it gives a vital snapshot into
the thinking of the British and Loyalist "Ultras" who even at this late
stage of the war believed victory, or at least honourable reconciliation,
was worth pursuing. Perhaps most remarkably the document was not
one that emphasised military solutions to the conflict but civil and political ones. The solutions offered are sophisticated and thoughtful and
show Arnold in a fresh light from the blustering headstrong soldier of
tradition.

I break down here the central assertions of Arnold for the purposes
of clarity and debate. The actual document features no such breaks.
Arnold's style is, as one may suppose, both forthright and emphatic,
though some of his points are repetitive. I have tidied up his grammar
and spelling, and have left out some of his more pedestrian points, but
other than that the paper is as written.

Some of his contentions are undoubtedly wrong. Many are extraordinarily accurate and insightful. Like the man himself, it is a paper that
will split opinions. The judgments under Arnold's narrative are the author's own and are not intended to be conclusive, rather a starting point
for debate. It is for *Journal of the American Revolution* readers to decide
how different the war may have been if the British had had had time
to engage Arnold's plan in full, but there is no doubt that as a summary
of British policy failings in America it stands up to rigorous scrutiny.

> Great Britain was deceived at the commencement of the American
> troubles when she trusted to what some wrote: that the discontents
> were confined to a small faction. Her measures thus became inadequate
> to her ends.[3]

Correct. And a bold assertion with which to begin the paper, for it
was commissioned by George III who was the leading proponent of
the opinion that the rebellion was the work of a few cynical individuals
and not a populist uprising. The British military response to a
widespread rebellion was therefore never likely to be adequate. Even at

3. Ibid., 419.

its height, the crown had upwards of 22,000 British regular troops at its disposal in North America to combat the rebellion, supplemented by several thousand German auxiliaries. An additional 25,000 Loyalists, faithful to Great Britain, participated in the conflict as well.[4] What Arnold didn't mention is that this insufficiency was as much a failure of logistics as it was a political blunder. The British simply didn't have the capability to put more troops into the field. More importantly, they didn't expect they would need too. Arnold is probably referencing the American secretary Lord Dartmouth who believed that limited coercion would "prevent bloodshed by overwhelming the radical leaders of the mob" while at the same time, strengthening the determination of those elements variously described as the "better sort" or the "right thinking" colonists.[5] Dartmouth's view was undoubtedly the prevailing one in Britain at the beginning of the war.

> There are those who now allege that she has few or no friends in America; and if they are believed, she will be a second time and more fatally deluded. Such accounts should be listened to with great jealousy, because they proceed from Ignorance or *bad* design, and lead to despair; and the severance of the Empire will be the ruin of it, and of every part of it.[6]

Correct. The Loyalist communities in the colonies remained remarkably consistent in their support for the crown throughout the war's long course. Indeed it could be argued that their attachment to a military solution was almost as firm as the King's himself. There is little evidence that this position faltered substantially after Yorktown. Arnold is wrong however in proclaiming that the loss of the American colonies would lead to the overall destruction of the nascent British Empire. It has been long accepted that the defeat in America was actually the making of the empire; merely moving Britain's focus from the west to the east.[7]

> That a great Majority of the Americans are averse to the separation is a truth supported by every kind of proof of which the subject is capable.[8]

4. Author Don N. Hagist podcast, Ben Franklin's World episode 47.
5. Kenneth Coleman, "On Lord Dartmouth and the American Revolution," *Georgia Review*, Spring 1968.
6. Arnold, *The Life of Benedict Arnold*, 419.
7. There have been numerous recent publications on the effect the loss of the American colonies had on the British Empire. See Maya Jasanoff, *Liberty's Exiles: The Loss of America and the Remaking of the British Empire* (London Harper Collins, 2011).
8. Arnold, *The Life of Benedict Arnold*, 419.

Incorrect. Arnold was presumably hoping to curry favour with the King through this statement. As a senior Continental commander who had operated in many of the colonies, he was undoubtedly aware that even in those states with sizable Loyalist communities such as New York, Georgia and Jersey they were never in a "great majority." Tellingly he offers no examples of his "every kind of proof."

> It is a Demonstration that the friends of the restoration are most numerous if the fact be admitted that the elections are everywhere attended by a minority, and this has been the case ever since the overtures of 1778. If it was not believed to be so, how should we account for the resort of so many thousands to the King's lines? What induces them to quit their estates, families and friends, and risk their own lives? It would be the greatest of all paradoxes to find them staking everything dear to them, upon their preference of the royal cause to the Congressional protection, if they knew the latter to be supported by the general voice.[9]

Confused. Though Arnold was correct to point out the sacrifices of the Loyalists as proof of their sustained and earnest support, the conclusion he reached is debatable. His assertion that "elections are everywhere attended by a minority" to back up his argument that this "de facto" signified a lack of support in Congress and the rebellion is tenuous at best.

> It was because . . . the multitude . . . were not consulted on the propriety of declaring Independence in 1776, nor on the confederation to authorise foreign alliances in 1777, nor on the rejection of the British overtures in 1778. Every one of these events actually made accessions to the number of the Loyalists and frittered down the Independent Party, . . . the minority increased in cruelty as they lessened in numbers.. the barbarities begot by their fears, disgusting others, and working with general calamities . . . The zealots . . . for protracting the war, are really . . . a very small proportion of the continent."[10]

Incorrect. This is perhaps the most personal part of the paper. Arnold's use of the words "barbarities," "disgust," "cruelty," "calamities" and "zealots" illustrates the angry state of mind that encouraged his rejection of the Patriot cause. His passion, however, seems to have coloured his logic. His claim that "the multitude" were not consulted is both naive and disingenuous. Congress did debate all of these issues

9. Ibid.
10. Ibid., 420.

and insofar as they were able to make democratic decisions in an age before universal suffrage, did so.[11]

> If it is thought . . . that the Rebels are everywhere an inveterate majority, and the Loyalists few and timid . . . I reply that this timidity should be called diffidence and arises from causes easily to be removed by a change in the Conduct of the War, which the American Loyalists have all along disapproved.[12]

Debatable. Arnold's contention here is a direct contradiction to the one most famously voiced by Charles Earl Cornwallis who regarded the Loyalists mainly as "quiet men."[13] Indeed Cornwallis went so far as to directly blame his failure in North Carolina as "not (from) a want of force to protect a rising of our friends. But by their timidity and unwillingness to take a useful and active part." Arnold clearly took the opposite view. In defence of Cornwallis, the "diffidence" Arnold relates undoubtedly revealed itself at crucial times during the war when a lack of confidence and organisation from the king's advocates compared poorly with the zeal and action of the Patriots. However, though Arnold believed this outlook could be transformed by a change of conduct in the war (presumably to a more aggressive one) he gives no explanation as to how this was to be accomplished "easily."

> It would be a tedious and invidious task to indulge in particular remarks, upon the Inactivity and misdirection of the King's arms; I leave it to others.[14]

Cynical. Arnold was both a patron of, and friend to Henry Clinton and Charles Cornwallis and was naturally averse to criticising them by name. Despite this he couldn't help bringing to the king's attention the army's "inactivity" (Clinton) and "misdirection" (Cornwallis), the unwritten conclusion being, of course, that he could lead it better.

> Has any attempt been made to set up the civil authority in any part of America, where the usurpation was beaten down? Certainly not and

---

11. "That the people wait for us to lead the way . . . That they are in favour of the measure, tho' the instructions given by some of their representatives are not." Notes of Proceedings in the Continental Congress, 7 June to 1 August 1776.
12. Arnold, *The Life of Benedict Arnold*, 420.
13. The National Archives Kew London holds the Cornwallis Papers. He is scornful of the Loyalists in much of his private correspondence. Wynnsborough to Balfour, November 17, 1780, appreciates his help; various comment on the situation, scornful remarks about loyalists, PRO 30/11/82/55-56.
14. Arnold, *The Life of Benedict Arnold*, 420.

till this is attended to, the Loyalists, in general, will not, nor indeed can give any essential assistance to the royal arms.[15]

Correct. This is Arnold's most telling criticism of British policy in America. In just one paragraph he isolates the fundamental failing of her strategy during the war. The British sought a military solution to a political problem. British generals were essentially given overarching powers in any state under British military control akin to those that Union generals later possessed in the postbellum Confederate south. This was a massively inefficient and tedious way to maintain control, and Arnold was correct in pointing out it dampened the enthusiasm of Loyalists while concentrating Patriot and neutral sentiment against the crown.

> He has ... no objection to serve in the militia within his own colony, under officers who are of it ... and to assist in supporting its government and defending himself in it and may perhaps pursue the Rebel out of it ... But for this purpose, the Civil Authority ... must first be set up, and without it, Great Britain can neither be benefited by his councils, his purse, nor his arms.[16]

Correct. Once again Arnold was exact in his censure of British policy. His particular reference to Loyalists not being governed or led by men of their own state may have been self-serving, but it was also accurate. Britain's failure to fully trust the Loyalists to administer or lead themselves in arms was in retrospect the biggest failing of the war. As Arnold points out, Loyalists didn't have confidence in the British army to protect them while concurrently administering the laws of the land.

> Is there a county in England, that thus circumstanced, would act otherwise, and be ... under the direction of an army? ... of an army too, addicted to plunder, and often willing to suppose a friend to be a Rebel, for the sake of what he has got, or they have seized?[17]

Correct. This is a vicious though valid criticism of both the army and British strategy. He pointed out, astutely, that no Englishman would ever stand for such a military occupation at home. Especially one that not infrequently resorted to plunder or arbitrary decree. Is it, therefore, any wonder that Loyalists were subdued and Whigs incensed?

15. Arnold, *The Life of Benedict Arnold*, 421.
16. Ibid.
17. Ibid.

Congress took advantage of our folly in leaving that Province to a military police . . . (but) wholly inadequate to a Province. Left to a state of nature, the soldiery began to insult . . . Robberies sprang up. The injured under the late usurpation avenged themselves upon their oppressors. The slaves left their masters, and the whole Province was prepared to resign all hope of Government for the common protection before the Congressional troops, arrived to increase the Confusion . . . If South Carolina is not lost, it is ruined; so that the only advantage we draw from all our operations in that quarter is the lesson it teaches . . . of consulting their salvation from destruction by a timely reconciliation with the mother country.[18]

Correct. Not only was much of South Carolina governed by what Arnold deemed a "military police," there were not even enough of them! He touches on the vicious civil war that sprang up as a result; a state of affairs that managed to both alienate her friends and offer succour to the rebels. His forthright plea for the British to consult with the local population and allow it to govern itself in order to seek a political reconciliation was never acted on.

The Congress is utterly become bankrupt not a bill of theirs now has any credit, and the only currency is hard money. This must be set down to the distrust began and propagated by the Loyalists; for the depreciation commenced in 1777. "Old money old price", was the vulgar cantatum of the friends of government, from the first moment of the paper emission in 1775."[19]

Exaggerated. This is a thought-provoking aside from Arnold. The near worthlessness of American currency he put down to the refusal of Loyalists to accept it as specie. However, this seems far too sophisticated and organised a resistance, principally because Continental money was distrusted by Patriots as much as everyone else. Though there were Loyalist attempts to undermine its value by counterfeiting, there is no evidence it was ever a concerted Loyalist tactic aimed at undermining Congress.[20]

The difficulty of forcing the militia into the field; the sanguinary laws of the usurpers; the mutiny and desertion of their regular troops; and various other topics might be mentioned as proofs of the declension

18. Ibid., 422.
19. Ibid.
20. The continental currency depreciated badly during the war, giving rise to the famous phrase "not worth a continental." A primary problem was that monetary policy was not coordinated between Congress and the states, which continued to issue bills of credit.

of the Party, with decisive confessions in the intercepted letters of the
Rebels. In a word, but for the late French aid, the Rebellion had sunk
under its own weakness.[21]

Exaggerated. Though all of the problems Arnold lists were genuine
concerns for Washington and Congress, it would be hard to conclude
that the rebellion was "sunk"—even without vital French aid.

> I say nothing upon the delicate enquiry which the disaster in Vir-
> ginia will lead to. It is material, however, to remark, that if the rebels
> deserve any advantage from it, "twill be as it shall affect the Councils
> of Great Britain this Winter.[22]

Interesting. Arnold is suggesting here that militarily the Americans
would gain little from the surrender at Yorktown. His contention that
it would be much more likely that the defeat would affect the political
will of Parliament turned out to be accurate. However, his contemptuous dismissal that an entire British army's surrender would not mate-
rially alter the ground war is more than a little dissembling.

> It is impossible for Washington to detach to Green, a force sufficient
> for the reduction of Charlestown; though he may and doubtless is in
> strength to ruin his friends as well as ours in the Southern Country.[23]

Correct. Charleston remained in British hands throughout the rest
of the war and was never seriously challenged. However, Washington
placed less emphasis on the southern theatre and after Yorktown realised he possessed the luxury of time; merely having to maintain the
status quo for victory to inevitably follow.

> By the complete detachment of Vermont from the rebel interest,
> and the reduction of the Highland forts early in the spring, much may
> be expected in the next campaign; especially since the New Yorkers in
> general, and a very great proportion of the country between them and
> the Connecticut River, are known to be very favorably inclined to the
> reunion.[24]

Optimistic. Few commanders would have had a better knowledge
of the tactical importance of the Highland forts. He also had first-hand
experience of the politically volatile situation in Vermont where the
British had sent military incursions and conducted secret negotiations

21. Arnold, *The Life of Benedict Arnold*, 422.
22. Ibid., 423.
23. Ibid., 424
24. Ibid.

with the Vermonters to re-join the British Empire. Arnold was additionally correct in his assessment that much of Lower New York and Westchester was sympathetic to the British.

However, his assurance that Vermont could be won over politically or that the Highlands could be reduced militarily when neither had happened in the preceding six years, seems both naive and overconfident.

> To authorize the Crown to appoint commissioners to come to a final agreement with the Colonies, or either of them . . . new peace commissioners should have every power of the crown for the appointment of officers, from Governors downwards, such guardians have been heretofore wanting. If they have a council, as I think they should have, to prevent the indelicacy of altercation, regard should be had to their tempers, standing and friendships in this country, as well as to their address and knowledge of its affairs."[25]

Deluded. This passage exemplifies some of the worst traits in Arnold's personality. There is no doubt that he was lobbying to be appointed as one of the "commissioners," noting that they should be men who had "standing" in the colonies as well as "knowledge of its affairs." His personal self-seeking went further in attempting to persuade the crown to grant these individuals almost unlimited powers, not just to negotiate with the States as a unit or singularly (a shrewd political suggestion incidentally) but also to allow them absolute patronage to appoint officers at every level. Though he suggested there should be a council, this clearly would be little more than a sinecure under the control of the said "commissioners."

The proposal is deluded on two fronts. Firstly Congress would have had little truck in negotiating anything with such a heinous traitor, let alone a peace settlement. More importantly, Great Britain was a constitutional democracy wherein the powers for reconciliation and patronage were held solely by Parliament. Early in the war, during the first attempted peace negotiations, the Howe brothers were constrained on what they could and could not negotiate with Congress. This limited authority made it a virtual certainty that nothing would come of their convention. This was true later of Lord Carlisle's commission. So hamstrung was Carlisle that he bitterly declared his negotiations "a mixture of ridicule, nullity, and embarrassments."[26]

---

25. Ibid., 426.
26. William Willcox, *Portrait of a General: Sir Henry Clinton in the War of Independence* (New York: Alfred A Knopf, 1964), 230.

It would be highly unlikely then, that the King or Lord North would grant almost autocratic powers to a handful of Loyalists. Though Arnold teasingly calls these new appointees "guardians," free from governmental restraint they would have inevitably become dictators – and wasn't that in good part what the rebellion had been all about in the first place?

> It cannot be worth the pains of stating arguments against the flimsy proposal of some for evacuating New York, the common centre, by means of the Hudson, of the British, Canadian and Indian interests in America . . . Nor against the wilder scheme . . . for yielding independence to all the continent, to the northward and eastward of a line of forts from the head of Elk River to Delaware, weakly relying upon a bargain, for the quick possession and retention of the Southern Provinces; for the produce of the latter, can be no equivalent for the loss of that commerce of the former.. to say nothing of the insecurity of the tenure . . . those districts would acquire very soon after Great Britain's acquiescence in the impairing of that monopoly by which she has been aggrandized."[27]

Fascinating. This is the most interesting "what if" of the paper. There were many in Britain who argued that her forces should abandon New York and retreat to hold a line from Quebec to Halifax. She would then reinforce the southern provinces where Lord Germaine had been convinced enough Loyalists remained for them to govern successfully. Arnold rightly ridiculed this proposal. His argument that the retention of the southern colonies, if her northern neighbours were lost, would be pointless and counterproductive is a shrewd one. Not only would they be permanently in thrall economically, but they would also be militarily insecure with the British merely postponing troubles for future generations to deal with.

His "all or nothing" guidance was actually the one the British eventually took. Unfortunately for Arnold's proposal, however, the Treaty of Paris acknowledged not the "all" of his paper but the "nothing" he dreaded.

27. Ibid., 427.

The Strange Case of
"Charles de Weissenstein"

RICHARD WERTHER

Early one morning in late June 1778, an unknown passerby tossed a package of documents that clanged against the gate at Benjamin Franklin's home in Passy, France.[1] In it was a letter addressed to Franklin dated June 16, 1778 from one "Charles de Weissenstein," writing from Brussels. In addition to the letter, the package contained two other documents, titled *Project for Allaying the Present Ferments in North America* and *An Outline of the Future Government in America.* The flurry of activity that followed provides a unique window into the state of both American and British thinking on the Revolution at the time and the nature of the alliance between France and America. It also provided bit of drama: a clandestine rendezvous that turned into a police chase. Was this now nearly forgotten incident a sideshow, almost comical if the issue at hand was not so serious, or was it a serious attempt to facilitate reconciliation between Great Britain and America? It's worth revisiting what happened.

The creation of plans designed to keep America in the British empire or otherwise end the war was practically a cottage industry during this period, so by itself the appearance of yet one more plan was not unusual, even if the method of delivery was a bit out of the ordinary. Many of these proposals were offered anonymously, so the fact that "Charles de Weissenstein" was quickly recognized as a fictional name was also unexceptional. However, upon further examination something about the contents of this package seemed different and worth more serious consideration.

1. Massachusetts History Online. Adams Papers, Diary of John Adams, 4: 150, www.mass hist.org/publications/adams-papers/index.php/view/DJA04d106, accessed March 9, 2018.

In mid-1778 Great Britain was licking her wounds from the crushing loss at Saratoga in late 1777. Besides thwarting of the British plan to divide the colonies along the Hudson corridor, this defeat gave the Americans legitimacy on the world stage, opening possibilities for alliances and badly-needed loans, both of which soon materialized with France. On the home front, their flagging war fortunes increased division politically and in popular opinion. Even among war supporters, criticism of military tactics and strategy became more strident.

The French alliance, signed in Paris on February 6, 1778 and ratified by Congress on May 2, had fundamentally changed the complexion of the conflict. With France in the fray, and Spain and The Netherlands likely to follow, Britain found itself in a world war. The need to defend other interests around the globe, such as Gibraltar and the West Indies, necessarily diminished the importance of the situation in the rebellious American colonies.[2] They had dispatched the Carlisle Commission to America in yet another attempt for a negotiated settlement. At home the ministry continued to waffle about recognizing (and therefore legitimizing) the American Congress and, most critically, about whether to recognize American independence. The Commission arrived in America in June 1778, scarcely a month after Congress ratified the French alliance. In the opinion of some, "if the Peace Commission under the Earl of Carlisle had reached America before news of the French alliance, its terms might well have been accepted."[3] Such is the importance of timing in history.

The Americans, despite the exhilaration of the victory at Saratoga, had their own issues. Their depleted military was limping out of the miserable winter in Valley Forge, not fully breaking camp until June. Since the British seizure of Philadelphia in late 1777, Congress was operating out of York, Pennsylvania. The performance of Washington's forces in the Pennsylvania battles of late 1777 defending Philadelphia had been dismal. A defeat of Howe around Philadelphia, coupled with the Saratoga outcome, might have brought more palatable peace overtures from the British. In summary, American fortunes were on the upswing, but there was a long slog still ahead.

The Carlisle Commission was aware of the French alliance but immediately shocked by the news that a British evacuation of Philadelphia

2. Leland G. Stauber, *The American Revolution, A Grand Mistake* (Amherst, NY: Prometheus Books, 2010), 187.
3. Samuel E. Morison, Henry S. Commager, and William E. Leuchtenburg, *The Growth of the American Republic—Volume 1* (New York: Oxford University Press, 1980), via Google Books, 194.

was imminent.[4] They offered a package to the Congress, still holed up in York. The terms provided for American self-government and representation in Parliament, but not recognition of America's independence.[5] Because of the latter omission, hardliners kept Congress unmoved. Meanwhile, across the ocean in France, the de Weissenstein drama unfurled.

THE LETTER

The package that hit the gate at Passy that day in June included a six-page handwritten letter, in English, from "de Weissenstein." According to John Adams, Franklin identified in the letter earmarks of it having come from the King himself, though neither Adams nor Franklin ever recorded what traits the latter saw that suggested such a thing. This attribution to the King could be genuine or, as historian Neil L. York suggests, the irreverent Franklin may have been having a little fun with the ever-earnest Adams. York writes: "Franklin's comments probably had more to do with the strained relations between the two diplomats than any belief on Franklin's part that the King had been privy to the plan. Adams, insecure and jealous of Franklin's status, may have just gotten on the Pennsylvanian's nerves."[6]

The cover page of the letter started with the admonition to "Read this in private and before you look at the other papers—but don't be imprudent enough to let anyone see it before you have considered it privately."[7] Starting on a positive note, de Weissenstein identifying himself as an Englishman who, while fond of order, was "no[t] yet one who is an idolatrous worshipper of passive obedience to the divine Right of Kings." He flattered Franklin as "a Philosopher, whom nature, industry, and a long experience have united to form, and to mature. It

4. Nathan R. Einhorn, "The Reception of the British Peace Offer of 1778," *Pennsylvania History* Vol. 16, No. 3, July 1949, 202, journals.psu.edu/phj/article/viewFile/21936/21705, accessed March 24, 2018.

5. Samuel Eliot Morrison, ed., *Sources and Documents Illustrating the American Revolution and the Formation of the Federal Constitution, 1764-1788* (New York: Oxford University Press, 1965). Pages 176-203 provide a complete text of the instructions issued to the Carlisle Commission.

6. Neil L. York, "Benjamin Franklin, the Mysterious 'Charles de Weissenstein,' and Britain's Failure to Coax Revolutionary Americans back into the Empire," in Paul E. Kerry and Matthew S. Holland, eds., *Benjamin Franklin's Intellectual World* (Madison, NJ: Fairleigh Dickinson University Press, 2012), 45. I attempted to correspond with York to clarify his opinions on this and see if he had further information about it but was unsuccessful.

7. "Charles de Weissenstein" to Benjamin Franklin, June 16, 1778, Founders Online, founders.archives.gov/documents/Franklin/01-26-02-0574, accessed March 9, 2018.

is to you therefore I apply." He went on to acknowledge the errors of the British regime, whose acts amounted to a "Stupid narrow-minded Despotism."[8]

The tone then darkened as the writer turned his sights on the French alliance, arguing that the French were untrustworthy and would eventually turn on America:

> The Progress of this new alliance is easily foreseen . . . For the present, and for a year or two to come, ye will obtain the most ample promises, and ready acquiescence. Then will come evasions to your applications, contemptuous delays, and of a sudden, a declaration that ye must shift for Yourselves. . . In that there may probably be a great Mistake, but with respect to America there can be no such Error, for when will she be able to combat France, and compell her to adhere to Treaties.[9]

Hitting closer to home, de Weissenstein dismissed both America's ability to win the war and then to defend itself as an independent nation. This struck at the heart of what the patriots had considered the starting point in any credible negotiation—recognition of America's independence:

> It is one thing to elude the Combat, another to vanquish Your adversary. The Maintenance of a Standing Army, and the Creation of a Regular Navy are not within the Compass of an inconsiderable revenue, and thinly peopled Country nor can attend the efforts of a few years, be activity and success as favorable as imagination can paint. Yet without these, your rising state will neither be in a capacity to secure itself from Hostile ravages, acquire new alliances, or preserve to any beneficial purpose, that which is already formed . . . Our Title to the Empire is indisputable, and will be asserted either by ourselves, or successors whenever occasion presents. We may stop a while in our pursuit to recover breath, but shall assuredly resume our career again.[10]

The denial of independence ended any serious consideration Franklin may have had of the proposal, if he even lasted that far. We shall later see his vitriolic response.

Where the plot thickened was in the conditions for response outlined in the letter. Franklin was asked to bring his reply to the Cathedral of Notre Dame between 12:00 and 1:00 PM on July 6 or July 9 and drop

8. "Charles de Weissenstein" to Benjamin Franklin, June 16, 1778, Founders Online, founders.archives.gov/documents/Franklin/01-26-02-0574, accessed March 9, 2018.
9. Ibid.
10. Ibid.

it off where a courier for de Weissenstein would be by the altar, "having a Paper in his hand as if drawing or taking notes."[11] Franklin was to drop the response there and then leave immediately. If unable to access this part of the cathedral (which was gated off in places), Franklin was to locate a person in one of the aisles "who will have a Rose, either in his Hat, which he will hold in his hand up to his face, or else in the buttonhole of his waistcoat."[12]

The courier would have no awareness of what he was carrying, and de Weissenstein wished to keep his identity masked:

> It matters very little for you in this state of busyness to indulge your curiosity in knowing who I am. I can serve you more effectually while invisible. If I succeed, perhaps I may never reveal myself; If I fail, surely my intentions merit some consideration from Men professing Patriotism.[13]

Franklin and Adams immediately broke the privacy request and brought the letter to their new ally, in the person of the French Foreign Minister, the Comte de Vergennes. Together they hatched a plan to bring in Paris police to stake out the pickup spot and attempt to apprehend the person picking up the documents, with hopes of using him to find out the identity of de Weissenstein. The police report, in French, still exists and with help of a neighbor who translated the document for me, I can report what happened next.[14] But first let's discuss the rest of de Weissenstein's proposal.

THE PROPOSALS

The attachments to the letter detailed two aspects of a reconciliation plan: how the transition would take place and how the new government would be structured. *Project for allaying the present ferments in North America* dealt with the first topic. Totaling eighteen articles, it detailed logistics such as the secrecy around the agreement (the first six articles were never to be released, the rest could be published once the agreement was consummated), safe passage to England for American nego-

---

11. Ibid.
12. Ibid.
13. Ibid.
14. Harvard University Library Online. pds.lib.harvard.edu/pds/view/422649875?n=1 &imagesize=1200&jp2Res=0.5&printThumbnails=no&oldpds, accessed March 9, 2018. This is the digitized scan of the original police report, handwritten and in French. It somehow ended up in the papers of Arthur Lee, another member of the American diplomatic team in France. I am indebted to my multilingual neighbor, Karen Motz, for graciously agreeing to decipher the handwriting and provide the English translation, as well as some clarifications and interpretations.

tiators while a state of war still existed, and how the suspension of arms would take place. By far the most interesting articles were numbers four and eight. Article four discussed how American leaders of the rebellion would be indemnified and kept safe from reprisals. In a component that was anathema to American notions of equality, it proposed the creation of an American hereditary peerage, going as far as to list four names of people who would become peers and receive permanent pensions. They were Adams, John Hancock, George Washington, and Franklin. The agreement also made provisions for the designation of others to be added to that list.[15] Article eight, brief but important, discussed how America's newly minted ally would be cast off, stating simply:

> The crown shall take upon itself to adjust the treaty between America and France which shall be laid before his Majesty in entire for his full information with respect thereto. A mode of notifying it to the court of France shall be settled.[16]

Great outline of the future governments in North America laid out in thirteen articles "A great and solemn compact . . . to be registered in the archives of every state of America" that would be "perpetual and irrevocable but by the free and mutual consent of both countries." The agreement would leave the governments of the existing colonies (states) in place but stipulated that the legislatures swear allegiance to the King. Further, it cancelled all existing laws promulgated by Parliament with respect to America, thus removing the major causes of the rebellion. It proposed to establish a Supreme Continental Court which would have jurisdiction over all the colonies and whose decisions could be appealed only to the House of Lords. It provided for an upper house Congress, a body that would be called into session every seven years or sooner, all at the King's discretion. All military operations would be placed under the Crown, with America to pay its share of the cost on a population-

---

15. Benjamin Franklin Stevens, *Facsimiles of manuscripts in European archives relating to America, 1773-1783*, Volume XXVI (London: Malby & Sons,1889). I accessed this book at the Hatcher Graduate Library, University of Michigan. The letter, the "Plan of Reconciliation," and "Outline of Future Government" were exhibits 835, 836, and 837 respectively. Based on the sequence of exhibits in the Stevens' collection, 835, 836, and 837 should have appeared in Volume VIII, but a notation in that volume indicates they are included in Volume XXVI. The reason for this move in unclear. The letter itself (Exhibit 835), and Franklin's unsent response are also transcribed and annotated in The Founders Online, but I could not find digitized versions of the attachments. I transcribed these myself from the handwritten versions.
16. Stevens, exhibit 836.

based pro rata allocation to the individual states, with stiff penalties for non-payment. The balance dealt with trade and tariff issues.[17] Interestingly, unlike many of the other proposals for a new continental government, there was no provision for any American-based executive function, no American president.

THE (UNSENT) REPLY

The failure to recognize America's independence probably doomed de Weissenstein's proposal from the start. Further, Franklin was no friend of the British ministry (or they of him), still smarting four years after his famous dressing down by Alexander Wedderburn in front of the Privy Council. Hence Franklin's reply, which addressed only three of the articles in the attachments, dripped with venom and anger that overshadowed his point-by-point refutation of de Weissenstein's proposals. As the plan was to share the draft reply first with Vergennes, Franklin may have been laying it on even thicker to demonstrate to his French partner America's devotion to their newly formed alliance.

The opening salvos laid into the British ministry:

> As to my future Fame, I am content to rest it on my past and present Conduct, without seeking an Addition to it in the crooked dark Paths you propose to me, where I should most certainly lose it. This your solemn Address would therefore have been more properly made to your Sovereign and his venal Parliament. He and they who wickedly began and madly continue a War for the Desolation of America, are alone accountable for the Consequences.
>
> But I thank you for letting me know a little of your Mind, that even if the Parliament should acknowledge our Independency, the Act would not be binding to Posterity, and that your Nation would resume, and prosecute the Claim as soon as they found it convenient. We suspected before, that from the Influence of your Passions, and your present Malice against us, you would not be actually bound by your conciliatory Acts longer than till they had serv'd their purpose of inducing us to disband our Forces[18]

The de Weissenstein proposal for the establishment of an American peerage was another major target of Franklin's wrath; he may have seen it as one indication of the King's involvement:

17. Stevens, exhibit 837.
18. Franklin to "Charles de Weissenstein," July 1, 1778, Founders Online, founders. archives.gov/documents/Franklin/01-27-02-0002, accessed March 9, 2018.

... you offer us Hope, the Hope of PLACES, PENSIONS and PEERAGES. These (judging from yourselves) you think are Motives irresistable. This Offer, Sir, to corrupt us is with me your Credential; it convinces me that you are not a private Volunteer in this Negociation. It bears the Stamp of British-Court-Character. It is even the Signature of your King...We must then pay the Salaries in order to bribe ourselves with these Places. But you will give us PENSIONS! probably to be paid too out of your expected American Revenue ... PEERAGES! — Alas, Sir, our long Observation of the vast and servile Majority of your Peers, voting constantly for every Measure propos'd by a Minister, however weak or wicked, leave us small Respect for that Title.[19]

This letter was first given to Vergennes. He apparently elected to let the matter lie; the letter was never delivered at the Notre Dame rendezvous. As far as can be determined, no formal notification about this proposal was relayed to Congress or anyone else in America. Adams did refer to it in passing in a letter to Congressman Elbridge Gerry, talking in general about British peace overtures and adding, "we had an Example, here last Week ... A long Letter, containing a Project for an Agreement with America, was thrown into one of our Grates ... There are Reasons to believe, that it came with the Privity of the King." Like Franklin, Adams zeroed in on the peerage issue, stating that while the letter was "Full of Flattery," it was also full of bribery,

> proposing that a Number not exceeding two hundred American Peers should be made, and that such as had stood foremost, and suffered most, and made most Enemies in this Contest, as Adams, Handcock, Washington and Franklin by Name, should be of the Number ... Ask our Friend [who Adams is referring to is not clear], if he should like to be a Peer?[20]

He also referred to Franklin's caustic response, saying, "Dr. Franklin ... sent an Answer, in which they have received a Dose that will make them sick."[21] In this he was wrong, as Franklin's response never got past Vergennes, but he was right about how the British would have reacted. Later, as part of a characteristically long, rambling screed about the letter in his diaries ("An aristocracy of American peers!"), Adams called

19. Franklin to "Charles de Weissenstein," July 1, 1778, Founders Online, founders. archives.gov/documents/Franklin/01-27-02-0002, accessed March 9, 2018.
20. Massachusetts History Online. Adams Papers, Diary of John Adams, Volume 4, www.masshist.org/publications/adams-papers/index.php/view/DJA04d106, 149, accessed March 9, 2018.
21. Ibid., 150.

the letter "very weak and absurd and betrayed a gross Ignorance of the Genius of American People."[22]

THE STAKEOUT

The Paris police did indeed stake out the drop-off point, the Cathedral of Notre Dame, as requested by Vergennes. There was no intent to hand over any reply. A copy of the police report documenting the incident, dated July 7, 1778, was relayed to Franklin soon thereafter. The officer in charge "went to the church of Notre Dame yesterday at 11am with three bodyguards whom I posted inside and outside to observe the stranger of interest and those who would come and accost him."[23] The stranger showed up at "12:00 sharp" and found his movement restricted by the "iron gates" referred to in the de Weissenstein letter.[24] These gates locked off various shrines within the cathedral which contained exhibits of value (statues, vases, etc.). According to the report "a man sweeping the floor came up to offer to let the stranger inside" some of these areas, and the stranger "had the sweeper open seven or eight of these."[25] As advertised, the stranger then wandered around the area "examining the chapels [exhibits] and scribbled or wrote in short bursts" on some paper he carried. At 1:15, "seeing no one, the stranger left." The police proceeded to tail him past several streets (covering roughly one to one and a half miles), the subject "looking as though he were dreaming [preoccupied or deep in thought]." The pursuit ended at the Luxembourg Hotel.[26]

At the hotel, they at last confronted the man, and "learned that he was Monsieur Jennings, Captain of the Guards of the King of England about four or five years ago." They further learned "his father had been a minister in the court of some other land." They described Jennings as "between the ages of 36 and 40, about 5'2" in height, with extremely blond hair . . . a very thin face and a swarthy or tanned complexion." In his stay at the hotel (he arrived June 20) he had reportedly seen no one.[27] The suspect was not arrested, there being nothing to charge him with, and the police followed up no further. He left the country shortly thereafter.

22. Ibid., 150.
23. Police report translation, see note 14.
24. Ibid.
25. Ibid.
26. Ibid.
27. Ibid.

One added twist to the mystery: At the bottom of the police report is written, in a comment apparently added later in different handwriting and in English "The above is doubtless a fabrication."[28]

WHO WAS CHARLES DE WEISSENSTEIN?

Franklin, Adams, and Vergennes all thought that the man the police tailed was "Charles de Weissenstein" himself. The German name "Weissenstein" means literally "white stone" in English. Applied to a person, it means a person with white hair, beard, or skin.[29] This meshes with the "blond hair" cited in the police report, though not so much with the "swarthy or tanned complexion." Also, "Charles" may have come from the name of Jennings' son.[30]

Building on what the police discovered, speculation was that the deliverer, but not the writer, was Sir Philip Jennings (1722–1788), a former major in the horse guards (1741–1770) and a current member of Parliament.[31] He was also known as Philip Jennings-Clerke and served in Parliament under that name from 1768 to 1788. Parliament was not in session during his time in France. He was granted a baronetcy by the King in 1774, 1st Baronet of Duddlestone Hall, that after his death passed briefly to son Charles, who died four months later, ending the line.[32] He was remembered by one colleague as "a man of unquestionable integrity, but not endowed with superior parts,"[33] and by another commentator as "one of the most persevering men in any business he chose to undertake."[34] His support in Parliament for conciliatory measures toward America (including recognition of the Continental Congress) lends credence to his involvement in this affair.[35] I could find no

28. Police report translation, see note 14.

29. Museum of the Jewish People: Beit Hadfutsot website, dbs.bh.org.il/familyname/ weissenstein, accessed April 18, 2017.

30. York, "Benjamin Franklin, the Mysterious 'Charles de Weissenstein,'" 67n11. In this note, York also mentions the observation of historian Richard Reeves from the New Forest Visitors Center (Foxlease) that perhaps the "white" in Weissenstein is a reference to "the white paint used on the stucco façade of the Georgian mansion at Cox lease (now Fox lease)." Fox lease, or Foxlease, was the mansion owned by Jennings. This seems to me a stretch, but it's possible.

31. Franklin to "Charles de Weissenstein," July 1, 1778, Founders Online, Footnote 4. Interestingly, Adams, writing years later, recalled that the man was named "was Col. (Mc) Fitz something, an Irish name," demonstrating how poor historical memory can sometimes be!

32. Sylvanus Urban, *The Gentlemen's Magazine and Historical Chronicle*, Volume 58, Part 1 (London: John Nichols, 1788), Google Books, 372.

33. York, "Benjamin Franklin, the Mysterious 'Charles de Weissenstein,'" 66n10.

34. Urban, *The Gentlemen's Magazine*, 176.

35. York, "Benjamin Franklin, the Mysterious 'Charles de Weissenstein,'", 67-68n20.

records of what Jennings-Clerke looked like or how tall he was, so was unable to corroborate the description in the police report. He would have been fifty-five or fifty-six years old at the time, significantly older than the police estimate of thirty-six to forty. His father was also an MP and though he had no service in a foreign land his father-in-law, Charles Thompson, was a member of His Majesty's Council in Jamaica until 1711.[36]

Jennings-Clerke opposed the war, stating in Parliament in late 1777:

> Having constantly opposed the American war from the commence-ment of it as thinking it might and ought to have been avoided, and for other reasons which I have frequently offered in this House . . . it will not be wondered at that I should now refuse to give my assent to those parts of the Address which are to convey assurances to the Throne of our intentions to furnish means of prolonging and continuing the war.[37]

CLOSING THOUGHTS

The first question must be: Did this event occur? Despite the notation on the police report, the correspondence of Franklin and Adams and the diaries of the latter indicate that it did. Yet they never reported it to Congress, meaning that if it was real, Adams and Franklin didn't take it very seriously. The letter writer's arrogant comments regarding both the recognition of American independence and the alliance with France rendered it unworthy of serious consideration and rendered moot both the questions of who wrote the proposal and whether any serious action should be taken. Jennings-Clerke, assuming he was "de Weissenstein," was a ten-year MP and member of the King's guard and thus a person of some standing. Was he acting on his own or in an of-ficial capacity and, if the latter, at whose behest? Franklin professed to have thought the letter had the King's fingerprints on it; perhaps the Carlisle Commission was the public channel to the Franklin back-channel? Being in France, Franklin would offer much quicker return communication, but given his poor relationship with the crown, would

36. *Calendar of State Papers, Colonial, British and the West Indies*: Volume 25, 1710-1711, 351-361, Originally published by His Majesty's Stationery Office, London, 1924, British History Online, www.british-history.ac.uk/cal-state-papers/colonial/america-west-indies/vol25/pp351-361, accessed March 25, 2018.

37. The History of Parliament website, www.historyofparliamentonline.org/volume/1754-1790/member/jennings-philip-1722-88#footnote6_pqo9q64, accessed March 25, 2018. Original source is John Almon, a bookseller and pamphleteer in this period who published registers of parliamentary sessions.

the King even try to negotiate with him? The instructions to the Carlisle Commission authorized them to make concessions like some of those in the de Weissenstein proposals, though, significantly, two of the major items, establishment of an American peerage and disposing of the French treaty, were not mentioned[38] (the latter perhaps because the treaty was agreed to just before the Commission's departure to America).

In my opinion, the King would not attempt to treat with Franklin at this point (although a subsequent ministry under him would do so under different circumstances in 1783),[39] so Jennings-Clerke was either acting on his own or on the orders of a lower level authority. Does all this make the whole affair irrelevant? In some ways perhaps, but it is one of the more colorful demonstrations of the British regime's continued resistance when it came to American independence, even in light of military defeats and the Franco-American alliance. Additionally, the proposal of an American peerage demonstrates a serious misunderstanding of the American mind. This blindness as it pertained to American motives, and the hard line taken by the British throughout the revolution, provides good insight into the causes of the British loss of the American colonies.

38. Morrison., *Sources and Documents Illustrating*, based on my review of Commission instructions on pages 176-203.
39. Stauber, *The American Revolution*, 196.

China and the American Revolution

❧ SIMON HILL ❧

Historians are aware that imperial China had ties to the American Revolution. Indeed, James Fichter wrote that "tea, though an Asian commodity, helped bring about American independence." Tea, which was shipped from China into Britain and then re-exported to Britain's American colonies, formed part of Britain's controversial taxation agenda for the said colonies during the 1760s and 1770s. Therefore, this commodity was often ridiculed by the colonists. Fichter also commented on how, post-1783, the newly independent United States developed trading relations with China (beforehand they had been largely prevented from doing so by Britain's regulatory Navigation Acts).[1] In due course, these American merchants proved formidable commercial rivals to their European counterparts trading in the East. The impact of the American War (1775-1783) upon British commerce at the Chinese port of Canton has also been studied.[2]

China's ties to the American Revolution and War of Independence often remains over-looked in textbooks and popular histories of the subject. These publications mention how the war gradually escalated between 1777 and 1780 to include the French, Spanish and Dutch as belligerents against Britain. Henceforth, this clash of European empires generated a "war beyond America" reaching the West Indies, Africa and India.[3] Yet China—one of the most powerful nations during the

1. James R. Fichter, *So Great a Proffit: How the East Indies Trade Transformed Anglo-American Capitalism* (Cambridge, MA: Harvard University Press, 2010), 7.
2. Patrick Tuck, ed., *Britain and the China Trade 1635-1842 Volume 2: The Chronicles of the East India Company Trading to China 1635-1834 by H.B Morse* (London: Routledge, 2000), 1-93 and Earl Hampton Pritchard, *The Crucial Years of Early Anglo-Chinese Relations 1750-1800* (New York: Octagon, 1970), 147, 187, 190, 193, 212-30.
3. Francis D. Cogliano, *Revolutionary America 1763-1815: A Political History* (London: Routledge, 1999), 31-44, 46-8, 92, and Stephen Conway, *The War of American Independence 1775-1783* (London: Arnold, 1995), 133-58.

eighteenth century—is rarely incorporated into these texts. Highlighting China's ties to the origins of the American Revolution, analysing how the war affected British trade at Canton, and determining what the consequences were for the Eastern trades after 1783, further develops the view that the American Revolution had global implications.

CHINESE TEA: A CONTRIBUTOR TO REVOLUTION

The English (later British) East India Company had traded with China since the seventeenth century, and enjoyed the monopoly of British trading interests with the East. By the eighteenth century Bengal in India was the Company's primary trading destination, and, because of their relative geographical proximities, the southern Chinese port of Canton and Bengal became economically aligned. Canton also became the only Chinese port open to European commerce by the 1760s. Hence East India Company (EIC) ships sailed between both destinations, and the Company also chartered private vessels under special licenses between India and China (the country trade). Goods and manufactures from British vessels sent to China were used to purchase Chinese silk and tea, which in turn were exported back to Britain. From the Chinese perspective, thirteen commercial firms (Hongs) were the sole legitimate agents of trade with the Western nations transacting business at Canton. At various times these Hongs had formed a guild (Cohong) to strengthen their positions. This guild had been disbanded in 1771, but was later resurrected in 1782 and lasted until 1842.[4]

By the 1760s the EIC was facing mounting financial difficulties. This was partially caused by the organisation's gradual transformation from being a trading company to a military-territorial power with considerable interests in India. Henceforth, Westminster passed several pieces of legislation designed to improve the Company's affairs—admittedly with mixed results.[5] In the words of one historian, "Tea lay at the heart of all these problems." Goods that the Company exported from Bengal were rarely in sufficient demand in China. This prevented the profits from these sales in China from being used to purchase larger amounts of tea. To counteract this, the Company shipped bullion to China—which succeeded in increasing the amount of Chinese tea

4. Immanuel C.Y. Hsu, *The Rise of Modern China* (Oxford: Oxford University Press, 1995), 139-63.
5. H.V. Bowen, "British India 1765-1813: The Metropolitan Context," in *Oxford History of the British Empire Volume 2: The Eighteenth Century*, ed. P.J. Marshall (Oxford: Oxford University Press 1998), 530-50; H-Cheung and L.H. Mui, "Smuggling and the British Tea trade before 1784," *American Historical Review*, 74, 1 (1968), 44-73; and Philip Lawson, *The East India Company: A History* (London: Longman, 1993), 86-143.

being imported into Britain between 1768 and 1772. Regardless, this strategy would only prove effective in increasing EIC revenues if British domestic consumption of "legal" tea was boosted. Yet teas shipped into Britain on EIC vessels were subject to high duties, which in turn encouraged the smuggling of cheaper "illegal" tea from mainland Europe into the United Kingdom (mainland European nations imported Chinese tea, and this was not subject to high duties). In a bid to increase EIC revenues, some British duties on legal teas were removed during the late 1760s. Whilst British tea consumption grew between 1767 and 1768, the longer-term results were less promising. Between 1768 and 1772 there was no great increase in the amount of tea sold by the Company, and this commodity piled up in warehouses. The inability of the EIC to solve this predicament was due to continued importation of tea from Canton, smuggling of illegal teas, and problems in America.[6]

Although duties on tea had been reduced in Britain in 1767, an import duty was levied upon all tea shipped into Britain's North American colonies. This proved to be a contentious decision. In 1765 Westminster had introduced the Stamp Act, which levied duties on printed goods in America (London regarded this as a necessary step to ease budgetary pressures caused by the Seven Years War of 1756-1763). However, the colonists opposed the Stamp Act, claiming that it was "taxation without representation"—the settlers were not directly represented at Westminster. In due course Britain repealed these stamp duties, but the issue of raising revenue to fill Britain's financial blackhole did not disappear. During the later 1760s the Townshend programme introduced additional revenue-raising schemes in the colonies, and again this was not well received by the settlers. Thus, in 1770, these newer duties were repealed except for the one on tea (Britain sought to retain a symbolic statement of Parliamentary authority over America). The 1773 Tea Act also changed the way that this commodity was sold in the colonies, attempting to under-cut middlemen and thus making tea cheaper in America. Ironically, this re-opened the vexed question of taxation without representation.

Tea was disliked by many (though not all) colonists due to what it supposedly represented—taxation without representation and the corruption of monopoly, both of which were viewed as threats to political and economic freedom. The Sons of Liberty famously demonstrated their opposition to tea by dumping this commodity into Boston Harbour in 1773. In response, London closed Boston until compensation

---

6. H.V. Bowen, *Revenue and Reform: The Indian problem in British politics 1757-1773* (Cambridge: Cambridge University Press, 1991), 107-10, 121-5.

for the destroyed merchandise was paid. Tea encouraged further polar-
isation of opinions. Because of their criticism of the EIC, monopoly,
and tea, many American Patriots were drawn towards free trade. Conversely, drinking tea in the colonies symbolised one's loyalty to Britain.[7]
Combined, these factors accelerated the deterioration of Anglo-American relations—resulting in warfare in 1775. Thus, whilst the American
Revolution was caused by several factors, disputes over what Chinese
tea represented played a part.[8]

THE WAR BEYOND AMERICA

Initially, this military conflict was confined primarily to North America
and the Caribbean, and therefore did not spill over to Asia. However,
circumstances changed after 1777. That year British troops were defeated at Saratoga in upstate New York, which encouraged France to
ally itself with the American Rebels (Paris sought to avenge its defeat
at the hands of Britain during the Seven Years War). Then in 1779 and
1780, respectively, the Spanish and Dutch empires began fighting the
British. Madrid hoped to regain Gibraltar from Britain. Equally, London believed that the Netherlands was supplying the United States and
France with military equipment, and the Dutch were upset by British
seizures of their ships. This helped precipitate the Fourth Anglo-Dutch
War. Consequently, a conflict that had begun in North America now
escalated around the globe.

India—a territory long subject to European imperial rivalry—was
the first Asian country to be affected by such escalations. When conflict
erupted between Britain and France (America's ally) in 1777/1778, the
British EIC sought to take advantage of the situation on the subcon-
tinent. The Company's troops occupied French possessions in India,
such as Pondicherry. Circumstances intensified in 1780 when Haidar
Ali of Mysore (a French ally) attacked his pro-British rival the Nawab
of Carnatic. Haidar subsequently forced the British into embarrassing
retreats. Then in 1781 news of the Anglo-Dutch War reached India,
and several Dutch possessions (including Negapatam in India and
Trincomalee in Ceylon) fell to the British. Still, in 1782 the French
managed to re-take Trincomalee.

7. Fichter, *So Great a Proffit*, 7-30.
8. See Gwenda Morgan, *The Debate on the American Revolution* (Manchester: Manchester
University Press, 2007).

This expansion of the war affected maritime trading routes in the Indian Ocean and South China Sea. EIC vessels sailing between Atlantic and Eastern destinations (including Canton) had to traverse these war-zones. Shipping patterns necessarily changed as a result. If word spread that an enemy vessel was cruising near an intended destination, then other vessels altered course.[9] Inevitably, British shipping was captured. By 1781 the Dutch were posting vessels at the Cape of Good Hope (South Africa) to intercept British shipping returning from India and China. Any British vessels that were captured were conveyed to Dutch Batavia.[10] The British also went on the offensive, which included sending vessels on scouting missions into Asia waters, and unleashing privateers.[11]

By June 5, 1779, news of these developments had reached the British supercargoes—representatives responsible for overseeing cargo and its sale—at Canton. On that day they entered the fall of Pondicherry into their records.[12] Furthermore, by December these residents received a letter confirming the "commotions in Europe and America." Most significantly, the British at Canton realised that these escalations would directly threaten their business prospects. In 1779 the supercargoes wrote that the enemy had sent cruisers "chiefly into the tract of Chinese and eastern traders . . . for the capture of ships returning from China."[13] Unsurprisingly, Britons at Canton were much relieved to hear of the eventual restoration of peace. In summer 1783 Canton received "important intelligence" that the peace preliminaries between Britain, France, Spain and the United States had been signed at Versailles.[14] Amidst this backdrop, there is little evidence in surviving EIC records that the United States was directly involved in the eastern war. There is only a brief reference to American cargoes being found on a Spanish vessel that had been captured near Macao.[15] But certainly, a war that had originated in America catalysed other conflicts around the globe.

9. Canton Consultations, January 15, 1782, British Library (hereafter BL), India Office Records (hereafter IOR), IOR/G/12/73.
10. *Whitehall Evening Post*, July 28, 1781.
11. Canton Consultations, August 15, 1781, BL, IOR/G/12/72. Also see *Morning Chronicle and London Advertiser*, October 3, 1778.
12. Canton Consultations and Letter Book, June 5, 1779, BL, IOR/G/12/65.
13. Canton Consultations, December 18, 1779, BL, IOR/G/12/66.
14. Canton Consultations, July 16, 1783 and August 11, 1783, BL, IOR/G/12/77. The Dutch did not reach a peace settlement until 1784.
15. Canton Consultations, September 13, 1780, BL, IOR/G/12/70.

BRITISH TRADE AT CANTON

The arrival of war in eastern waters affected the long-standing trading relationship between Britain and China. Measurement of this economic activity is made challenging by considering a wide range of factors, including the number of vessels sailing to Canton, as well as the value of imports, exports, and profits. Figures annually fluctuated depending upon which criteria were being measured. Nevertheless, there were four general phases to British trade at Canton during the period of the American War. Firstly, there was a period of relative calm—one might even say growth. Secondly, whilst business continued there were emerging problems (including warfare). The result was both good and bad trading years. Thirdly, there was a clear decline in commerce towards the end of the war. Finally, in the post-war years British trade with Canton still oscillated but gradually recovered.

A range of figures illustrates this broad quadruple pattern, including the total value of exports from China by the EIC. This figure initially rose from 625,257 Taels (Chinese currency) to 1,486,677 Taels between 1774–75 and 1777–78, respectively. The second phase of mixed trade was demonstrated with a reduction to 1,031,278 Taels in 1779–80, and a good year with 2,026,042 Taels in 1780–81. The third phase of highly disrupted trade registered in 1782–83, with a much reduced value of 796,371 Taels. Finally, in the post-war period the total value of EIC exports from China improved to reach over 1 million Taels in 1783–84. Figures in Pound Sterling confirm the broad quadruple structure. The net profit of the EIC upon its China trade (above 4 per cent interest) was valued at £241,646 in 1775–76. The following year it had risen to £282,850. The second phase of mixed trade showed profits of over £344,000 in 1779–80, reducing to £130,074 profit for 1780-81. Profits then dropped significantly in 1781–82 to under £100,000. Figures from the post-war period varied, but reached a clear high of over £1,000,000 profit in 1784–85.[16] In terms of the number of EIC vessels arriving in China per year, it rose from five in 1775 to nine in 1777. A second phase of mixed figures witnessed a reduction back down to five arrivals in 1779, but an increase to twelve in 1780. 1782 heralded the start of the third phase with a major reduction back down to five vessels. Finally, in the post-war years there was a recovery to reach a new high of nineteen sailings in 1785.[17]

Qualitative evidence suggests a relatively benign trading environment in Canton at the start of the conflict. Indeed, when the American

16. Pritchard, *Crucial Years of Early Anglo-Chinese Relations*, 391-402.
17. Tuck, *Britain and the China Trade*, 436-9.

War commenced in 1775 it had little impact in Asia. Granted, at that time the British expressed some trepidation at the rumoured reintroduction of the Cohong—but this did not materialise until 1782. Henceforth, the British supercargoes at Canton essentially went about their business as usual. This involved dealing with matters such as tracking cargoes and preventing damage to merchandise. British records for China in 1776 also noted that the "books [were] being balanced."[18]

The second phase of mixed trade with profits and losses emerged during the later 1770s, and continued into the early 1780s. In 1777 a correspondence from Madras, India, to the supercargoes in Canton was optimistic: you "do not tell us you will be in want of any further assistance at present we trust the supplies now sent to you will be sufficient."[19] Additionally, there seems to have been positive shipping news. By October 1780 twelve British ships had already arrived at Canton, and more were expected that season. The same good fortune extended to private vessels: "The number of Ships from China belonging to the Country trade exceeded this year what they were . . . last . . . It has indeed been the good fortune of the merchants that they have suffered but little since the commencement of the war."[20] However, there were some problems during these years. In September 1779 the Canton supercargoes recorded that there were challenges in India (presumably the spread of warfare), and therefore Madras could not send supplies to Canton.[21] Consequently, there was less money for the British supercargoes at Canton to purchase Chinese goods for export. The most pressing problem for the British in China during the late 1770s and early 1780s was the outstanding debts owed to them by the Hong. The British attributed this partially to the end of the Cohong in 1771. Indeed, the termination of this association had encouraged individuals not previously involved in overseas trade to engage in this line of business, creating "several bad debts."[22] British residents also blamed these problems upon the "folly and vanity" of several Hong merchants, as well as to the "oppression" of the officials who sought revenue for their Emperor.

In late-1779 the British frigate *Sea Horse* arrived at Canton, for the first of two occasions, with orders to recover these bad debts. The

18. Canton Consultations, June 14, 1775, July 4, 1775, July 10, 1775, August 19, 1775 and January 29, 1776, BL, IOR/G/12/58.
19. Canton Letter Book, July 25, 1777, BL, IOR/G/12/60.
20. Canton Consultations, September 4, 1780 and October 29, 1780, BL, IOR/ G/12/70.
21. Canton Consultations, September 19, 1779, BL, IOR/G/12/65.
22. Canton Consultations, May 3, 1777, BL, IOR, G/12/60.

British supercargoes were horrified by this, fearing that Chinese officials would either not receive the ship's captain or that they would not
answer favourably. Therefore, the supercargoes tried to prevent the *Sea
Horse's* captain from delivering a letter of intent to the Hoppo (superintendent of maritime customs).[23] Ultimately, Beijing ruled that the
property of the offending Hongs be auctioned off with surpluses being
forwarded to the British as compensation.[24]

By the 1780s, a third phase associated with declining trade manifested itself. One factor behind this downturn was the eventual restoration of the Cohong guild in 1782. The British supercargoes now
complained that "Prices are very low comparatively to those which
might be obtained if it were not for . . . monopoly . . . this shows us as
in what a far worse Situation the Trade is at present than in the time
of any former monopoly."[25] But there were other factors at work too—
namely the expansion of the war. One of the fronts was the "War on
the two coasts" in India, involving British troops against Mysore and
the Marathas (the EIC had been engaged in conflict with the latter
since 1775). This situation adversely affected the British in China, as
British troops in India were consuming supplies originally intended for
Canton.[26] Hence the supercargoes in China had to endure a "want of
funds," which meant that they could not purchase goods and "the Company's Trade [was] in danger of great Embarrassment."[27]

Nor was the Dutch war well-received. Some British vessels were
sailing home from the East "totally unacquainted" with the outbreak
of these particular hostilities. Unsurprisingly, this "greatly alarmed . . .
English merchants."[28] At Canton itself there was a decrease in the
country trade, occasioned by the "great Expense and risk which attends
Navigation." This was a reference to the increased cost of maritime in-
surance during wartime. Equally, the British supercargoes at Canton
faced stiff competition from European powers that were neutral during
the American War. British supercargoes angrily noted that the Danes
and Swedes "will not fix Terms until we declare ours, that they may
take the advantage of offering a penny more, or four or six months
shorter period in their Bills."[29]

23. Canton Letter Book, September 19, 1779 and September 24, 1779, BL, IOR/G/12/68.
24. "The English Demand Payment of Debts Owed their Merchants," March 1780, in *A
Documentary Chronicle of Sino-Western Relations 1644-1820*, ed. Lo-Shu Fu (Tuscon: University of Arizona Press, 1966), 291-2.
25. Canton Consultations, October 20, 1781, BL, IOR/G/12/72.
26. Canton Consultations, May 18, 1783, BL, IOR/G/12/77.
27. Canton Consultations, October 31, 1781, BL, IOR/G/12/72.
28. *London Courant Westminster Chronicle and Daily Advertiser*, October 27, 1781.
29. Canton Consultations, October 24, 1781, BL, IOR/G/12/72.

The British response to this potentially disastrous situation was varied. One approach was to request additional convoy provision for vessels sailing to Canton. But in late 1781 British Adm. Richard Hughes refused to send his vessels to convoy Britain's China ships through the Straits of Malacca, fearing the risks of separating his squadron whilst confronting both the French and Dutch fleets.[30] The supercargoes also sought renewed financial assistance from India, but on November 2, 1782 the supercargoes acknowledged that virtually "no assistance can be expected from" India due to the war. So, the British supercargoes purchased Chinese items in bulk—but due to the absence of shipping these cargoes were "laying on hand to their great detriment." An indication of how precarious the situation had become was that the British were prepared to sell opium in China. Granted, British China merchants had sold this substance since the 1750s—but it was frowned upon by Chinese authorities.[31]

The fourth and final stage marked a gradual recovery in British trade with China during the post-war years. Granted, this did not happen smoothly. In 1784 British supercargoes lamented that the "situation [in Canton] is intolerable . . . The management of the European trade lies entirely in the mercenary hands of a company called the Con-hang. It is composed of ten interlopers."[32] There were also fears that the price of Chinese tea would fall due to the large stockpiles of the commodity in British and European warehouses. Therefore, the British Parliament passed the 1784 Commutation Act—which slashed duties on tea, and helped boost tea sales in Britain over the next few years.[33]

BRITISH INTERACTIONS WITH THEIR EUROPEAN RIVALS AND THE CHI-
NESE

Like the British, mainland European powers had traded with China prior to the American War. How did these nations interact with their commercial and military rivals at Canton during the war years? There were examples of cordial behaviour, such as the British supercargoes meeting their Danish, Swedish and Dutch counterparts to discuss debts.[34] But equally there were several instances of controversial be-

30. Canton Consultations, October 1, 1781, BL, IOR/G/12/72.
31. Canton Consultations, November 2, 1782 and November 25, 1782, BL, IOR/G/12/76. Also Paul Van Dyke, The *Canton Trade: Life and Enterprise on the China Coast 1700-1845* (Hong Kong: Hong Kong University Press, 2007), 121.
32. *Morning Herald and Daily Advertiser*, November 10, 1784.
33. H-Cheung and L.H. Mui, "William Pitt and the Enforcement of the Commutation Act 1784-1788," *English Historical Review*, 76, 300 (1961), 447-65. Also Pritchard, *Crucial Years of Early Anglo-Chinese Relations*, 146-51.
34. Canton Diary of the Chinese Debts, February 16, 1780, BL, IOR/G/12/68.

haviour. For example, in 1779 drunken British sailors insulted the French flag at Canton by cutting it down from the mast.[35] The British also clashed with the Dutch. After the commencement of the Anglo-Dutch War, in September 1781 the crew of a British country ship seized a Dutch vessel near Canton. A boarding party of fifteen men lowered the Dutch colors, and hoisted up the Union Jack.[36] Rarely did these events escalate much further, as the Chinese simply did not allow them to. During the September 1781 incident, the local authorities deployed troops to prevent the captured vessel from departing the port. The Chinese also warned that their "Emperor [Qianlong] will not suffer . . . bring[ing] war into his Dominions—and that whoever does so in future shall be treated as an enemy."

Often, the British supercargoes regarded these Chinese proclamations as empty threats.[37] After all, the Hong still needed to trade with foreign nations to supply gifts to the Emperor. Yet the British knew that they should not cross a certain line. If an incident involved the loss of life then the supercargoes feared a far harsher Chinese response. During another altercation between British and Dutch sailors in 1781, the former cut down a flag stand that almost fell into a factory, which might have resulted in several deaths. Fortunately, this did not happen and the British realised that they had been very lucky: "extremely bad consequences might have happened had any lives been lost."[38]

THE LONG-TERM IMPACT OF THE AMERICAN WAR IN THE EAST

By 1783 peace was restored, and the United States achieved its independence. American citizens were now free to openly trade with Asia. The following year the *Empress of China* became the first American vessel to reach Canton. As Fichter has pointed out, this "new U.S. commercial presence was greater, more sustained, and spread across more of the Indies than anything that had emanated from North America before." Yet, ironically, part of the reason for this successful American commercial expansion was that the former colonists worked with their former colonial masters. British and American traders in Asia were obviously competitors, but they also transacted business together.[39]

As for the British, despite the loss of the thirteen colonies their global empire remained largely intact in 1783. In some respects their Canton trade would improve during the post-war environment. The

35. *St. James's Chronicle or the British Evening Post*, September 4, 1779.
36. Canton Consultations, September 8-28, 1781, BL, IOR/G/12/72.
37. Canton Consultations, September 28, 1781 and August 21, 1781, BL, IOR/G/12/72.
38. Canton Consultations, December 29, 1781, BL, IOR/G/12/73.
39. Fichter, *So Great a Proffit*, 2-4.

reduction of duties as part of the 1784 Commutation Act increased British consumption of tea. Nevertheless, several problems remained. In reducing duties on tea, the Westminster government's revenue from the tea trade declined. Nor had the EIC's dire financial position improved during the hard-fought years of global warfare. Moreover, British traders in China faced several challenges as a result of the Versailles Treaty. The British were clearly concerned by the arrival of the Americans in Chinese waters: "several articles that are the products of their country [the United States] . . . sell for as much, if not more, than they will require for their returning cargoes . . . make no doubt that in seven or eight years hence they may send as many more, without draining their country of silver."[40] Nor was it just the emerging American presence in China that worried British traders. Writing of the Portuguese in Macao (who had been effectively neutral during the war): "The Trade of Macao is . . . greatly improved from the unavoidable advantages thrown their way by the Dutch War . . . [they are] the most happy for a lucrative commerce they have now purchased three large country ships for the Trade to Batavia and the Malay Ports from which the English ships must now be excluded."[41] Yet another problem for the British supercargoes at Canton was that they had not controlled all Britons in Chinese waters during the war. One such individual was Capt. John McClary of the country vessel *Dadaloy*. In May 1781 he seized an allegedly Spanish vessel that had departed Macao (this coincided with the war against Madrid). Then the owners of the captured vessel claimed that it was Portuguese, and hence ineligible as a prize. The Portuguese governor of Macao also demanded its return. This incident created a serious problem for the British supercargoes. On the one hand they sent their apologies to the Portuguese, but on the other they stressed that because the *Dadaloy* was a country vessel, "we do not Pretend any Power over Captain McClary." McClary continued to prowl Chinese waters, capturing a Dutch vessel later in the year. Predictably, the Dutch claimed that this was an illegal act in a neutral port such as Canton. The Chinese also wanted McClary restrained. Eventually, the vessel was returned to the Dutch (although McClary did not return all of the ship's contents).[42]

Evidently the British in Canton were dispirited: "in no part of the world . . . are English subjects . . . left so devoid of protection."[43] Thus,

---

40. *Whitehall Evening Post*, December 7, 1784.
41. Canton Consultations, December 20, 1781, BL, IOR/G/12/73.
42. Canton Consultations, May 20-June 1, 1781, August 21-29, 1781, BL, IOR/G/12/72.
43. Canton Consultations, January 22. 1782, BL, IOR/G/12/73.

in attempt to resolve these difficulties the British supercargoes sought to establish greater control over country ships—an issue that made progress in 1786 by way of parliamentary statute.[44] Moreover, the supercargoes considered using greater force in Canton. Fearing for their personal safety, on December 20, 1781 they wrote: "we are driven to Macao by the Chinese and cannot escape from it without mortification . . . should we . . . be imprisoned by the infatuation of the people of Macao & the Chinese refuse interfering; we know of no alternative but using the Force of our ships to release us: which is a predicament so highly unbecoming our situation, that we are extremely sorry . . . we should find ourselves in it."[45]

Of course, in the short-term there was no realistic prospect of the British successfully asserting more influence in China. In 1784 a gunner from the British vessel *Lady Hughes* fired a salute in Canton that accidentally killed some Chinese. The man went into hiding, and in a show of strength Chinese officials deployed troops and took a British hostage as leverage to force the supercargoes to hand over the gunner. These "uncommonly hard measures" lasted for several days, and in the end the hostage was released unharmed.[46] The gunner was also handed over to the Chinese, but was subsequently executed. Beijing used this incident to "discipline the foreigners."[47] In an attempt to strengthen their position in China, Britain also sent delegations to Beijing to discuss the prospect of establishing a diplomatic dialogue between both nations. The most famous of these, the 1793 Macartney Mission, produced little of substance. Instead, China's Qianlong Emperor asserted that "We [China] possess all things . . . and have no use for [Britain's] manufactures."[48] Thus, it would not be until well after the American Revolutionary War that Britain could assert greater influence in China. Owing to advances in Britain's Industrial Revolution and gradual Chinese dynastic decline (although imperial China would endure until 1911), Britain would defeat China during the 1839–1842 Opium War, and thereafter open several Chinese ports to British commerce.[49]

---

44. Pritchard, *Crucial Years of Early Anglo-Chinese Relations*, 224.

45. Canton Consultations, December 20, 1781, BL, IOR/G/12/73.

46. Canton Consultations, 9 December 1784, BL, IOR/G/12/79.

47. "Two Chinese Killed by an English Gunner," December 23, 1784 in *A Documentary Chronicle of Sino-Western Relations 1644-1820*, ed. Lo-Shu Fu (Tuscon: University of Arizona Press, 1966), 297-8.

48. See Robert Bickers, ed., *Ritual and Diplomacy: The Macartney Mission to China 1792-1794* (London: Wellsweep, 1993).

49. Peter Lowe, *Britain in the Far East: A Survey from 1819 to the Present* (London: Longmans, 1984), 8-18.

Allen McLane—Revolutionary War Intelligence Officer and Spy

࿓ KEN DAIGLER ࿓

There is often confusion in terms when discussing individuals involved in intelligence activities. For example, intelligence officers are often referred to as spies, and while this is occasionally the case, it is not the norm. A spy is an individual with access, through location, occupation or relationship, to information of value regarding an adversary. In most cases the intelligence officer is the person who recruits and directs the activities of spies. During the Revolutionary War the term "intelligence officer" wasn't used, but military officers did perform that role. Allen McLane was a rare individual who, during the course of his service in the Continental Army, functioned both as an intelligence officer and as a spy.

McLane joined Caesar Rodney's Delaware militia battalion as a lieutenant in September 1775, and his unit was involved in heavy combat during the army's retreat from Long Island and New York City. He was also involved in the successful attacks on Trenton and Princeton. He was promoted to the rank of Continental Army captain in January 1777.[1] Shortly thereafter, McLane returned to Delaware and raised a mounted company which would operate as an independent scouting and reconnaissance unit for Washington.

McLane's first documented involvement in intelligence collection against the British began in early 1777 when Gen. Thomas Mifflin, at the orders of Washington, began to establish an intelligence collection capability in the Philadelphia area. After the disastrous New York campaign, Washington recognized that intelligence collection was as nec-

---

1. George Washington to Allan McLane, December 31, 1781, Founders Online, National Archives, founders.archives.gov/documents/Washington/99-01-02-07612, accessed December 21, 2013.

essary for the army's survival as his equally pressing logistical and man-power problems. He also recognized that Philadelphia, the de facto colonial capital and home of the Continental Congress, would be a target of the British forces and he did not want to be ignorant of their activities there as he had been in the New York campaign.

McLane's intelligence activities were both overt and covert. His unit's military role to scout British defensive positions and remain alert to any British offensive movement represented his overt role. It also provided cover for his debriefing of human sources to report on British activities. In a letter from Washington to McLane dated March 28, 1777, he was told "I therefore depend upon your keeping a very good look out upon their line, and gaining every intelligence from people coming out of town."[2] At this point, McLane was only involved in debriefing people, but as Washington wanted more detailed information that would soon change.

After the British victory at the Battle of Brandywine, which Washington admitted was partially due to poor intelligence on his part,[3] in a letter dated on October 29 he sent McLane a detailed list of information he hoped to receive.

1st What number of troops supposed to be in Genl Howe's Army, and how disposed of?
2nd What works thrown up in and about the City, & what cannon in them?
3rd Have any detachments been made over to Jersey, & for what purpose?
4th How many men have they sent over there, & how many pieces of cannon?
5th What kind of cannon, whether field pieces or larger cannon?
6th What preparations are they making on the water, are they fitting out Ships, Gallies, fire rafts, or floating batteries?
7th Do they think they can stay in Philadelphia, if their shipping cannot pass the forts?
8th Are they resolved to make any farther attempts on both the Forts or either of them, and in what way, whether by storm or siege?
9th Can you discover whether they will attempt anything against the Forts and where? Observe carefully the preparations making on the river, and along the wharves, it is of great importance to know the time or near it.

2. Washington to McLane, March 28, 1777, *The Writings of George Washington from the Original Manuscript Sources*, Library of Congress, Vol. 7: 327.
3. Washington to the Continental Congress, September 11, 1777, George Washington Papers, Revolutionary War Series, Vol. 9:207.

10th Is there any talk of leaving Philada and by what route, observe carefully what they are doing with their wagons, whether their baggage is packed up, and in what directions their wagons receive?

11th Are the Tories, and friends of the British Army, under much apprehensions of their leaving Town, and what preparations are they making to remove themselves, or their effects?

12th For what purpose is it understood, the bridge is thrown over the middle ferry, and what force is kept on the West side of the Schuylkill?

13th Has the bridge been injured by the late storm, or is it passable?

14th Where are the Grenadiers, Light Infantry, and Rangers, and are they making any preparations to move?

15th What number of men are sent over to Carpenters, and province Islands, and how often are they relieved?

16th In what condition are those banks since the late rain-Can wagons and Carriages pass, so as to transport provisions and Stores from the Ships to the Town?

17th In what conditions are the Troops for provisions, and in what articles is there the greatest scarcity?

18th How are the Inhabitants situated for provisions?

19th What impression has the new of Genl Burgoyne's surrender made on the British Army?

20th Is there any conversation in the British Army, or among the Inhabitants, of Genl Howe's coming out to meet Genl Washington?

21st What is the British Army now employed about? Note carefully the prices of every thing.

22nd Does continental money rise or fall in value, in the Town?

23rd Can you learn whether there are any preparations making or any intentions to go up the Delaware, to burn the Frigates & Vessels there?

24th Find out what duty the Soldiers do, and whether they are contented, How many nights in the week, are they in bed?

25th Enquire particularly into the treatment of the prisoners, in the new Goal, so that if necessary you make oath of it!

26th Do they compel any to enlist by starving or otherwise ill treating them?

27th Find out how far the redoubts between Delaware and Schuylkill are apart, and whether there are lines, or abattis between the redoubts.[4]

Considering the broad scope of information Washington wanted it was obvious to McLane that regular scouting activities alone would not be sufficient. He would need reporting from people specifically tasked

4. Questions for Capt. Allen McLane, October 29, 1777, Founders Online, National Archives, founders.archives.gov/documents/Washington/03-12-02-0043, accessed December 21, 2013.

to seek out this information from observations within the city and by conversations with British officials, military personnel and local Tories. He began to identify individuals who could fulfill such roles and how to motivate them to do so.

In late November, Washington responded to a request from McLane asking permission to pay certain individuals to spy for him:

> I have this moment received your Letter containing the Proposals of some of the Inhabitants near the Enemys Lines—I will undoubtedly accept their Offers of Service provided they give in a list of their names, and engage to be under the absolute command for the time specified of such Officer as I shall appoint—this precaution is necessary, for otherwise they may receive the Public Money without preforming the Duty expected of them.[5]

A few days later, on November 28, Washington alerted McLane to the possibility of a British attack, and asked him specifically to obtain intelligence on British plans and intentions:

> I have certain information that Lord Cornwallis returned from Jersy Yesterday, and 'tis said they intent an Attack upon the Army with their Joint Force before Genl Greene can rejoin us. I therefore depend upon your keeping a very good look out upon their line, and gaining every intelligence from people coming out of town, that I may have the earliest Notice of their Movements or Intentions.[6]

In early December, McLane was able to provide intelligence, confirming information from other sources, that gave Washington advanced notice of the British movement towards the army's position at Whitemarsh, Pennsylvania.[7] This reporting allowed Washington to prepare the Continental Army for what he hoped would be a set-piece battle similar to Bunker Hill, at which he could defeat the British or at least burden them with heavy causalities. After several days of clashes, however, General Howe withdrew to Philadelphia, and the Continental Army marched to their winter quarters at Valley Forge.

During early 1778 it became apparent that the British might evacuate Philadelphia and McLane watched closely for any such indications of enemy movement. By early May, Washington expected the British to move soon, and McLane was instructed to increase his debriefings

5. Washington to McLane, November 22, 1777, Founder Online, National Archives, founders.archives.gov/documents/Washington/03-12-02, accessed December 21, 2013.
6. Washington to McLane, November 28, 1777, The Writings of George Washington, Vol. 10:118.
7. Allen McLane Papers, BV McLane, MS1817, New-York Historical Society.

of persons entering or departing the city. He was to report all intelligence obtained and the time he obtained it. He was also instructed to send daily reports of this information to Washington very morning.[8]

Later that month Washington sent General Lafayette to Barren Hill, near Whitemarsh, to observe British activities and their defensive lines. This was an exposed position, and he was accompanied by only a small force. When the British learned of his forward location a plan was formulated to try and capture him. Considering Lafayette's close relationship to the French monarchy, his capture would be a serious diplomatic blow to the newly formalized French-American alliance. Once again, McLane was able to identify British preparations and learn their objective, and warned Lafayette in time for him to escape capture.[9]

As the British departed Philadelphia on June 18, 1778, McLane led a small party into the city to confirm their departure. He captured several British officers who dallied with their local female companions a bit too long.[10] It is also probable that Washington selected McLane as the first officer to enter the city because of the need to protect American intelligence operatives who had reported on British plans and activities through close association with them. Unless protected, these individuals would become targets of revenge for their "cooperation with the enemy" by local patriots who would not have known of their intelligence activities for the American cause.

In the following year McLane was involved, as a soldier, an intelligence officer and a spy, in two battles, Stony Point and Paulus Hook. At Stony Point in July 1779, Washington ordered Gen. Anthony Wayne to attack the British position on the west side of the Hudson River. As the British post appeared to be well defended, Washington suggested Wayne conduct a detailed reconnaissance of the position with the help of Continental engineering officers. He further suggested that even better intelligence could be obtained if a man could be sent into the position to personally observe the force and its situation. McLane agreed to play the role of a rather simple-minded relative of a local woman who had been given permission to visit Stony Point to see her son, who had recently defected to the British from a local militia unit. While the mother spoke with her son, McLane wandered about the post, noting defensive positions, numbers of troops and the garrison's

8. Alexander Clough to McLane, May 1778, Orders, image 756, memory.loc.gov.ammem/mgwquery.html, accessed August 3, 2014.
9. Allen McLane Papers.
10. Edward G. Lengel, *General George Washington: A Military Life* (New York: Random House, 2005), 291-292.

security procedures at night.[11] When he returned to Wayne's headquarters, the general combined McLane's information with the engineering officers' observations of the terrain and defensive works, and formulated a plan for a night bayonet assault by way of a shallow area of the river. The surprise attack was successful, resulting in the capture of most of the British garrison with only a few American causalities.

The next month, on August 16, Major Henry "Light Horse Harry" Lee sent McLane to reconnoiter the British fort at Paulus Hook, New Jersey. The fort served as a base for British and Loyalist raids into New Jersey and thus was a constant irritation to American forces. While observing activities at the fort, and its defenses, McLane was able to capture two British soldiers. His comprehensive debriefing of these men, combined with his personal observations of the fort, provided valuable intelligence that assisted Lee in planning a successful attack in the early hours of August 19.[12] American losses were minimal, while the enemy suffered numerous causalities and over one hundred and fifty prisoners were captured.

In the fall of 1781 Washington sent McLane to the New York City area to meet with a spy connected with the Culper Ring, the large and sophisticated American collection effort centered in the region. This was a very important agent, the Tory printer James Rivington, who had social and business access to senior British officials and military officers in the city. Details of McLane's actions with Rivington have not been uncovered, but it is known that McLane received from Rivington the British naval signal book, which contained the code used by the British fleet to coordinate its movements. How, when and from whom Rivington obtained the book remains unknown. The book was subsequently provided to the French Fleet operating to keep the British bottled up at Yorktown.[13] The book may have provided information of value to the French.

McLane resigned from the army later that year, and at the end of the year Washington, in a December 31 letter, wrote, "I can testify that he distinguished himself highly as a brave and enterprising partiz[an]."[14] Typical of Washington's practice of not recording specifics of intelligence activities, he made no mention of McLane's contributions in the intelligence field.

11. Allen McLane Papers, entry dated July 2, 1779.
12. Allen McLane Papers, entry dated August 16, 1779.
13. Allen McLane Papers.
14. Washington to McLane, December 31, 1781, Founders Online, National Archives, founders.archives.gov/documents/Washington/99-01-02-07612, accessed December 21, 2013.

Elias Boudinot IV: America's First Commissary General of Prisoners

JOSEPH WROBLEWSKI

"The prisoner of war is one of the most tragic figures in any conflict."
—Larry G. Bowman[1]

Various studies have placed the number of Americans taken prisoner during the American Revolution anywhere from 18,000 to 20,000, with 8,500 to 12,000 dying in captivity.[2] The harsh treatment of Americans taken by the British began after the Battle of Bunker Hill when twenty Americans out of the thirty-one taken captive were reported to have died in prison.[3] The Continental Congress's first action to deal with the problem of prisoners of war was on October 6, 1776 when it authorized each state to deal with prisoners taken in their state and to negotiate exchanges for its own citizens.[4]

On December 3, 1776, Gen. William Howe reported that during the New York and New Jersey Campaigns the British captured 4,430

1. Larry G. Bowman, *Captive Americans: Prisoners in the American Revolution* (Athens: Ohio University Press, 1976), 3. "One of three taken captive perished during the long struggle ...The 33 percent overall death rate was not to be in any of the nation's wars until the recent Korean Conflict." Richard H. Ammerman, *Treatment of American Prisoners in the Revolution*, NJ Historical Society, vol. 78, 1960, 257.
2. Howard Peckham, *Toll of Independence* (Chicago: University of Chicago, 1974), 130.
3. Bowman, *Captive Americans*, 6. For a good overview of fate of prisoners of war on both sides see: Gary Shattuck and Don N. Hagist, "10 Facts About Prisoners of War," *Journal of the American Revolution*, April 27, 2015.
4. Major General Henry G. Corbin and Raphael P. Thian, *Legislative History of the General Staff of the Army of the United States, 1775 to 1901* (Washington, DC: Government Printing Office, 1901), 639. Found at *books.google.com; Congressional Serial Set*. Also found at this site are all the resolves of Congress regarding the Commissary General of Prisoners, 1776–1782. It is interesting to note that Elisha Boudinot, Elias's younger brother, was appointed Commissary of Prisoners for New Jersey in December 1778.

American troops. He noted that he released about 2,000 enlisted men, mainly militia, telling them to return to their homes.[5] This still left him with 2,000 prisoners, to be held in what was an already overcrowded New York City. With no special prisoner of war camps, the prisoners were held in local jails, various warehouses, particularly sugarhouses, churches, and most infamously, the prison ships anchored in Wallabout Bay, Brooklyn. According to British custom, prisoners of war were allotted two-thirds the daily ration of a British soldier. The British did not feel responsible for supplying prisoners with any "amenities" such as clothing, bedding, firewood, etc.; these were to be provided by their own countrymen.[6]

Gen. George Washington called upon Congress to set up a centralized authority to deal with the handling of prisoners of war. On December 27, 1776 Congress authorized the establishment of the post of Commissary General of Prisoners. Washington's first choice for the position, Col. Clarence Cox, a quartermaster commissary with the Pennsylvania Militia, turned down the offer. Then on April 1, 1777 from his Morristown, New Jersey Headquarters, Washington sent the following letter:

> Sir, I am authorizd by Congress to appoint a Commissary of Prisoners … I intend to annex another duty to this Office; and that is, the procuring of Intelligence. The Gentleman ingaged in the department of Commissary of Prisoners will have as much leizure, and better oppertunities, than most other Officers in the Army, to obtain knowledge of the Enemys Situation—Motions—and (as far as may be) designs. Thus Sir, in concise terms, have I given you a sketch of the duties of, and my expectations from, a Commissary of Prisoners; and now, give me leave to ask, if you will accept the Appointment? With very great esteem and regard, I am—Sir Yr Most Obedt Servt. Go: Washington[7]

The letter was sent to Elias Boudinot IV, a leading lawyer and Whig politician from New Jersey. At first Boudinot, just as Colonel Cox, turned down the offer. But the Commander-in-Chief retorted with an impassioned plea: "That if men of character and influence would not come forward and join him in his exertions, all would be lost."[8]

---

5. Bowman, *Captive Americans*, 12.
6. Bowman, *Captive Americans*, 18.
7. George Washington to Elias Boudinot, April 1, 1777, *Founders Online*, National Archives, founders.archives.gov. Spelling as found in the original.
8. Ibid., fn. 3.

Boudinot then relented and became the Continental Army's first Commissary General of Prisoners.[9]

Elias Boudinot IV was descended from French Huguenots. His father (known as Elias III) was a silversmith who apprenticed in New York City, then went to the island of Antigua. There he married Catherine Williams and eventually moved to Philadelphia where on May 2, 1740 Elias IV was born. In 1753 the family relocated to Princeton, New Jersey where Elias III purchased a tavern, was named postmaster and occasionally practiced his silversmithing. Elias IV took up the study of law under the tutelage of Richard Stockton, who in 1757 married his sister Annis Boudinot.[10] In 1760, at the age of twenty, Boudinot was admitted to the Bar in New Jersey, then moved to Elizabethtown where he established what was to become a very successful law practice.[11] In 1762 Boudinot, who has been described as physically attractive, tall, handsome, elegant, eloquent and emotional, married Hannah Stockton, the sister of his mentor and brother-in-law Richard Stockton. With this marriage, Elias raised himself in colonial society and established lifelong contacts.[12]

Evidence of Boudinot's commitment to the Patriot cause was indicated in that he headed Essex County's Committee of Correspondence and was a delegate from Essex County to New Jersey's extralegal Provincial Congress. As late as April 1776, Elias opposed Independence and felt there still could be reconciliation with the Crown. He opposed Dr. John Witherspoon's call for New Jersey declaring its independence, and to Witherspoon's astonishment Boudinot's plea for restraint carried the day.[13] However, with the British arrival at New

9. On June 6, 1777 Congress confirmed Boudinot's appointment with the pay ($60 per month) and rations of a colonel, retroactive to May 15, 1777, although Boudinot accepted on April 15, 1777. See, *Legislative History of the General Staff of the Army of the United States, 1775 to 1901*, 639.

10. Richard Stockton was one of the five signers of the Declaration of Independence from New Jersey.

11. One of the oldest towns in New Jersey, today it is Elizabeth, New Jersey; while it is presently located in and the county seat of Union County, at the time of the American Revolution it was part of Essex County.

12. Donald W. Whisenhunt, *Elias Boudinot* (Trenton: New Jersey Historical Commission, 1975), 9-10.

13. Elias Boudinot, *The Life, Public Services, Addresses and Letters of Elias Boudinot, L.L.*, Jane J. Boudinot, ed. (Cambridge: The Riverside Press, 1896), 14-22, archives.org.

York Harbor in the June and July 1776, Boudinot became fully committed to the Patriot cause and to Independence.[14]

When Elias Boudinot became the commissary of prisoners he faced a number of daunting tasks. His responsibilities included seeing that British and Hessian prisoners of war were securely housed and their physical needs taken care of until prisoner exchanges could be arranged. He also had to supplement the rations and basic amenities of Americans held by the British. Finally, in Washington's "job description" for the position, the commissary was to "procure intelligence," making him the head of a spy network.[15]

From the start, Elias Boudinot believed his tasks as commissary of prisoners were almost insurmountable. In his journal he noted:

> Soon after I had entered on my department, the applications of the Prisoners were so numerous and their distress so urgent, that I exerted every nerve to obtain supplies but in vain—Excepting £600 I had rec'd from the Secret Committee in Bills of Exchange, at my first entrance into the Office—I could not by any means get a single farthing more, except in Continental Money, which was of no avail in New York.[16]

Describing the dire situation to General Washington, Boudinot told him there was no way he could help the prisoners except by borrowing money on his personal credit and from friends, to which he said Washington replied,

> He greatly encouraged me to the attempt, promising me that if I finally met with any loss, he would divide it with me—On this I began to afford them some supplies of Provisions over and above what the Enemy afforded them, which was very small & very indifferent.[17]

To help perform his duties, Boudinot was at first allotted two deputies (rank of major, pay $50 per month); later this was increased to five and by the end of the war, there was a deputy in each state. One of the first people that Boudinot turned to was Lewis Pintard, a wealthy

---

14. When future Gov. William Livingston was named brigadier and commander of the East Jersey Militia he named Boudinot as an aide-de-camp. With the British in New York, Boudinot moved his family to a farm he owned in Basking Ridge, New Jersey; the town was also the home of William Alexander (Lord Stirling). Barbara L. Clark, *The Story of Elias Boudinot IV, his family, his friends and his country* (Philadelphia: Dorrance Press, 1977), 45.

15. The commissary of prisoners reported directly to George Washington and in Congress he answered to the Board of War and the Secret Committee.

16. Elias Boudinot, *Journal or Historical Record of American Events during the The Revolutionary War* (Philadelphia: Frederick Bourquin, 1894), 10.

17. Ibid.

Elias Boudinot, mezzotint, c. 1798. (*New York Public Library*)

New York merchant, to whom he happened to be related by marriage. Boudinot offered him a commission as one of his deputies but Pintard turned it down, stating that if he had any "official" status, General Howe would most likely refuse him permission to remain in New York City. Instead he acted as Boudinot's unofficial deputy or agent. For the rest of the war, Lewis Pintard did much to help the American prisoners of war held in New York.[18] On the British side, General Howe appointed a Loyalist from Massachusetts, Joshua Loring, their Commissary General of Prisoners.[19]

With the maneuvering and skirmishing that accompanied General Howe's decision to capture Philadelphia (the British entered the city unopposed on September 26. 1777) and then with the Battle of Germantown on October 4, 1777, the British had another 500 prisoners

18. Burrows, *Captive Americans*, 85-86. Also, see Joseph Lee Boyle, *"Their Distress is almost intolerable," The Elias Boudinot Letterbook 1777-1778"* (Westminster, MD: Stackpole Books, 2008), 4, 7, et.al. (check index for all correspondences from Boudinot to Pintard).
19. Joshua Loring's wife Elizabeth Lloyd, also from Massachusetts, has been characterized as the mistress of General Howe; while it has been accepted that she was Howe's mistress, there are no factual accounts of this relationship being more then companionship. Stephen Davidson, *The Redcoat and the Scarlet Woman: Part Two*, "Loyalist Trails" 2010-31: August 1, 2010.

of war who were held in Philadelphia.[20] To deal with these prisoners, Howe appointed a Philadelphia Loyalist, Henry Hugh Fergusson, as Deputy Commissary of Prisoners for Philadelphia. Ironically, Fergusson's wife Elizabeth Graeme, a noted poetess of the era, was a good friend of the Boudinots, especially with Elias's sister Annis, who in her own right was one of the leading poets of colonial and Revolutionary America.[21]

Elias Boudinot's term as commissary of prisoners was to reach a climax during the winter of 1777 and 1778.

In December 1777, the New Jersey Legislature elected him a representative to the Continental Congress. Due to proposed meetings with the British over the treatment of prisoners and with the difficulty in finding a replacement Commissary, he did not actually take his seat in Congress until July 1778.[22] While an elected member of Congress, Boudinot continued his duties as commissary of prisoners and before he resigned his commission, he oversaw significant actions to help improve the lot of American prisoners of war.

The first big change happened when General Howe moved his headquarters to Philadelphia. Gen. Sir Henry Clinton was left with command of the British and Hessian troops stationed in New York. He gave permission for Boudinot to enter New York City and meet American prisoners without restriction.[23] From February 3 to February 17, 1778, the American commissary of prisoners visited and interviewed prisoners of war. The first person he met with was Gen. Charles Lee, who had been held since December 1776; Lee was living in a pri-

20. George Adam Boyd, *Elias Boudinot: Patriot and Statesman 1740—1821* (New York: Greenwood Press Reprint, 1969), 40. While Colonel Boudinot was on Washington's staff and was usually with the General at his headquarters, he was not at Brandywine for it was reported that on September 7, 1777 outside of Wilmington, his horse tripped, he was thrown and supposedly was unconscious for seven hours. He went on sick leave back to New Jersey; returned to duty in late October.

21. Burrows, *Forgotten Patriots,* 121. For an interesting insight to Elizabeth Graeme and some of the consequences of marrying Fergusson, see Larry E. Tise, *The American Counterrevolution: A Retreat from Liberty, 1783-1800* (Mechanicsburg, PA: Stackpole Books, 1998), Chapter 10, 161-168.

22. Col. Francis Johnson, 5th Regiment, Pennsylvania Line, was offered the position, but turned down; it was then offered to Maj. John Beatty, 3rd Regiment, Pennsylvania Line, who did accept. Beatty was taken prisoner of war at the surrender of Fort Washington. Beatty served from May 1778 - April1780. Following John Beatty the other commissaries of prisoners were: Col. Joseph Ward (April 15, 1780) and Abraham Skinner (September 15, 1780).

23. Boyle, *Letterbook,* 52. While in New York City he stayed with his agent Lewis Pintard.

vate residence in the city and negotiations were underway for his exchange.[24]

Next he went to the New Jail, more commonly referred to as the Provost, where about thirty prominent prisoners both military and civilian were being held.[25] While at the Provost, he met with the notorious British Provost Marshal, William Cunningham to complain of the harsh treatment of the prisoners under his care. Supposedly, Cunningham did not deny the accusations, but rather boasted of his harsh treatment of the rebels.[26]

Also on his agenda were visits to the various sugarhouses and other places of confinement. One of the places where he found the prisoners in deep distress was the *Eglise du St. Esprit*, the Huguenot Church where his father had been baptized. There he found well over 300 prisoners who complained that they were so crowded that they all couldn't lay down at the same time. They stated that since October they were given no firewood and as a result they burned all the pews, doors and window frames. They had to "eat raw pork."[27]

After his visits to prisoners being held in New York City, he traveled to Long Island where some 235 officers were paroled and living in private residences. In these meetings, the officers reported that they were well treated. The one group of prisoners he was not allowed to meet with were those held on the prison ships. These prisoners were under the jurisdiction of the Royal Navy and Commodore William Hotham, the naval commander of New York, refused him permission. He noted, "There are 58 Officers and 62 SeaMen on board the Prison Ships, who suffer greatly and die daily."[28]

Before Boudinot left he met with Commissary Loring and other British officers. At this meeting they notified Boudinot that many of

24. General Lee was finally exchanged on April 21, 1778 for Gen. Richard Prescott.

25. The most prominent prisoner held at the Provost Jail at this time was Ethan Allen. The Provost was where Boudinot's brother-in-law, Richard Stockton, the only signer of the Declaration of Independence arrested by the British, was held for a month or two (December 1776 –January 1777). After Boudinot's complaint of the officers being held in "close confinement" in the Provost, Clinton agreed to parole them to Long Island.

26. William Cunningham, who is often referred to as "the notorious" Provost Marshal, served General Howe by running prisoner of war installations, first in New York City then in Philadelphia. For an overview of Cunningham's life see: *William Cunningham: The Provost Marshal*, accessgenealogy.com, July 15, 2011.

27. Boyd, *Elias Boudinot: Patriot and Statesman 1740—1821*, 59.

28. Most of the prisoners being held on the ships were privateers captured at sea. After Boudinot left New York, the Royal Navy gave Lewis Pintard permission to send these prisoners supplemental rations. David L. Sterling, *Prisoners of War in New York; A Report by Elias Boudinot*, William and Mary Quarterly, vol. 13, no. 3, July 1956, 376-392.

the American officers were in arrears of the $2/day board they were expected to pay for their upkeep while on parole.[29] Further, they threatened that unless this debt was paid, they would revoke the paroles and return the officers to either the prisoner compounds in the city or to the prison ships. To avoid this, Boudinot pledged to pay all of the officers' board debt back to December and to continue to pay the board in the future. One of the ways he planned to pay these expenses was for Americans to send flour and wheat to New York City where Pintard would sell it and the proceeds would be used to pay the prisoners expenses; the British agreed to this arrangement.[30]

To further insure that the prisoners' needs were seen to, Elias Boudinot's final action before he left New York was to borrow funds on his personal credit to "Furnish 300 officers with handsome suits of cloaths each and 1100 men a plain suit. Also, Blanketts, shirts, etc. and added to their provisions a full half day of Rations Bread and Beef per day for upwards to 15 months."[31]

While Boudinot was on his inspection of prisoner conditions in New York City, General Howe, on February 5, 1778, sent General Washington a proposal to hold a meeting to come up with an agreement for a general exchange of prisoners. In response, Washington sent a message to Boudinot that when he finished in New York he was to return to "Camp" (Valley Forge) and take part in these negotiations.

The negotiations began at Germantown on March 31, 1778, were adjourned and then resumed at Newtown, Bucks County, on April 6. These meetings lasted ten days. While both sides agreed on some items on the agenda, the main sticking point continued to be the implication that a formal prisoner cartel would have on the recognition of American Independence. Since neither side would give on this point, the result was once again a failure to reach an agreement. With the collapse of the negotiations, Boudinot left Valley Forge and went to Morristown where he believed he was undertaking his last mission as commissary of prisoners.

---

29. The sum of $2 per day board was agreed by both sides as what a paroled officer would be charged for his upkeep.
30. Boyle, *"Their Distress,"* 55.
31. William W. Attenbury, *Elias Boudinot: Reminiscences of the American Revolution*, Read before the Huguenot Society, February 15, 1894, 24, babel.hathitrust.org. Also see: Helen Jordan, "Colonel Elias Boudinot in New York City, February, 1778," *Pennsylvania Magazine of History and Biography* 24 (1900): 453–66. Online at: archive.org.

There he met Lt. Col. Archibald Campbell, a British officer on parole and slated to be exchanged.[32] With permission from the British, the pair went to New York City where Campbell was formally exchanged for Ethan Allen. While in New York, Boudinot arranged the exchange of seventy-five officers and fifty-nine privates. Upon completion of this mission and believing his resignation was effective as of May 11, 1778, he let General Washington know that he was getting his accounts in order; however, he was soon to learn that his service as commissary of prisoners was not yet at an end.

On May 23, 1778, Washington sent him a message to return to "Camp":

> This renders your immediate presence at Camp necessary; which I therefore request Col. Francis Johnson has been nominated to succeed you in your department; but he has not yet accepted the appointment. In any case, your presence and assistance are indispensable, as your successor could not be at once sufficiently acquainted with the state of the department to execute with propriety a matter of such extent and importance, as that which now calls for your attention; and indeed you ought to be sometime with him to communicate the necessary information concerning it, and put him in a train, because General Howe came up with a new proposal for a general exchange of prisoners.[33]

Boudinot did not arrive back at Valley Forge until June 5 and on the next day, both he and his replacement, Col. John Beatty, went to Germantown to meet with Commissary Loring. At this meeting, Loring officially informed them the British were evacuating Philadelphia and the new commander-in-chief, Sir Henry Clinton, would prefer to exchange the prisoners held in Philadelphia rather than send them by ship to New York. The one sticking point from the American point of view was that they felt it would be unfair to those prisoners in New York who were in captivity for a longer period of time. To this Loring stated the prisoners in Philadelphia might be paroled and the actual exchange based on seniority of captivity could be worked out at a latter date. On June 8, 1778, Boudinot agreed to the terms.[34]

---

32. Lt. Col. Archibald Campbell, of the 71st Highlanders, captured when his transport *George* mistakenly entered Boston Harbor, June 16, 1776. Following his exchange he took part of the capture of Savannah in 1779. He was appointed Governor of Jamaica, in 1782, then Governor of Madras from 1786-1789; he died in Scotland in 1791. See: J.L. Bell, boston1775.blogspot.com/2015/07/a-tolerable-cannonade-ensued.html, July 22, 2015. See also: Boyd, *Elias Boudinot: Patriot and Statesman*, 63.
33. Washington to Boudinot, May 23, 1778, *Founders Online: Letters.*
34. Boudinot to Washington, June 28, 1778, *Founders Online: Letters.*

By June 16, Boudinot had in his custody all the British prisoners being held in Reading and Easton, Pennsylvania, but there was a snag because most of the Hessians had been sent to Lancaster County where they were hired out to work on farms. Boudinot indicated that it would take more time to round up all of these men and a number of them did not wish to rejoin their regiments. By this time Boudinot was informed that the American prisoners had been boarded transports and the evacuation was to begin the next day. He was then informed that the British privates slated for exchange were to be forwarded to Staten Island. At this, Boudinot felt the British were acting in bad faith and the entire exchange was called off.[35]

Following the failure of this prisoner exchange and the British evacuation of Philadelphia, Elias Boudinot's time as commissary of prisoners came to an end. He took his seat in Congress, attending his first session on July 7, 1778. Boudinot reported in his journal that one of the reasons he accepted the position was George Washington's counseling him:

> I was chosen a member of Congress but continued in the army till June, when George Washington, knowing I was near $30,000 in advance for the prisoners, urged me to go and take my seat in Congress, where I might get some of the hard money received from General Burgoyne before it was all expended, for if it was once gone; I should be totally ruined.[36]

Upon taking his seat, one of the first things that Boudinot did was present to Congress his account of the money he forwarded for the care of the prisoners in New York from his personal credit. Congressmen Richard Henry Lee and William Duer, on the Account Committee, agreed to Boudinot's claim and ordered a warrant in the form of hard specie to the amount of $26,000 be issued to Boudinot. Before it was presented, however, Congressmen Francis Dana (Massachusetts) and Henry Marchant (Rhode Island) vehemently opposed this payment. They stated that "Mr. Boudinot had taken up this money at the instance of Gen'l Washington, without the approbation of Congress, he had no right to be paid but in Continental money as other Creditors of Congress."[37] Boudinot angrily replied that he borrowed the money

35. Ibid.
36. Boudinot, *Journal*, 68-69. Boudinot notes here how he formed a plan for General Burgoyne to pay for the upkeep of the Saratoga prisoners and in the beginning of 1778 Congress received $40,000 in "hard money."
37. Boudinot, *Journal*, 70.

on his own credit and he would go home, sell his property to meet his creditors' demands as far as it would go and then send word that there would be no more credit available for the care of the prisoners in New York from him.

After ten days he reported that he received word from New York that the misery of the prisoners was now increased, and he read the letter he received from his agent (most likely Pintard). Boudinot reported there was an emotional outcry from members, Congress then voted unanimously to approve a warrant for £10,000 specie, which he immediately forwarded to New York to resume caring for the American prisoners of war.[38] In August, after serving less than two months, Boudinot left Philadelphia and did not return to Congress. In New Jersey as a private citizen, he returned to his law practice and the restoring of his financial stability. His respite from public service only lasted until 1781.

The United States, now being governed by the Articles of Confederation, saw Elias Boudinot once again chosen as a representative from New Jersey. In 1782, he was elected by Congress as it President, which under the Articles was the closest position to a chief executive. In 1783, as President of the Congress, Boudinot led Congress when it met in Princeton (June–November) and the signing of the Treaty of Paris (September 3, 1783), which officially recognized American Independence.[39]

While Boudinot did not take part in the adopting of the United States Constitution, he favored it and was elected to the House of Representatives from New Jersey (1789 to 1795). From 1795 to 1805 he was the director of the United States Mint, his last public position. In retirement he turned to religion and was one of the founders and first President of the American Bible Society. Elias Boudinot died in 1821 and was interred at the St. Mary's Episcopal Church Cemetery, Bordentown, New Jersey.

---

38. Boudinot, *Reminiscences*, 24.

39. The move was because 300–400 Continental soldiers marched to Philadelphia and threatened Congress with violence if they didn't receive their back pay. When Boudinot's request for the Pennsylvania Militia to provide Congress protection was denied, they adjourned to Princeton. See: Boudinot, *The Life*, "Mutiny of Pennsylvania Troops," 329-30.

Compelled to Row: Blacks on Royal Navy Galleys during the American Revolution

❦ CHARLES R. FOY ❦

For many persons, their only knowledge of galleys and the men who rowed them comes from movies set in ancient times such as *Ben-Hur*. Suffice it to say, depictions of galleys and their crews in movies are often historically inaccurate. It would come as a surprise to most that galleys were used by both sides during the American Revolution, as there is a noticeable paucity of scholarship on Royal Navy galleys during the war.[1] Given that galleys were small, typically having crews of thirty to forty men, rarely played central roles in important naval battles, and were either sold or broken up by 1786, this lack of academic interest is not unexpected. An analysis of the role of Blacks on British naval galleys during the American Revolution shows that the Royal Navy was "brutally pragmatic" in how it employed men of African ancestry and demonstrates that, in their treatment of Blacks, officers of galleys generally adhered to customs of the regions in which they served.[2]

USE OF GALLEYS

At the start of the American Revolution American Rebels lacked a standing navy. Although they were ultimately successful in building a small fleet of frigates, Rebel naval forces were predominately shallow-

---

1. For example, there is no discussion of British eighteenth century naval galleys in N.A.M. Rodgers' *The Command of the Ocean: A Naval History of Britain, 1649-1815* (New York: W.W. Norton, 2005).
2. Simon Schama, *Rough Crossings: Britain, the Slaves and the Atlantic Revolution* (New York: HarperCollins, 2006), 13 and 168; Charles R. Foy, "The Royal Navy's Employment of Black Mariners and Maritime Workers, 1754-1783," *International Maritime History Journal*, 28, no. 1 (Feb. 2016), 6-35.

draft vessels such as whaling boats, barges, and galleys.[3] The American galleys had considerable success in shallow waters with commanders using knowledge of local waters to capture larger British ships, as did Capt. Ebenzeer Dayton, when in April 1778 his three armed galleys captured the British sloops *Fanny* and *Endeavour* in New York's Great South Bay. More impressively, in October 1776, Benedict Arnold's deft employment of row galleys in his small flotilla of vessels on Lake Champlain was critical in his ability to fight Gen. Guy Carelton's far larger fleet of twenty-five armed ships, four hundred bateaux, and numerous Native American canoes.[4]

Although British men-of-war ships enabled the movement of tens of thousands of troops and the capture of major cities, vessels that could maneuver in North America's coastal waters were needed to compete with American shallow-draft vessels. Whaleboats, barges, and galleys were regularly used by British forces in North American waters to conduct raids and attack American positions.[5] Even in major campaigns, such as the 1778 capture of Philadelphia, galleys and barges played a critical role in clearing inland waters, in this case the Delaware River, to permit the movement of larger men-of-war.

Particularly during its campaigns in the Carolinas and Georgia (1776–1783), the Royal Navy relied upon galleys. Ironically, Royal Navy galleys were captured from American forces or purchased from private sellers, not built at the Royal dockyard in New York. Obtaining galleys was critical for the Royal Navy as American forces were said to have "very considerable Armed Naval Forces" built expressly for the purpose of "protecting and defending" southern lakes, rivers, and inlets.[6] To counter Americans' local knowledge of shallow coastal waters the Royal Navy recruited Blacks, enslaved and free, to maintain, crew, and pilot the galleys. In doing so, the navy understood that in the Americas prior to the Revolution, enslaved Blacks regularly rowed barges and galleys, and could do so for the King. The four Blacks whom Rhode Islander John Brown hired for "8 days rowing the Barge" were unremarkable in

3. The Continental navy only had thirteen ships, all of which were by 1778 out of commission.

4. *Naval Documents of the American Revolution* ("*NDAR*") (Washington, DC: Government Printing Office, 1962-), 5:1 and 6:1237.

5. George E. Buker and Richard Apley Martin, "Governor Tonyn's Brown-Water Navy: East Florida during the American Revolution, 1775-1778," *The Florida Historical Quarterly* 58, No. 1 (Jul. 1979), 58-71.

6. Prescott to Lord Cornwallis, Nov. 22, 1779, Cornwallis Papers, PRO 30/55/20/41, The National Archives, Kew, England (TNA); Georgia Executive Council, Apr. 3, 1778, *NDAR* 12:28-29.

that it was common for Blacks to do such work in the Western Atlantic.[7]

NATURE OF GALLEY CREWS

Black maritime workers were crucial in order for galleys to operate. Enslaved maritime artisans worked regularly to keep Royal Navy galleys in waters off the Carolinas, Georgia, and Florida in working condition. For example, in October 1780 Paul Pritchard hired fourteen Black carpenters and caulkers to the Royal Navy to refit HM Galley *Adder* at Hobcaw, South Carolina. Similarly, the Navy relied upon enslaved maritime artificers, men like Punch and Lewis, to keep HM Galley *Arbuthnot* and their other galleys in the southern North American waters sea-worthy.[8] Earlier in 1780 twenty-seven enslaved caulkers and shipwrights, including Tom, Dennison Sam, Punch, Cork and twenty-two other Black artisans, entered onto HM Galley *Scourge* at Hobcaw to repair the vessel. The Royal Navy utilized enslaved carpenters, caulkers, and shipwrights not only in the Carolinas and Georgia, but in St. Augustine, Florida, as well. In its considerable use of enslaved artisans to maintain its galleys the Royal Navy was, as it had been in the Caribbean throughout the eighteenth century, reliant upon Black labor to keep its vessels afloat.[9]

Black pilots were also critical to Royal Navy galleys' operations. Pilots occupied a singular place in maritime hierarchy by controlling ships despite not being officers. By doing so, they inverted the usual American white–Black social hierarchy and were threatening to white naval officers. Despite this threatening inversion of social conventions, Black pilots operated throughout the western Atlantic, steering valuable merchant ships, boats, and Royal Navy men-of-war through dangerous shallow waters. Naval officials and other whites accepted this inversion of established racial hierarchy because pilots of African ancestry had particular knowledge of American waters and navigational skills that made them, in the words of one British official, "capable of Conducting the Fleet safe." Their service in the Royal Navy included directing its galleys in North American waters. For example, between 1779 and

7. John Brown Papers, Historical Society of Pennsylvania, AM 8180, p. 12.
8. HM Galley *Adder* Muster, 1780-1782, ADM 36/10384, TNA. When and where the Royal Navy employed enslaved maritime artisans was largely a function of local customs, environmental conditions and whether white artisans were available. Foy, "The Royal Navy's Employment of Black Mariners and Maritime Workers, 1754-1783," 6-35.
9. HM Galley *Scourge* Muster, 1779-1780, ADM 36/10427, TNA; HM Galley *Arburthnot* Muster, 1783, ADM 36/10426, TNA; Foy, "The Royal Navy's Employment of Black Mariners and Maritime Workers, 1754-1783," 24-25.

1788 there were not less than five Black pilots—Webster, Jermmy, Johannes, Dublin, and Boomery—aboard HM Galley *Scourge* as it operated along the southeast coast of North America. Similarly, in 1781 a "Negro Man named Trap" was hired onto HM Galley *Fire Fly* to serve as its pilot in Georgian waters. Black pilots directing the operation of the King's galleys was an exception to the usual circumstance in the Royal Navy, i.e., that Blacks rarely obtained officer status or positions of authority.[10]

Other European navies often employed slaves, seamen who failed to appear for compulsory naval duty, religious dissenters, and captured enemy seamen to row their galleys. Enslaved men could be regularly found working on French, Spanish, or Portuguese galleys. Maritime historians traditionally associate service on galleys with marginalized peoples, not something most think of when considering the lives of seamen of the Georgian Royal Navy. Instead, as N. A. M. Rodger noted about the medieval Royal Navy, most historians have believed Royal Navy oarsmen were "not slaves but free men." But in fact, slaves did work on Royal Navy galleys during the American Revolution. Fewer than five percent of all Royal Navy crewmen on the North American coast during the American Revolution were Black, but there were more than twice as many Blacks on Royal Navy galleys in the waters off Georgia, the Carolinas, and Florida—12.3 percent of such crews.[11]

Why did Blacks work on Royal Navy galleys during the American Revolution at twice the rate they worked on other Royal Navy vessels? A review of galley musters and related documents indicates three reasons for this: the hiring out of slaves to the Royal Navy by Loyalists; impressment of free black seamen by galley commanders; and fugitive slaves seeking freedom.

10. Kevin Dawson, "Enslaved Ship Pilots in the Age of Revolutions: Challenging notions of race and slavery between the boundaries of land and sea," *Journal of Social History*, 47, no. 1 (Fall 2013), 71-72; HM Galley *Scourge* Muster, 1779-1780, ADM 36/10427, TNA; John Gambier to Sir George Pocock, March 30, 1762, ADM 1/237, f. 51, TNA; Douglas Hamilton, "'A most active, enterprising officer': Captain John Perkins, the Royal Navy and the boundaries of slavery and liberty in the Caribbean," *Slavery & Abolition* (May 2017), 2; Foy, "The Royal Navy's Employment of Black Mariners and Maritime Workers, 1754-1783," 15-16.

11. Jean Martielhe, *The Huguenot Galley Slaves* (New York, 1867), Chap. 6; *London Evening Post*, Oct. 7, 1741; Carla Rahn Phillips, "The Life Blood of the Navy': Recruiting Sailors in Eighteenth Century Spain," *Mariner's Mirror*, 87 no. 4 (2001), 421; Mariana Candido, "Different Slave Journeys: Enslaved African Seamen on Board of Portuguese Ships, c. 1760 1820s," *Slavery & Abolition*, 31, no. 3 (Sept. 2010), 399; N. A. M. Rodger, *The Safeguard of the Sea: A Naval History of Britain, 660-1649* (New York: W. W. Norton, 1999).

With the turbulence of war disrupting the slave economies of Georgia and the Carolinas and large numbers of slaves running away to take advantage of freedom offered them pursuant to Dunmore's Proclamation, Loyalist slave owners sought certainty and profit by hiring out bondsmen to the Royal Navy. Admittedly, doing so meant risking losing their investment in their slaves should the bondsmen die, be captured, or desert. But many of these Loyalists would have been familiar with such risks; hiring slaves onto privateers, patroons, and merchant ships was a common practice in North American colonies prior to the American Revolution. This would have made some Loyalist slave owners, in a world of increasing chaos in which both British and American forces regularly took slaves from plantations, predisposed to the reasonable risk of having the King pay a regular wage for bondsmen.[12] To cite but one example, when HM Galley *Cornwallis* was captured in 1780 by the American privateer brig *Ariel*, seven enslaved oarsmen were found on board. Dick, Joe, Andrew, Caesar, Thomas Carey, Perter, and Hamden were hired out to the Royal Navy by six different Virginian slave masters. These Loyalist Virginians hoped to benefit from their slaves rowing for the King. Due to the *Cornwallis* being captured these six slave masters instead lost their bondsmen. The unfortunate Black sailors were, however, the real losers in this circumstance, as they were sold as prize goods in Puerto Rico, returning them into enslavement in a far off and unfamiliar environment. Thus, it was Black seamen who bore the greatest risk of service on galleys, not their slave owners.[13]

The unattractiveness of service on galleys is evident from the extraordinarily high desertion rates from these vessels. During the wars of the eighteenth century the Royal Navy's overall desertion rate "hovered around 7 percent," although during the American Revolution there was a spike above ten percent.[14] Thus, when Lieutenant James Every commanded HM Galley *Adder* from 1780 to 1783, during which time over nineteen percent of the galley's crew deserted, he may have felt unlucky as he suffered almost twice the Navy's usual rate of runaways. Yet among galleys in North America during the Revolution, the *Adder* had the lowest desertion rate. Andrew Law, during his difficult

12. Charles R. Foy, "Seeking Freedom in the Atlantic World, 1713-1783," *Early American Studies: An Interdisciplinary Journal*, 4:1 (Spring 2006), 53, 60, 65; Philip D. Morgan, *Slave Counterpoint: Black Culture in the Eighteenth-Century Chesapeake & Lowcountry* (Chapel Hill: University of North Carolina Press, 1998), 238.
13. *Virginia Gazette* (Dixon & Nicolson), March 3, 1781.
14. Denver Brunsman, "Men of War: British Sailors and the Impressment Paradox," *Journal of Early Modern History* 14 (2014), 19.

year commanding HM Galley *Comet*, saw seventy-eight percent of his crew flee, while the unfortunate Tylston Woollam, commander of HM Galley *Vindictive*, lost ninety percent of his crew. Woollam was only able to keep the *Vindictive* operating by impressing almost his entire crew in southern ports.[15]

Among the sixteen Royal Navy galleys on the North American station for which musters could be located, the average desertion rate was 51.8 percent, with the eight galleys operating in southern waters averaging 53.7 percent.[16] These high desertion rates undoubtedly reflect seamen's dissatisfaction with work on galleys. Unlike on a man-of-war, where "the whip of the lash contributed little to" the often "intricate tasks on a sailing vessel," brute force was more often the rule on galleys.[17]

Despite galleys' critical role in supporting troops along inland and coastal waterways, the need for precise sequencing of rowing resulting in disciplining of crew, the physical demands of galley service, the infrequent obtaining of prize monies by galley crews, and the lack of shelter for most seamen on galleys, made assignment on these vessels unattractive to many seamen. The lack of appeal of service on naval galleys can be seen by the not insignificant number of elderly mariners who served on such vessels. The presence of elderly seamen in a particular maritime job, be it cook or galley oarsman, was a "mark of exceptional poverty," as older men who normally would have shifted to less physically demanding land-based jobs were compelled to continue to go to sea and work at jobs other mariners avoided.[18]

15. HM Galley *Comet*, Muster, 1780-81, ADM 36/10258, TNA; and HM Galley *Vindictive*, Muster, 1779, ADM 36/10429, TNA.

16. HM Galley *Arbuthnot*, Muster, 1780-81, ADM 36/10213, TNA; HM Galley *Clinton*, Muster, 1779, ADM 36/9965, TNA; HM Galley *Comet*, Muster, 1780-81, ADM 36/10258, TNA; HM Galley *Cornwallis*, Muster, 1777-80, ADM 36/10259, TNA; HM Galley *Delaware*, Muster, 1777-79, ADM 36/10139, TNA; HM Galley *Dependence*, Muster, 1777-79, ADM 36/8508, TNA; HM Galley *Hamond*, Muster, 1780-82, ADM 36/9972, TNA; HM Galley *Philadelphia*, Muster, 1778-81, ADM 36/9932, TNA; HM Galley *Scourge*, Muster, 1779-80, ADM 36/10427, TNA; HM Galley *Vaughan*, Muster, 1779-81, ADM 36/10395, TNA; HM Galley *Vindictive*, Muster, 1779, ADM 36/10429, TNA; HM Galley *Viper*, Muster, 1780-83, ADM 36/10390, TNA; and HM Galley *Vixen*, Muster, 1779-83, ADM 36/10389, TNA.

17. Brunsman, "Men of War: British Sailors and the Impressment Paradox," 34.

18. Daniel Vickers with Vince Walsh, *Young Men and the Sea: Yankee Seafarers in the Age of Sail* (New Haven: Yale University Press, 2005), 119. See also Cheryl A. Fury, ed., *The Social History of English Seamen, 1485-1649* (Woodbridge: Boydell Press, 2012), 269.

On some Royal Navy galleys, it appears that old men were employed as a last measure when commanders were unable to maintain full complements. For example, during 1782 HM Galley *Arbuthnot* had experienced a greater than 80 percent desertion rate. In December alone, eighteen sailors, or over one-half of the galley's crew, deserted. In January 1783 Lt. Tylston Woollam became the galley's commander. With desertion rates remaining extremely high in April 1783 Woollam took on board the *Arbuthnot* seven elderly sailors: forty-year-old Hugh Sherrard, forty-six-year-old William Gaines, forty-seven-year-old John Shabar, forty-year-old Thomas Black, forty-five-year-old John Close, forty-year-old Francis Roberts, and forty-one-year-old John Bevan. They joined forty-year-old Thomas Arbuthnot, forty-two-year-old John Rusdale, forty-eight-year-old Dennis McCarty, forty-four-year-old Peter Farleigh, and forty-eight-year-old John Ball. Such older men were hardly ideal galley crew members. And as they comprised 30 percent of the galley's forty-man complement, Lieutenant Woollam's choice in having these elderly men come aboard the galley evidences his rather desperate attempts to complete the manning of his vessel. The galley *Adder* similarly relied upon elderly men to fill its complement. While operating off of South Carolina in 1780 and 1781, eight men fifty years of age or older served on the galley, the oldest being William Lynch, a seventy-four-year-old seaman. The *Adder*'s reliance upon old salts became even more extreme in 1782 when eighty-three-year-old Joseph George became a member of the galley's crew.[19]

It is against this background of most seamen not wanting to work on galleys and slaves being hired onto these vessels that one needs to consider the impressment of free Black seamen onto Royal Navy galleys during the American Revolution. Leading maritime historians have asserted "impressment was a step up for many Black seamen." This "step up" was in large part because, within the Anglo-American Atlantic, captured Black sailors were assumed to be slaves, whether they were or not, making them vulnerable to being treated as prizes and sold into slavery. As Gov. Robert Hunter of New York observed in 1712, when Black seamen were captured by British ships the men were sold into slavery as prize goods "by reason of their colour." This presumption would be applied by British Admiralty Court officials throughout the Atlantic and some officials would continue to utilize this standard at

19. HM Galley *Arbuthnot*, Muster, 1783-1786, 36/10426, TNA; HM Galley *Adder*, Muster, 1782, ADM 36/10384, TNA.

the end of the eighteenth century.[20] When impressed onto naval vessels Blacks were provided with equal wages and protected from enslavement and the anxiety that possible enslavement caused for seamen of African ancestry. And yet while it was undoubtedly true that coerced naval service could be an improvement for Blacks, particularly for enslaved seamen, stressing this overlooks that impressment could, and in fact did, act to worsen conditions for many free Black seamen on galleys during the American Revolution.

White sailors were often protected against press gangs by local residents willing to engage in violent confrontation with the gangs. There were hundreds of such affrays in the second half of the eighteenth century.[21] The fear of becoming "Impressment Widows" lead women to take to the streets to protect their husbands and lovers. However, when Blacks were impressed, few whites were willing to confront press gangs on their behalf. And their family and kin doing so would have been dangerous, particularly in slave colonies such as Georgia, the Carolinas, or East Florida.

Impressment was often described by white seamen as a form of "galley slavery" common to that in Turkey or Algiers.[22] In Tory Georgia impressment of slaves was seen as a necessary measure to deal with the threat of Rebel forces. By 1780 Loyalists were required to furnish, as needed, slaves to the royal government. Most worked on building and maintaining fortifications, but others, as did one group of 134 slaves, dragged row-boats over land, while others rowed on galleys.[23]

Impressed free Black seamen could be found on many of the navy's galleys. Scipio Cornelius, Prince William, Neptune Chance, and America Shipjack on HM Galley *Delaware*, Prince Vaughan on HM Galley *Vaughan*, Polydore, Dublin, James Dick, and Thomas Arbuthnot on HM Galley *Arbuthnot*, Hercules Romney on HM Galley *Comet* and Thomas Prince on HM Galley *Scourge* all found themselves compelled

20. Brunsman, *Evil Necessity*, 122; Bolster, *Black Jacks*, 30-323, 71-72; Charles R. Foy, "Eighteenth-Century Prize Negroes: From Britain to America," *Slavery and Abolition* 31:3 (Sept. 2010): 381; Opinion of John Straker of the Vice-Admiralty Court, 1795, Papers of Adm. Sir Benjamin Caldwell, National Maritime Museum, Greenwich, UK, CAL 127.
21. Nicholas Rogers, *The Press Gang: Naval Impressment and its opponents in Georgian Britain* (New York: Continuum, 2007), 39.
22. Leon Fink, *Sweatshops at Sea: Merchant Seamen in the World's First Globalized Industry* (Chapel Hill: University of North Carolina Press, 2011), 13.
23. Benjamin Quarles, *The Negro in the American Revolution* (Chapel Hill: University of North Carolina Press, 1996), 137; Michael Lee Lanning, *African Americans in the Revolutionary War* (New York: Citadel Press, 2005), 210.

by press gangs to serve the King. It was, however, the experience of impressed free Black sailors on the galley *Vindictive* that best illustrates the scale of impressment of free Blacks onto naval galleys and how men of African ancestry resisted coerced labor at sea. In 1779, while in waters off Georgia, the *Vindictive* twice impressed groups of free Black seamen. First on June 28 and then again on September 10, the galley's commander, Lt. Tylston Woollam, had free Blacks impressed at Savannah onto the galley. These press sweeps resulted in a vessel in which the entire crew was Black and its officers were white. Of the thirty free Blacks impressed onto the *Vindictive*, all but Michael Luise, Illasure, and Harry deserted the galley when the vessel returned to Savannah, many doing so within two days of the galley docking. It is likely that the twenty-seven seamen of African ancestry who fled the galley shared John Marrant's view that being impressed caused a "lamentable stupor" that left them "cold and dead."[24] The deserting Black seamen undoubtedly were tired of being forced to work in what they must have considered to be slave-like conditions. But they also probably were weary of Lieutenant Woollam's command, which they likely experienced as inept. Unlike other galley commanders in North American waters, such as John Brown and Sidney Smith, who went on to distinguished naval careers as admirals, Lieutenant Woollam never rose above commanding a galley, never passed the lieutenant's exam, and after the Revolution never again served in the Navy.[25]

NOT COMPELLED TO ROW

There was one group of Blacks serving on Royal Navy galleys who were not "compelled to row:" runaway slaves. For fugitives, service on a Royal Navy vessel, even a galley, could result in permanent freedom.[26] In less than two weeks in July 1782 Quash, Ned, Billy, Harry, Sam, Ceasar, Joco, Jacob, Snow, London, George, Jack, and Bristol all "deserted from

24. HM Galley *Vindictive*, Muster, 1779, ADM 36/10429, TNA; John Marrant, *Narrative of the Lord's Wonderful Dealings* (London, 1785), 94. Historians dispute whether Marrant served in the Royal Navy. Vincent Carretta, "Black Seamen and Soldiers," *18th Century Studies* 36, No. 3 (Fall 2014), 1500-153. However, his characterization of how a free Black might have felt about being impressed is still a useful tool in contextualizing the experiences of Black seamen.
25. Bruno Pappalardo, *Royal Navy Lieutenant's Passing Certificates, 1691-1902* (Kew, UK: List and Index Society, 2002). The vast majority of galley commanders on the North American coast did not pass the Lieutenant's Exam, a clear indication that galley commanders, Brown and Smith, notwithstanding, were not the best of the navy's officers.
26. Charles R. Foy, "Possibilities & Limits for Freedom: Maritime Fugitives in British North America, ca. 1713-1783," in *Gender, Race, Ethnicity, and Power in Maritime America* (Mystic, CT, 2008), 43-54.

the Rebels," i.e. fled their South Carolinian masters, and made their way onto HM Galley *Adder*.[27] Given that the *Adder* at this time only had between eighteen and twenty men, without the thirteen runaways the galley could not have operated against American forces. Some of these men deserted from the *Adder*, finding, like the impressed free Blacks on the *Vindictive*, that service on a galley was not to their liking. But others, such as Quash, Ned, Billy, and Harry, subsequently found themselves discharged at St. Augustine as free men. For these former bondsmen, as for hundreds of Black Loyalists, the Royal Navy served as a conduit to freedom.

Unfortunately, runaways who served on galleys could also find themselves "returned to [their] owner[s]." A number of former slaves, having found freedom on naval galleys, lost their freedom when the vessels returned to ports from which they had fled. Thus, in November 1779 when HM Galley *Scourge* returned to Port Royal, South Carolina, Prince, Coffee, and seven other Blacks on the galley were returned to enslavement when their former masters came to the wharves to reclaim them. The *Scourge* was hardly the only naval galley which returned runaways to their masters. In 1783 HM Galley *Arbuthnot* impressed many of its crew while in Savannah and St. Augustine. Two years later, James Dick, an African-born able-bodied seaman, Nicholas March, and Thomas Black, St. Augustine-born seamen, were all discharged at St. Augustine for "being a Slave." Dublin and Polydore were similarly discharged from the *Arbuthnot* at St. Augustine. As were other Black Royal Navy seamen who were discharged "for being a slave," these Black sailors were returned to their slave masters despite having served in the Royal Navy for more than two years. In returning runaways to their Loyalist owners the navy reinforced Georgian and Carolinian slave culture. Thus, while fugitives from "Rebels" might have found service on galleys an avenue to freedom, many runaways from Loyalists achieved only temporary freedom from enslavement by their time on navy galleys.[28]

CONCLUSION

If there was a clear glass ceiling for Blacks in the Georgian Royal Navy such that obtaining the post of captain was achieved by only by one

---

27. HM Galley *Adder*, Muster 1782, ADM 36/10384, TNA.
28. HM Galley *Scourge*, Muster 1779-1780, ADM 36/10427, TNA; HM Galley *Arbuthnot* Muster, 1783-86, ADM 36/10426, TNA. The return of former slaves by navy officers was hardly limited to those serving on Royal Navy galleys. Foy, "The Royal Navy's Employment of Black Mariners and Maritime Workers, 1754-1783," 14.

exceptional Black sailor in the eighteenth century, a similar but reverse dynamic worked when it came to avoiding one of the most difficult naval assignments: rowing a naval galley. As the musters of the *Scourge, Vindictive*, and other Royal Navy galleys operating in North American waters indicate, whites did all they could to avoid working on galleys while Blacks found themselves impressed or hired out for such back-breaking work, and runaway slaves who entered navy galleys often found themselves re-enslaved. In this, as in many other avenues of life in the British Atlantic, Black seamen were often disadvantaged solely due to the color of their skin.[29]

29. Enslavement of captured free Black seamen was not uncommon in the eighteenth century. Foy, "Eighteenth-Century Prize Negroes," 379-393.

John the Painter:
Terrorist for America

LARS HEDBOR

Upon our arrival, I did behold a most curious Sight, which gave me further Cause to wonder about the true Safety we might here enjoy. Above the entrance to the Harbor of this town there stands upon the Gibbet a most piteous set of remains, being the last mortal pieces of a most heinous Criminal, lately caught in these parts. He was known as Jack the Painter, and upon declaring his attachment to the Violent Cause of Rebellion in America that we have just escaped, he did undertake to commit Acts of destruction upon these shores. He succeeded only in firing the rope-house at the Royal Navy's great Shipyards here, but even that caused a great Disruption and Upset in these parts. It comes as small Comfort to my distressed Mind that he was captured in due course, and brought to a Swift and certain End, his corpse left to Dangle here as a visible Warning to all who might Conceive of a mis-placed Notion to follow his example.

—*The Break, Tales From a Revolution: Nova-Scotia*

The mizzenmast of HMS *Arethusa* rose over sixty-four feet high into the spring morning, forming a gallows the likes of which had never before been seen on England's fair shores. It had been unbolted from the ship where she lay at anchor in Portsmouth harbor, and raised for this purpose both to enable the unprecedented throngs to witness the fate of the condemned, and also because his crimes were felt to have been a particular assault upon the Royal Navy.[1]

---

1. "Dockyard Timeline: 1776—Jack the Painter," Portsmouth Royal Dockyard, 2015, accessed January 16, 2016, portsmouthdockyard.org.uk/timeline/details/1776-jack-the-painter.

James Aitken, a disheveled-looking, redheaded Scotsman, was drawn in chains on a wagon toward the site of his impending execution, and his date with infamy. Most of the residents of Portsmouth, and more from the surrounding towns crowded into the public square, amounting to as many as 20,000 witnesses to this moment in history.

As Aitken neared the gallows, his wagon was directed to pass by the burnt-out ruins of an immense structure within the walls of the naval storeyard. The prior fall, it had bustled with activity, as scores of workers labored within its walls, winding and twisting mile upon mile of hempen rope for His Majesty's ships' rigging and anchors. The lines that had issued forth from the now-ruined building had helped the Royal Navy impose a cordon around the ports of rebellious cities in the American colonies, and the loss of this facility was but one stroke in a series of attacks to further impede the ability of the navy to impose the King's will upon his unruly subjects across the sea.

What thoughts must have passed through Aitken's mind as he looked one last time upon the culmination of many months' planning? A sense of satisfaction, perhaps, that he had been able to succeed at the plot? Or disappointment that he had been foiled in accomplishing more that he had planned, by chance and by the spreading terror that he had, in fact, sought to cause? Or, perhaps, a sense that he had at last risen above the difficult years of his childhood and the habits of petty crime into which he'd fallen, to commit acts which had inflamed the sentiments of the British public against the American cause, and had, in some measurable way, changed history?

Alternatively, were his thoughts no more orderly than those of any other madman, filled with self-important aggrandizement of his role in sowing terror across England, from her shipyards to the seat of power? It is impossible to know with complete certainty, but he left behind an uncharacteristically rich record of how he wanted posterity to think of him.

James Aitken (variously known as "John," "Jack the Painter," "John the Painter," and a variety of aliases that he adopted throughout his career including James Hill, James Boswell and James Hind) was born in Edinburgh in 1752, the eighth of twelve children in a large Scottish family. When he was still just a boy, his father died, and John was admitted to a charity school set up by George Heriot for the benefit of fatherless children. Intended to give such unfortunates the advantages of a top-notch education, it was a relatively strict, if effective, institution.

Aitken spent his days in regimented studies and devotions, lasting from seven in the morning until eight at night. Time was provided for

JAMES AITKEN,
alias
JOHN the PAINTER.

Frontispiece to *The trial at large of James Hill, otherwise James Hind, otherwise James Aitken, commonly known by the name of John the Painter*, published in 1777. (*John Carter Brown Library*)

"innocent diversions" and "visiting with friends," but these privileges could be revoked for bad behavior. [2]

However, his apprenticeship with a painter was unfortunate. The market for house painters was both saturated and shrinking in 1767, when he started his career.[3] Although he clearly absorbed the practical aspects of his craft, John just as clearly found it difficult to support himself.

To supplement his income as an itinerant worker, he turned to crime, stealing from shops, travelers, and homes. Worse, he later admitted to having raped a woman who was alone with her sheep in the countryside.[4] During this period of his life, he clearly developed the habit of taking what he wanted, without regard for anything resembling what his peers might have considered moral or right.

2. *Regulations for George Heriot's Hospital* (Edinburgh, 1795), 25-27, books.google.com/ books?id=oSJeAAAAcAAJ, accessed April 2, 2018.

3. Jessica Warner, *John the Painter: Terrorist of the American Revolution: A Brief Account of His Short Life, from His Birth in Edinburgh, Anno 1752, to His Death, by Hanging, in Portsmouth, Anno 1777: To Which Was Once Appended a Meditation on the Eternal Foolishness of Young Men* (New York: Thunders Mouth Press, 2004), 32.

4. James Aitken, *The Life of James Aitken, Commonly Called John the Painter, An Incendiary Who Was Tried at the Castle of Winchester on Thursday the 7th Day of March 1777 and Convicted of Setting Fire to His Majesty's Dockyard at Portsmouth, Exhibiting a Detail of Facts of the Utmost Importance to Great Britain* (London: J. Wilkes, 1777), 32, books.google.com/ books?id=-BNlAAAAcAAJ, accessed April 2, 2018.

As did many who had a criminal background for which they wished to escape prosecution, he decided to leave behind known hardships of home for the unknown opportunities of the colonies, signing on as an indentured servant. He failed to find the riches and ease he sought on these shores, and though the historical record is silent on his exact activities in America, he later claimed to have traveled fairly extensively through the colonies.[5]

This was the mid-1770s, and revolutionary fervor was rising among the restive colonials. Many of the newspapers and pamphlets that he would have encountered on the streets and in the shops rang with denunciations of the King and Parliament, as well as lurid tales of the depredations of British troops who were sent to quell their rowdy subjects.

By the time Aitken returned to England, open rebellion was at hand in the colonies, and he began to devise a plan to make his mark on history, while striking a blow against the society that he blamed for his own hardships.

He had pretty clearly lost his fear of capture, either because enough time had passed since his youthful misdeeds that he did not expect anyone to be looking for him anymore, or because his appearance had changed with a few years' maturity.

In any event, he apparently traveled throughout Britain, and even went so far as to visit Paris; what means of support he found for these activities is unrecorded, but his earlier career leaves us with little doubt that he continued to pursue a variety of criminal activities.

In Paris, he sought and received an audience with the American mission there. He met with Silas Deane—who was there primarily to convince the French to enter the war fully in support of the United States—and the American apparently listened with a mixture of disbelief and interest to the young Scotsman's wild scheme.

Aitken laid out an elaborate plan of attacks, starting with a campaign of arson against British naval bases up and down the coast, throwing in attacks elsewhere as necessary to sow terror and confusion throughout the nation.

His background as a painter's apprentice taught him the many opportunities for flaming disaster attendant to that line of work, and his preparations reflected that. However, he would take additional, fiendishly inventive steps to ensure the success of his plans.

Building on the painters' techniques of grinding pigments into fine powders, he would produce readily-ignited charcoal powder, which he

5. Aitken, *The Life of James Aitken*, 17-19.

would use to spread the flames. However, to solve the problem of starting a fire and still escaping the hoped-for conflagration, he had assembled a device that featured a candle in a box to serve as a sort of timed fuse, with a base filled with turpentine; the theory was that as the flame burned down to the level of the highly flammable fluid, an explosion would result, spreading fire to all that surrounded the device.

He is thought to have shown this infernal device to Deane, as he made the case for official (even if clandestine) American support for his plan. Deane appears to have taken the young man's measure, and concluded that his scheme had little chance of success, but that if Aitken did pull it off, he would, indeed, significantly affect the progress of the war.

While he did not give the Scotsman everything he asked, Deane did offer American support to the plan in the form of a few pounds in cash, but he also gave Aitken a passport in the name of the King of France, executed by the Comte de Vergennes, assuring his safe passage back to England.[6]

Aitken returned across the English Channel and hired a couple of tinsmiths to build a number of the devices he'd designed; only a single shop came through for him, though, and he had to content himself with just one incendiary device.

The events after this point are related in Aitken's own jailhouse confession. On the 5th of December, 1776, Aitken arrived in Portsmouth and began his reconnaissance. He snuck into the dockyard there, and first set up his device in storehouse, having soaked a bale of hemp with turpentine and gunpowder. He did not ignite it, however, as he wanted to see whether he could arrange for an even larger conflagration elsewhere in the sprawling facility.

He found a likely-looking spot in the ropehouse, an immense structure over 1,000 feet long, where rope was braided from individual threads of hemp into the monstrous lines used to work the Royal Navy's warships. Here was a target worth investing some time in, and Aitken later said that he set a careful tinder pile, again adding turpentine and powder.

When he attempted to light it, however, the tinder was too damp, and he spent so long trying to start the fire that he found himself locked into the structure. He abandoned the attempt for the night, and had to pound on the door until he could convince someone to let him out. His credulous rescuer believed his story of innocent curiosity, and Aitken was able to return to his lodgings for the night.

6. Ibid., 35.

After attempting (and failing) to set fire to his boarding house, Aitken was able to again gain access to the warehouse and ropehouse. This time, he was able to light his device (though the hemp around it prevented it from working) and the tinder he'd set up the prior day— it was a complete success, from his point of view.

As he hurried out of the dockyard before the fire could be detected, he bumped into an acquaintance, and was so worried that he'd been recognized that he decided to flee the city entirely. He was able to see the dockyards ablaze as he departed, and it was with some self-satis-faction that he reported to the contact that Deane had given him.

There, he met with another great disappointment, however, as the shocked Dr. Bancroft—a double agent[7] in London—not only said that he had heard nothing of the plot from Deane, but was, in fact, a faithful subject of the British Crown. Bancroft turned him out, for fear of being exposed as an American spy, and Aitken drafted a warning to Deane that the Bancroft could not be trusted.

Despite not having been rewarded with the riches he hoped for, Aitken moved on to Plymouth, where he hoped to expand upon his reign of terror. There, he found security tightened in response to the fire at Portsmouth, and after an abortive incursion into the dockyard there, he fled to Bristol.

There, he set several incendiary devices in one night, all of which failed, but the townspeople were now on edge. When another device did succeed in burning down several warehouses, the resulting uproar spawned arrests and copycats, continuing long after Aitken was far from town. Fear rose that Bristol had been targeted by a coordinated conspiracy of Whigs favorable to the American cause.

The panic spread when Aitken's original failed incendiary was dis-covered buried in the hemp at Portsmouth, and a rash of what might have been ordinarily dismissed as normal misfortunes were conflated into a French or Spanish plot—or an American one.

Alarms were raised at ports all over Britain, and huge rewards of £500, and then £1,000 were posted. The response in Liverpool was typ-ical:

> . . . it was resolved that a strong and efficient watch be set every night from five o'clock in the evening, till seven o'clock in the morning, to patrol round the docks and through the town. Owners, masters, and others interested, were recommended to have their ships carefully

7. Thomas J. Schaeper, *Edward Bancroft: Scientist, Author, Spy.* (New Haven: Yale University Press, 2011), 54.

watched, the persons in charge not to be allowed any candle-light or fires aboard during their watch . . . A strict lookout was kept on all loitering persons being in or coming into the town, and the inhabitants who had lodgers whom they eyed with suspicion, were invited to impart those suspicions to the authorities—an excellent opportunity to settle old scores.[8]

By the time Aitken's luck ran out, in the aftermath of yet another bungled burglary, the reward for his capture had risen to well over £2,000 in all, and he was finally taken in by a jailer who had recognized him since he had been casing the last shop he burgled.[9] The jailer was unjustly cheated out of his reward by a strategic prosecution who relied on charges related to the crimes committed *before* the rewards were posted.[10]

Between Aitken's arsonist tools—which were found on him—and the testimony of an acquaintance who had seen him in Portsmouth in the wake of the fire there, Aitken's fate was little in doubt, and his conviction and sentence were a foregone conclusion by the time the court met for his trial.

In the days before the trial, Aitken was at first wildly uncooperative, even refusing to give his correct name. Once he became convinced that he was bound for the gallows, he was persuaded by a publisher to dictate his entire confession in exchange for money to improve his conditions of imprisonment.

This confession was not only a means of answering the many questions raised by his deranged actions (and putting some money in the pocket of the publisher), but also doubtless served to allay the fears of the British people that they were under attack on their own soil.

His unlikely "last words" were published along with this confession:

> Good people, I am now going to suffer for a crime, the heinousness of which deserves a more severe punishment than what is going to be inflicted. My life has been long forfeited by the innumerable felonies I have formerly committed, but I hope God, in his great mercy, will forgive me; and 1 hope the public, whom I have much injured, will carry their resentment no further, but forgive me, as I forgive all the world, and pray for me that I may have forgiveness above. I have made a faith-

---

8. Gomer Williams, "Privateers of the American War of Independence," *History of the Liverpool Privateers and Letter of Marque: With an Account of the Liverpool Slave Trade* (New York: Routledge, 2013), 8.

9. Aitken, *The Life of James Aitken*, 59.

10. Warner, *John the Painter*, 191.

ful confession of every transaction of my life from my infancy to the present time, particularly the malicious intention I had of destroying all the dock yards in this kingdom, which I have delivered to Mr. White, and desired him to have printed for the satisfaction of the public. I die with no enmity in my heart to his majesty and government, but wish the ministry success in all their undertakings; and I hope my untimely end will be warning to all persons, not to commit the like atrocious offence.

James Aitken's actions likely helped to inflame the passions of the British people against their American cousins, and rather than helping the movement toward American independence, his violence gave the Colonies' enemies in Parliament the support they needed to prosecute the war with even more vigor.

In the end, just as in more recent history, Aitken's terrorism failed to convince anyone of the justice of the cause in whose name it was undertaken. It did, however, serve to increase the perception among the British people that the cause of American independence was a mortal threat to their personal safety and security. For all his claims to have been striking against Britain on behalf of America, Aitken likely did us far more harm than good.

How to be a Revolutionary War Spy Master

❄ DON N. HAGIST ❄

George Washington is credited with being a great spy master, and the feats of his Culper spy ring have become famous. How did he learn this clandestine craft? Although he had military experience, prior to 1775 he hadn't served in the headquarters and staff positions that were usually the hub of intelligence gathering activities. But Washington had other experienced men around him, and he also had the resource through which officers in all of the era's armies learned much of their trade: books.

Many military textbooks were available in the English language during the eighteenth century, many readily available from printers and booksellers in America. Anyone who could read could easily learn the theory of marching maneuvers, tactics, fortification, and other aspects of the military arts. There was no one book devoted solely to intelligence gathering, but some texts included sections and chapters on the subject, providing common-sense general instructions on the employment of spies. With a few good books, every officer of rank on both sides of the conflict had the rudiments of spycraft at his fingertips.

An example is in a popular mid-century work, *Military Instructions by the King of Prussia*. Written by the great military thinker Frederick II of Prussia and published in German in 1748, an English-language edition appeared in London in 1762.[1] The twelfth chapter, or article, is called, "Of Spies, how they are to be employed on every Occasion, and in what Manner we are to learn Intelligence of the Enemy." It begins with the observation, "If we were acquainted beforehand with the intentions of the enemy, we should always be more than a match for

---

1. *Military Instructions by the King of Prussia*, T. Forster, trans. (London, 1762), 31-33.

him even with an inferior force. It is an advantage which all generals are anxious to procure, but very few obtain." The chapter continues,

> Spies may be divided into several classes: 1st, common people who choose to be employed in such concern; 2dly, double spies; 3dly, spies of consequence; 4thly, those who are compelled to take up the unpleasant business.
>
> The common gentry, viz. peasants, mechanics, priests, &c. which are sent into the camp, can only be employed to discover where the enemy is: and their reports are generally so incongruous and obscure, as rather to increase our uncertainties than lessen them.
>
> The intelligence of deserters is, for the most part, not much more to be depended on. A soldier knows very well what is going forward in his own regiment, but nothing farther. The hussars being detached in front, and absent the greatest part of their time from the army, are often ignorant on which side it is encamped. Nevertheless, their reports must be committed to paper, as the only means of turning them to any advantage.
>
> *Double* spies are used to convey false intelligence to the enemy.

The author gives examples from European campaigns—of providing a known spy with false information to lure an opponent into a trap; of a postmaster paid to open and copy letters; of a king's secretary who was discovered to be a spy, and was then regularly provided with deceptive information. During the American Revolution, James Armistead was among the "common people" who successfully infiltrated an enemy camp and became a "spy of consequence."

In spite of having doubted the value of information from deserters, Frederick II recommended using soldiers posing as deserters to send bogus information:

> When we wish to gain intelligence of the enemy, or give him a false impression of our situation and circumstances, we employ a trusty soldier to go from our camp to that of the enemy, and report what we wish to have believed. He may also be made the bearer of hand-bills calculated to encourage desertion. Having completed his business, he may take a circuitous march and return to camp.

This is akin to the activities of American spy Daniel Bissell, who went so far as to enlist in a Loyalist regiment. Frederick II also suggested a similar technique, forcing a prominent citizen to go to the enemy headquarters on some pretense or another, with a spy posing as a servant in tow. Effecting this requires coercion by holding the family or property of the citizen as hostages, which the author admitted to be "a harsh and cruel practice." Capt. Allen McLane used an approach like this when he posed as the simple-minded son of a civilian visitor to gain intelligence about the British post at Stony Point.

Frederick's final advice about spies is particularly important:

> I must farther add, that in the payment of spies, we ought to be generous, even to a degree of extravagance. That man certainly deserves to be well rewarded, who risks his neck to do you service,

Maurice Count de Saxe was another highly regarded military mind; his *Reveries, or Memoirs concerning the Art of War* appeared in English in 1759.[2] Saxe's chapter 10, "Of Spies and Guides," was more succinct than Frederick II's, but offered much of the same guidance:

> One cannot bestow too much attention in the procuring of spies and guides. M. de Montecuculli says, that they serve as eyes to the head, and that they are equally as essential to a commander. Which observation of his is certainly very just. Money therefore should never be wanting, upon a proper occasion; for the acquisition of such as are good, is cheap at any price. They are to be taken out of the country in which the war is carried on, selecting those only who are active and intelligent, and dispersing them every where; amongst the general officers of the enemy, amongst his sutlers, and, above all, amongst the purveyors of provisions; because their stores, magazines, and other preparations, furnish the best intelligence concerning his real design.
>
> The spies are not to know one another; and are to consist of various ranks or orders; some to associate with the soldiers; others to follow the army, under the disguise of pedlars: but it is necessary that all of them should be admitted to the knowledge of some one belonging to the first order of their fraternity; from whom they may occasionally receive any thing that is to be conveyed to the general who pays them. This charge must be committed to one who is both faithful and ingenious; obliging him to render an account of himself every day, and guarding, as much as possible, against his being corrupted.

One of the recommended guises, that of a peddler, was used by the British spy Ann Bates, while the American Lt. Lewis Costigin managed to send intelligence information while a prisoner of war in New York City.

Saxe concluded his remarks with this wise observation:

2. Maurice Count de Saxe, *Reveries, or Memoirs concerning the Art of War* (Edinburgh: Sands, Donaldson, Murray and Cochran, 1759), 216-218.

I shall not insist any longer upon this subject; which, upon the whole, is a detail that depends upon a great variety of circumstances, from which a general, by his prudence and intrigues, will be able to reap great advantages.

Washington is not known to have owned a copy of Saxe's *Reveries*,[3] but he did own a book by Thomas Simes, one of the most prolific British military authors of the era, in which Saxe's section on spies was reprinted verbatim.[4]

Another book in Washington's library, one which he recommended to his subordinates, was *Essay on the Art of War*, a 1761 English translation of a 1754 French volume. The section entitled "Of the General of an Army"[5] includes this succinct advice about spies:

> A General should spare no Trouble or Expence to be well informed of every Thing that passes with the Enemy, either by Means of Parties, or of Spies whom he should pay well, if he would be well served: Nothing is more absolutely necessary or more useful than Spies, who Strada, with Reason, calls the Eyes and Ears of princes: We see in Scripture, that God himself commanded Moses to send out Spies to the Land of Promise, and all the Instructions a General can possibly give to the Spies he employs, are to be found in the thirteenth Chapter of Numbers.

The last sentence is worthy of a message from a spy, giving not direct guidance but a reference to another source for the information. Numbers 13 reads (approximately, depending on which translation is used),

> Go up through the Negev and on into the hill country. See what the land is like and whether the people who live there are strong or weak, few or many. What kind of land do they live in? Is it good or bad? What kind of towns do they live in? Are they unwalled or fortified? How is the soil? Is it fertile or poor? Are there trees in it or not? Do your best to bring back some of the fruit of the land.

In other words, instruct your spies to gather whatever information might be useful. That's obvious, but it's not enough guidance to develop an intelligence program.

3. Per the listing at www.librarything.com/catalog/GeorgeWashington.
4. Thomas Simes, *The Military Guide for Young Officers* (Philadelphia, 1776; originally printed London, 1772), 10-11. In this book, Simes did not cite Saxe as the source of the material on spies, but he did do so in his previous work, *The Military Medley* (Dublin, 1767), 169.
5. *Essay on the Art of War* (London: A. Millar, Strand, 1761), 31-32.

Essay on the Art of War goes on, however, to present much more detailed information about how spies should operate, and how they should be managed; here we see many of the methods used in some way or another by Washington throughout the war:[6]

> As to Spies, those you employ should be Persons of Capacity, able to know the Strength of a Fortification or Intrenchment, either from its natural Situation or from Art; what Extent of Ground a certain Number of Infantry or Cavalry occupy commonly either in Camp or on March, according to the different Fronts in which they march, and at one Glance of their Eye be able to comprehend nearly the Strength of a Camp or Post where the Enemy are lodged; and how many Cavalry or Infantry they have in their Camp or on their March, without being obliged to count the Tents or the Regiments.
>
> The Subjects of a neutral Prince are those who run the least Risk in serving as Spies; for under Pretence of Travelling or Traffic they can pass unsuspected from one Country to the other.
>
> You may also have some Officer in the Enemy's Camp, or other Person of Ability in the Neighbourhood, who informs you of what you want to know. As often as you write to him, you can use the Cypher and Composition mentioned, letting nothing appear but a few Lines on any indifferent Subject, and subscribing the Letter with the Name of a Relation, Countryman, or Friend, of the person intrusted; so that if it is intercepted nothing appears, but one Friend writing to another on indifferent subjects, or Family Affairs.
>
> You will have warned the person intrusted, that if the Enemy send out a small Detachment, or try an Expedition of little Importance, he need not advise you of it; that you may not expose your Spies for Trifles. You may also have Spies among the Enemy, by making ten or twelve of your own Soldiers desert, chusing those in whom you can trust, and who possess something in their Country, or leave their Wives or Children as Pledges of their Fidelity: Name to each the particular Regiment in which he shall inlist, and let him know, that whenever a Person shall give him a Watch-word agreed on, he shall directly bring to you the Letter or any Intelligence that Person shall give him. These Soldiers should not know each other, and ought each to have a different Watch-word; so that if one is taken or proves unfaithful, the rest may not be in Danger. Neither should you name the Person of the Enemy's Army with whom you are in Intelligence, nor give him any Mark to know him by. It is sufficient they have Orders to return when their Watch-word is given them. After having taken these Precautions, you write to

6. Ibid., 213-217.

the Person intrusted, that in such a Regiment there is such a Man whom you have sent there, whom he may know by such a Mark, Name, or watch-words and describing in the same Manner the rest who have deserted for that Purpose. If your Correspondent has only a Letter to send you, it is not necessary he discover himself by giving it with his own Hand: But having exactly observed the Marks by which the Soldier is to be known, he can send him the Watch-word and Letter by another trusty Person: Or if the case admits of it without Inconvenience, he can wait till Night, and when it is dark, in Disguise, passing by the Soldier, give the Watch-word and Letter. We only mention this Sort of Spies not to omit any thing; though it appears to be extremely difficult to have certain Intelligence by Means so complicated.

It is of great Importance to gain some of those employed in the Enemy's Secretary of State's Office, in that of the Secretary at War, or of the General in Chief, who give you Intelligence of the Resolutions taken. There are different Ways to succeed in this, needless here to mention. A Golden Key opens every Lock.

In general you must endeavour to draw Intelligence and Instructions from the Spies by every possible Means, but never open yourself to them. You should employ several for the same Subject, who are absolutely ignorant of each other, never see them but in private, make them talk on different subjects; let them speak a great deal, but say you little, in order to discover their Character, and what they are fit to be employed in; then set other Spies on them, to discover if they are not employed on both Sides.

If you would execute an Enterprize, after believing from the concurrent Reports of several Spies, that they have told Truth, carry them however along with you separately. You may also gain Intelligence from the People of the Country, whom Traffic or their own private Affairs draw to the Camp, or the Towns, who sometimes become Spies without knowing it, as do the prisoners, from whom also you may artfully draw Intelligence in general Conversation. The first of these, the People of the Country, should never be questioned; but artful sensible People should be employed, who, without any seeming curiosity, lead them to talk on different Subjects, and insensibly draw from them those things you want to be informed of.

When you would know from a Prisoner what passes in the Army or Country he belongs to, send before-hand to the same Ward, in the prison where he is to be confined, a person in whom you can trust, who speaks the Enemy's Language, is drest in their Manner, and who in every respect bears the Marks of a Prisoner. If there are several Prisoners, they must be separated in different Wards, in each of which there should be such a person, who will draw from the Prisoners whatever you want to know, and thus you will also know how far they all agree in what they say. But it is proper to have questioned the prisoners before Hand, of what Regiment, Town, or Province they are, that the supposed Prisoner may not announce himself to be of the same, and so be discovered; for it is certain, that if the Prisoner believes the other to be really in the same Situation with himself, a very few Hours Conversation serves to draw from him every thing he knows with regard to the Army or Place where he served.

The Spies you may have from the Monasteries in Catholic Countries are the best and surest. The Government of Consciences is a secret Empire which none can penetrate, and which penetrates every where. The Employment of this sort of Spies is infallible, where a Town is occupied by a Prince of a different Religion, or in a Country which has changed its Sovereign. Women are also serviceable either to get into a Town, to examine what passes in a Camp, or to carry Letters, because they are less suspected than Men.

You may also, in order to discover in Part what passes in the Enemy's Country, make a Soldier desert who has Address, and in whom you can trust; who enters at one Part of the Enemy's Frontier, and demands of the first Party of the Enemy's Troops he meets, a Pass to take Service in any Regiment of the Army, or of any Detachment, which he knows at that time to be at the other Extremity of this Frontier, in order to observe exactly during his March all that passes, and after having arrived at the Army, and narrowly and at his Ease examined every thing, he shall again desert to your Country.

You may also be informed of the Disposition of the Enemy's Camp, or such other Particulars as it is important for you to be instructed in, by feigning some Pretence to send an Officer to confer with the Enemy's General, who shall be accompanied by intelligent Persons, drest like Servants, who, while their pretended Master is in Conference with the General, on those Affairs for which he seems to be sent, shall carefully, though seemingly with Indifference, observe those things you want to be informed of.

These techniques were available not only to Washington, but to any officer who could read the original French or the English translation of this widely-printed volume. It should be no surprise, then, that George Washington was an excellent spymaster—he owned a copy of the instruction book.

Pierre Landais, the War's Most Enigmatic Naval Captain

❖ LOUIS ARTHUR NORTON ❖

One American Revolutionary War naval captain, Pierre Landais, appeared paranoid and somewhat deranged. Landais was a French merchantman lieutenant who trafficked arms to America for entrepreneur Pierre Augustin Caron de Beaumarchais.[1] Beaumarchais created a fictitious trading enterprise called *Hortalez et Cie* that channeled French arms to the Americans via colonial West Indian *entrepôrts*.[2] Once there, the arms were sold to American agents. When Landais left the smuggling trade, he became an honorary citizen of Massachusetts and subsequently, on June 18, 1778, was given command of the American warship *Alliance,* named to honor America's new alliance with France.[3] He and his ship were assigned to an American squadron under the hot-blooded John Paul Jones whose initial impression of Landais was that he was "a sensible and well-informed man."[4]

John Adams, who had been a commissioner in France, spent a good deal of time in Landais's company. Adams found him to be an enigma; frustrated in his ambitions, disappointed in love, unable to win the affection of his officers or hold their respect, and consumed by jealousy. An entry in Adam's diary for May 12, 1779 noted that Landais "is jeal-

---

1. Michael Crawford, ed. *Naval Documents of the American Revolution* (Washington, DC: Government Printing Office, 1996), 10: 961-2. Note: The name Landais is spelled variously as Lundy, Landai and Landi in documents of this period.

2. Beaumarchais was a French Renaissance man who, during his extraordinary life, was a satirist, playwright, musician, publisher, watchmaker, inventor, diplomat, spy, arms dealer, financier, revolutionary and botanist/horticulturist.

3. Landais's French 20-gun ship was the *Heureux* whose name was later changed to the *Flamand.*

4. John Paul Jones to Benjamin Franklin, May 14, 1779, Benjamin Franklin Papers, American Philosophical Society: Philadelphia, PA., XIV, 110.

ous of every Thing. Jealous of every Body . . . he knows not how to treat his officers, nor his passengers, nor any Body else . . . There is in this man an Inactivity and an Indecisiveness that will ruin him. He is bewildered . . . an embarrassed Mind." Adams found Landais a mystified man, constantly talking about imaginary plots against him. Adams visited the *Alliance* and "had the pleasure to restore this ship to peace and harmony," but predicted that when he left, "all [officers and crew] will become unhappy again." He further predicted, "Landais will never accomplish any great thing . . . This man . . . has a littleness in his mien and air. His face is small and sharp so that you form a mean opinion of him from the first sign."[5]

On August 25, 1779 Landais had his first open disagreement with Jones. They were at sea, and the commodore was troubled because several of his squadron's small boats were lost in the Irish coast's dense fog. Landais, aggressive in his hunt for enemy vessels, wanted to chase a prize into these treacherous waters. Jones feared that he might also lose the badly needed *Alliance* and ordered Landais to stay with the fleet. The Frenchman argued that he had the right to follow his own "opinion in chasing when and where he thought proper and in every other matter."[6] Jones tried to mollify Landais, expressing his concern about the hazards that faced *Alliance* in the area's fog and turbulent seas. Landais then said that the loss of the small boats was the result of Jones's incompetence. John Paul Jones, in fury, responded that Landais had slandered his superior officer. This enmity produced an affront to the honor of each according to the code of eighteenth century gentlemanly behavior. The piqued Landais then challenged Jones to a duel with swords. The choice of the sword as the dueling weapon would give Landais, raised in the French tradition of swordsmanship, a distinct advantage.[7] Jones was also outraged, but managed to subdue his anger to a higher virtue—the sense of duty when on a mission. Even though both men were hot headed, Jones suggested that they suspend the duel until they were on land.

Crews of most ships during the Revolutionary War period were very international. Neutral ports around the North Atlantic abounded and

---

5. Lyman Hyman Butterfield, Leonard C. Faber, Wendell D. Garrett, eds. *Autobiography of John Adams* (Cambridge, MA: Belknap Press of Harvard University Press, 1961), 2:368.
6. Evan Thomas, *John Paul Jones, Sailor, Hero, Father of the American Navy* (New York Simon and Schuster, 2003), 170.
7. According to the formal dueling code the challenged person, if he accepts, has the choice of weapons. Since Jones essentially refused the challenge by putting it off, the sword issue may only have been Landais's way of continuing his threat to Jones.

prizes captured at sea were frequently taken to the nearest port as a *guerre de course*. Once the ship had been disposed of, the prize crews that sailed them were occasionally left to fend for themselves. They were usually free to sign on to any available ship that might take them to a more desirable port. In this way, a burgeoning population of maritime nomads grew on the high seas with little sense of morality or allegiance. Jones's flagship, the *Bonhomme Richard*, had such a multinational crew. They were difficult to control because of divided loyalties and so "a group of rogues guard [each] other."[8]

On one mission the squadron was in search of British shipping in the Bay of Biscay. The *Bonhomme Richard* and the *Alliance*, blinded by a squall, emerged from the turbulent weather on a collision course. Hearing shouts from the *Bonhomme Richard*'s bow watch, Landais assumed that some of the *Bonhomme Richard*'s ex-British sailors had become mutinous. Rather than changing course, Landais descended into his cabin to arm himself. The bowsprit of the *Bonhomme Richard* tore into the *Alliance*'s rigging and damaged her mizzenmast. Jones happened to be off watch asleep in his cabin. The collision awoke him and he quickly relieved the officer of the deck and too charge. This incident was unintentional, but served to heighten the tension between the two captains.

On September 23, 1779, in the North Sea off Flamborough Head, England, the American squadron came across the 44-gun *Serapis*, her consort the *Countess of Scarborough*, and a convoy of forty-four small merchant vessels that were carrying naval stores. The poorly armed merchantmen hastily headed for the nearest British port. As evening approached, a bright full moon rose from the sea. Jones made a lantern signal to the *Alliance* to join the *Bonhomme Richard* in the upcoming battle so that they would have a numerical advantage, but Landais stayed his course, ignoring Jones's order. The *Serapis* fired first, blasting the *Bonhomme Richard* with a broadside. The *Serapis*'s greater weight of shot wounded or killed many members of the *Bonhomme Richard*'s gun crews, thereby taking away much of its firepower. In addition, the *Bonhomme Richard*'s hull was breached in several places and her rudder badly damaged. The moon illuminated the battle scene as the *Alliance* finally sailed into the fray. The warship rounded the stern of the *Bonhomme Richard* and the bow of the *Serapis* and fired a broadside of grapeshot that struck both vessels. Most of the damage, however, was

8. Gerard W. Gawalt, John R. Sellers, eds., *John Paul Jones' Memoir of the American Revolution Presented to King Louis XVI of France* (Washington, DC: American Revolutionary Bicentennial Office, Library of Congress, 1979), 29.

The action off Flamborough Head, by Thomas Mitchell, 1780. The *Bonhomme Richard* is center exchanging fire with the *Serapis*, while the *Alliance*, far right, fires a broadside into both ships. (*US Naval History and Heritage Command*)

done to the *Bonhomme Richard*. The *Alliance* then changed course, returned to the two stricken ships and discharged another grapeshot broadside into the bow of the *Bonhomme Richard* wounding many Americans on deck or in the rigging. In desperation Jones ordered identity signal lanterns hoisted aloft to sway the *Alliance* from firing again. In spite of the highly visible lanterns, around ten o'clock the *Alliance* closed once again to engage the two ships that were locked in combat. Landais ordered yet another grapeshot broadside to be indiscriminately fired.

The commander of the *Serapis* was appalled at the slaughter onboard the American vessel and knew that the *Bonhomme Richard* was in danger of sinking. Yet in battle the line between bravado and desperation can be thin. With the two ships literally locked together in combat, sharp shooting marines fired from the *Bonhomme Richard*'s fighting tops, raking *Serapis* with gunfire and devastating the vulnerable British sailors on deck. Jones and his crew continued to fight tenaciously, even as their ship was sinking beneath them. Finally, the British Union Jack of the *Serapis* struck and the ship capitulated. The next morning the American ensign could be seen flying from both the *Bonhomme Richard* and the vanquished *Serapis*. As the rest of the American squadron rejoined Jones, they likely heard a few choice comments about what had transpired during the battle. From the bloodstained deck of the *Serapis*, the survivors of both the American and British vessels watched the sea finally engulf the *Bonhomme Richard.* "After the battle Landais confided to one of the French colonels that his intention was to help *Serapis* sink the *Richard,* to capture and board the British frigate and emerge victor of the battle. Later he had the impudence to claim that his broadsides forced [the *Serapis*] to strike."[9]

Jones stated in his memoir, "Captain Landais, a man of the most unhappy temper, not only behaved with disrespect to the commander, but soon assumed to act as he pleased, and as an independent commander, refusing to obey the signals of the Commodore, giving chase where or how he thought fit, and availing himself of any pretext to leave the squadron which he finally did."[10]

Once ashore in the Netherlands Jones accused Landais of incompetence for his haphazard firing of grapeshot that ravaged the crews of both contesting vessels. Landais was unapologetic and unremorseful for his actions. Later, at a chance meeting with Jones in an Amsterdam tavern, Landais reminded the commodore that they had agreed to a duel once they were onshore. Jones again avoided the challenge by saying their differences would be appropriately settled in a court-martial in the United States. Meanwhile Jones had Landais relieved of command of the *Alliance,* assuming command of his antagonist's ship. The loss of command further infuriated Landais. Jones felt that the morale on the *Alliance* was in disarray. The crew was disorderly and officers were continually drinking grog. This led to subordination and neglect of the vessel.

Impressed by Jones's exploits over the British, King Louis XVI of France conferred the title of *Chevalier de l'Ordre du Merite Militaire* on Jones, an honor also coveted by Landais. Meanwhile Landais became obsessed with forcing a duel with Jones, pursuing him on the streets of L'Orient, his sword readily at hand. This proved to be more of an annoyance than a provocative.

In another effort to aggravate Jones, Landais endeavored to reassemble his former officers and crew of the *Alliance* to regain his lost command and sail back to America. The men of the *Alliance* were split between those who were loyal to Landias and others loyal to Jones. Benjamin Franklin, United States Minister to France, intervened between the contending factions by jesting, "Capt. Jones loved close fighting, Capt. Landais was skillful at keeping out of harm's way, and that

9. Samuel Eliot Morison, *John Paul Jones: A Sailor's Biography* (Boston: Little, Brown and Company, 1959), 235.
10. John Paul Jones, *Memoirs of Rear-Admiral Paul Jones* (London: Simpkin and Marshall, 1830), 1: 163.

therefore you thought yourselves safer with the latter."[11] Franklin, however warned Jones that Landais would be very troublesome as long as they were in the same place. Jones responded, "The general conduct of Landais was that of a malignant madman, as much incited by the prevailing influence of frenzy as actuated by deliberate villainy."[12]

Not long after this Franklin suspended Landais's commission as a consequence of Captain Jones's complaint about Frenchman's cowardice and bad conduct. Landais was ordered to Paris, but before he set out he sent a written challenge to a duel to Captain Cottineau, commander of one of Jones's American Squadron ships the *Pallais*. Cottineau accepted the encounter and they went on shore with their seconds for a swordfight. Landis was the victor, leaving Cottineau was seriously wounded.

Although Jones was justified in his complaint to Franklin, the political climate made it unwise to take disciplinary action in France against a French officer, even though he held an American commission. The Frenchman was not cashiered from naval service and he had the brashness to insist that Jones return the command of the *Alliance* to him even though Franklin had given the ship to Jones. Some political intrigues and feuds among the American commissioners in France—Franklin, Arthur Lee, and Silas Deane —helped Landais get away with this misadventure.

Despite ample evidence of Landais's instability, incompetence, and possible perfidy, Lee, who had a long-standing dispute with Deane and Franklin, supported the Frenchman's claim to the command of the *Alliance*. Lee informed Jones that Franklin had no authority to relieve Landais of the command of a frigate assigned to him by Congress.

With Lee's reassurance and his intense envy of Paul Jones, Landais plotted to get his warship back. On June 13, when he learned that Jones had gone ashore, he boarded the ship in L'Orient Harbor. He mustered the officers who had previously served under him on the quarterdeck while all Jones's officers were below at dinner. After rallying them, Landais was greeted with loud huzzas. Jones's former officers were summoned on deck where Landais read them the commission issued to him by Congress. He then ordered ashore officers of the late *Bonhomme Richard* who did not acknowledge his authority. Landais did not, however, allow any of the crew to leave. Some of Jones's former

11. Franklin to the Officers of the *Alliance*, June 12, 1780, in William B. Wilcox and Barbara B. Oberg, eds. *Benjamin Franklin Papers* (New Haven, CT: Yale University Press), 32: 508.
12. Jones. *Memoirs of Rear-Admiral Paul Jones*, 1: 192.

men seemed happy about the upheaval. They were dissatisfied with Jones because he delayed in distributing prize money from recent ship captures and was also a notorious martinet. Those who were displeased with Landais's usurpation of command were put in irons and thrown in the hold with the rats and ballast.

Jones became furious when he learned he had been outfoxed. Midshipman Nathaniel Fanning, a former Jones officer wrote, "his passion knew no bounds; and in the first paroxysm of his rage he acted more like a madman than a conqueror."[13] Once he regained his composure, Jones behaved with circumspection. Instead of confronting Landais he chose to travel to Paris to obtain official authorization to regain command of the *Alliance* from both the American and French governments. Franklin provided him a written directive explicitly ordering Landais to immediately vacate the ship and the French Minister of Marine, M. de Sartine, issued a Royal Warrant for Landais's arrest.

Landais did not remain idle. When Jones returned from Paris on June 20, he found that the *Alliance* had been moved from L'Orient to nearby Port Louis. Jones called upon the captain of the port with his two orders to prevent *Alliance*'s escape. A chained log-boom was promptly moved across mouth of the harbor blocking Landais's exit. In addition, a gunboat armed with three 24-pounders was ordered to stand by to prevent his escape. The commander of the harbor's citadel that comprised two forts was also to fire on the frigate if Landais attempted to pass. To physically retake the *Alliance*, Jones was provided with a small flotilla of three row galleys, about one hundred soldiers from the garrison and some one hundred marines.

Curiously the usually aggressive Jones refrained from joining the expedition. When Landais was called upon to yield the frigate, he replied: "If you come within reach of my cannons I will sink you."[14] Apparently intimidated, the task force withdrew and returned to port. Accusing the officers of the port of acting more like women than men, surprisingly John Paul Jones acquiesced, reversing the order to fire upon the *Alliance* and having the boom removed. He later justified his change of heart by saying he did not want to be responsible for bloodshed between allied subjects of France and America.

Not all officers aboard the *Alliance* enthusiastically supported Landais's seizure of power. Leading the defiance was Capt. Matthew Parke, commander of the ship's marines, who agreed to defend the ship

13. Nathaniel Fanning, *Fanning's Narrative: The Memoirs of Nathanial Fanning 1778-1778* (Bedford, MA: Applewood Books; originally published 1913), 76.
14. Ibid., 77.

but objected to the way command of the ship had occurred. Landais regarded this as defiance of his authority and ordered the purser, Nathaniel Blodget, to keep a watch on Captain Parke and if he displayed disloyalty to the captain, he was to run his sword through him. Blodget considered this order bewildering and told Landais he would not obey it. Still feeling threatened while in Port Louis, on June 21 Landais had Parke confined in his quarters with the intention of releasing him once the ship was at sea. On July 8 the boom was removed allowing *Alliance* to slip out to sea, but disorder soon appeared.

Landais grew restless and slept very little while at sea. He was distrustful of his own officers, and gave them a good deal of anguish by continuously creating unnecessary difficulties and stirring up imaginary ones. Nobody aboard ship was exempt from his mercurial moods including the five passengers, most prominent of whom was Landais's staunch supporter Arthur Lee. The returning American envoy had taken along a private cargo of goods for his personal profit, but at government expense. One day at dinner Lee complained about Landais's ungentlemanly conduct at the dinner table. He responded that in essence that he was captain of the ship and would do as he pleased. That response confounded Lee. He said that he never disputed Landais as captain of the ship, but he was not used to being so mistreated. Landais however resorted to threats once again. He said that when they reached shore Lee should have his pistols loaded, implying that Lee should be prepared to have a duel with the Frenchman.

Landais's eccentricities kept the ship in a constant turmoil. As an example, before *Alliance* sailed from Boston for France on their initial voyage, the officers had insured a supply of fresh meat for the long journey by using their own funds to purchase swine as their own property. Once at sea Landais bizarrely demanded that one half of the pigs belonged to him because he owned the boar that fathered them. His officers were then ordered to abstain from killing any of them without his permission.

On the trip back to America Landais became increasing more abusive and tactlessly reprimanded his officers before the crew. On the night of July 13, Landais appeared on the quarterdeck and gave the ship's first officer, Lt. J. A. Degge, a public scolding for not keeping the ship with the wind astern. Before that Degge had been a loyal Landais supporter, but now visibly upset by the abuse, the lieutenant ordered the men to cut off all the weather braces. Landais disliked the tone of his voice and ordered Degge to go below, but the lieutenant refused, responding that he would had rather be in hell than sail with a man he could not please. This produced what must have been a bizarre scene of Landais chasing Degge around the deck. The Frenchman instructed Captain Parke of the marines to arrest the lieutenant, but Degge armed himself, went into the wardroom and stayed below.

It was not long before the passengers, officers and crew grew dismayed with the captain and a series of calamities developed. The first occurred on the morning of August 5 when many of the ship's company came to the quarterdeck and asked why had he had ordered sail taken up since the wind was fair that morning. Shortening sail did not seem the best way to get to the Grand Banks. Was he not proceeding to America? Landais was shocked by the insubordinate attitude of the crew and asked the men whether or not they intended to obey him. They responded that they would as long as he immediately proceeded to America. The Captain stubbornly gave no such order, so the men went forward and began to hoist as much sail as they could. Enraged at their rebelliousness, Landais shouted to his third lieutenant to lower the foretopsail that had been hoisted. The officer tried to obey the order, but the crew prevented him from doing so.

Then Landais ordered his marines put under arms at once to enforce his orders. Captain Parke, a consistent anti-Landais stalwart, called the roll of marines, but not a single man came aft. This meant that a state of mutiny now existed with the crew in control of the ship. The officers and passengers grew exceedingly apprehensive and Landais became indecisive. An officer asked the captain what to do when so many were against him. Landais did not know the answer so he went below, thus allowing the crew to make sail and take charge of the ship.

The next day, at 10 A.M., the *Alliance* sounded bottom at thirty-five fathoms. That meant they were on the Grand Banks off Newfoundland. The crew had been provided with fishing tackle so they could supplement the ship's rations with fresh fish and the men threw their lines overboard to catch as many as they could. Landais ascended onto the quarterdeck and ostensibly out of shear contrariness ordered all the fish that had been caught thrown back into the sea and to make sail once again. That evening Samuel Guild, the ship's surgeon, protested, pointing out that the stores for the sick were nearly exhausted and that a number of them needed nourishing food. Landais argued in turn that if the men stopped to fish the trip would be delayed and thus they would consume more of the precious stores. Guild pointed out that since they were off the Grand Banks, the crew needed just two hours to catch a supply sufficient for the remainder of the voyage. Landais curtly replied that he would stop for nothing. Landais returned to his cabin, feigning sickness; he threw himself on his bunk and pretended to sleep.

The officers of the *Alliance* now encountered increasing difficulty getting the crew to perform their duty. They requested Landais to head for the nearest American port, but he refused, insisting that his orders were to go to Philadelphia. With increased muttering several crewmen proposed to the officers that they change the ship's course to Boston. When the officers refused, a large part of the ship's company assembled on deck and declared that if they encountered an enemy ship, they would not fire a single broadside against the challenger if the *Alliance* would not sail to Boston, warning that they would spike the ship's guns should a hostile ship come alongside. During this mutinous altercation Landais did not come on deck.

At about dawn the next morning the officers composed a carefully written report on the dangerous condition of the ship. They presented it to Landais in his cabin, but he refused to have the paper read. He only cried out that he had orders to go to Philadelphia and that is where he intended to go. The officers progressively looked upon the captain as having relinquished his command. Since he refused to assist them, they thought that it was time to think about choosing somebody else to take command. The officers then wrote out and signed a statement that attested to the alarming situation aboard the frigate. The discontent of the people had become most serious. Landais declined to receive any communication from his officers and shouted at any delegation that entreated him.

The officers now held a meeting and stated that they would rather be hanged for bringing the ship into any safe port than be taken by an inferior foe's force and conveyed to the enemy's port. The passengers then gave their opinion that a competent officer should be designated as commander to conduct the ship to the United States.

Acting with considerable caution and recording every move they made, the officers chose Lieutenant Degge to take over the command. Degge was the only officer commissioned by Congress on board except for Landais. With understandable reluctance the lieutenant accepted, but only after the other officers on board gave him their orders in writing. Captain Landais never left his cabin after that time, only to reappear when the ship came in sight of land.

When the *Alliance* reached Boston, the Navy Board for the Eastern District directed Captain Parke to deliver a letter ordering Landais to leave the ship and to turn over his cabin and furniture to Capt. John Barry, the ship's new commander. When Parke attempted to carry out the order, Landais threatened to shoot the marine officer. Finally, a sergeant and two men broke into the cabin and hauled the captain off the ship.

Once ashore, Landais filed formal charges of mutiny against the officers and passengers who supported their mutinous behavior. The Marine Committee of Congress instructed the Navy Board in Boston to hold a court of inquiry into Landais's conduct from reassuming command of the *Alliance* at L'Orient until his arrival in Boston. The commissioners also directed the board to identify the mutiny's ringleaders for a probable court-martial.

The verdict of the court was a foregone conclusion. Parke was acquitted, but Landais was judged guilty of four charges. His sentence was to have his commission revoked and be declared unqualified for service in the American navy.

POSTSCRIPT

After the American Revolution Landais returned to Revolutionary France and was given command of a warship in 1792. Mutinies broke out among the crews of his assigned fleet forcing Landais to put into Brest. His commission was revoked on October 26, 1793. In November 1797 he returned to New York to press his claims for prizes captured by the *Alliance* in 1779. In 1806 Congress paid him four thousand dollars, but his bid for further remuneration failed in the Senate in 1815. He spent his remaining years impoverished in New York City.

An American Sea Captain Encounters Horatio Nelson— And Lives to Tell the Tale

❋ DAVID D. KINDY ❋

Few sea captains could claim they crossed bowsprits with Lord Nelson and sailed away—ship and cargo intact—but Nathaniel Carver of Plymouth, Massachusetts, was one who did. Not only did he survive the encounter, the American received a letter of commendation from the man who would later be remembered as the "Hero of Trafalgar."

This unusual event occurred in the summer of 1782 just off Cape Cod. The outcome of the American Revolution was all but decided at this point. A year earlier, George Washington had forced the surrender of British forces under Lord Cornwallis at the Battle of Yorktown, and in April 1782, peace negotiations had begun in Paris between England and its former American colonies.

Combat operations, however, had not ceased, though they were definitely on the downswing. On the ocean, smaller craft still needed to be careful that they did not sail into harm's way—that is, any larger armed vessels on the prowl for easy prizes.

On July 14, Carver was on a return voyage from North Carolina. The Plymouth captain was in command of the *Harmony*, a small schooner hauling corn from the southern states. Some reports identify

SOURCES: William T. Davis *History of the Town of Plymouth with a Sketch of the Origin and Growth of Separatism* (Philadelphia: J.W. Lewis & Co., 1885); *Biographical Review Containing Life Sketches of Leading Citizens of Plymouth County, Massachusetts* (Boston: Biographical Review Publishing Company, 1897); *Representative Men and Old Families of Southeastern Massachusetts* (Chicago: J.H. Beers & Co., 1912); Sir Harris Nicolas, ed., *The Despatches and Letters of Admiral Lord Viscount Nelson* edited by (London: Henry Colburn, Publisher, 1845); Edwin L. Miller, ed., *Robert Southey's Life of Nelson* edited by (London: Longmans, Green and Co., 1898).

his vessel as a fishing boat, which it may have been, but it is likely she was serving as a merchantman on this particular trip.

As luck would have it, Captain Carver's schooner caught the attention of the HMS *Albemarle*, a twenty-eight-gun, sixth rate frigate under the command of none other than Horatio Nelson, then a junior officer in the Royal Navy. Nelson, a lieutenant, was on his way back to Quebec after a rather unsuccessful cruise to raid American shipping and to hunt for pesky privateers.

On this summer day, Nelson brought Carver onboard his vessel and ordered the American to serve as pilot through the treacherous shores in and around Cape Cod. Filled with shoals, sandbars and rock outcroppings, this notorious region is often referred to as the "Graveyard of the Atlantic"—and for good reason. Over the past 500 years, the complex coastline along Cape Cod, Martha's Vineyard, and Nantucket has claimed thousands of shipwrecks, which is precisely why Carver was such a valuable asset to Nelson. The American captain's knowledge of the local waters would be extremely helpful as the *Albemarle* continued its mission in the seas off New England.

Undoubtedly, Captain Carver was aware of the capabilities of his captor. The British lieutenant had scored several small successes as a captain of tenders and also as master and commander of the HMS *Badger*, a brig with twelve guns.

Of course, this was not the Nelson of legend that Carver encountered. He was not yet a lord, nor even an admiral. Horatio Nelson was twenty-three and captaining only his second ship. Ahead of him still lay fame and glory. This remarkable leader with a unique understanding of strategy and the ability to create unconventional tactics in the heat of bloody conflicts was just beginning his march into history.

Nelson would go on to become one of Britain's most famous naval war heroes. His presence of command in battle resulted in several decisive victories for England and cemented the notion that "Britannia rules the waves." And he was not afraid to put his own life on the line. Nelson lost sight in his right eye in combat off the island of Corsica in 1794 and most of his right arm in a rare defeat in the Canary Islands in 1797.

At the Battle of Copenhagen in 1801, then-Vice Admiral Nelson was leading his ships into battle against a formidable fleet of Danes and Norwegians. The British flagship signaled for him to retreat but Nelson put his telescope to his blind eye and said, "I really do not see the signal!" He then resumed the battle and led Britain to victory. Thus, "turning a blind eye" entered the English lexicon.

Nelson would go on to strike fear into the French fleet during the Napoleonic Wars. His boldness and aggressive attacks decimated the enemy and resulted in major naval triumphs for England. His crowning moment came at Trafalgar in 1805, when the Royal Navy crushed the French fleet and ended Napoleon's dream of conquering the British Isles. At the beginning of the battle, Nelson sent a stirring signal to his ships: "England expects that every man will do his duty." Ever since, this stalwart expression has been the country's motto during times of duress.

Trafalgar was also the end of Nelson. He was mortally wounded by a sharpshooter as his flagship, the famed HMS *Victory*, moved in to deliver a death-dealing broadside to a French vessel. Nelson was buried with full honors at a state funeral. Today, his likeness stands atop the Nelson Column at Trafalgar Square in Westminster to remember his heroic sacrifice.

However, that was all in the future. In 1782, Nelson was just coming of age. And now, with Captain Carver serving as an able pilot, he was able to continue his raid.

For the next month, Nelson had Carver help him navigate the bays—Boston, Massachusetts and Cape Cod—while the *Albemarle* harassed American merchantmen and challenged the French fleet in Boston Harbor to sail forth and do battle. Under the command of Louis-Philippe de Vaudreuil, the French ships finally took notice of this upstart Englishman and began the hunt.

With Carver's assistance, Nelson led four French ships of the line and a frigate on a merry chase from Boston Harbor, around Cape Cod, and down to Vineyard Sound. Rather than fleeing his enemy, the English lieutenant was trying to induce a mistake by the French admiral so he could lessen the stacked odds against him and make it a fair fight.

Captain Carver's local knowledge proved advantageous. The American was able to direct Nelson through a series of shoals where the deeper-draft French ships dared not follow. Once past these hazards, Nelson noticed the French flagship had become separated from the rest of the fleet. The English lieutenant ordered his crew to shorten sail and came about to engage the enemy. The French admiral—even with at least 40 more cannon—thought better of the situation and made a tactical retreat.

Following this event, Nelson sailed the *Albemarle* back to Plymouth and returned Carver and his crew to their homeport. The English lieutenant kept the *Harmony* to serve as a tender. Carver reported the incident to the schooner's owner, Thomas Davis of Plymouth, who was determined to recover his vessel.

Davis loaded fresh meats and provisions on another boat, and then he and Carver sailed out to meet Nelson. They pulled alongside the *Albemarle* and shouted that they had brought the lieutenant a gift. Nelson welcomed them aboard. He was pleased to receive fresh food and vegetables since he had been at sea for several months and was in desperate need of resupply, especially with the ever-present threat of scurvy hanging overhead.

Nelson invited Davis and Carver to join him for dinner in the captain's quarters. Not a word was spoken about the return of the ship. Following the meal, the lieutenant called for his writing desk and wrote the following certificate (spelling and punctuation appear as on the actual manuscript):

> These are to certify that I took the schooner *Harmony* Nathaniel Carver master belonging to Plymouth, but on acct of his good services have given him up his vessel again.
> Dated onb His Majestys Ship *Albemarle* 17 August, 1782, in Boston Bay
>
> HORATIO NELSON

The letter was a "Get out of Jail" card for Davis and Carver. It guaranteed the *Harmony* would not be troubled during any future encounters with the Royal Navy. Nelson then handed over the certificate and released the schooner back to the possession of its owner and master.

The Davis family kept the letter. Immediately after the American Revolution, it was seen as a novelty—a kind of a war souvenir from a quirky moment between two warring nations. However, it soon became a prized possession as Nelson's acclaim began to rise.

The certificate was passed through the family for generations, eventually being framed and hanging prominently on the wall for all to see. For some time, it was believed to be the only signature of Nelson in the United States.

The certificate was unknown in England until 1852, when Abbott Lawrence, minister to the Court of St. James, happened to mention it in conversation with a professor of history at the University of Edinburgh. The professor was astounded because he was unaware Nelson had served in North America during the Revolution. He did not believe the story until a copy of the certificate was later presented.

William T. Davis, the great-grandson of Thomas Davis, eventually came to own the letter and wrote about it in one of his many history books about Plymouth. The Davis descendant was clearly proud of his family's legacy and even shared the story with British historian Robert Southey, who included the event in "The Life of Nelson," the first definitive biography of the admiral, which was published in 1886.

The whereabouts of the original certificate are unknown today but believed to still be in the possession of the Davis family. A facsimile resides at the Hedge House, headquarters of the Plymouth Antiquarian Society in Plymouth, Massachusetts. Replete with remarkable penmanship and the flourishes of the later First Viscount Nelson, First Duke of Bronté, it is a fascinating link to a nearly forgotten moment of the American Revolution—a brief encounter when hostilities were temporarily suspended and enemies could treat each other with respect.

Slavery Through the Eyes of Revolutionary Generals

❊❦ GENE PROCKNOW ❦❊

Generally when people think about slavery in the United States, they harken back to the Civil War period when Northern states had abolished slavery and slavery was the center of the southern plantation economy. However, during the Revolutionary era, the noxious institution of slavery prospered in both Northern and Southern states. While there were substantially more slaves in the Southern states, legalized slavery was condoned and rife throughout all thirteen colonies. Among the white population, slavery was widely accepted with only hints of the upcoming nineteenth-century abolition movement.

Slave ownership by the richest segment of society typified the Revolutionary era institution of slavery. Wealthy individuals and those with leadership positions in the community employed slaves in agriculture, manufacturing and household services. As a group, the Continental Army major generals fit the definition of people who were most likely to own slaves.[1] Looking at the major generals' views on slavery and their slave ownership is a window on how the entire leadership class and population viewed slavery.

Not counting George Washington, there were twenty-nine major generals, of which twenty-three lived before or after the war in the United States.[2] Over half of these major generals owned slaves, which

1. As the most senior army officers, the Continental Army major generals as group were representative of the highest level of authority and responsibility within Revolutionary America.
2. The six other major generals are foreign volunteers who served in the Continental Army and returned to their homeland or did not survive the war. I did include in the twenty-three major generals Prussian volunteer Frederick von Steuben as he purchased a large tract of land in New York State after the war and had the opportunity to engage in slavery (but never did).

is a bit lower in proportion to the slave owning signers of the Declaration of Independence. While certainly a small percentage, the proportion of the major generals who advocated ending slavery is not certain.[3] The contradiction between fighting for political liberty and fighting for personal liberty did not seem to manifest itself (or be important enough) in the minds of this group of Revolutionary leaders.

What complicated the situation for the major generals, however, is that they were faced with severe manpower shortages and had to decide whether to recruit slaves into the army. During an October 1775 council of war, George Washington and seven current and future major generals considered the question of enlisting both freed and enslaved African Americans. They "agreed unanimously to reject all slaves and by a great majority to reject all Negroes altogether."[4] At the same time, Brig. Gen. (later Maj. Gen.) John Thomas disagreed and welcomed Blacks into the ranks, saying in a letter to John Adams, "we have Some Negros, but I Look on them in General Equally Servicable with other men, for Fatigue and in Action; many of them have Proved themselves brave."[5] With his back to the wall during the 1777 Saratoga campaign, Philip Schuyler, a New York major general, complained to Maj. Gen. William Heath on the quality of his reinforcements, stating, "one third of the few that have been sent are boys, aged men and negroes, who disgrace our arms." Raising the contradiction of slaves fighting for white people's freedom, Schuyler went on to say, "Is it consistent with the Sons of Freedom to trust their all to be defended by slaves?"[6]

As the war continued longer than expected and the need for additional soldiers increased, Thomas's point of view won out and most major generals changed their views to freely enlist both free and enslaved African Americans. Even large slaveholders such as Maj. Gen. William Smallwood actively advocated for enlistment of enslaved people. In the end, major generals had to rely on slaves. Up to ten percent of the Continental Army were free and enslaved African Americans,

---

3. For a listing of Continental Army major generals and statistics on slave ownership and views, see http://researchingtheamericanrevolution.com/major-generals/.

4. George Washington, *The Papers of George Washington. 2 2: Revolutionary War Series September - December 1775*, William Wright Abbot and Dorothy Twohig, ed. (Charlottesville, VA: University Press of Virginia, 1987), 125.

5. Thomas to John Adams, October 24, 1775, https://founders.archives.gov/?q=%20Recipient%3A%22Adams%2C%20John%22%20Author%3A%22Thomas%2C%20John%22&s=1111311111&sa=thomas&r=1, accessed October 5, 2017.

6. Philip Schuyler to William Heath, July 28, 1777, *Collections of the Massachusetts Historical Society*, Seventh Series, Vol. IV (Boston, MA: Published by the Society, 1904), 135-6.

especially in the later years of the war and among the Continental line outside of the deep south.[7]

Contrary to popular perceptions, both Northerners and Southerners owned slaves. All six of the major generals from states south of the Mason Dixon line owned slaves while five out of seventeen Northern major generals owned slaves. Rather than regionalism, slave ownership most closely correlated with income; the wealthiest major generals owned slaves. Similar to civilian slave owners, the major generals either used slaves as exploited labor or as house servants.

Other than George Washington, Maj. Gen. William Moultrie, owner of a prosperous South Carolina planation, owned the largest number of slaves with over two hundred. The war ravaged his plantation, however, and he died both penniless and without slaves. Other large slave owning major generals include William Smallwood (fifty-six slaves), Adam Stephen (thirty slaves) and Robert Howe (thirty slaves), all southerners. With the exception of Maj. Gen. Philip Schuyler (thirteen slaves), Northern major general slave owners tended to own at most a handful of slaves.

A number of the major generals were guilty of hypocrisy when it came to slavery. Raised a Rhode Island Quaker but not practicing by the outset of the rebellion, Nathanael Greene owned slaves during the war and may have brought them with him on campaign.[8] When military exigencies became extreme, however, he strongly advocated for slave enlistment.[9] Further, after the Revolution, the states of South Carolina and Georgia rewarded his military services by deeding him sequestered loyalist plantations. Greene stated that he was forced to use slaves to make those properties financially successful. Like others, Greene changed his views on slavery when it suited his economic interests. Another example of hypocrisy is the case of Alexander Mc-Dougall. As a pre-war merchant he bought and sold slaves and he owned at least one slave by the name of Colerain.[10] Joining the nascent

7. For a good analysis of the role of blacks in fighting for American independence, see Judith L. Van Buskirk, *Standing in Their Own Light: African American Patriots in the American Revolution*, Campaigns and Commanders, volume 59 (Norman, OK: University of Oklahoma Press, 2017).

8. Nathanael Greene, *The Papers of General Nathanael Greene* (Chapel Hill, NC: Published for the Rhode Island Historical Society [by] the University of North Carolina Press, 1976), Volume VI, 93.

9. Greene to Washington, March 9, 1782, *Founders Online*, National Archives, http://founders.archives.gov/documents/Washington/99-01-02-07940.

10. Bibliographic Directory of the United States Congress 1774—Present, http://bioguide.congress.gov/scripts/guidedisplay.pl?index=M000415, accessed October 3, 2017.

New York Manumission Society later in life, McDougall may have had a change in heart. It is not clear whether he continued to own slaves after the war and while a member, as there were other slaveholders in the Manumission Society,[11] including its principal founder, John Jay.[12]

Israel Putnam was the only major general to have likely freed his slaves prior to the onset of Revolutionary hostilities. As with most other events in Putnam's life, it is hard to separate fact from fiction and notable events from embellishment. A mid-nineteenth century biographer recounted a story about Putnam helping subdue a Connecticut neighbor's unruly slave. To prove a point, Putnam placed a single noose around the necks of both master and slave, thereby ending the dispute.[13] Later, there was a story about Putnam rescuing a slave named simply Dick from mistreatment by his Cuban masters in 1762. Putnam returned to Connecticut with Dick who functioned as a freely employed manservant for the rest of Putnam's life.[14]

One would have thought that fighting for the ideals of the Revolution and having African American soldiers serving under them would have changed the views of slave-owning major generals. With one partial exception, this appears not to have been the case. Horatio Gates has been praised for freeing all slaves who operated his Virginia plantation called Travelers Rest shortly after the war.[15] However, closer examination reveals that this is a misstatement. Actually, per the terms of a September 14, 1790 deed of sale, Gates sold his slaves for £800 with the stipulation that five would be free after five years and the remaining eleven when they reached the age of twenty-eight.[16] Financially, it became easier for Gates to manumit his slaves as he became wealthy through marriage to his second wife. While this is a much different story than commonly reported, none of the other major generals took steps while living, no matter the motivations, to emancipate their slaves.

11. The New York African Free School, https://www.nyhistory.org/web/africanfreeschool/history/manumission-society.html, accessed October 3, 2017.

12. Joanne Retano, *The Restless City: A Short History of New York from Colonial Times to the Present* (New York: Routledge, 2010), 29.

13. William Cutter, *The Life of Gen. Putnam*, 4th ed. (Boston: John Philbrick, 1854), 29–30.

14. George L. Clark, *The History of Connecticut: Its people and Institutions* (New York: G.P. Putnam & Sons, 1914), 157.

15. Samuel White Patterson, *Horatio Gates Defender of American Liberties* (New York: Columbia University Press, 1941), 368.

16. Paul David Nelson, *General Horatio Gates: A Biography* (Baton Rouge: Louisiana State University Press, 1976), 288.

Certainly, Washington freed his (though not Martha's) slaves at the time of his death. Several major generals including Richard Montgomery, Charles Lee and Adam Stephen bequeathed their slaves to heirs. The other slave owners' last wills and testaments cite only property to be bequeathed with the assumption that slaves would be divided just like other property. Two large pre-war slaveholders, William Moultrie and Robert Howe, died destitute and likely sold all of their slaves prior to death to discharge debts.

Only Samuel Holden Parsons, Arthur St. Clair and William Heath publically expressed opposition to slavery or to the expansion of slave-owning territory, all of them never have owned slaves during their lifetimes. After the Revolution, both Parsons and St. Clair politically advocated the prohibition of slavery in the Northwest Territories.[17] Moving from Connecticut, Parsons became a leading settler in the Ohio region and later Washington appointed him as a territorial judge. Parsons's opposition was widely known and lent support to those opposing slavery as the 1787 Northwest Ordinance was drafted.[18] In 1802, St. Clair made an impassioned speech in Cincinnati supporting the prohibition of slavery when forming the laws of the new state of Ohio.[19] Parsons's and St. Clair's efforts were instrumental in defeating Thomas Jefferson and the Democratic-Republican efforts to open the territory north of the Ohio River to slavery. While his views were more nuanced, William Heath publically opposed slavery during the 1787 Massachusetts Constitutional Convention. Although Heath did not believe it possible to eradicate existing slavery due to the states' rights provisions of the Constitution, he opposed any expansion of territories allowing slavery and prognosticated that slavery would wither away due to the non-importation clause and likely decline in economic productivity.[20]

In posterity, biographers have sought to burnish the reputations of our most revered Revolutionary War generals. Several biographers ig-

17. There are sources which lack supporting citations that allege Arthur St. Clair owned and even purchased slaves during his tenure as Northwest Territorial governor. For an example, see, http://www.lib.niu.edu/1998/iht519802.html.
18. Charles S. Hall, *Life And Letters of Samuel Holden Parsons Major General in the Continental Army and Chief Judge of the Southwestern Territory 1787-1789* (Binghamton, NY: Otseningo Publishing Col., 1905), 606.
19. William Henry Smith, ed., *The St. Clair Papers. The Life and Public Services of Arthur St. Clair Soldier of the Revolutionary War, President of the Continental Congress and Governor of the North-Western Territory with His Correspondence and Other Papers* (Cincinnati: Robert Clarke & Co., 1882), 587–90.
20. Debate in Massachusetts Ratifying Convention, http://press-pubs.uchicago.edu/founders/documents/a1_9_1s11.html, accessed October 3, 2017.

nored their slave ownership or played it down. For example, Philip Schuyler's highly comprehensive biographer Don R. Gerlach ignored his slave ownership all together.[21] A good example of playing down slave ownership is the David Mattern biography of Benjamin Lincoln in which the author attempts to put a good face on Lincoln's slave ownership by asserting that Northern slavery was not as bad as Southern slavery. Further, Mattern concludes that as a result of his Southern campaign, Lincoln changed his views to oppose slavery.[22] William Moultrie's biographer C. L. Bragg even goes so far as to depict him as a benevolent slave master who engendered loyalty and commitment from the enslaved.[23] While abhorrent today, this view that "some slavery was better than other slavery" has survived for a long time.

What biographers do recount are the major generals' attempts to employ slaves as military assets. After the initial period of non-use, most major generals engaged slaves as soldiers, laborers or servants and actively sought ways to inhibit slaves from fleeing to the British lines. In some cases, they advocated granting freedom in exchange for enlistment. This was especially the case in the southern theater where the numbers of soldiers were few, recruitment was difficult, and there was a high proportion of slaves in the population. Maj. Gen. Nathanael Greene even offered a persuasive pecuniary argument to the governor of South Carolina that arming blacks would allow the Patriots to recapture from the British the most agriculturally fertile regions and restore the war ravaged economy. Notwithstanding the economically compelling argument, the South Carolina Patriot politicians feared a slave uprising more and dismissed Greene's proposal.[24]

Beyond noting the ownership of slaves and their military value, biographies rarely discuss the major generals' views on slavery. Perhaps this is because slavery was so widely accepted during the Revolutionary period that it is not considered notable or a controversial issue. Another factor maybe that with only a few exceptions, the major generals lost considerable wealth during the war and were largely financially unsuccessful after the war; therefore they did not have the economic capacity

21. Don R. Gerlach, *Proud Patriot: Philip Schuyler and the War of Independence, 1775-1783* (Syracuse, NY: Syracuse University Press, 1987); Don R. Gerlach, *Philip Schuyler and the American Revolution in New York, 1733-1777* (Lincoln: University of Nebraska Press, 1964).
22. David B. Mattern, *Benjamin Lincoln and the American Revolution* (Columbia, SC: University of South Carolina Press, 1998), 19.
23. C. L. Bragg, *Crescent Moon over Carolina: William Moultrie and American Liberty* (Columbia, SC: The University of South Carolina Press, 2013), 12.
24. Van Buskirk, *Standing in Their Own Light*, 169.

to purchase slaves. Most importantly, the incongruity of leading both free and enslaved soldiers in the fight for liberty and freedom from oppression is proof of the prevailing wide spread support for slavery in all segments of the Revolutionary era population.

In rare and nuanced cases such as Benjamin Lincoln or Horatio Gates, military service may have altered a few major generals' opinions on slavery. As a group, however, their views were consistent with other prominent leaders in society. They fought for independence and freedom from "British slavery" but not for the freedom of enslaved African Americans.

Our Man in Minorca:
Lewis Littlepage, American Volunteer with the Spanish Armed Forces

❀ LARRIE D. FERREIRO ❀

The Revolutionary War was fought on a global scale, with six nation states engaged in battles across three continents and two oceans. Volunteers from many European nations came to the United States to fight alongside the American insurgents: Antoine Félix Wuibert and the Marquis de Lafayette from France, Jordi Farragut from Spain and Thaddeus Kosciuszko from Poland, to name but a few. By contrast, only a handful of Americans fought under foreign flags against the British enemy: the merchant Oliver Pollock, who was aide-de-camp for Bernardo de Gálvez during his Southern campaigns 1779-1781; Alexander Gillon of the South Carolina Navy, who in 1782 served in a Spanish force that captured Nassau in the Bahamas; and Lewis Littlepage, a Virginian in the household of John Jay in Madrid, while Jay was vainly attempting to forge a formal alliance between the United States and Spain. During his sojourn in Spain, Littlepage served under the Spanish flag in two land assaults, one in Minorca and one in Gibraltar, and in one naval battle at Cape Spartel, pitting French and Spanish forces against Britain. By all accounts he acquitted himself well, before beginning a new career as a diplomat for the Polish crown to European courts.

Lewis Littlepage was born near Richmond, Virginia on December 19, 1762 to Elizabeth Lewis Littlepage and James Littlepage. His place of birth is variously recorded as Hanover County or New Kent County. His father died when Lewis was just four years old, leaving Elizabeth's brother as guardian for her two children. Eight years later Elizabeth married Lewis Holladay, the man she had originally hired as her farm overseer, with whom she had two more children. Lewis Littlepage had a happy childhood, and at age sixteen attended William and Mary College in Williamsburg, where he studied the classics. This was the year 1778, when the War of American Independence was still being fought mostly in the northern states. Within a few months that all changed, as the British brought the fight to the Chesapeake Bay with a raiding party led by George Collier and Edward Mathew in May 1779. Littlepage was among the William and Mary students who fought against the British troops before they withdrew to New York. This apparently gave the otherwise studious Littlepage his taste for grand adventure, for in January 1780—having just turned seventeen years old—he was on a ship bound for Europe to experience the war at first hand.[1]

Littlepage's family had secured his passage aboard one of the merchant ships carrying tobacco from Virginia to France in order to pay for arms and munitions that French merchants had obtained for the insurgents. At the same time, some influential friends of the family also persuaded John Jay, who had just been appointed by the Congress to travel to Spain to seek an alliance, to receive Littlepage as a paying guest and take him under his wing during his diplomatic overtures. Jay arrived in Spain in January 1780 with his secretary William Carmichael, where they began an ultimately unsuccessful bid for Spanish recognition of the nascent United States of America. Littlepage debarked in Nantes, France a few weeks later, where he took rooms at a boarding house. One of his neighbors, the Massachusetts businessman (and chronicler of the Revolution) Elkanah Watson was suitably impressed with the teenager, describing him as "of a fine manly figure, with a dark, penetrating black eye, and a physiognomy peculiar and striking . . . [and] esteemed a prodigy of genius."[2]

Littlepage's genius was apparently limited to academia, for when he finally arrived in John Jay's household in Madrid in October 1780, he became singularly foolhardy in his dealings with his esteemed guardian. Jay assumed he was grooming an up-and-coming lawyer like himself, and that his expenses for this training would be adequately reimbursed. Littlepage instead saw this arrangement as carte blanche to achieve personal glory and spent Jay's money quite freely without any arrangements for repayment. This resulted in a very public back-and-forth bat-

---

1. Much of this information is from two biographies of Littlepage: Curtis Caroll Davis, *The King's Chevalier: A Biography of Lewis Littlepage* (Indianapolis, IN: Bobbs-Merrill, 1961); and a descendant of the subject's family, Nell Holladay Boand, *Lewis Littlepage* (Richmond, VA: Whittet & Shepperson, 1970).
2. Elkanah Watson, *Men and Times of the Revolution; Or, Memoirs of Elkanah Watson, including Journals of Travels in Europe and America, From 1777 to 1842* (New York: Dana and Company, 1856), 132.

tle of pamphlets, printed after the end of the war, in which each party slandered the other's deeds and reputation.[3]

While Littlepage was still a student at William and Mary, France and Spain had signed the "Treaty of Defense and Offensive Alliance against England" at the Spanish palace of Aranjuez on April 12, 1779. This military alliance joined the French and Spanish navies in a series of operations against the vaunted British navy. Their first mutual effort that summer, a combined armada to invade Britain, failed because of lack of coordination and a massive outbreak of dysentery aboard the ships. By 1781 the disease had dissipated, and the two navies began working efficiently together, a sort of NATO before NATO. That year, two major joint operations were planned. The first was a successful combined assault on Pensacola, which drove the British from West Florida in May. The second was the recovery of the Mediterranean island of Minorca, which had been transferred from Spanish to British rule after the Seven Years' War.

In the early summer of 1781, the combined assault fleet was gathered in Cádiz, Spain. The naval forces were commanded by the French Lieutenant-General of the Navy (roughly equivalent to vice admiral) Luc Urbain Du Bouëxic, comte de Guichen, and by the Spanish Captain-General (admiral equivalent) Luis de Córdova y Córdova, both of whom had learned hard lessons on joint operations from the failed attempt to invade Britain. Commanding the ground forces would be Louis des Balbes de Berton, Duc de Crillon. Crillon was an ideal choice to lead a joint campaign; he had been a French lieutenant-general in the first part of the Seven Years' War, before transferring in 1762 with the same rank into Spanish service.

Littlepage had followed these preparations with great interest, and against Jay's express wishes he petitioned the Duc de Crillon to volunteer as an aide-de-camp. On June 19, 1781 King Carlos III granted permission for "Don Luis Litelpage, distinguished young man from the American Provinces who is here to learn the language and to study," permission to join the Minorca campaign. William Carmichael was as surprised as John Jay by this, for as he noted several days later to Ben-

3. John Jay, *Letters, being the whole of the correspondence between the Hon. John Jay, Esquire, and Mr. Lewis Littlepage. A young man whom Mr. Jay, when in Spain patronized and took into his family* (New York: Francis Childs, 1786); Lewis Littlepage, *Answer to a pamphlet, containing the correspondence between the Honorable John Jay, secretary for foreign affairs; and Lewis Littlepage, Esquire, of Virginia* (New York: Francis Childs, 1786); Frank W. Brecher, *Securing American independence: John Jay and the French alliance* (Westport, CT: Praeger, 2003), 55-56; Chris R. Pullen, *The talented Mr. Littlepage & The Spirit of '76: An American character study,* Master's Thesis, Harrisonburg, VA: James Madison University, 2010, 5.

jamin Franklin, "[Littlepage's] application to serve was particularly
agreeable & he was received when many volunteers of rank who offered
were refused." Littlepage was placed on Crillon's staff under the direct
supervision of Capitán-General (roughly-five star) Miguel de la Grúa
Talamanca Branciforte. On July 21 the massive flotilla began departing
the Bay of Cádiz, fifty-eight ships of the line and seventy-five transports carrying 8,000 troops. Britain's navy was at that time spread across
the English Channel, the North Sea, New York, the West Indies and
the East Indies; they had no more ships left to confront such a massive
fleet, or to reinforce the British garrison on Minorca.[4]

The combined Spanish-French force landed near the capital of
Mahón on August 20. The British troops retreated to the citadel of
Fort San Felipe, where according to Littlepage, they were "very liberal
of their powder," with almost 500 cannon and 2,400 troops to man
them. Crillon established a blockade of the city and citadel, while further Spanish and French reinforcements arrived in October. He now
had 14,000 men to occupy the entire island and lay siege to San Felipe,
whose garrison endured months of almost constant bombardment
while succumbing to diseases like scurvy. When the British finally
hoisted a white flag in February 1782, only 600 men were fit enough
to walk out unaided. The victors were appalled by the near-skeletons
they had to carry out of the citadel and nurse back to health; the vanquished boasted that their captors could take little credit for seizing a
hospital. Littlepage, who left few records of his battle experiences (but
sent many letters to Jay asking for more funds), returned to Madrid in
April 1782. A few days later, John Jay departed Madrid to join Benjamin Franklin in Paris, since he had not succeeded in convincing the
Spanish court to formally ally with the Americans. William Carmichael
was now head of the delegation.[5]

With the fall of Minorca, the only British stronghold left in the
Mediterranean was Gibraltar. Britain had captured the Spanish
promontory in August 1704 during the War of the Spanish Succession,
and ever since then, Spain had been trying to recover it. After Spain
and France had joined forces in 1779 and carried the war to Britain,
the Spanish also laid siege to Gibraltar in an attempt to starve the inhabitants out. Britain had managed to break the naval blockade and
resupply the garrison several times, allowing them to hold out. Now

4. William Carmichael to Benjamin Franklin from, Madrid, June 26, 1781, founders.
archives.gov/documents/Franklin/01-35-02-0144#BNFN-01-35-02-0144-fn-0004-ptr.
5. Siege of Minorca: Larrie D. Ferreiro, *Brothers at Arms: American Independence and the
Men of France and Spain Who Saved It* (New York: Alfred A. Knopf, 2016), 286-288.

"Vue générale de l'assaut des batteries flottantes sur Gibraltar, le 13 septembre 1782." (*Anne S. K. Brown Military Collection, Brown University Library*)

the Spanish and French turned their attention to concluding the three-year-long blockade and siege. The fall of Minorca had freed up many thousands of Spanish and French troops to join the siege of Gibraltar and prepare for a grand assault to break the backs of the British occupiers, once and for all. In June 1782, the Duc de Crillon was back in Madrid to accept his commission and receive his orders to lead the assault against Gibraltar.

The concept for the assault decided in Madrid was simple if also far-sighted: since the most vulnerable part of the Gibraltar fortification was its western side, facing the Bay of Algeciras, the Spanish would build and deploy a series of armored floating batteries to pummel the British defenses and open up a breach for an amphibious assault to follow. These batteries were warship hulks, built with reinforced roofs to shield against British gunfire. In a clever innovation to guard against the well-known use of red-hot shot (cannon balls which had been heated in a furnace prior to firing), the batteries were fitted with pump-fed seawater pipes which ran the length of each ship to continually wet down the wooden structures, in order to prevent them from catching fire.

Even while in Minorca, Littlepage had known that an assault upon Gibraltar was next and he was eager to participate in it; as he said to Jay on March 25, 1782, "I must own my military Quixotism is not yet abated, and I could wish to assist at the Gibraltar business."[6] He once

6. Jay, *Letters*, 51.

again petitioned Crillon to join his entourage as aide-de-camp, and once again Carlos III granted his wish, this time with Carmichael's blessing. In June 1782, "Luis Litlpese," as the Spanish memoranda named him, arrived at Crillon's headquarters, where preparations for the final assault began. As a member of Crillon's fifty-man staff, Littlepage would have had his hands full with the planning necessary to bring the full force of the combined forces to bear on the British positions. By September 1782, over 35,000 Spanish and French troops and sailors surrounded Gibraltar, with the Spanish-French fleet of Córdova and Guichen moored across the bay in Algeciras. On Friday, September 13, 1782 at 7:00 AM, the floating batteries were towed into a line opposite Gibraltar's western fortifications. Littlepage was aboard *Talla Piedra*, armed with twenty-eight guns and 700 crew, primarily French, led by Karl Heinrich von Nassau-Siegen, Prince of Nassau. By 10:00 a.m. they had moored about a thousand yards out and began opening fire, while the British fired back from behind their fortified walls and tunnels. At first, neither side did much damage; the Spanish shot battered the walls but did not silence the guns, while the red-hot British artillery bounced off the sloping roofs of the floating batteries without setting anything ablaze. As it turned out later, *Talla Piedra* was the only one of all the batteries on which the sailors continued to pump water to moisten the structures throughout the fight.

As the afternoon wore on the battle began to turn against the Spanish floating batteries. Some began to catch fire as the seawater pipes ran dry, while their crews were unable to maneuver out of harm's way. Great clouds of smoke covered the ships. Across the bay, Córdova, the senior naval commander, watched inertly, unwilling to bring his ships into battle —at first because he did not want to expose his highly flammable ships to the red-hot shot, then because the wind was wrong, then because it became too late to assist. By late afternoon the floating batteries had all but ceased fire, and at midnight, Córdova ordered the floating batteries to be burned so as not to fall into enemy hands. Littlepage noted that "The *Talla Piedra* burnt to the water's edge and sunk about 1:00 in the morning of the 14th of September, after having lain upwards of fourteen hours under the fire of Gibraltar." Nassau, Littlepage and the surviving crew made their way back to shore. At 5:00 AM the flames began reaching the powder magazines of the remaining batteries, and one by one they blew up, the eruptions lofting enormous mushroom clouds a thousand feet into the sky. The next day, almost a thousand bodies from the floating batteries began washing up on the Gibraltar shoreline. The Spanish bombardment had failed utterly, and there was no attempt at an amphibious assault. Despite months of careful planning, the actual operation was rushed and uncoordinated, and Britain held on to Gibraltar after the end of the war, as it does even today.[7]

The assault was over, but the naval battles were not. On October 10 a British fleet under Richard Howe arrived at Gibraltar on the heels of a storm which decimated the blockading Spanish - French fleet. Howe resupplied the British garrison for what would turn out to be the last time, before setting sail back to Britain the following week. The Spanish and French gave chase, though their ships, without coppered-plated bottoms, were too slow to overtake Howe. The two fleets exchanged long-range fire most of the night. Littlepage, given permission by Crillon to board the seventy-gun *San Rafael* in the reserve squadron, had a commanding view of the battle from the quarterdeck and sketched the action for his commanding officer, later noting to Crillon that they "chased [the British] the entire night in battle formation" before Howe broke off and continued home. This exchange took place just a few miles off Cape Spartel in Morocco, within sight of Cape Trafalgar where French, Spanish and British fleets would meet again twenty-three years later in a battle that would rewrite world history.[8]

Littlepage returned to Cádiz at the end of October. By then his reputation had preceded him. Soon after the end of the siege of Gibraltar, William Carmichael wrote to Robert R. Livingston, then U. S. Secretary of Foreign Affairs, "I cannot conclude, without mentioning that a Mr. Littlepage, from Virginia, has acquired reputation by his gallant conduct in the expedition against Mahon, where he served as Aid-de-camp to the Duc de Crillon, and since at Gibraltar, where he acted in the same capacity. The Prince de Nassau, with whom he served as a volunteer on board his floating battery, rendered public justice to his character at Court." Within weeks Littlepage also found favor with the newly-arrived Marquis de Lafayette, who had come back from the Yorktown campaign the previous year and was helping prepare for the combined French-Spanish assault on Jamaica the following spring. Lafayette invited Littlepage to join this campaign, but by February

7. Siege of Gibraltar: Watson, *Men and Times of the Revolution*, 132-133; Davis, *The King's Chevalier*, 60-72; Ferreiro, *Brothers at Arms*, 288-291; Sarah Travers Lewis Scott Anderson, *Lewises, Meriwethers, and their kin: Lewises and Meriwethers with their tracings through the families whose records are herein contained* (Richmond, VA: Dietz Press, 1938), 386-387.

8. Battle of Cape Spartel: Davis, *The King's Chevalier*, 72-73; José María Blanco Núñez, *La Armada Española en la Segunda Mitad del Siglo XVIII (The Spanish Navy in the Second Half of the 18th Century)* (Madrid: IZAR Construcciones Navales, 2004), 160-163.

1783 the preliminary peace treaties had been signed and the campaign was called off.[9]

Littlepage's career after the end of the War of American Independence was filled with intrigue and adventure. After accompanying Lafayette to Paris, and the Prince of Nassau to Poland, he was invited by King Stanisław August Poniatowski to join the Polish court. Littlepage by then was deeply in debt to John Jay and others, and accepted the offer as perhaps the only way to stay solvent. He took a leave of absence in 1785 to settle his business affairs in Virginia, before moving back to Poland. On November 8, 1785 he dined at Mount Vernon with George Washington, who later wrote in his diary, "This Captn. Littlepage has been Aid de Camp to the Duke de Crillon—was at the Sieges of Fort St. Phillip (on the Island of Minorca) and Gibraltar; and is an extraordinary character."[10]

Lewis Littlepage spent the next fifteen years in service to the Polish crown, carrying out diplomatic missions to Russia and France. He finally returned to the United States in late 1801, but he was never able to use his extensive diplomatic experience in the further service of his own country; just months after his return, on July 19, 1802, Lewis Littlepage died at age thirty-nine in Fredericksburg, Virginia, apparently after a long illness. Unmarried and without children, he was buried in the Masonic Cemetery in the city, where his grave is still visible today.[11]

9. William Carmichael to Robert R. Livingston. St. Ildefonso, September 29, 1782, in Jared Sparks, *The diplomatic correspondence of the American Revolution* (Washington, DC: J.C. Rives, 1857), 5: 102; Davis, *The King's Chevalier*, 74-75.

10. Boand, *Lewis Littlepage*, 52-91; *The Diaries of George Washington*, November 1785, founders.archives.gov/documents/Washington/01-04-02-0002-0011.

11. Grave No.183, Masonic Cemetery, Corner of Charles St. and George St., Fredericksburg, VA, www.findagrave.com/memorial/5004843/lewis-littlepage.

Patrick Tonyn: Britain's Most Effective Revolutionary-Era Royal Governor

❧ JIM PIECUCH ❧

Even among historians of the American Revolution, the name of East Florida's royal governor, Patrick Tonyn, is all but unknown. However, Tonyn proved himself to be the crown's most effective governor in mainland North America during the Revolutionary era. Tonyn's leadership was not only instrumental in maintaining British control of East Florida, but he also brought significant pressure to bear on colonies to the northward that had joined the rebellion while successfully dealing with challenges from pro-Revolutionary elements within East Florida. His astute diplomacy to maintain an alliance with the Creeks and Seminoles, efforts to make his province a refuge for thousands of Loyalists from other colonies, and his organization of loyal refugees into military units enabled East Florida to withstand three rebel invasions while threatening the Revolutionaries' control of southern Georgia. Tonyn's achievements were even more remarkable because he received little guidance from his superiors in London, and therefore had to create his own policies to deal with both external and internal threats to East Florida.

Tonyn was born in 1725, possibly in Ireland, although nearly nothing is known of his life before he was commissioned an officer in the 6th (Inniskilling) Regiment of Dragoons at the age of nineteen. He was promoted to captain in May 1751 and fought in Germany during the Seven Years' War, including participation at the Battle of Minden on August 1, 1759. In 1761 he was promoted to lieutenant colonel in the 104th Regiment of Foot. At the end of the war, Spain ceded Florida to Great Britain; British officials divided the territory into two separate provinces, East and West Florida, with the former consisting of the peninsula bordered by the St. Mary's River on the north and the

Apalachicola River to the west. Tonyn was granted 20,000 acres in East Florida in 1767 as a reward for his military service. He was later appointed royal governor of the province and arrived at the capital, St. Augustine, on March 1, 1774.[1]

Upon Tonyn's arrival, he found the small province to be on a solid economic footing. Of East Florida's approximately three thousand non-Indian inhabitants, about one half were African American slaves. Most of the slaves labored on plantations along the St. Mary's and St. John's Rivers, while another thousand or so indentured servants from Europe, mostly Roman Catholic Minorcans, worked on Andrew Turnbull's plantation at New Smyrna, south of St. Augustine. Trade with the province's Indians was profitable, and the plantations produced lumber, turpentine, rice, and indigo for export.[2]

Tonyn assumed the governorship less than three months after the Boston Tea Party ignited the final round of sparks that would lead to revolution in America. Perhaps because of his military background as well as his understanding of his duty as royal governor, Tonyn was determined to keep his province loyal to Great Britain. He apparently found no evidence of rebellious sentiments in the province during his first months there, as he wrote to the Earl of Dartmouth, Secretary of State for the American Department, that the controversy over the 1773 Tea Act could have been avoided entirely by shipping the tea to St. Augustine, where merchants would have paid the tax without protest and could then have shipped the tea to other American colonies. His assertion had merit, given that East Floridians had made no protests against the Stamp Act of 1765 or any other parliamentary legislation that had caused such a furor in the colonies to the northward. The fact that East Florida had no elected legislature to serve as a voice for its inhabitants, and would not have such a body until 1781, may have contributed to the colony's passive response to British taxation.[3]

While Tonyn believed that East Florida's settlers were reliably loyal, as the Revolution began he worried about the political sentiments of some of the colony's leaders. Lt. Gov. John Moultrie, a South Carolina native, was the brother of William Moultrie, who supported the rebellion and rose to the rank of brigadier general in the Continental Army.

1. Daniel S. Murphree, "Patrick Tonyn," in H.C.G. Matthew and Brian Harrison, eds., *Oxford Dictionary of National Biography*, Vol. 55 (Oxford, UK: Oxford University Press, 2004), 4-5; J. Leitch Wright, Jr., *Florida in the American Revolution* (Gainesville: University Presses of Florida, 1975), 1-2.
2. Wright, *Florida in the Revolution*, 3-7, 15; Burton Barrs, *East Florida in the American Revolution* (Jacksonville, FL: Guild Press, 1932), 3.
3. Wright, *Florida in the Revolution*, 17-18.

Another South Carolinian, William Drayton, served as East Florida's chief justice, and was related to rebel firebrand William Henry Drayton. Turnbull, a member of the council, chafed under what he considered Tonyn's authoritarian rule, and his wealth gave him an added degree of influence.[4] Under such circumstances, it was not surprising that Tonyn chose to wield power with little consideration for the views of other provincial luminaries.

In the summer of 1775, Tonyn informed the Earl of Dartmouth that reports from South Carolina described "every excess of outrage and sedition" in that province, and that Gov. Sir James Wright's position in Georgia was precarious. Tonyn added that widespread accounts indicated that the South Carolinians intended to invade East Florida, and that he would "put everything in the best state of defense" despite the small number of troops available.[5] A letter from William Henry Drayton reporting on rebel activities in Charleston to William Drayton in St. Augustine, that Tonyn intercepted, added to the governor's worries.[6] So too did a request from Virginia's royal governor, Lord Dunmore, in September. Dunmore asked Tonyn for troops from the East Florida garrison to strengthen his forces conducting raids in Chesapeake Bay, and Tonyn reluctantly agreed to send a detachment of the 14th Regiment, but not the entire number of troops that Dunmore had requested. Tonyn noted that his force was so small that "the province is absolutely defenceless; the garrison so inconsiderable that the fort [Castle St. Mark, formerly the Spanish Castillo de San Marcos] alone can be guarded, not defended in any very formidable manner." The governor added that he had met with a prominent Creek emissary and was working to garner support from that powerful Indian nation, and reminded Dartmouth "of the importance to Great Britain of this province in the present circumstances."[7]

Fortunately for Tonyn and the British, the rumored rebel invasion of East Florida did not occur in 1775; instead, loyalism in the province was bolstered by an influx of refugees, most from Georgia and the Carolinas. Tonyn encouraged immigration by offering land grants to Loyalists, promising to make East Florida "an asylum to the friends of the [British] Constitution." The majority of immigrants were small farmers

4. Ibid., 20-21.
5. Patrick Tonyn to the Earl of Dartmouth, July 1, 1775, in K. G. Davies, ed., *Documents of the American Revolution, 1770-1783 (Colonial Office Series)*, Vol. 11 (Dublin: Irish University Press, 1976), 30-31.
6. William H. Drayton to William Drayton, July 4, 1775, in Davies, *Documents*, 11: 36-37.
7. Tonyn to Dartmouth, September 15, 1775, in Davies, *Documents*, 11:107-109.

eager to escape rebel persecution, but several planters came to the province with their slaves, along with some merchants and Anglican ministers. Parliament's prohibition on the rebellious colonies' right to trade with the rest of the British Empire spurred the growth of agriculture and the production of naval stores for export to the West Indies and to supply the royal navy, allowing most Loyalist newcomers to support themselves.[8]

The influx of refugees created an administrative problem for Tonyn. While East Florida had an abundance of land, much of it had been granted to absentee owners. The governor referred the problem to officials in London, where it was decided in March 1777 that the ownership of any granted lands that had remained empty or undeveloped for three years or longer reverted to the crown. This upheld Tonyn's policy of granting portions of the absentees' holdings to refugees. The governor also intervened to prevent food shortages while the new arrivals established farms. Many immigrants had brought provisions and livestock with them to East Florida, while loyalists in some of the revolted colonies managed to ship grain to St. Augustine. However, military officials seized much of these foodstuffs on the grounds that they violated the parliamentary embargo on trade with the rebels. On his own initiative, Tonyn issued licenses to loyalists that enabled them to circumvent the embargo and thus provide urgently needed food supplies for the province's inhabitants.[9]

The anticipated rebel attack on East Florida became increasingly likely in the spring of 1776. Rebels from Georgia destroyed several plantations on the St. Mary's River in May, and launched additional raids in July and August. The main invasion began in the latter month, under Maj. Gen. Charles Lee, commander of the Continental Army in the Southern Department. Lee's Georgians, South Carolinians, and Virginians managed to advance a detachment as far south as the St. John's River, where they plundered some plantations, but the main force never proceeded farther than Sunbury, Georgia, where sickness and supply shortages forced them to halt.[10]

---

8. Wright, *Florida in the Revolution*, 22, 23-24; Wilbur H. Siebert, *Loyalists in East Florida, 1774-1785: The Most Important Documents Pertaining Thereto Edited with an Accompanying Narrative*, 2 Vols. (Deland: Florida State Historical Society, 1929), 1:23-24.

9. Siebert, *Loyalists in East Florida*, 1:48-50; Carole Watterson Troxler, "Refuge, Resistance, and Reward: The Southern Loyalists' Claim on East Florida," *Journal of Southern History*, Vol. 55, No. 4 (Nov. 1989), 569.

10. Martha Condray Searcy, *The Georgia-Florida Contest in the American Revolution, 1776-1778* (University: University of Alabama Press, 1985), 34-36, 43-44, 50, 54-56, 61-62; Charles E. Bennett and David R. Lennon, *A Quest for Glory: Major General Robert Howe and the American Revolution* (Chapel Hill: University of North Carolina Press, 1991), 48-50.

The rebels' actions spurred Tonyn into taking measures he had promised more than a year earlier to secure the province. In August, the same month as the rebels began their ill-fated invasion, Tonyn organized a battalion of militia for provincial defense. He planned to raise four companies from among the residents of St. Augustine, two of settlers along the St. John's River, and four companies of blacks. Lieutenant Governor Moultrie was appointed colonel commanding the unit.[11]

By this time Tonyn considered Moultrie to be reliable in his loyalty to Britain, because of the lieutenant governor's role in political disputes that had nearly fractured the provincial government. Tonyn informed Lord George Germain, Dartmouth's successor as head of the American Department, in April that "since my arrival in this province I have labored most assiduously to extinguish the jarring flames of party and faction by every lenient measure." The effort had failed, and Tonyn suspended Chief Justice Drayton for what the governor considered improper conduct, noting that a longstanding "enmity had subsisted between Mr Moultrie and Mr Drayton." Tonyn hoped that Drayton's suspension would serve as a lesson to Andrew Turnbull, who had angered the governor for various reasons, including collaborating with Georgia rebel Jonathan Bryan to make a private purchase of Indian land. Turnbull instead vocally supported Drayton, and in a meeting of the provincial council, became involved in an argument with Moultrie during which Turnbull declared "that America was in the right, the King's ministers in the wrong, that Lord North would answer with his head." Shortly afterward, Turnbull left the province.[12] Moultrie's opposition to Drayton and Turnbull apparently reassured Tonyn that his lieutenant governor was trustworthy.

Tonyn had also been working to maintain a strong alliance with the Creeks and the Seminoles, who were nominally still part of the Creek confederacy, since he believed Indian assistance was crucial to his province's defense. On April 20 he wrote to David Taitt, Southern Indian Superintendent John Stuart's deputy to the Creeks, to warn about possible rebel efforts to win over that nation. Tonyn urged Taitt to take steps to maintain Creek support for Britain.[13] Two months later, Tonyn wrote to Maj. Gen. Henry Clinton, who commanded the land force of a British expedition to the southern colonies, asserting that "the assistance they [the Indians] would be of to His Majesty's service is very

11. Tonyn to Lord George Germain, August 21, 1776, in Davies, *Documents*, Vol. 12 (1976), 186-187.

12. Tonyn to Germain, April 2, 1776, in Davies, *Documents*, 12:104-105.

13. Tonyn to David Taitt, April 20, 1776, in Davies, *Documents*, 12:108-110.

great. . . . The Americans are a thousand times more in dread of the savages than of any European troops. Why not avail of their help?" Tonyn complained that both Stuart and British officials were too slow in employing the Indians, and declared that even though East Florida's garrison consisted of only part of the 14th Regiment, "three small companies of the 16th regiment," and three companies of the 60th, some of these troops and the Seminoles could, by attacking Georgia, create "a powerful diversion" to assist Clinton's operations.[14] The Seminole leader, Ahaya of Cuscowilla, known to the British as Cowkeeper, was a staunch ally of the crown and had pledged to assist in the defense of East Florida.[15] Clinton did not follow Tonyn's advice, but Germain did express his pleasure at "the favorable disposition" of the Indians in a letter to the governor and praised Tonyn's willingness to assist the army in its operations.[16]

Although the governor undertook defensive preparations, his views regarding the use of Indians and regulars to strike Georgia demonstrated his preference for taking the offensive against the rebels. In February 1776, Tonyn had asked Thomas Brown, a South Carolina loyalist who had escaped to St. Augustine after surviving a violent attack by the rebels, to assess "the disposition, strength and resources of the inhabitants upon the frontiers" of the southern provinces to determine what assistance British forces might receive if they mounted an attack in the backcountry. Brown observed that "an attempt to raise the friends to government" without Indian assistance "will not only be attended with extreme danger, but perhaps [be] impracticable." However, Brown believed that a strong force of Loyalists and Indians would be able to recruit "2 or 3000 men in South Carolina . . . in the course of a month," adding that Georgia "from its defenceless state will make but a poor resistance; by its reduction, the province of South Carolina may be attacked in the weakest part." Brown recommended the capture of Augusta, Georgia, and Fort Charlotte in South Carolina to open a line of communication from North Carolina to East Florida and provide bases for further operations.[17]

Tonyn did not put Brown's plan into effect, but his long service in the British army did not make him inflexible with regard to military tactics, rather, he "adapted with startling flexibility to the type of war-

14. Tonyn to Henry Clinton, June 8, 1776, in Davies, *Documents*, 12: 147-150.
15. John Stuart to Germain, November 24, 1776, in Davies, *Documents*, 12:253.
16. Germain to Tonyn, June 12, 1776, in Lord George Germain Papers, Vol. 4, William L. Clements Library, Ann Arbor, MI.
17. Thomas Brown to Tonyn, February 1776, in Davies, *Documents*, 12:69-73.

fare he was required to wage." Using his authority as commander-in-chief of his province, the governor organized refugee volunteers into two battalions of provincial troops, the South Carolina Royalists, and the East Florida or King's Rangers, commissioning Brown lieutenant colonel commandant of the latter unit. In October 1776 Brown struck into Georgia, burning rebel plantations at Beard's Bluff and south of the Altamaha River.[18]

Brown undertook another raid in February 1777, leading a mixed force of Rangers and Indians to raid into Georgia with support from 160 regulars from the St. Augustine garrison. Brown's party captured Fort McIntosh on February 18 before the regulars arrived; the troops then skirmished with rebel forces while pushing to the Altamaha River, allowing Brown to round up some two thousand head of cattle to feed East Florida's populace before the British withdrew.[19]

The supplies obtained by Brown did little to ameliorate the hunger and difficult living and working conditions that plagued the Minorcan laborers at Turnbull's New Smyrna plantation. Turnbull's overseers continued their policy of harshly treating the workers. Rumors circulated that the dissatisfied Minorcans were seeking aid from the rebels in Georgia, leading some nearby planters to advise Tonyn to prepare to confine the workers if the rebels or Spaniards invaded East Florida. The Minorcans sent two delegations to St. Augustine in March and April 1777 to lay their complaints before the governor. Tonyn ordered Attorney General Arthur Gordon and Chief Justice Henry Yonge to investigate the situation, with the result that the provincial court ordered the Minorcans released from their indentures. Turnbull's attorneys reluctantly complied, and most of the workers moved to the vicinity of St. Augustine, where the governor provided them with land. Tonyn had judiciously eliminated a potential internal threat to East Florida's security and ended the abuses practiced at Turnbull's plantation.[20]

Turnbull, however, simmered over this perceived injustice, and in December he complained to Germain of what he considered Tonyn's authoritarian policies. Tonyn, declared Turnbull, had chosen "to interfere in a most arbitrary and illegal Manner between the Proprietors and Settlers at Smyrnea, which not only deranged the affairs of the Settle-

18. Searcy, *Georgia-Florida Contest*, 37-38, 68; Edward J. Cashin, *The King's Ranger: Thomas Brown and the American Revolution on the Southern Frontier* (New York: Fordham University Press, 1999), 49, 59, 61.

19. Searcy, *Georgia-Florida Contest*, 84-88; Cashin, *King's Ranger*, 61-62.

20. Kenneth H. Beeson, Jr., "Janas in British East Florida," *Florida Historical Quarterly*, Vol. 44, Nos. 1 and 2 (July-October, 1965), 131-132.

ment at that Time, but also established a firm Belief among these Men (being all brought from despotick Governments) that the Governour of the Province had all Power over them, and not the Proprietors." As a result, Turnbull claimed, when he returned to East Florida he found some of the workers had become "idle and mutinous." He added that Lieutenant Governor Moultrie and other provincial leaders "were present, when the first Attack was made on our Contracts and private Property by Govr. Tonyn." Although Turnbull claimed that he had "resolved to live on good Terms with the Governour," he had now concluded that Tonyn had the fixed intention "of breaking up the Smyrnea Settlement in the Hopes, as I was then informed, that he and his Connections would have the Advantage" of relocating "the most industrious of these Families" to their own plantations, in order to profit from the Minorcans' labor.[21] Germain did not respond to Turnbull's complaint.

The governor did not need such distractions, because Brown's successful March raid convinced the rebels to mount another invasion of East Florida in the belief that the seizure of St. Augustine would end the threat from the southward. With the reluctant concurrence of Maj. Gen. Robert Howe, the new commander of the southern Continental Army, a two-pronged land and sea force set out, with the former reaching the St. Mary's River on May 12. Two days later, Indians captured over one hundred horses from the rebel camp, and the American commander, Col. John Baker, shifted his camp to Thomas Creek. Brown attacked the two hundred rebels on May 17 with an equal number of Rangers and Indians, forcing the invaders to retreat into a detachment of one hundred British regulars sent to cooperate with Brown. Three Americans were killed and thirty-one captured, and when the seaborne units reached Amelia Island the next day, the overall commander of the invasion force, Col. Samuel Elbert, decided that the operation stood no chance of success. He ordered a withdrawal on May 26.[22]

With the rebel threat ended, Tonyn ordered Brown to resume the attacks on Georgia, and the Rangers and Indians made repeated forays into the southernmost rebel state. Georgian Joseph Clay complained in late September that the raiders had "for some Months past been continually making incursions into our State," and "not the smallest Check has ever been given to these People."[23] Tonyn, still eager to carry the

21. Andrew Turnbull to Germain, December 8, 1777, Germain Papers, Clements Library.
22. Searcy, *Georgia-Florida Contest*, 89, 92-96; Bennett and Lennon, *Quest for Glory*, 62; Charles C. Jones, Jr., *The Life and Services of the Honorable Maj. Gen. Samuel Elbert of Georgia* (Cambridge, MA: Riverside Press, 1887), 12.
23. Joseph Clay to Henry Laurens, September 29, 1777, in Joseph Clay, *Letters of Joseph Clay, Merchant of Savannah, 1776-1793*, in *Collections of the Georgia Historical Society*, Vol. 8 (Savannah: Georgia Historical Society, 1913), 40.

war to the enemy, was not satisfied. In December he wrote Germain that it was "a matter of great concern to me that a thousand men should remain in inaction in this province . . . while a contemptible lawless rabble ingloriously exult in the subjection and ruin of the friends of government in Georgia."[24]

Brown's successes continued into 1778; his greatest victory was the capture of Fort Barrington on the Altamaha River on March 13. The Rangers and Indians' operations reinforced Tonyn's conviction that his forces alone were capable of subduing Georgia. The following month he wrote to Gen. Sir William Howe, emphasizing the "numberless inconveniences from acting always on the defensive." Tonyn suggested that with the troops in the St. Augustine garrison, along with "the Rangers and Indians, the province of Georgia may be taken in possession." After that was accomplished, communications could be opened with the loyalists in the South Carolina backcountry, and if they proved sufficiently numerous, "I apprehend that province would soon be compelled to subjection," the governor declared.[25]

Howe, who had recently resigned the command in America, did not reply to Tonyn's proposal, and meanwhile the rebels mounted yet another invasion of East Florida. This time the operation began more successfully, when rebel troops dispersed a party of Rangers, forcing Brown to abandon and burn Fort Tonyn on the St. Mary's River. On June 30 Brown's Rangers, assisted by some regulars, repulsed a party of some one hundred mounted Georgians. After several weeks of occasional minor skirmishing, the rebels retreated on July 14. In his report to Germain, Tonyn praised the performance of the Rangers and Seminoles in repelling the invasion, and informed the American Secretary that he would "meditate on the necessary preparations for the conquest of Georgia and Carolina when Lord [Richard] Howe and Sir Henry Clinton's operations are turned that way, that all our assistance may be in readiness."[26]

No sooner had the rebels left East Florida than Brown renewed his attacks on Georgia. "We are again very much infested with Tonyns Banditti Stealing our Horses & Negroes & doing us all the Mischief

24. Tonyn to Germain, December 26, 1777, in Davies, *Documents*, Vol. 14 (1976), 275-277.
25. Thomas Brown to Tonyn, March 13, 1778, and Tonyn to William Howe, April 6, 1778, in Sir Guy Carleton Papers (Headquarters Papers of the British Army in America), Vol. 9:1014, Vol. 10:1073, microfilm, David Library of the American Revolution, Washington Crossing, PA.
26. Brown to Tonyn, June 30, 1778, Carleton Papers, 11:1247; Cashin, *King's Ranger*, 77-78; Searcy, *Georgia-Florida Contest*, 142, 144-147; Tonyn to Germain, July 24, 1778, in Davies, *Documents*, Vol. 15 (1976), 168-169.

they can," Clay lamented in early September. Later in the month, he reported that "the Floridians & Indians by their Robberies & Murders keep us in a continual State of Alarm."[27]

The rebel threat to East Florida was eliminated when a British expedition from New York captured Savannah in December. In January 1779 these troops were reinforced by units from St. Augustine. With his province now secure, Tonyn was able to report to Germain in July that "many industrious persons have by planting considerably increased their fortunes," and that exports of timber, naval stores, and other goods were thriving. The governor was less pleased by the inhabitants' demands for a provincial legislature, which Tonyn attributed to "the factious and disaffected." Yet he noted that this "malignant spirit hath almost subsided," and expressed a hope that an elected assembly could prove beneficial. The governor added that he continued to promote privateering and that East Florida's privateers had not only "accumulated wealth" but seriously distressed the rebels.[28]

In January 1780, Germain instructed Tonyn to proceed with electing an assembly, and advised the governor that the legislature's first priority should be to pass a law to provide revenue for the province's expenses, which had been paid by the British government since East Florida had been established.[29] By December, Tonyn had still not called for elections, although he told Germain that "the growth of the province depends much upon" the creation of a legislature. The governor reported that abundant crops of corn and large herds of cattle had resulted in a drop in food prices, but complained that since the British capture of Charleston in May 1780, much merchant shipping had been diverted to that port and at St. Augustine "there is a great quantity of naval stores on hand for want of ships to carry them off." He also reported that Lt. Gen. Charles, Earl Cornwallis, had exiled some thirty prominent South Carolina rebels to East Florida, and assured the American Secretary that "these incendiaries can do little mischief here."[30]

One reason for Tonyn's delay in calling for the election of a legislature may have been the growing threat to East Florida following Spain's entry into the war in 1779. In addition to a possible seaborne threat from the Spanish base at Havana, Cuba, a military expedition from New Orleans had begun the conquest of neighboring West Florida.

27. Clay to Henry Laurens, Sept. 9, 1778; Clay to John Lewis Gervais, September 25, 1778, in Clay, *Letters*, 106, 109.
28. Tonyn to Germain, July 3, 1779, in Davies, *Documents*, Vol. 17 (1977), 155-156.
29. Germain to Tonyn, January 19, 1780, in Davies, *Documents*, Vol. 18 (1978), 40-43.
30. Tonyn to Germain, December 9, 1780, in Davies, *Documents*, 18:252-255.

Lt. Col. Alured Clarke, whom Cornwallis had assigned to direct the defense of Georgia and East Florida, visited St. Augustine in August 1780 and reported that "with the addition of a few redoubts . . . and a supply of such ordnance stores as appear deficient," the town would be in "as good a state of defence as the nature of its situation . . . will admit of." Clarke was less impressed with the provincial troops in the garrison, describing them as "totally undisciplined, and not the most trusty." He also asked Cornwallis to "adopt some mode of preventing any difficulties that might otherwise arrise between Governor Tonyn and myself relative to the command in East Florida, for, though nothing but the greatest kindness and civility has yet taken place between us," Clarke's concerns about his relationship with the governor had been aroused on his arrival, when Tonyn informed him that "it was customary for the Governor to take the command when a brigadier [general] was not in the province."[31] Cornwallis assured Clarke that "there can be no doubt" of the command "being vested in you."[32] Nevertheless, Tonyn clearly still understood his role as commander-in-chief of the province in a literal sense.

Security issues were not Tonyn's only concern, for Turnbull was still assailing the governor for the loss of his labor force at New Smyrna. Turnbull had again gone to England after his 1777 visit to East Florida, but by March 1780 he was back in St. Augustine, from whence he wrote to the Earl of Shelburne to complain that his settlement had been "most insidiously broke up in my Absence from the Province by Govr. Tonyn, plundered afterwards by American Privateers, and partly burnt by a Rover from Cuba." The frustrated planter added that "I have long wished to finish my Affairs here, that I might quit a Province, where great Wrongs (added to every kind of Protection having been repeatedly refused to me by Govr. Tonyn) convinced me, that I was an Object of his Resentment and Oppression." Turnbull stated that he had complained repeatedly to Germain of the injustices he had suffered from "Tonyn and his Tool Moultrie," without ever receiving a reply, and asked Shelburne to recommend him to Cornwallis, in hopes of obtaining a civil appointment in another province. In another vitriolic passage, Turnbull wrote that if the current king's ministers were re-

---

31. Alured Clarke to Lord Cornwallis, August 20, 1780, in Ian Saberton, ed., *The Cornwallis Papers: The Campaigns of 1780 and 1781 in the Southern Theatre of the American Revolutionary War*, 6 vols. (Uckfield, UK: Naval and Military Press, 2010), 2:292-293.
32. Cornwallis to Clarke, September 5, 1780, in Saberton, *Cornwallis Papers*, 2:302.

placed by honest men, he would like Shelburne to "influence a Removal of such a Tyrant and Oppressor from this Government."[33]

After the British captured Charleston, South Carolina, in May 1780, Turnbull settled there, and apparently Shelburne did intercede with Cornwallis, who appointed Turnbull's eldest son Nichol commissary of provisions. The appointment angered Tonyn, who informed Cornwallis that the elder Turnbull had been overtly sympathetic to the rebel prisoners exiled to St. Augustine and told the general "that I could have wished that some of His Majesty's well affected subjects had been rewarded with the appointment . . . instead of Mr [Nichol] Turnbull, who with his father have been in constant opposition to Government." Tonyn's assessment of the Turnbulls' political opinions was accurate, for both remained in America after the war.[34]

After this round of controversy involving Turnbull and his son, Tonyn shifted his attention to the possibility of a Spanish attack on his province. In January 1781, Thomas Forbes, who had been sent to Havana to arrange the exchange of twenty-five prisoners from the 60th Regiment, returned with intelligence of Spanish activities in Cuba and West Florida. Lieutenant Colonel Clarke pronounced Forbes "a sensible young man" and was convinced of "the authenticity of his information," which Tonyn relayed to Cornwallis. According to Forbes, the Spaniards were "confident of success" in their operations against Pensacola, and were therefore "determined to attack this province, for which purpose preparations are making, and four ships of the line, three frigates, and twelve new gallies, each . . . calculated for the East Florida navigation, it was thought might be ready to sail in March with six regiments and irregulars together amounting to five thousand men."[35] To augment the province's defenses, Tonyn held a conference with the Seminoles and gave them a generous quantity of presents, for which he requested reimbursement from the army. The Seminoles gave Tonyn "the strongest assurances of friendship and assistance against all our enemies," and agreed to post lookouts along the coast southward from St. Augustine to warn of any approaching naval force.[36]

Tonyn also found time at last to proceed with the election of a legislature, and he informed Germain on July 30, 1781, that "the repre-

33. Turnbull to the Earl of Shelburne, March 14, 1780, Earl of Shelburne Papers, Vol. 66, Clements Library.
34. Tonyn to Cornwallis, November 24, 1780, in Saberton, ed., *Cornwallis Papers*, 3:433-434.
35. Clarke to Cornwallis, January 26, 1781; Tonyn to Cornwallis, January 29, 1781, in Saberton, ed., *Cornwallis Papers*, 5:332, 337.
36. Tonyn to Cornwallis, May 5, 1781, in Saberton, ed., *Cornwallis Papers*, 5:353.

sentatives in the Commons House are the most respectable of the inhabitants and well affected to His Majesty's person and government, and have fully evinced by their conduct in a legislative capacity the sincerity of their warm professions of loyalty."[37]

At the time Tonyn wrote, however, the military situation had taken an unfavorable turn for the British. Spanish forces captured Pensacola in May to complete their conquest of West Florida, while Brown had been forced to surrender the post at Augusta, Georgia, in June, thus confining the British in that province to the coast. Facing threats from Spain in the west and by sea from Cuba, and from the rebels by land from the north, Tonyn took measures to insure Indian assistance and strengthen the militia, but found himself thwarted by a shortage of funds for the Indian Department and a lack of cooperation from army officers, who refused to provide arms and gunpowder to the militia or provisions for the Indians. The prospects for a successful defense of the province in case of invasion appeared bleak to Tonyn.[38]

Fortunately for the governor and East Floridians, the feared invasion never materialized. However, as the war drew to a close following Cornwallis's surrender at Yorktown, Virginia, the peace negotiations produced a result that military operations had not accomplished: the treaty between Britain and Spain ceded both East and West Florida to the Spaniards.[39] Although no definitive treaty had yet been signed when the new British commander in North America, Gen. Sir Guy Carleton, arrived in New York in 1782, he nonetheless ordered the evacuation of all British posts in the South, including St. Augustine. A few months later, after considering the complexity of relocating so many Loyalists, Carleton changed his mind and decided to hold St. Augustine. On June 20 Maj. Gen. Alexander Leslie, who had replaced Cornwallis in command of the southern theater, relayed Carleton's new instructions to Tonyn. Carleton's "enquiries into the strength and situation" of St. Augustine, Leslie wrote, had convinced him that it could be defended for some time, "which might afford a more favourable opportunity for the Inhabitants to make an advantageous disposal or arrangement of their property, in case a future necessity should require the relinquishment of the Province, and at the same time afford a convenient refuge" for the loyalists who were about to be evacuated from Georgia.[40] Tonyn shared the good news with members of the council

37. Tonyn to Germain, July 30, 1781, in Davies, *Documents*, Vol. 19 (1979), 204.
38. Tonyn to Germain, December 31, 1781, in Davies, *Documents*, 19:290-292.
39. Wright, *Florida in the Revolution*, 122-123.
40. Alexander Leslie to Tonyn, June 20, 1782, Alexander Leslie Letterbook, microfilm, South Carolina Department of Archives and History, Columbia.

and assembly on July 23, and the two houses in turn sent an address to Tonyn praising his leadership and asking him to express their gratitude to Carleton and Leslie.[41]

By November 1782, Tonyn reported to the Earl of Shelburne that 2165 Loyalist refugees with 3340 slaves had arrived in East Florida from Georgia and South Carolina, in addition to "many hundred" who had come earlier, "driven from their homes . . . without provisions, money, clothing or implements of agriculture, and in the most deplorable circumstances." The governor had provided them with food and tools from the garrison's stocks, so that they were presently "doing well." He was providing land to the more recent arrivals, but worried that the provincial economy was endangered because "no merchants will purchase" East Florida's products "owing to the want of shipping and the consternation occasioned by the alarm of evacuating the province." Tonyn urged the government to contract with "intelligent merchants" who could purchase the large quantities of turpentine and lumber awaiting export. The military situation also vexed Tonyn, who noted that there were only four hundred provincial troops available to defend East Florida, and called attention to "several inconveniences which have arisen from the extensive authority exercised by the commanding officers of His Majesty's troops in this province and the circumscribed power of the civil governor." He reminded Shelburne that he was still an army officer, "animated with military ardour and ambitious of serving my country in that capacity"; Tonyn did not think such a role was "incompatible" with his position as civil governor and instead observed that if his authority was reduced by the actions of other officers in the province, it might prove harmful to the king's service.[42] The governor had not relinquished his belief that he was and should continue to be East Florida's commander-in-chief.

By the time the final treaty was signed in 1783 ceding East Florida to Spain, more than 12,000 Loyalists had resettled in the province. News of the cession struck a cruel blow to their morale, as they had been working to establish themselves in East Florida in the belief that Britain would retain the colony. Tonyn remarked that the people were "quite at a loss how to dispose of themselves." The Spanish government generously allowed those who wished to leave the time needed to settle

41. Tonyn to the East Florida Council and Tonyn to the East Florida Assembly, July 23, 1782, and the Address of Both Houses to Tonyn, August 16, 1782, Leslie Letterbook, SC Dept. of Archives and History.
42. Tonyn to Shelburne, November 14, 1782, in Davies, *Documents*, Vol. 21 (1981), 136-137.

their affairs, and until November 1785, when the final evacuation occurred, Tonyn governed East Florida jointly with Vizente Manuel de
Zespedes, with the Spaniard working from St. Augustine while Tonyn
moved to the St. Mary's River. The two governors were able to cooperate fairly well despite their complex situation.[43]

For more than a decade Tonyn had provided East Florida with
forceful, capable leadership, even if he had alienated many people by
his independent, even stubborn, manner. Tonyn had kept East Florida
in the British Empire until the peace treaty ceded the province to
Spain. He had successfully if harshly dealt with the internal political
threats posed by Drayton and Turnbull, defended his province from
three rebel invasions, strengthened alliances with the Indians and created provincial forces that carried the war to the enemy, resolved the
plight of the Minorcans, and established a legislature. Almost all of this
had been accomplished without direction from his superiors in London, who were preoccupied with issues in other theaters of the conflict.
Tonyn may have been abrasive and reluctant to include others in his
decision-making, yet his accomplishments made him the most successful royal governor on the North American mainland during the Revolution. Certainly, none of his counterparts accomplished more with so
few resources.

43. Tonyn to Thomas Townshend, May 15, 1783, in Davies, *Documents*, 21:167; Wright,
Florida in the Revolution, 135, 138.

The Most Extraordinary Murder

❀❦ CHAIM M. ROSENBERG ❦❀

On July 2, 1778, the Commonwealth of Massachusetts hanged Bathsheba Ruggles Spooner and Continental soldier Ezra Ross, together with British soldiers Sgt. James Buchanan and Pvt. William Brooks. They had been convicted of the murder of Bathsheba's husband, Joshua Spooner, in "the most extraordinary crime ever perpetrated in New England."[1] The trial was the first capital case of the new nation. Bathsheba Ruggles Spooner, favorite daughter of the Loyalist Timothy Ruggles, was the first woman to be hanged in the United States of America following the declaration of independence. The execution of the five-months pregnant woman reflected strong anti-Loyalist sentiment, and "personal vengeance on the part of a high-ranking official was also a motive in that infamous hanging."[2]

Timothy Ruggles, Bathsheba's father, was the fifth generation of the Ruggles family in the New World. Born in 1711, he graduated Harvard College in 1732 and established a law practice. In 1753 he moved his family to a 400-acre farm in the new town of Hardwick, west of Worcester, Massachusetts. Ruggles played a major role in the French and Indian War and was awarded the rank of brigadier general. In 1762 he was appointed chief justice of the court of common pleas in Worcester. Ruggles served in 1762 and 1763 as speaker of the Massachusetts General Court. The young John Adams, who trained in the law while living in Worcester, admired the haughty judge Ruggles' quickness of mind, the strength of his thoughts and expressions, and the boldness of his opinions. "His honor is strict . . . People approached him with

1. *Boston Independent Chronicle*, March 12, 1778.
2. Deborah Navas, "New Light on the Bathsheba Spooner Execution," *Proceedings of the Massachusetts Historical Society*, Third Series. Vol. 108 (1996), 115-122.

dread and terror," wrote Adams in 1759. At the height of his career, Timothy Ruggles was appointed president of the Stamp Tax conference held in New York City in October 1765, but he refused to add his signature to a petition critical of the king's government for imposing taxes without the knowledge and approval of his subjects. Ruggles saw in the document the seeds of rebellion and bloodshed, and opposed it out of a sense of duty. For this act the General Court of Massachusetts censored him; his once-sterling reputation plummeted. "His behavior was very dishonorable. [Ruggles] is held in utter contempt and derision by the whole continent," wrote John Adams in 1775.[3] Timothy Ruggles was once "one of the most distinguished citizens of the Province of Massachusetts Bay." But after he declared his allegiance to the king he was regarded "as the worst of traitors and his name held in the utmost abhorrence . . . No man in Massachusetts was regarded as so inimical to the cause of rebellion as general [Timothy] Ruggles." Many of his erstwhile friends and family opposed him, including his brother Benjamin who came to regard him as "an enemy of his country." Five of his nephews, including his namesake Lt. Timothy Ruggles, joined general Washington's army. In 1774 his Hardwick home was attacked and his cattle poisoned. Ruggles accused the rebels of using the pretense of "being friends of liberty [to commit] enormous outrages upon persons property . . . of his Majesty's peaceful subjects." Threatened in central Massachusetts, Ruggles rode the one hundred miles to Dartmouth "but patriots would not tolerate his presence anywhere," forcing him to seek shelter in British-occupied Boston.[4] Ruggles established the Loyal American Associators to protect Loyalists from abuse and to openly display allegiance to the crown. He gathered together only 200 followers, mainly wealthy Boston merchants. In March 1776 he departed Boston with the British fleet and followed the army and navy to Staten Island to further aid the British cause.[5] In September 1778, the Massachusetts Banishment Act listed 300 people accused of joining the enemy. After former governors Thomas Hutchinson and Francis Bernard, and former lieutenant governor Thomas Oliver, the name of Timothy Ruggles is the fourth on the list of traitors. Massachusetts confiscated all Timothy Ruggles' properties.[6]

3. Charles Francis Adams, *The Works of John Adams, Second President of the United States, Volume 4* (Boston: Little & Brown, 1857), 33.
4. Ray Raphael and Marie Raphael, *The Spirit of '74; How the American Revolution Began.* (New York: New Press, 2015), 87-88.
5. Henry Stoddard Ruggles, *General Timothy Ruggles* (Boston: Privately Printed, 1897).
6. James Henry Stark, *The Loyalists of Massachusetts and the Other Side of the American Revolution* (Boston: James H. Stark, 1909), 225-228.

Four of Ruggles' daughters, including Bathsheba, had married before the rebellion and remained in America. Born in 1746, Bathsheba wed Joshua Spooner on January 15, 1766 and went to live with him in Brookfield, eleven miles southeast of her parents' homestead in Hardwick. Joshua Spooner was "in character a feeble man," abusive and a heavy drinker. The beautiful Bathsheba was intelligent and high-spirited, but "her passions had never been properly restrained."[7] By 1774 she was the mother of four children but separated from her beloved Loyalist father and trapped in a loveless marriage to Joshua Spooner, for whom she had developed an "utter aversion."

In March 1777, a young soldier named Ezra Ross came to Brookfield. The sixteen year-old and four of his brothers from a respectable Ipswich, Massachusetts, family had joined the American army at the start of the war. After the Siege of Boston and the British evacuation in March 1776, Ross followed Gen. George Washington to New York and to Trenton, New Jersey. After completing his enlistment, Ezra set out by foot on the arduous 300-mile journey to return to his home in Ipswich. Passing through Brookfield he had "a severe fit of illness" and was taken into the Spooner home where Bathsheba showed him "every kindness" on the path to recovery. Besotted by Bathsheba, the handsome youngster came again to Brookfield in August on his way to support the Americans at Fort Ticonderoga. After the American victory at Saratoga, young Ezra made haste to the Spooner home and was often seen out riding with the beautiful Bathsheba, a woman twice his age. Passions flowed and Bathsheba became pregnant by young Ezra. With adultery considered sinful and divorce well nigh impossible, Bathsheba plotted to get rid of her husband. Promising to marry her young lover, Bathsheba asked Ezra to poison Joshua Spooner by pouring aqua fortis (nitric acid) into his grog. Ezra refused and left Bathsheba to her fate.[8]

The British army that surrendered at Saratoga, meanwhile, gave up their arms, crossed the Hudson River and marched into Massachusetts "to be quartered in, near or as convenient as possible to Boston" while awaiting their embarkation back to Europe. The march across New England in October and November was arduous; conditions in the Berkshires were tough with driving rain, mud and then snow. Carts broke down, "others stuck fast, horses tumbling with their loads of lug-

7. Peleg William Chandler, *The Trial of Bathsheba Spooner and Others. Volume 2* (Boston: Timothy A. Carter, 1844.
8. Deborah Navas, *Murdered by his Wife* (Amherst, Massachusetts: University of Massachusetts Press, 2001).

gage."[9] Along the way to Boston, a large number of Burgoyne's troops deserted, among them two soldiers of the 9th Regiment of Foot. James Buchanan, a Scottish sergeant in his early thirties, was "of decent education and good appearance" and had left his family behind in Montreal when he set out on the fateful 1777 campaign.[10] William Brooks was from Wednesbury, Staffordshire, was twenty-seven years old, and had had a bizarre experience during his regiment's voyage to America in 1776:

> April 20th. Our ship sailing at the rate of five miles an hour, a soldier whose name was Brooks, leaped off the forecastle into the ocean; the vessel in a moment made her way over him, and he arose at the stern. He immediately with all his might, swam from the ship. The men who were upon the deck alarmed the captain and officers, who had just sat down to dinner; the ship was ordered to be put about, and the boat hoisted out, and manned, the unfortunate man was soon overtaken, and it was with difficulty that the sailors could force him into the boat. When he was brought back he was ordered between decks, and a centinel placed over him; the next morning he was in a high fever, and continued very bad the remainder of the voyage. The fear of punishment was the cause of this desperate action, as the day before he had stolen a shirt from one of his messmates knapsacks.[11]

Early in February 1778, Buchanan and Brooks were passing through Brookfield on their way to Springfield in search of work. Desperate to kill her husband before her pregnancy showed, Bathsheba sent her servant to invite the bedraggled British soldiers into her home for food, rest and comfort. With Joshua Spooner away on a business trip, Bathsheba ensnared Buchanan and Brooks with a warm welcome into an American home in the midst of the war. They were delighted to learn that Bathsheba "had a great regard for the [British] army, as her father was in it, and one of her brothers." Bathsheba seduced Brooks the way she had earlier seduced Ezra Ross. Brooks was seen with his head laid "upon Mrs. Spooner's neck and, oftentimes, his hands round her waist." Offering the British deserters one thousand dollars, clothing and the alluring prospect of sex, Bathsheba "made a direct proposal to

9. Thomas Fleming, "Gentleman Johnny's Wandering Army," *American Heritage* December 1972, Volume 24, Issue 1.

10. "The Dying Declaration of James Buchanan, Ezra Ross and William Brooks," in Navas, *Murdered by his Wife*, 211-218.

11. Don N. Hagist, *A British Soldier's Story: Roger Lamb's Narrative of the American Revolution* (Baraboo, WI: Ballindalloch Press, 2004). There was only one man named Brooks in the regiment at that time. Muster rolls, 9th Regiment of Foot, WO 12/2653.

these entire strangers to murder her husband, which they agreed to do on the first favorable opportunity." Enjoying great comfort for eleven days in the grand Spooner home, Buchanan and Brooks little thought "of the bait the seducer of souls was laying for us."[12] Circumstances changed dramatically when Joshua Spooner returned; angry to find the British soldiers in his home, he ordered them to leave. Bathsheba concealed them in the barn and provided them with food, to await the opportunity to murder Joshua Spooner. On March 1, Ezra Ross "either by accident or design" arrived at the Spooner house. He had never met Buchanan or Brooks before, but the beguiling Bathsheba inveigled him into the murder plot.

Joshua Spooner spent that evening with his pals at Cooley's Tavern, a quarter-mile from his house. He left the tavern between eight and nine o'clock. Returning home he was attacked by William Brooks, who beat him to death while Buchanan and Ross were "aiding, abetting, comforting and maintaining the aforesaid Brooks." Bathsheba "invited, moved, abetted, counseled and procured" the murder of her husband. The men dragged Joshua's body out of the house and dumped it down the well (Bathsheba planned to say that her husband had gotten up during the night to draw water from the well and had accidently fallen in and drowned), but they left telltale evidence such as Joshua's crumpled hat, blood on the snow, footsteps, and heaps of snow next to the well. Bathsheba and the three men burned Joshua Spooner's bloodstained clothing. Bathsheba opened her family's money box and gave the men a down-payment of two hundred dollars together with Joshua's fresh clothing, and off the three fled into the night, making their way to Worcester.[13]

The following day, Buchanan, Brooks and Ross were apprehended. Between them they had Joshua Spooner's shirt, jacket, breeches, saddlebags, his ring, watch and a pair of silver buckles with Spooner's initials on them. The men also had the wads of money given them by Bathsheba. She and the men readily confessed to the murder and were clapped into prison. Their trail took place in Worcester on April 27, with chief justice William Cushing officiating, aided by associate justices David Sewall and James Sullivan (future governor of Massachusetts), with a jury of twelve men. Leading the prosecution was attorney for the Commonwealth Robert Treat Paine (a signer of the Declaration of Independence). Levi Lincoln (future lieutenant governor of Massa-

12. Chandler, *The Trial of Bathsheba Spooner*, 35.
13. Ibid., 12-13.

chusetts, and a distant relative of Abraham Lincoln) was the attorney for the accused.

Lincoln reminded the jury that the case was "the first capital trial since the establishment of the government." He entreated the jurors to put aside "all feeling and prejudice . . . all political feelings." "This doubtless," wrote Peleg Chandler, "was an allusion to the vibrant prejudice at that time in Massachusetts against Mrs. Spooner's father on account of his political course." Born of high rank, well educated and accomplished, the mother of four children and now four months pregnant, Bathsheba had been trapped in an abusive marriage. With her father and brothers aiding the enemies of the nation, she had nowhere to go and had orchestrated "a most horrible crime." Bathsheba was "not in a state of mind which rendered her guilty," claimed Lincoln.

The whole murder trial took a mere sixteen hours. Despite the insanity plea, the jury found Bathsheba Ruggles Spooner, Ezra Ross, James Buchanan and William Brooks, guilty of murder. Chief Justice William Cushing pronounced the penalty: death by hanging. Execution was set for June 4.

Ezra Ross's aged parents submitted an appeal to save his life. "At the first instance of bloodshed" they had sent five sons to fight for the American cause. Four sons fought at Bunker Hill, and three (including Ezra) had marched southwards with General Washington. One of their sons was killed in battle. The Ross family claimed that their boy, far from the security and guidance of his family, was seduced "by a lewd and artful woman" to take part in the gruesome murder.

Bathsheba Ruggles Spooner made no appeals to save her own life. At the close of May 1778, she informed the court that she "was soon to become a mother [and] the child I bear was lawfully begotten. I am earnestly desirous of being spared till I shall be delivered of it." Execution was postponed to allow time for Bathsheba to be medically examined. Believing that Bathsheba sympathized with her Loyalist father in his politics, the two male-midwives and twelve matrons who examined her concluded that she "was not quick with child."[14] Deputy secretary John Avery Jr. signed the final warrant of execution set for July 2, 1778. An ardent patriot and member of the Sons of Liberty, Avery was guided by a deep animosity towards Bathsheba's father, Timothy Ruggles.[15]

14. Herbert M. Sawyer, *History of the Department of Police in Worcester, Massachusetts from 1874-1900* (Worcester: Worcester Police Relief Association, 1900), 26.
15. Navas, "New Light on the Bathsheba Spooner Execution," 1996.

On the appointed day, "an immense throng of people" numbering 5,000, coming from near and far, assembled in Worcester to witness the hanging of the four murderers. Escorted by an armed guard of one hundred men, the prisoners were brought out by cart to the hanging place, close to the courthouse where Timothy Ruggles had served as chief justice. After the three men were hanged, the rope was place around Bathsheba's neck. With her face covered, Bathsheba acknowledged her guilt. Taking the sheriff William Greenleaf by the hand, she said: "My dear Sir, I am ready. In a little time I expect to be in bliss and but a few years must elapse when I hope I shall see you and my other friends." And she was hanged till she was dead. Post-mortem revealed a five-month, perfectly formed male fetus, an innocent victim put to death with the guilty.

Whether Bathsheba Spooner was insane, and whether the state of Massachusetts wrongfully hanged a five-months pregnant woman to punish her Loyalist father, have long been debated. In 1889, Samuel Swett Green offered evidence that "for a long time Bathsheba had been a markedly eccentric woman" and her daughter (also named Bathsheba) "had been hopelessly crazy for many years."[16]

Timothy Ruggles was in New York when his daughter Bathsheba was hanged. Well into his sixties, he no longer played a significant role in the affairs of his country. With the British defeat in 1783, Ruggles and three of his sons, Timothy Jr., John and Richard, went into exile to Nova Scotia. In gratitude for his loyalty and to compensate him for the loss of his Massachusetts properties, the British government awarded him 1,000 acres near the town of Wilmot in Annapolis County. Timothy Ruggles chose Resurgam (I will rise again) as the motto of Nova Scotia. There he lived out the remainder of his life, dying in 1793 at the age of eighty-two.

16. Samuel Swett Green, *Bathsheba Spooner: incidental remarks made at the annual meeting of the American Antiquarian Society held in Worcester, October 22, 1888* (Worcester: Charles Hamilton, 1889).

Moravians in the Middle: The Gnadenhutten Massacre

⁂ ERIC STERNER ⁂

In 1782, six months after Cornwallis's surrender at Yorktown, Patriot militiamen committed one of the most heinous war crimes of the Revolutionary War. On March 8, between 100 and 200 militia and frontiersmen from western Pennsylvania slaughtered nearly 100 peaceful Indians at the small village of Gnadenhutten, on the Tuscarawas River in present day Ohio.[1] The Indians, largely Delaware and Munsey who adopted the pacifist Christianity preached by Moravian missionaries, had struggled to navigate the political currents of violence on the American frontier for years. To the west, British authorities at Detroit sought to mobilize the Ohio tribes (Miami, Shawnee, Huron, Wyandot, Delaware, and Mingo) to raid across the Ohio River into the American settlements in Kentucky, western Virginia, and western Pennsylvania. To the east, Continental, state, and local officials based at Fort Pitt struggled to resist the Indian raids by building frontier forts and conducting punitive raids against Indian settlements. The Moravian Indians were stuck squarely in the middle, trying to appease both sides. Ultimately, their attempt at neutrality led both sides to resent their presence in the no-man's land of eastern Ohio. Both sides resolved to do something about it, destroying the Moravian community on the Tuscarawas in the process.

Moravian missionaries started working in North America in the early eighteenth century and began their sustained work west of the

---

1. At the time of the Revolution, the Tuscarawas was called the Muskingum and most contemporary source material refers to the river along which the villages were located as the Muskingum. Today, however, the river is named Tuscarawas and becomes the Muskingum where the Tuscarawas and Walhonding Rivers join at Coshocton, Ohio. This article refers to the river as the Tuscarawas, but some direct quotations still use the eighteenth century name.

Appalachians when John Heckewelder began preaching on Beaver Creek in April 1770.² David Zeisberger, an experienced missionary, arrived in March 1771, having determined that his flock in eastern Pennsylvania could only be safe when removed from the evils of broader society.³ By May 1772, Zeisberger had established a community of Christian Delaware and Munsey, founding a town named New Schoenbrunn (Fine Spring) on the Tuscarawas River in Ohio. More followed from Pennsylvania's Susquehanna River in the summer and then Heckewelder led his group to the Tuscarawas the following spring. Within a year of its founding, New Schoenbrunn had grown so crowded that many of the Indians flocking there established a new town downriver, naming it Gnadenhutten.⁴ The settlements flourished as more converts joined from the Delaware tribe nearby, which also afforded them a degree of protection from Indian raids.

Unfortunately, Dunmore's War (1773–1774) between Virginia and the Ohio tribes did not leave the neutral Moravians and Delaware untouched.⁵ Shawnee, Wyandot, and Mingo raiding parties fighting the Virginians often hovered around New Schoenbrunn and Gnadenhutten, where they might find vulnerable traders, or perhaps missionaries.⁶ Wrote one nineteenth century historian, "During its continuance the settlements scarcely enjoyed a single day of rest. As the savages were greatly inflamed against the white people, the missionaries themselves were often in danger of their lives. Numerous troops of warriors marched through the settlements, —some upon murdering expeditions;

2. C.C. Mitchener, ed., *Ohio Annals: Historical Events in the Tuscarawas and Muskingum Valleys, and in Other Portions of the State of Ohio* (Dayton, OH: Thomas W. Odell, 1876), 84. The missionary Frederick Christian Post had visited the area in 1762 but did not stay long due to the French and Indian War. But, when Heckewelder and Zeisberger arrived, Post had already introduced local Delaware to the Moravian faith.
3. Mitchener, *Ohio Annals*, 83. In his history of the Moravian missionaries working among Native Americans in the mid-Atlantic states, Moravian missionary John Heckewelder noted that they were the subjects of constant persecution by colonial authorities, often suspected by their neighbors of collusion with raiders from the Iroquois Confederation. See John Heckewelder, *A Narrative of the Mission of the United Brethren among the Delaware and Mohegan Indians from its Commencement, in the Year 1740, to the Close of the Year 1808* (Philadelphia: M'Carty & Davis, 1820), 17-67. See also, Thomas Verenna, "The Darker Side of the Militia," *Journal of the American Revolution*, February 26, 2014, allthingsliberty.com/2014/02/the-darker-side-of-the-militia/, accessed January 13, 2018.
4. Mitchener, *Ohio Annals*, 89.
5. Heckewelder, *Narrative of the Mission*, 135.
6. Mitchener, *Ohio Annals*, 93-94; Samuel P. Hildreth, *Contributions to the Early History of the North-West Including the Moravian Missions in Ohio* (Cincinnati: Poe and Hitchcock, 1864), 93.

others returning with scalps and prisoners, —often threatening that both places should soon be surprised, and burned to the ground."[7] The pattern would cause difficulty for the Moravians again.

Isolated from the early months of the American Revolution, the Moravians continued to flourish and established a third town, Lichtenau, closer to the new center of Delaware power at Goshochking (Coshocton) in April 1776.[8] Zeisberger and Heckewelder both moved there to better conduct their mission to the Delaware, a rich source of new converts. As the year progressed, American Indian commissioners sought to maintain neutrality among the Indians. British commissioners, however, sought to enlist the Western tribes and the Iroquois nations of upstate New York in their cause. While the Iroquois inclined toward war, the Western tribes (Wyandot, Mingo, Huron, and Shawnee) hesitated and the Delaware (unsuccessfully) sought to maintain peace west and north of the Ohio River. When Delaware peace delegates were turned away at Detroit, they and the Moravians found themselves squarely in the middle, but as yet unassailed by either side.[9]

Neutrality was a difficult position to maintain. Indian raiding parties and white traders occasionally passing through made both sides suspicious.[10] American militia and frontier settlers suspected the Moravians might be sustaining Indian raiders; the British and western tribes suspected the Moravians were feeding intelligence to the Americans at Fort Pitt. Both were true, but reflected a Moravian policy of appeasement rather than duplicity. In 1777, reports reached the Moravian villages that the western Indians around Detroit would no longer accept neutrality and that those Indians who did not take up the hatchet against the Americans would be viewed as siding with them.[11] For their part, the Delaware nation blamed Indian aggressiveness on the British at Detroit, and threatened to go to war against them if they did not stop pushing the Wyandot, Huron, Mingo, and Shawnee Indians to go to war against the Americans.[12]

Tensions grew so bad on the frontier, that in 1777 and 1778 the Moravians abandoned both New Schoenbrunn and Gnadenhutten for

---

7. William M. Willett, *Scenes in the Wilderness: Authentic Narrative of the Labours and Sufferings of the Moravian Missionaries among the North American Indians* (New York: G. Lane & P.P. Sandford, 1842), 35.

8. Heckewelder, *Narrative of the Mission*, 143.

9. Ibid., 145.

10. Ibid., 147-149; Hildreth, *Contributions to the Early History of the North-West*, 99.

11. Heckewelder, *Narrative of the Mission*, 151.

12. Ibid., 154.

greater safety in Lichtenau, closer to the seat of Delaware power.[13] Unfortunately, and inadvertently, this only drew them into the politics of war. For example, in 1777, a Wyandot war party arrived in the Delaware capital, reportedly intent on raiding Lichtenau and either seizing or killing the missionaries there. Rather than fighting, the pacifist Moravians responded by attempting to appease the Wyandot with a feast. Meanwhile, anti-American agents had been circulating in the towns, seeking to incite individual Moravians to join them in raids and finding a receptive audience among some until the missionaries intervened.[14] In 1778, the Delaware signed a treaty with the Americans, promising neutrality, causing internal splits between war and peace factions in the tribe. Nevertheless, in 1778-1779, Wyandot and Mingo war parties continued moving through areas near the Moravian settlements, often purposely passing through the villages.[15] Moravians were well aware that such acts would not dispose the Americans kindly toward them and rumors of an American attack on the Moravians circulated as readily as rumors of potential attack by the Wyandot or Huron.[16] At the same time, the Moravians notified the Americans at Fort Pitt when war parties stopped in their towns and occasionally forwarded intelligence useful to the American war effort.[17] But, the policy of neutrality satisfied no one. Pro-war factions on the British and Indian side blamed the Moravians for constraining their efforts to mobilize the western tribes, while American settlers blamed the Moravians for sustaining cross-river raiding parties. Meanwhile, raids across the Ohio continued, only further inflaming passions on both sides and exacerbating hostility toward the Moravian villages among frontier settlers.[18]

For the next few years, groups of Moravians drifted in and out of New Schoenbrunn and Gnadenhutten, which, after all, contained tilled

13. Willett, *Scenes in the Wilderness*, 142-143.

14. Mitchener, *Ohio Annals*, 121-122.

15. Heckewelder, Narrative of a Mission, 167, 194-195.

16. Ibid., 160-165.

17. Ibid., 239-240; Rev. David Zeisberger to General Hand, November 16, 1777, in Rueben Gold Thwaites, ed., *Frontier Defense on the Upper Ohio, 1777-1778*, Draper Series, Vol. III (Madison, WI: Wisconsin Historical Society, 1912), 164-165.

18. Ruben Gold Thwaites, ed., *Chronicles of Border Warfare, or A History of the Settlement by the Whites, of North Western Virginia, and of the Indian Wars and Massacres in that section of the State with Reflections, Anecdotes, &c.* (Cincinnati: Stewart & Kidd Company, 1912), 300. The original version of this book under the same title, by Alexander Scott Whithers, was originally published in Clarksburg, Virginia by Joseph Israel in 1831. The work will hereafter be cited as Whithers, *Chronicles of Border Warfare*, but the pagination is from the 1912 edition annotated by Thwaites.

fields, homes, storehouses, and the like, only to hastily abandon them upon the rumor that an Indian or American war party had set out to destroy them. In 1780, even Lichtenau became insecure and the Moravians abandoned it for a new settlement near Gnadenhutten, which they named Salem.[19] Meanwhile, a portion of the Delaware war faction, led by "Captain Pipe," as he was known among whites, left its capital and settled in Upper Sandusky, considerably closer to British power at Detroit.[20] Pro-peace Delaware began to seek the protection of the Continental Army at Fort Pitt. As the Delaware split into more explicitly pro-war and pro-peace camps, their protection of the Moravian settlements dissipated.

Things did not improve in 1781. With the collapse of Delaware cohesion, the Moravians found themselves increasingly isolated and operating in a no-man's land between the western Indians and the Americans. Raiding parties continued to travel in and around their towns on raids, solidifying the enmity and suspicion Americans felt toward them. In the spring of 1781, Colonel Daniel Brodhead, the Continental commander at Fort Pitt, led a punitive raid west responding to a major Indian raid earlier that year and ostensibly aimed at the Delaware, whose split had caused the collapse of the 1778 Treaty.[21] The idea of a raid appears to have arisen with the militia, which then prevailed upon Brodhead to lead it. The Colonel had just led a campaign up the Allegheny River and now led 150 Continentals plus 134 militia toward the Muskingum and Tuscarawas.

When the force arrived outside Salem, Brodhead faced a dilemma. The militia wanted to destroy the town, but Brodhead opted instead to send a note to the missionaries asking a representative to join him in camp. Heckewelder went. Brodhead informed the missionary that he was conducting operations against hostile Indians at the forks, meaning the old Delaware capital at Coshocton. The Colonel wanted to know whether there were any Moravians about, as it was his wish to avoid conflict with them.[22] After facing down a group of militia determined to destroy the Moravian towns, Brodhead proceeded to Coshocton and destroyed Indian crops there. The Christian Indians had dodged a major attack, but just barely and only through the determination of a Continental colonel whose troops outnumbered the militia.

19. Willett, *Scenes in the Wilerness*, 144; Heckewelder, *Narrative of the Mission*, 209; Hildreth, *Contributions to the Early History of the North-West*, 110-111.
20. Heckewelder, *Narrative of the Mission*, 214.
21. Whithers, *Chronicles of Border Warfare*, 299-300.
22. Heckewelder, *Narrative of a Mission*, 213-214; Whithers, *Chronicles of Border Warfare*, 300-301.

In August 1781, a large war party of western Indians (Huron, Wyandot, Pipe's Delaware, plus a few Shawnee, Mohegan, and Ottawa) in company with a British officer arrived at the Moravian towns, attempted to persuade the Moravians to move to the Detroit area and demanded that the missionaries be turned over to them.[23] Eventually, on September 2, Wyandots with the party seized several of the missionaries, including Heckewelder and Zeisberger.[24] The British officer eventually released them, but continued to pressure the Moravians to depart as the warlike Indians from the northwest despoiled crops, livestock, and possessions at will. As a group, the Moravians finally submitted to pressure and agreed to emigrate, abandoning "Schoenbrunn, Gnadenhutten, and Salem, with much heaviness of heart and great regret, leaving in them the larger portion of their possessions."[25] Captain Pipe and his band of Delaware, who had already emigrated west, were the designated escort on the long journey to the Wyandot area along the upper Sandusky River, in western Ohio.[26]

The Moravians arrived on October 11 and began to put up huts and houses for the winter, while scrounging supplies for the winter and to feed those livestock they had managed to drive from the Tuscarawas River. Though they had promised a secure and bountiful home along the Sandusky, the western Indians made no provision to feed or house the Moravians, who faced a desperate situation and the prospects of starvation over the winter. The lack of food caused some disorder among the flock, although Zeisberger was somewhat cryptic about its nature.[27] In all likelihood, British agents and their Indian allies continued earlier efforts to recruit warriors from the Moravian community. By the end of the month, the British commander at Detroit, Major Arent Schuyler De Peyster, summoned the missionaries there, splitting them from their congregation.[28] At Detroit, De Peyster examined them about their relationship with the Continental Congress, then allowed them to return to the Sandusky. In their absence, Indians from the local tribes (Wyandot, Huron, and Pipe's Delaware) appeared to make progress among the missionaries' converted Indians. Zeisberger wrote, "Satan rages . . . not only from without, but also from within. For in

23. Hildreth, *Contributions to the Early History of the North-West*, 118-119; Heckewelder, *Narrative of the Mission*, 231-242.
24. Eugene Bliss, translator and editor, *Diary of David Zeisberger: A Moravian Missionary among the Indians of Ohio, Volume I* (Cincinnati: Robert Clarke & Co, 1885), 11-12.
25. Hildreth, *Contributions to the Early History of the North-West*, 124.
26. Heckewelder, *Narrative of the Mission*, 275.
27. Bliss, *Diary of David Zeisberger*, 54.
28. Ibid., 29; Heckewelder, *Narrative of a Mission*, 285.

the church there were people who upheld them in their false dispositions and applauded them, who wished to establish by force that wicked
life of his and heathenism. If we oppose them they become angry and
set on the wild Indians against us . . . Such a change has now come in
the Indian church that the bad, wicked people can not be cast out, but
they wish to be there and to cause harm in the church, for they in the
wild towns have occasion enough therefor and no one would say any
thing to them about their sinful life."[29]

Back on the Muskingum and Tuscarawas, the militia finally set out
to do what Colonel Brodhead had prevented them from doing in the
spring, namely, destroying the Moravian presence on the Tuscarawas.
Pennsylvania militia under Col. David Williamson arrived at the now
abandoned Moravian towns intent on either driving the Moravians farther from the Ohio river and American settlements, or making the entire lot prisoner and removing them to Fort Pitt.[30] So, it came as
something of a surprise when they found the towns abandoned.
Williamson rounded up the few Indians he could find in the area and
took them to Fort Pitt, from which they were eventually released.

Throughout the winter of 1781-1782, the Moravians on the Sandusky suffered under poor conditions. Groups of Moravians made their
way sporadically back to the towns they had abandoned on the Tuscarawas, namely to gather crops they had sown the previous spring and
collect supplies and possessions they had been forced to leave behind
when removed in October.[31] In general, they planned to collect corn in
the fields and then store it underground in the forest nearby, from
where it might be drawn as needs demanded. Originally, they had
planned to camp well away from the towns, but, believing them relatively safe, moved closer and lived among their old homes while they
worked.

Unfortunately, as the season progressed, the job of shuttling back
and forth between the Sandusky and Tuscarawas grew increasingly
risky. In the late-winter and early-spring, the Native Americans
launched several raids across the Ohio, north and south of the fort at
Wheeling. Everywhere, the pattern was the same: isolated settlements

29. Bliss, *Diary of David Zeisberger*, 56-57.

30. Whithers, *Chronicles of Border Warfare*, 313-314; Williamson, of Washington County,
Pennsylvania, was lieutenant colonel, 3rd Battalion, Pennsylvania Militia, raised in the area
around Donegal Township. Item 13, Militia Officers Index Cards, 1775-1800, Pennsylvania State Archives, Archives Records Information Access System (ARIAS), www.digita-
larchives.state.pa.us/archive.asp, accessed January 13, 2018.

31. Heckewelder, *Narrative of a Mission*, 311; Bliss, *Diary of David Zeisberger*, 29.

and houses would be struck and the occupants killed or carried off, while the responding militia could only briefly pursue a raiding force and determine that "Indians" had done it, without necessarily distinguishing among the tribal affiliations of the raiders. According to one historian writing early in the nineteenth century:

> The early period in the spring at which irruptions were frequently made by the savages upon the frontier, had induced a belief, that if the Moravian Indians did not participate in the bloody deeds of their red brethren, yet that they afforded to them shelter and protection from the inclemency of winter, and thus enabled them, by their greater proximity to the white settlements, to commence depredations earlier than they otherwise could. The consequence of this belief was, the engendering in the minds of many, a spirit of hostility towards those Indians; occasionally threatening a serious result to them. Reports too, were in circulation, proceeding from restored captives, at war with the general pacific profession of the Moravians, and which, whether true or false, served to heighten the acrimony of feeling towards them, until the militia of a portion of the frontier came to the determination of breaking up the villages on the Muskingum.[32]

The Moravians gathering and storing crops at Gnadenhutten had some awareness of the ongoing Indian raids. Back on the Sandusky, the missionaries noted at least one war party leaving the area in February.[33] As the work party toiled at Gnadenhutten, a small war party from the Sandusky had crossed the Ohio and raided local settlements in Pennsylvania.[34] In February, the war party had attacked the homestead of the Robert Wallace family and was returning westward. It camped near Gnadenhutten where warriors informed the working Moravians that they had captured a woman and a child, who they had impaled on stakes on the western side of the Ohio River.[35] A prisoner

32. Whithers, *Chronicles of Border Warfare*, 313-314.
33. Bliss, *Diary of David Zeisberger*, 67.
34. Heckewelder, *Narrative of a Mission*, 312; James II McMechen, *Legends of the Ohio Valley or Thrilling Incidents of Indian Warfare* (Wheeling, WV: West Virginia Printing Company, 1887), 46.
35. Heckewelder, *Narrative of a Mission*, 312; Whithers, *Chronicles of Border Warfare*, 319. Some sources name the family as that of David or William Wallace, understandable as they were all related. See Joseph Doddridge, *Notes on the Settlement and Indian Wars of the Western Parts of Virginia and Pennsylvania from 1763 to 1783* (Pittsburgh: John S. Ritenour and Wm. T. Lindsey, 1912), 188. This is the third printing of a collection of articles printed initially in the Wellsburg, Virginia *Gazzette* in 1824. Doddridge settles on Robert. Doddridge, *Notes on the Settlement*, 200. Sources conflict about whether the militia found Mrs.

with them warned the Moravians that the militia would pursue them and pass through Gnadenhutten.[36]

The February raids triggered a quick response from the Pennsylvania militia, which understood that Moravian Indians had been returning to their towns. Simply put, militiamen collectively decided to act on their 1781 intentions to destroy the Moravian presence along the Tuscarawas.[37] Subsequent historians argued that their intentions were much as Brodhead's had been: destroy the villages and crops, then remove the Moravians from the region by bringing them as prisoners to Fort Pitt.[38] (Ostensibly, the militia would remove the Moravians for their protection from warlike Indians farther west; the mirror image of the rationale that the western tribes had offered for removing the Moravians in the fall of 1781!) Some 160 men gathered in western Pennsylvania, mounted on their own horses and bearing personal arms, then formally mustered at Mingo Bottom, on the Ohio River just below present-day Steubenville. As earlier, they elected David Williamson to command as their colonel. The expedition set out for the Moravian villages on March 4, 1782, arriving on the Tuscarawas on March 5 and camping for the night.[39]

At Fort Pitt, Gen. William Irvine had replaced Daniel Brodhead and then departed the fort to seek assistance for the frontier in Philadelphia, leaving his deputy, Col. John Gibson, in command. Gibson, learning that the militia was marching on the Moravian villages, dispatched a messenger to warn the Indians there. He arrived too late.[40]

On the 6th, Williamson divided his forces into two columns. One would cross the river and attack from the west, from which it could also prevent escape. The other would divide into three parts and approach the town through the woods, striking it from north, south, and east.[41] Williamson's dispositions made the militia highly vulnerable to

---

Wallace's body, but Doddridge believes they did not and dismisses the brutal slaying of Wallace's family as a cause of the subsequent massacre. A family history indicates the Wyandot attacked Robert Wallace's family while he was away, capturing his wife and three children, then later impaling her on a stake while killing and mutilating one infant child. See F.S. Reader, *Some Pioneers of Washington County, PA: A Family History* (New Brighton, PA: F.S. Reader & Son, 1902), 40-41.

36. *The History of Tuscarawas County, Ohio* (Chicago: Warner, Beers & Co., 1884), 96.
37. Ibid., 295-296.
38. Whithers, *Chronicles of Border Warfare*, 321.
39. *The History of Tuscarawas County*, 295.
40. Ibid., 296.
41. Doddridge, *Notes on the Settlement and Indian Wars*, 189.

attack, suggesting that he did not fear such military measures from the Christian community. For their part, the working Moravians were confident of their innocence in the attacks across the Ohio and did not fear the oncoming militia.

The first column lacked canoes to cross the river. One man volunteered to swim it and recovered a sugar trough, which the group used to begin crossing men. Several stripped and swam, placing their clothes, weapons, and powder in the trough, and then pulling it along with them.[42] When a small group had crossed, sixteen strong by most accounts, it encountered Joseph Shabosh, who was out searching for a horse, and promptly killed, then scalped him.[43] Sources disagree whether he was shot first, or simply bludgeoned to death. The most popular story is that he was initially shot in the arm, breaking it, and then executed by gunfire afterward.[44] This group then encountered Indians working in the cornfields west of the river, hailed them as friends, and escorted them to the town, telling them they would be taken to Fort Pitt as prisoners, but where they would be fed. Not fearing for their safety, the Moravians working in the fields went along peacefully.[45] On the west side of the river, John Martin and his son, both Christian Indians, observed the party returning to Gnadenhutten. Martin sent his son to Gnadenhutten, while he went to Salem to apprise the Indians working there of events.[46]

Meanwhile, the second column, which had divided into three parts and remained on the east bank of the Tuscarawas, arrived at Gnadenhutten.[47] On the way, this group encountered Indians using a canoe on the Tuscarawas and killed them.[48] Jacob, Joseph Shabosh's brother, saw this murder from a distance and promptly fled.[49] They also found

---

42. *The History of Tuscarawas County*, 296.

43. Mitchener, *Ohio Annals*, 160; Willett, *Scenes in the Wilderness*, 182; *The History of Tuscarawas County*, 296. Whithers, *Chronicles of Border Warfare*, 322. Whithers and *The History of Tuscarawas County* have Shabosh being shot in the arm and then to death, which would have likely alarmed others. Whithers makes no mention of a peaceful meeting between Indians in the cornfields and this first division.

44. Doddridge, *Notes on the Settlement and Indian Wars*, 189n1. According to Doddridge, Charles Bilderback of Virginia fired the fatal shot and scalped Shabosh. Indians later captured him and his wife, took them to the site of Shabosh's murder, and executed Charles there in 1789.

45. Mitchener, *Ohio Annals*, 161.

46. Ibid., 161.

47. Ibid.

48. *The History of Tuscarawas County*, 296. One may have been Shabosh's wife. Whithers, *Chronicles of Border Warfare*, 322.

49. *The History of Tuscarawas County*, 296-299; Mitchener, *Ohio Annals*, 160.

Joseph Shabosh's wife hiding at the river's edge and killed her.[50] The group then approached the town proper and began mingling in a reasonably friendly fashion with the Indians there.

John Martin made quick time to Salem, where he informed the Indians there that he believed their wants would be satisfied by the Americans around Fort Pitt. They appointed two men to travel to Gnadenhutten with Martin to collect further information. Friendly mingling among the Indians there seemed to confirm Martin's belief.[51] Williamson sent Martin back to Salem with his compatriots and a militia detachment in order to retrieve the work parties there and assemble the entire body at Gnadenhutten.[52] After that party left, the militia deprived the Moravians in town of any dangerous implements (weapons, farm tools, etc.), seized, bound, and herded them into two buildings, men in one, women and children in the other.[53] The militia sent to Salem also received a welcome, behaved as friends, disarmed the Indians there, and moved the entire group back toward Gnadenhutten.[54] Upon their arrival, the Salem party discovered blood by the side of the river, but it was too late to turn back. The militia bound them and confined them to the two houses as well.[55] Realizing their peril, the Moravians began to pray and sing hymns.[56]

With the towns secured and the Moravians locked up, the militia did two things, although the order in which they occurred is less clear. First, the militia held a sham mob trial, perhaps trying to justify the action some of its members contemplated, work up the courage to do so, rationalize taking the Indian property that they seized, or some combination of all three. Basically, the militia pointed to the Indian property, such as horses, farm implements, and cooking utensils, and accused the Moravians of obtaining them on Indian raids.[57] Explanations and pleas of innocence fell on deaf ears.

Second, Williamson turned the fate of the Indians over to his men. Two nineteenth century accounts agree that the militia officers were unable, or perhaps unwilling, to make the decision themselves.[58] It's

50. Doddridge, *Notes on the Settlement and Indian Wars*, 192.
51. *The History of Tuscarawas County*, 299.
52. Mitchener, *Ohio Annals*, 161.
53. *The History of Tuscarawas County*, 299.
54. Ibid., 299; Bliss, *Diary of David Zeisberger*, 79.
55. Mitchener, *Ohio Annals*, 61. Willett, *Scenes in the Wilderness*, 183-184.
56. Bliss, *Diary of David Zeisberger*, 79.
57. Mitchener, *Ohio Annals*, 161; Willett, *Scenes in the Wilderness*, 184; *The History of Tuscarawas County*, 300.
58. Whithers, *Chronicles of Border Warfare*, 323; Mitchener, *Ohio Annals*, 162.

also possible that Williamson and his officers knew what would happen given the mood of the frontier communities and sought to absolve themselves of responsibility for the consequences. Williamson had the militia form a line, directing those men who were "inclined to mercy" to step forward. Of more than one hundred militiamen, only sixteen or eighteen stepped forward.[59] Finding themselves in a small minority, they left, although Williamson's whereabouts are unclear. One account has a woman with the community pleading with Williamson for their lives, only to be told he could do nothing.[60] There is some hint that Williamson was not popular with the militia due to his restraint in the towns the prior autumn and may have deferred to the armed body in order to restore it.[61]

The remaining militiamen commenced the work of murder. They began by separating several men supposed by the militia to be warriors and marched them out of town, planning to kill them at its edge. Two attempted to escape, but were killed in the process.[62] Back in town, the militia began braining the bound Moravians with a mallet in the houses in which they had been imprisoned, taking turns as each militiaman wearied. Then, they scalped their victims, left the houses, eventually returned to finish off any they found alive, and burned the buildings.[63] In this fashion, between the murders outside town and in the town, the frontier militia killed ninety-six unarmed people. Sixty-two were adults; the remaining thirty-four were children.[64] Their work completed, the militiamen looted the towns, investigated New Schoenbrunn, packed up, and set out to return to the Ohio.

As with most massacres, there were survivors. One young man named Thomas reportedly survived his scalping, hid among the dead bodies, crept out, then hid until darkness enabled him to make his way to the Sandusky trail. Similarly, a young boy imprisoned in a house with the women hid briefly in a cellar, then managed to escape through

59. Whithers, *Chronicles of Border Warfare*, 323; Mitchener, *Ohio Annals*, 162. Doddridge identifies sixteen men, who apparently did not announce their opposition to the death sentence when they returned home for fear of "public indignation." Doddridge, *Notes on the Settlement and Indian Wars*, 202n1. He also includes a missive from a descendent of one man present, which claims that his grand uncle opposed the death sentence. Counting him and Williamson, that would bring the total opposed to eighteen. Doddridge, *Notes on the Settlement and Indian Wars*, 202-203n2.
60. Bliss, *Diary of David Zeisberger*, 79-80.
61. Doddridge, *Notes on the Settlement and Indian Wars*, 199.
62. Ibid., 192.
63. Mitchener, ed., *Ohio Annals*, 162; Willett, *Scenes in the Wilderness*, 186.
64. Willett, *Scenes in the Wilderness*, 187.

a window as the house burned around him. A young boy with him got stuck in the window and burned to death. The two survivors fell in with the work party from New Schoenbrunn, already on its way back to Sandusky.[65] Most of the story of what happened in town comes from these two boys. It circulated among the communities along the Sandusky and was re-told by Heckewelder and Zeisberger, from whom most subsequent accounts drew their narratives.

Additional information about the movements of the militia comes from two messengers that the Moravians on the Upper Sandusky had sent to recall the work crews from the Tuscarawas. De Peyster had summoned the missionaries at Sandusky back to Detroit. One of their flock had sped eastward to recall the Moravians working the abandoned towns to say goodbye. As they packed and began departing, the New Schoenbrunn Moravians sent messengers to Gnadenhutten. Those messengers saw signs of a large body of mounted men in the area—the militia—and encountered Shabosh's body where the militia had left it. They then joined their friends, who were already west of the river for the night, reported what happened, and went back to New Schoenbrunn the next day while the main party continued westward. Seeing militia at New Schoenbrunn, the messengers finally caught up with their party on the way back to Sandusky.[66]

In addition to these witnesses, the returning militiamen themselves were, of course, aware of what they had done. Among some communities that had suffered at the hands of raids from the Sandusky area, the result was "highly gratifying to many," and the militiamen opposed to the murders did not announce their opposition upon returning home.[67] A third-hand account of Williamson's attitude quotes him as saying, "Should it be asked what sort of people composed this band of murderers, I answer, they were not all miscreants or vagabonds; many of them were men of the first standing in the country. Many of them had recently lost relations by the hands of the savage, and were burning with revenge. They cared little on whom they wreaked their vengeance, [just] so they were Indians."[68] The quote itself is suspect, but may reflect Williamson's attitude toward his fellow militiamen in his latter years.

65. Mitchener, *Ohio Annals*, 163; Willett, *Scenes in the Wilderness*, 189.
66. Willett, *Scenes in the Wilderness*, 190-191.
67. Whithers, *Chronicles of Border Warfare*, 327.
68. McMechen, *Legends of the Ohio Valley*, 48-49. The quote is nearly identical to an earlier account by Doddridge, who said he was acquainted with Williamson in the former's childhood, and is clearly Doddridge's conclusion and not a quote from Williamson. For a general overview of the changing attitudes of frontier settlers toward the native tribes along the frontier, see Darren R. Reid, "Anti-Indian Radicalisation in the Early American West, 1774-

Even if news of the massacre found a receptive audience among some settlers in western Pennsylvania, it was not well received at Fort Pitt. Brig. Gen. William Irvine, who had replaced Colonel Brodhead in command at Fort Pitt, was disgusted with the whole affair. Returning to the fort in late March, he wrote Commander-in-Chief George Washington, "things were in greater confusion than can well be conceived. The country people were, to all appearance, in a fit of frenzy. About three hundred had just returned from the Moravian towns, where they found about ninety men, women and children, all of whom they put to death, it is said, after cool deliberation and considering the matter for three days. The whole were collected into their church and tied when singing hymns."[69] He then relayed information about a militia plot to kill his deputy, Col. John Gibson, and the murder of two friendly Delaware Indians who had sought safety near the fort. When the militia launched another raid on the Indians in May, this time aimed at reaching the Sandusky and the tribes actually raiding across the Ohio, Irvine was clear to the commander, Col. William Crawford, who was not present at Gnadenhutten, that "it will be incumbent on you especially who will have the command, and on every individual, to act, in every instance, in such a manner as will reflect honor on, and add reputation to, the American arms—always having in view the law of arms, of nations, or independent states."[70] Irvine likely had the Gnadenhutten massacre in mind and wanted to avoid a repeat. In distant France, Benjamin Franklin wrote a correspondent in England, "the abominable Murders committed by some of the frontier People on the poor Moravian Indians, has given me infinite Pain and Vexation. The Dispensations of Providence in this World puzzle my weak Reason. I

1795," *Journal of the American Revolution*, June 19, 2017, allthingsliberty.com/ 2017/06/anti-indian-radicalisation-early-american-west-1774-1795/, accessed January 25, 2018.
69. Irvine to Washington, April 20, 1782, in C.W. Butterfield, ed., *Washington-Irvine Correspondence: The Official Letters Which Passed Between Washington and Brig.-Gen. William Irvine and Between Irvine and Others Concerning Military Affairs in the West from 1781 to 1783* (Madison, WI: David Atwood, 1882), 99.
70. Irvine's orders to the expedition commander, who was as yet to be determined when he wrote them, are contained in Irvine's Instructions, May 14, 1782, *Washington-Irvine Correspondence*, 118-119n1. After the failed May raid on the Sandusky, the story circulated that the militia intended to finish killing off the Moravians who had fled west. Participants denied that was their intention. Given that the Sandusky was the heart of power for many of the hostile Indian tribes and the fact that completing the work of destroying the Moravians would not provide additional security for the border, the story seems unlikely.

cannot comprehend why cruel Men should have been permitted thus to destroy their Fellow Creatures."[71]

Word of the massacre reached the missionaries on March 14, when an Indian returning with the Schoenbrunn party reported that the Indians at Salem and Gnadenhutten had been captured by the Americans and either taken to Fort Pitt or killed. Shabosh's murder was reported, likely by the messengers the New Schoenbrunn party had sent to Gnadenhutten before their own departure.[72] Zeisberger held out hope that the separated members of his flock had been taken to Fort Pitt, where they might find some measure of safety.[73] But, there was little opportunity to collect additional information, as he and his fellow missionaries set out for Detroit on the 15th per De Peyster's earlier summons. A more complete account had to wait until March 23, when two Indians bringing supplies for the trip to Detroit relayed the tales of the two boys who had escaped.[74]

The Gnadenhutten massacre has the ingredients of a simple morality play: land-hungry and depraved settlers slaughtered innocent Indians as the latter prayed for salvation. Nineteenth century histories of the massacre were content to let matters rest there. A history prepared for the dedication of a memorial at the site referred to the militia as "blood thirsty troops" and "murderers" and the Moravian Indians as "pious and unoffending."[75] Indeed, that was true in the main, but the massacre at Gnadenhutten represented the culmination of several antagonistic forces along the Ohio frontier and not just the work of bloodthirsty murderers: western tribes sought to provoke settler animosity toward the Moravians; Moravian attempts to appease both sides gave both sides reasons to object to their actions; poor communication between Continental authorities and the militia created tense command relationships among the Americans; frontier brutality on both sides was common and unexceptional at the time; and, the Moravians persisted in an area they knew was dangerous.

71. Benjamin Franklin to James Hutton, July 7, 1782, *Founders Online*, founders.archives .gov/?q=Moravian%20Period%3A%22Revolutionary%20War%22&s=1111311111&sa=&r =82&sr, accessed January 22, 2018.
72. Heckewelder, *Narrative of a Mission*, 287.
73. Bliss, *Diary of David Zeisberger*, 73.
74. Ibid., 78-80.
75. *A True History of the Massacre of Ninety-six Christian Indians, at Gnadenhutten, Ohio, March 8th, 1782* (New Philadelphia, OH: Gnadenhutten Monument Society, 1870), 9.

None of these factors excuse the cold-blooded mass murder of innocent people in Gnadenhutten. But, they highlight that it was not a mere spasm of inexplicable violence on the American frontier in wartime. It was the culmination of conflicting interests and decisions consistent with an intensifying pattern of brutality and violence on the frontier and a reminder that the birth of the United States had a darker side than many Americans like to admit.

Who Picked the Committees at the Constitutional Convention?

DAVID O. STEWART

Through four months in the summer of 1787, passionate arguments over political principles filled the Pennsylvania State House while hard-nosed political horse-trading buzzed in the taverns and drawing rooms of Philadelphia. Fifty-five American politicians were writing a new charter of government for the United States, the Constitution. They produced the longest-surviving constitutional republic in human history, and that summer has drawn the rapt attention of historians and legal scholars ever since.

One part of that constitutional story, however, has proved elusive. Although the debates among the delegates sometimes were electrifying and often were important, many of the most difficult questions were resolved by specially-appointed committees of a few delegates.[1]

Because key constitutional provisions were produced by committees, not on the convention floor, we might learn a good deal about the dynamics of the convention if we knew how the committee members were chosen. That, in turn might explain why certain delegates were included on a committee and why others were omitted. That could illuminate much about the attitudes of the delegates toward each other, and toward the challenging issues before them.

But we don't know how the delegates chose the members of each committee. Neither the convention nor any delegate left a record of the

---

1. *E.g.*, John R. Vile, "The Critical Role of Committees at the U.S. Constitutional Convention of 1787," *American Journal of Legal History*, 48:147 (2006). This article is the result of enlightened prodding and ideas of William Treanor, John Vile, Mary Sarah Bilder, John Mikhail, and Richard Beeman, for which the author is most grateful.

procedure they followed. The most likely answer, it turns out, has been hiding in plain sight all along.[2]

THE COMMITTEES

Two committees of five delegates handled the most daunting work of the summer: the Committee of Detail produced the first draft of the founding document; the Committee of Style produced the final draft. Despite their innocuous-sounding titles, those committees completed the essential work of synthesizing the elements of the founding document into a coherent whole.

In addition, eight "committees of eleven"—consisting of one delegate from each state then represented at the convention—resolved the thorniest questions of the summer, the ones that threatened to blow the convention up:

How to balance representation in the legislative branch between small and large states?

How to control the explosive risks of slavery, reassuring slaveholding states while not totally embracing the nefarious institution?

How to structure a presidency that had energy, but not monarchical power?

Many of the delegates who played key roles on the committees have largely been ignored by history: John Rutledge of South Carolina, Gouverneur Morris and James Wilson of Pennsylvania, and Edmund Randolph of Virginia. Rutledge chaired three critical committees, including the Committee of Detail, where Wilson and Randolph made important contributions. For the Committee of Style, Morris single-handedly wrote the final draft of the Constitution.

Through what process did the delegates choose these men to undertake the most delicate and important work of that summer?

Several answers to that question are possible: That the delegates chose members of committees by voting in their state delegations, with one vote for each state; or that each delegation chose the person who represented that state on a given committee; or that all the delegates voted together as individuals; or that they voted by different methods depending on the nature of the committee being selected.

---

2. In my book on James Madison, *Madison's Gift: Five Partnerships that Built America* (New York: Simon & Schuster, 2015), 337, I complained that despite considerable effort, I had not been able to figure out how the delegates chose committee members, and reported a consultation with three other scholars of the Convention (Richard Beeman, John Vile, and Mary Sarah Bilder) who expressed similar frustration. I have since continued to pick at that scab and herewith present the results of that work.

When the delegates voted on substantive matters at the Convention, they voted only as state delegations, with each state casting a single vote. That was always the practice in the Continental Congress, beginning in 1774. If a state had an even number of delegates who deadlocked on a motion, the state cast no vote on that motion. Voting by states gave extra influence to small states like Delaware, which were dwarfed in population and land mass by their larger siblings, Pennsylvania and Virginia. But per-state voting respected the principle of state sovereignty. So one possibility is that the delegates applied this familiar practice—one-state, one-vote—when choosing committee members.

Yet per-state voting would seem an odd practice to follow for the "committees of eleven," which included one delegate from each state. Why should Georgia delegates vote on which Massachusetts delegate, or which New York delegate, or which Maryland delegate, would serve on a committee? Would the Georgians even be able to make an informed judgment on which delegate had time or interest or background to be an effective member of that committee? Or which delegate best reflected the views of the other members of the state delegation? A far more plausible approach would be for each delegation to choose its own representative to those committees of eleven.

What about the two pivotal committees with only five members? It would be impossible for each state to choose one of its delegates for those committees, since no more than five states could have a member on each such committee. Consequently, the balloting for those committees was likely to have been on some other basis. Did the delegates vote in those instances as individual delegates, or as state delegations?

These questions have confounded decades of constitutional study, and the answers are important. The method of choosing committee members can shed important light on the mindset and intentions of the delegates at key points through the summer.

For example, the first "committee of eleven" addressed the issue that brought small states to the brink of abandoning the Convention: whether each state should have an equal vote in the national legislature, or whether legislative representation should be apportioned on the basis of state population or wealth.

For that first committee of eleven, the members representing the large states were, surprisingly, delegates who had not been pressing for proportional representation, even though proportional representation was in the interest of those states. Thus, two strong proponents of proportional representation—James Wilson of Pennsylvania and James Madison of Virginia—were passed over in favor of Ben Franklin and George Mason, respectively. Franklin and Mason had been far less engaged on the question, and might be expected to have been far more willing to compromise on it.[3] How did that happen?

If each state delegation chose its own committee member, then choosing Franklin and Mason were signals from the two largest states that they were open to compromise, no matter how passionate Wilson and Madison had been during floor debates. Alternatively, if the full convention chose the committee members by per-state votes, then the small states tilted the committee's membership in their favor by taking advantage of their greater numbers. Or, if the committee members were chosen by all delegates voting as individuals, then perhaps the small states enjoyed an edge because their delegations often were just as large as those of the large states, while there were more small states than large ones.

Which is true? Herewith the evidence.

THE FALSE LEADS

Because the Convention's proceedings were closed to the public, the first place to look for an answer is in the Convention's own records. The only official record is the journal maintained by William Jackson, secretary to the Convention. His work has sometimes been described as sloppy and sometimes has been defended, yet it remains the official source.[4] He did not try to create a transcript of the proceedings, but recorded only the motions and resolutions that were proposed and how they were decided.

A second source, sometimes accorded nearly official authority, is the record compiled by James Madison of Virginia, who set out to record the delegates' debates through the long sessions. Of lesser authority are the notes of Robert Yates of New York, who abandoned the convention after six weeks, and occasional notes taken by delegates including James McHenry of Maryland and Alexander Hamilton of New York.[5]

On its first day in session, the Convention appointed a three-member committee to develop the body's procedural rules. That committee, according to Jackson's journal, was chosen "by ballot." The Convention also selected Jackson as secretary, which Jackson recorded as also oc-

---

3. Vile, "The Critical Role of Committees," 159.
4. See Richard Beeman, *Plain, Honest Men: The Making of the American Constitution* (New York: Random House, 2009), 70 (calling Jackson "an exceptionally poor choice" as Secretary).
5. As explored in detail by Mary Sarah Bilder in *Madison's Hand: Revising the Constitutional Convention* (Cambridge: Harvard University Press, 2015), Madison somewhat obsessively revised—or even enhanced—his notes for years after the convention. That singular practice does not, however, affect the question addressed in this article.

curring by "ballot;" Madison's notes reflect that five states supported Jackson while two voted for another candidate. Madison, like Jackson, used the term "ballot" to describe the selection process.[6]

In its report, that three-person rules committee addressed the selection of committees by the convention. Committee members shall be, the report states, "appointed by ballot," with "the members who have the greatest number of ballots, although not a majority of the votes present, be the Committee."[7]

The rules specified that each state would cast one vote on substantive issues, but that rule sheds no light on the question whether, when choosing committees, the "ballots" or "votes" were to be cast by states or by individual members. The rules are silent on that point.[8] Remember that silence. It's important.

Further textual study encounters more silence. When recording the choice of the first "committee of eleven"—one from each state—Jackson's journal records the voting "by ballot;" Madison did also.[9] Yet, as noted above, having each state cast a vote for another state's committee member seems offensive to each state's sovereignty, and also cumbersome.

Moreover, never does any of the sources record the votes cast for individual committee members. Thus, we do not know if delegate X was chosen for committee Y by the votes of six states, or by the votes of twenty-one individual delegates; if such a record were available, it might reveal an interesting regional or philosophical pattern or alliance among the delegates. The records, however, disclose no such information.

The picture grows more vexing with the selection in late July of the five members of the Committee of Detail. Jackson's journal describes the Convention having "produced to ballot" for that panel, while Madison called it "a ballot for a committee."[10] As noted above, as a practical matter a five-member committee could not be chosen by having each state delegation choose a member, so all of the delegates voted—either by states or as individuals—for those committee members. Yet both

---

6. Max Farrand, ed., *The Records of the Federal Convention of 1787* (New Haven: Yale University Press, 1911), 1: 2, 1: 4 (May 25, 1787).

7. Ibid., 1: 9 (May 28, 1787). Ties, the report added, would be resolved in favor of the member "first on the list in the order of taking down the ballots." It is not clear how a member would come to be "first on the list." That may have referred to something as simple as alphabetical order; it may have referred to the custom of recording votes of states from north to south, from New Hampshire to Georgia. *E.g.*, Ibid., 1: 32 n.5.

8. Ibid., 1: 8 (May 28, 1787).

9. Ibid., 1: 509, 1: 516 (July 2, 1787).

10. Ibid., 2: 97, 2: 106 (July 24, 1787).

Jackson and Madison used the term "ballot" to describe the selection process for that smaller committee; they used the same term for the committees of eleven.

In short, the available texts from the convention provide no definitive answer. "Ballot" describes all of the occasions on which the delegates chose committee members, but that term does not reveal the nature of the voting contest. Voting by "ballot" could mean voting by states, by individual delegates, or sometimes by one method and sometimes by another.[11]

THE POWER OF PRECEDENT

With no clarity in the available texts, the remaining source is the practice of the American Congress since 1774, when the Continental Congress first convened. Many of the delegates were lawyers trained in the English common-law traditions, so they understood and accepted the logic of following prior precedent in legal matters.

In every Congress for thirteen years, as every delegate in Philadelphia knew, each state cast a single vote; the practice was incorporated in the Articles of Confederation, which took effect in 1781. The Articles also authorized Congress to appoint a "committee of the states" which would tend to business while Congress was in recess. Each state could have one member on a committee of the states. Congress also could create "such other committees . . . as may be necessary."[12]

Based on its practice since 1774, Congress in 1781 adopted two rules for exercising the power under the Articles to appoint "such other committees." For important issues, Rule 19 authorized the use of a "grand committee" with a member from each state. Rule 19 specifically stated that "each state shall nominate its member" of a grand committee. According to a leading study of congressional procedure, the Continental Congress always followed this practice in the years before the rule took effect.[13]

11. One scholar has suggested that the delegates voted as individuals on the selection of all committee members. Jack Rakove, *Original Meanings: Politics and Ideas in the Making of the Constitution* (New York: Knopf, 1996), 379n38. That assertion is supported, however, only by a citation to Madison's notes on the selection of the first "committee of eleven." Madison's entry on that occasion states only that the committee members were selected "by ballot," a term that both he and Jackson used to describe the selection of Jackson as Convention Secretary on May 25, when each state delegation cast one vote. Accordingly, use of the term "ballot" sheds no light on the question addressed in this article.
12. Articles of Confederation, Art. V, cl. 4; Art. IX, cl. 5.
13. Journals of the Continental Congress, 20: 479 (May 4, 1781); Calvin C. Jillson and Rick K. Wilson, *Congressional Dynamics: Structure Coordination, and Choice in the First American Congress, 1774-1789* (Stanford: Stanford University Press, 1994), 98.

But Congress also had made ample use of its residual power to create smaller committees, relying on them to address discrete problems and then to disband, often in a matter of a few days or a week. The proliferation of three-member and five-member committees was astonishing. In 1783 alone, Congress appointed 498 committees, or nearly four new committees in every three-day period; over eight years, Congress utilized an average of 280 committees each year.[14]

Congress's Rule 20 governed the choice of those smaller committees, stating that "the states shall ballot for small committees," adding that if the committee could not be completed with individuals receiving a majority vote (that is, the votes of seven states), the "*house* shall by a vote or votes determine the committee."[15] Although the "states" might cast an initial ballot for the members of small committees, it was mathematically impossible for more than one delegate to command a majority of state votes, which would leave at least two seats to be filled by the vote of the "house" (or four vacant seats for the five-man committees). Voting by individual ballot—by the "house"—surely was the predominant method for filling hundreds of committee seats every year.

Congress did not ordinarily record the voting on selection of committee members, but it did in February 1777, when it established a three-person committee to examine desertions from the army. Twenty-seven members of Congress were present that day; twenty-seven ballots were cast for members of the committee. The three delegates commanding the highest number of votes (nine votes, five votes, and five votes, respectively) were named to the committee.[16]

Indeed, in 1783 Congress amended Rule 20 to specify the procedure by which individual delegates voted for members of small committees. The ballots were to be completed by the delegates "from their seats," with one member from each delegation placing the ballots in a box that would be delivered to the president of Congress.[17]

This precedent—which was the contemporary reality well-known to the Convention delegates—provides a sensible template for projecting how the Constitutional Convention selected its committee members. The Convention's Committees of Eleven may be likened to the "grand committees" of Congress, with each delegation selecting the member who would represent that state on the committee. That pro-

14. Ibid., 96-97.
15. Journals of the Continental Congress, 20: 480 (May 4, 1781) (emphasis supplied).
16. Journals of the Continental Congress, 9: 109 n.1 (February 12, 1777); Jillson & Wilson, *Congressional Dynamics*, 66.
17. Journals of the Continental Congress, 24: 344 (May 15, 1783).

cedure preserved the prerogative of each state to determine which delegate would represent it, at a time when state prerogatives were jeal-
ously defended.

For smaller committees like the Committee of Detail and the Committee of Style, the delegates almost surely cast ballots as individual
members of the whole house, as the Continental Congress did when
choosing members of its small committees. Thus, a delegate from a
small state might be chosen—as William Samuel Johnson of Connecticut was voted onto the Committee of Style, and Oliver Ellsworth from
the same state on the Committee of Detail—solely because his talents
were thought to match the task facing the committee, while other
prominent delegations provided no delegates to that panel.

Only if the delegates voted as individuals within "the house" could
they have selected Alexander Hamilton for the Committee of Style.
The New York delegation could not choose Hamilton for that committee because New York was not even officially present at the Convention at that time. New York's legislature had specified that at least
two of its delegates had be present in order to cast the state's ballot at
the Convention, but Hamilton was the only New Yorker at the Pennsylvania State House after early July. With no state delegation to choose
him, Hamilton could have been chosen only by the vote of the individual delegates.[18]

These conclusions have the considerable virtue of matching congressional precedent and practice before 1787, which dictated many of
the procedures the Convention followed, including per-state voting
and closing its proceedings to the public. These conclusions have the
further virtue of making sense. That they are not grounded in an authoritative text of the Convention is a frustration, but not one that
should obscure the best available explanation of the committee selection
procedure.

18. The delegates voting for Hamilton plainly overlooked the further question of whether
he was even a member of the Convention if he was not part of a state delegation then present. George Washington, ever punctilious, noted that problem when he recorded in his
diary for September 17, 1787, that the Constitution had commanded the "unanimous as-
sent of 11 states and Colo. Hamilton's from New York (the only delegate from thence in
Convention)."

A Second Bonaparte:
Searching for the Character
of Alexander Hamilton

STEVEN C. HERTLER

Thomas Jefferson, that *American Sphinx*,[1] is perhaps Alexander Hamilton's only rival within the high pantheon of the founding generation for enigma. Hamilton's character recalls Giambologna's *The Rape of the Sabine Women*, a spiraling marble Renaissance masterpiece resident in Florence's Piazza Signoria, featuring three intertwined figures that can only be captured conclusively from a host of vantage points. We can ask, as did Douglas Ambrose in *The Many Faces of Alexander Hamilton: The Life and Legacy of America's Most Elusive Founding Father*:

> Was he a closet monarchist or a sincere republican? A victim of partisan politics or one of its most active promoters? A lackey for British interests or a foreign policy mastermind? An economic genius or a shill for special interests? The father of a vigorous national government or the destroyer of genuine federalism? A defender of governmental authority or a dangerous militarist?[2]

All complex persons with mixed motives require balanced interpretation. Napoleon, Sherman, Savonarola, and Castlereagh, are respectively known as either a Corsican ogre or Colossus of the Nineteenth Century, merchant of terror or Uncle Billy, heretic or prophet, and trai-

---

1. In the words of Joseph Ellis. J. J. Ellis, *American Sphinx: The Character of Thomas Jefferson* (New York: Knopf, 1997).
2. Douglas Ambrose, "Introduction: the life and many faces of Alexander Hamilton," in D. Ambrose & R. W. T. Martin, eds., *The Many Faces of Alexander Hamilton: The Life and Legacy of America's Most Elusive Founding Father* (New York: New York University Press, 2006), 1-22.

tor or representative, all depending on whether one is listening to the
Anglo-Americans or French, Southern separatists or Northern victors,
papist or purist, or Irish Catholics or English Protestants. In each case,
a very different narrative can be framed. This is the case at present with
Hamilton. Yet Hamilton is at least different in degree, necessitating
particular caution and circumspection before coming to characterolog-
ical conclusions.

With respect to Hamilton, one might come across Henry Cabot
Lodge's hagiography,[3] which sympathizer John Morse Jr. finds to be
an important volume due to Cabot's understanding of Federalism. Yet,
Morse reveals Hamilton and George Cabot, an ancestor of Henry
Cabot, to have been intimate friends. Morse then goes on to say,
"Knowing well that, if Mr. Lodge was very naturally inclined to make
a hero of Hamilton, he at least practiced a strictly intelligent and reasonable worship." This does not render Lodge's biography nugatory. If,
however, it is the only source of speculation on Hamilton, one will come
away with a highly stylized, and ultimately flawed, understanding of
the subject. On the other hand, exclusively reading J. P. Boyd's *Number
7: Alexander Hamilton's Secret Attempts to Control American Foreign Policy* would cause comparable skew in the other direction.[4] Thus, the lesson is to read both partisans and detractors. Political sympathies,
however, are not the only forces to balance against one another. There
is also the issue of zeitgeist. Historical personages are prone to being
celebrated or denigrated to the extent that their symbolism is congruent
or incongruent with the writer's own time, and the sentiments, policies
and positions then valued. Reading Lodge, Nathan Schachner,[5] Boyd,
Richard B. Morris,[6] Robert W. T. Martin,[7] Ambrose, John L. Harper,[8]
and John Ferling,[9] begins to cut across political poles and pendulous
swings. In doing this we replace the search for that rare unbiased and

3. H. C. Lodge, *Alexander Hamilton* (New York & Boston: Houghton Mifflin & Co, 1898).
4. Julian P. Boyd, *Number 7: Alexander Hamilton's Secret Attempts to Control American Foreign Policy* (Princeton: Princeton University Press, 1964).
5. Nathan Schachner, *Alexander Hamilton* (New York: D. Appleton-Century Co., 1946).
6. Richard B. Morris, *Seven Who Shaped Our Destiny: The Founding Fathers as Revolutionaries* (New York: Harper and Row, 1973).
7. Robert W. T. Martin, "Reforming Republicanism: Alexander Hamilton's Theory of Republican Citizenship and Press Liberty," in *The Many Faces of Alexander Hamilton*, 109-133.
8. J. L. Harper, *American Machiavelli: Alexander Hamilton and the origins of US foreign policy* (Cambridge: Cambridge University Press, 2004).
9. John E. Ferling *Jefferson and Hamilton: The Rivalry that Forged a Nation* (New York: Bloomsbury Press, 2013).

comprehensive source with a collection of sources, the biases of which oppose one another.

The principle of triangulation, as one might call this multiplication of perspective through pursuing diversified sources, can also be applied to original source writings of Hamilton and his contemporaries. Of course, it is important to read original writings from Hamilton, such as his many Federalist papers, and the writings of his partisans, such as James McHenry. Additionally, sympathetic but more objective associates like George Washington can provide balance. Also, Hamilton's character cannot be rendered without knowing the opinions of Aaron Burr, James Monroe, or Jefferson; the latter of whom wrote:

> I will not suffer my retirement to be clouded by the slanders of a man whose history, from the moment at which history can stoop to notice him, is a tissue of machinations against the liberty of the country which has not only received and given him bread, but heaped its honors on his head.[10]

With Hamilton, there is no question of ability, as there was no doubt of his ambition and genius. Further still, there are elements of his life and conduct that force the student of historical biography to jettison essentialist thinking, for Hamilton defies dichotomies such as good or evil, patriot or tyrant. For instance, looking to his marriage, a detractor can charge Hamilton with *hypergamy*[11] and *adultery*,[12] but without credibly being able to cast Hamilton in the role of a rake. Putting aside inquiries into his personal life, across his brilliant political career there are some critical junctions, the deep investigation of which affords particular insight into Hamilton's inner character: (1) The Newburg Conspiracy; (2) congressional investigations into his conduct as treasury secretary; (3) the election of 1800; (4) his attempted character assassination of John Adams; and (5) his efforts to suppress domestic rebellions. Through the aforementioned triangulation of sources and perspectives, these five pivotal moments within the nation's history emerge as best positioned to elucidate Hamilton's inner nature.

10. Thomas Jefferson to George Washington, September 9, 1792, Founders Online, founders.archives.gov/documents/Jefferson/01-24-02-0330.

11. *Hypergamy* is the act of marrying above one's status, which is characteristic of Hamilton who married into the Schuyler family.

12. This of course refers to the Maria Reynolds affair wherein Hamilton was, for all appearances, taken in by an unscrupulous husband and wife acting in concert so as to extort money via blackmail.

Therein, we may find the necessary portals into the inner man, specifically to determine whether he was *Catiline*[13] reincarnate or simply an *American Machiavelli.*[14]

THE NEWBURG CONSPIRACY

In Newburgh, New York in 1783, the infamous Newburgh Conspiracy was hatched wherein discontent among the rank and file infantry was to be harnessed to threaten the civil government, then in arrears. Hamilton's role therein betrays, at the very least, an instance of impetuosity and poor judgement. It seemed that Hamilton utterly lacked the virtue that induced such admiration of George Washington by George III, namely, the unequivocal subordination of military power to civilian authority. Then, as always, Washington would not allow the military to menace the civilian authority under whose auspices it served. Once Hamilton realized as much, he reversed course, distancing himself from what may well have been something between complicity and acquiescence. As Morris states, "Verily, Hamilton had learned a lot from the way in which Washington had handled the Newburgh crisis, and considering Hamilton's own devious role in that incident, his loud professions of virtue could easily have been prompted in part by a haste to clean his own muddied boots."[15]

At worst, it looked as though Hamilton urged Washington to weaponize the disaffected, but not disbanded, army against the Continental Congress. Going still further, according to Ferling, Hamilton's "fingerprints were all over the Newburgh Affair."[16] A reading of Ferling's reconstruction shows Hamilton seducing members of the Continental Army, those with pretension to higher power who at the same time were sympathetic to the army's dissatisfaction. Ferling puts this incident in context by studying the relationship between Washington and Hamilton. Ferling dismisses the approximation of a father-son relationship, such as that which seems to have truly been present between Washington and Lafayette. Instead, Ferling sees Hamilton as having no lost love for Washington, essentially using him opportunistically as a ladder upon which to climb to prominence and power. Washington, in turn, recognized Hamilton as a Machiavellian man who brooked no limit to his power, a man who brazenly pulled strings to bring about

13. Catiline refers to Lucius Sergius Catilina, a senator charged with attempted subversion of the Roman Republic. Hamilton defamed Aaron Burr as a Catiline. Nancy Isenberg, *Fallen Founder: The Life of Aaron Burr* (London: Penguin, 2007).
14. J. L. Harper, *American Machiavelli.*
15. Morris, *Seven Who Shaped Our Destiny*, 252.
16. John Ferling, *A Leap in the Dark: The Struggle to Create the American Republic* (New York: Oxford University Press, 2003), 439.

whatever outcome he deemed necessary, a man who would use most means to achieve his ends. Despite the degree to which this relationship was paternal or contentious, Washington certainly constrained the most dangerous excesses of Hamilton's nature. So long as Hamilton operated either under the aegis or constraint of Washington's superior moral compass, he furthered the ends of the republic.

CONGRESSIONAL INVESTIGATION

Hamilton's appointment as the first secretary treasurer placed the new nation's purse within his grasp. Given his willingness to subvert rules, laws and precedents, his contemporaries in the emerging opposition party assumed intrigue: "Convinced that Hamilton had aided and abetted corruption as Treasury Secretary, one of Jefferson's first acts as president was to order his Secretary of the Treasury, Albert Gallatin (1761-1849), to search the department's files for incriminating evidence."[17]

Even more interesting is the reaction to the evidence of their own investigation: "When none was found, Jefferson saw this not as an exoneration of Hamilton but as further evidence of his skill at deceit."[18]

That the convictions held against Hamilton were so strong as to prove immutable in the face of contrary evidence indicates a fundamental misunderstanding of Hamilton's character. Jefferson, and likely also Madison and others who would come to overtly identify as Republicans, saw in Hamilton the archrival—the Samson in the field. They mistook Hamilton's different vision of government for treasonous malevolence. The student of Hamilton is apt to make the same mistake. Stephen Brock speaks to this issue:

> It is easy to interpret every aspect of Hamilton's policy as part of a grand design to enrich a capitalist class at the expense of the people, but such a simplified view displays neither justice to the man nor an understanding of his problems. Politically the great desideratum was to attach to the national government enough powerful interest to make it effective; this rests upon three sensible assumptions, that the union could not be preserved without strong central government, that government could not be strong unless people wished it to be so, and that a material stake in good government was more valuable than vague well-wishing.[19]

17. Stephen Knott, "'Opposed in Death as in Life': Hamilton and Jefferson in American Memory," in *The Many Faces of Alexander Hamilton*, 28.
18. Ibid.
19 W. R. Brock, "The Ideas and Influence of Alexander Hamilton," in *British Essays in American History*, H. C. Allen and C. P. Hill, eds. (New York: St. Martin's Press, 1957), 204.

These are the complex motivations for assumption, and for Hamilton's actions as treasury secretary. One must note that, for all his pursuit of power and glory, Hamilton did not fiscally capitalize on his office.

THE ELECTION OF 1800

Though electioneering antics were evident in the election of 1796 in which Hamilton took part, the election of 1800 was so infamous as to elicit several book length narratives[20] and peer reviewed investigations.[21] While many of these sources focus on John Adams as incumbent and Jefferson as insurgent, Elkins and McKitrick's *The Age of Federalism* ably documents Hamilton's particular machinations. [22] Like other Arch-Federalists, Hamilton wanted a change of guard. Hamilton attempted to oust the uncontrollable and unpredictable Adams in favor of the more pliable Charles Pinckney. He toured New England to survey public opinion, finding that:

> Though the greatest number of strong minded men in New England are not only satisfied of the expediency of supporting Pinckney, as giving the best chance against Jefferson, but even prefer him to Adams; yet in the body of that people there is a strong personal attachment to this gentleman, and most of the leaders of the second class are so anxious for his re-election that it will be difficult to convince them that there is as much danger of its failure as there unquestionably is, or to induce them faithfully to cooperate in Mr. Pinckney, notwithstanding their common and strong dread of Jefferson.[23]

Elkins and McKitrick use the term *cabal* in describing the attempt to thwart Adams' reelection, though the word would be far too strong had it not been for what followed. If Hamilton had accepted that his efforts were unsuccessful, this would have amounted to a defensible wielding of political influence for personal gain and party good. Yet, he went further. Hamilton contacted John Jay, then governor of New

20. E. J. Larson, *A Magnificent Catastrophe: The Tumultuous Election of 1800, America's First Presidential Campaign*. (New York: Simon and Schuster, 2007); J. Ferling, *Adams vs. Jefferson: The Tumultuous Election of 1800* (New York: Oxford University Press); J. R. Sharp, *The Deadlocked Election of 1800: Jefferson, Burr, and the Union in the Balance* (Lawrence: University Press of Kansas, 2010).
21. J. B. Freeman, "The Election of 1800: A Study in the Logic of Political Change," *The Yale Law Journal*, *108*(8) (1999), 1959-1994; C. O. Lerche, "Jefferson and the Election of 1800: A Case Study in the Political Smear," *The William and Mary Quarterly: A Magazine of Early American History* (1948), 467-491; D. R. Egerton, "Gabriel's Conspiracy and the Election of 1800," *The Journal of Southern History*, *56*(2) (1990), 191-214.
22. S. Elkins & E. McKitrick, *The Age of Federalism*. (New York: Oxford University Press).
23. Ibid., 735.

York, "imploring him to reconvene the existing legislature and persuade it to enact a new law for choosing electors by district, which he thought might bring a Federalist majority."[24] The circumspect Jay ignored the missive, leaving it lie in his drawer. Drawing the distinction between Jay and Hamilton in this circumstance provides a compelling contrast. Unlike Hamilton, who was so unscrupulous and indiscreet as to make the request, Jay had the discretion to reject and suppress what was clearly capable of imperiling the infant nation's constitutional process.

CHARACTER ASSASSINATION OF ADAMS

As seen in many biographies of Hamilton and Adams, and as documented by Harper and by Elkins and McKitrick, Hamilton's attempted character assassination of Adams stands high even among the heightened and hyperbolic events of America's 1790s. As Harper details, the "calamitous attack on President John Adams is impossible to excuse, [and] difficult to explain."[25] In that this decision "backfired, destroying his reputation," it has been called, "the most lunatic political act of his life."[26] As quoted by Elkins and McKitrick, the *Aurora* announced:

> The pulsation given to the body politic, by Hamilton's precious letter, is felt from one end of the union to the other. Never was there a publication so strange in its structure, more destructive in its purposed end. It has confirmed facts that were before known, but held in doubt. It has displayed the treachery, not only of the writer, but of his adherents in the public counsels; and while it has thrown much false glare on the character of Mr. Adams, it has given some new and faithful traits also; but it has thrown a blaze of light on the real character and designs of the writer and his partisans.[27]

There was in this letter of Hamilton's a thoroughgoing rehearsal of deficiencies, both petty and substantive, all of which were supposed to relate to Adams to the end of casting doubt on his fitness for office. The author employed a range of pretenses as foils for his true motivation, which was nothing other than "private resentment."[28] In deescalating the quasi-war, instead of pressing it forth towards formally declared and vigorously prosecuted hostilities, Adams had obviated the need for the army Hamilton positioned himself to head; and in doing so Adams had deprived Hamilton of the opportunity war afforded for

---

24. Ibid., 734.
25. Harper, *American Machiavelli*, 225.
26. Elkins and McKitrick, *The Age of Federalism*, 736.
27. Ibid., 783.
28. Harper, *American Machiavelli*, 256.

advancement. War had raised Hamilton from obscurity; and it was war which was to elevate Hamilton beyond the reaches of his peak powers. If he accepted deescalation, Hamilton might have maintained the power to which he had attained. However, pressing forward with this scheme to replace Adams, Hamilton, as Harper documents, fell in the estimation of fellow federalists such as Robert Troup. More than this, the letter proved something of a Rorschach test, wherein some of Hamilton's own foibles and follies were projected, unsuccessfully, upon Adams, as can be seen in a letter from George Cabot to Hamilton: "I am bound to tell you that you are accused by respectable men of Egotism, & some very worthy & sensible men say you have exhibited the same vanity in your book [letter] which you charge as a dangerous quality & great weakness in Mr. Adams."[29]

THE SUPPRESSION OF DOMESTIC REBELLIONS

When young and obscure, Hamilton famously longed for a war, knowing that only in such times of flux could men make radical social advances. As a mature founder, Hamilton was bent on war. For instance, as discussed in the previous section, during the quasi-war, to justify heretofore unseen expenditures and armament,[30] he minimized the importance of the nation's three thousand mile ocean barrier. However, Hamilton did not reserve martial solutions for foreign foes. To the southerners he stoked fears of a slave insurrection, while he presented the specter of anarchic atheism to the religious.[31] For instance, as Newman states, in writing to William Loughton Smith of South Carolina, Hamilton spoke unflinchingly of manipulating public opinion and rousing fears: "The politician will consider this an important means of influencing Opinion, and will think it a valuable resource in a contest with France to set the Religious Ideas of his Countrymen in active Competition with the Atheistical tenets of their enemies."[32]

As one applies heat to metal to make it ductile, Hamilton hoped to apply fear to the people to make them manipulable. As Morris states,

> It was characteristic of Hamilton that throughout his life he was
> wont to prefer military solutions to political ones in times of emergency,
> whether it was to satisfy the officers and public creditors in 1783, or to

29. George Cabot to Hamilton, November 29, 1800, Founders Online, founders. archives.gov/documents/Hamilton/01-25-02-0122.
30. P. D. Newman, *Fries's Rebellion: The Enduring Struggle for the American Revolution* (Philadelphia: University of Pennsylvania Press, 2004).
31. Ibid.
32. Ibid., 63.

put down the wretched whiskey insurrectionaries a decade later, or to settle differences with France arising during President Adams's administration.[33]

In Morris's account of the Whiskey Rebellion, Hamilton simply emerges as autocratic, in that he wanted the Federal Government to appear as a leviathan against which no opposition could be mounted. Newman's account of Hamilton's role in Fries Rebellion is more sinister, suggesting Hamilton's willingness to trump up charges and use discontented citizens as tools to augment his martial power.

CONCLUSIONS

Some of the readings informing this survey suggest that many have been overly magnanimous in their judgement of Hamilton, as exampled by Lodge for one; but also as seen in the person of James Bryce, author of *The American Commonwealth*,[34] who delivered, according to Lord Acton, "a panegyric on Alexander Hamilton."[35] Then there was Talleyrand, who "assured Ticknor that he had never known his [Hamilton's] equal."[36] Likewise, Acton attests that Seward calls Hamilton, "The ablest and most effective statesman engaged in organizing and establishing the union;" Macmaster and Hoist thought him the "foremost genius among public men in the new world."[37] Such hyperbole is justified to the extent that Hamilton is judged on ability alone.

The principle of triangulation, inoculating us against mischaracterizations via the multiplication of perspective afforded by a multitude of sources, is a starting point in studying such a complex character. In a way, this approach is the literary analogue of the psychometric search for convergent evidence. For instance, in attempting to measure intelligence, it is the shared variance of those many intelligence tests that is purported to measure the latent construct of g or *general intelligence*. In this same way, we can discard one-time descriptions, obvious vituperations of lone detractors, uncharacteristic actions, and so forth, which are not replicated across time, writers, and sources. Alternatively, those features that are so replicated can more confidently be taken as core features of Hamilton's character. In making such a search, five junctures within Hamilton's life emerge as windows of analysis, as have herein

33. Morris, *Seven Who Shaped Our Destiny.*
34. James Bryce, *The American Commonwealth* (London, 1888).
35. J. E. E. Dalberg-Acton, *The History of Freedom and Other Essays* (New York: The Classics of Liberty Library, 1993, reprint of 1907 edition).
36. Ibid.
37. Ibid.

been reviewed. These must be surveyed personally and fully by anyone attempting to form their own conclusions. Further focus might be given to assumption, Hamilton's description of Julius Caesar as the greatest man that ever lived,[38] a forensic examination of Hamilton's role in New York politics, Hamilton's calculating use of dueling, or Hamilton's legal battle with the Philadelphia *Aurora*.[39]

At worst, more amoral than immoral, Hamilton played the part of the *Nietzschean* superman. "Hamilton," in the proper estimation of Ferling, "was an opportunist and a master of intrigue, orchestration, and manipulation."[40] From the perspective of modern personality science, Hamilton had a strong measure of *dark triad* traits, with *Machiavellianism* being more developed either than *narcissism* or *psychopathy*,[41] making him deserve J. L. Harper's appellation of *American Machiavelli*. Elkins and McKitrick seem to have come to a different conclusion:

> There was no question of Alexander Hamilton's immense ambition, his pride, his acute sense of personal honor, or his propensity for sweeping plans which nobody quite knew better how to execute than himself. He was fascinated by power and the uses of power. And yet one cannot quite project from this a picture of Hamilton as the calculating schemer. The cold Machiavellian, the crafty plotter, the man whose eye is on the main chance—this, for better or worse, was no part of Hamilton's character. The sheer ardor of the man, the impatience, the impulsiveness, the need to keep moving, all served to inhibit that calculating prudence which might have made a very different person of him.[42]

38. Hamilton's admiration for Julius Caesar continued throughout his life, giving credence to Jefferson's account of a visit Hamilton paid to the home of the Secretary of State in Philadelphia probably in the spring of 1791. Hamilton inquired about the portraits hanging on the wall. Jefferson identified the subjects as Sir Francis Bacon, Sir Isaac Newton, and John Locke, claiming them to be his "trinity of the three greatest men the world has ever produced." Hamilton was unimpressed. "The greatest man that ever lived," he remarked, "was Julius Caesar." Morris, *Seven Who Shaped Our Destiny*, 224.

39. See especially R. N. Rosenfeld, *American Aurora: A Democratic-Republican Returns. The Suppressed History of Our Nation's Beginning and the Heroic Newspaper that Tried to Report It* (New York: St. Martin's Press, 1997), 273.

40. Ferling, *A Leap in the Dark*, 439.

41. The dark triad includes Machiavellianism, psychopathy and narcissism; three traits which seem to cohere together in certain character types. For an example of extensive research on this topic see the following example sources: D. L., Paulhus & K. M. Williams, "The Dark Triad of Personality: Narcissism, Machiavellianism, and Psychopathy," *Journal of Research in Personality*, 36(6) (2002), 556-563; S. Jakobwitz & V. Egan, "The Dark Triad and Normal Personality Traits," *Personality and Individual Differences*, 40(2) (2006), 331-339; M. Wai & N. Tiliopoulos, "The Affective and Cognitive Empathic Nature of the Dark Triad of Personality," *Personality and Individual Differences*, 52(7) (2012), 794-799.

42. Elkins and McKitrick, *The Age of Federalism*, 99.

Still, it seems that Elkins and McKitrick dissent, only on the grounds of Hamilton's occasional inability to stay the course. Though he showed lapses in judgement and bursts of impulsivity that sometimes undermined his ends, he did indeed have Machiavellian plots and plans, many of which were successfully executed.

One finds insight into Hamilton's character among the Adams's; not John Adams [43] who was too close to events and too directly affected for clarity of judgement, but in his wife Abigail, who called Hamilton *a second Bonaparte;* a characterization that was later expanded upon by Henry Adams in a response to Lodge:

> You do not of course expect me to acquiesce entirely in your view of A. H. I dislike Hamilton because I always feel the adventurer in him. The very cause of your admiration is the cause of my distrust…From the first to the last words he wrote, I read always the same Napoleonic kind of adventuredom.[44]

43. It is said that John Adams's estimation of Hamilton was much more positive early on in the revolutionary process, prior to the two coming into direct competition. Thereafter the two "hated each other to a degree exceeded by no comparable enmity in the early life of the republic." Elkins and McKitrick, *The Age of Federalism*, 793. A composite of Adams's early estimations with those later formed might approach accuracy.
44. Knott, "'Opposed in Death as in Life'", 36.

Elias Hasket Derby: The Privateer Who Pioneered the Russian Trade

❧ NICK DELUCA ❧

At the height of his wealth and power in the 1780s, Elias Hasket Derby may have been seen around Salem, Massachusetts, or nearby Boston dressed in nothing less than absolute finery; sometimes donning a Sir Roger de Coverley coat, sometimes leaning on a gold-headed cane.[1]

Indeed, Derby was among the wealthiest men of his time and is considered to be the first American millionaire.[2] He accumulated his wealth by assisting his father in the family merchant shipping business, eventually inheriting it and turning it into a major global player. Derby's vessels achieved a number of seafaring milestones, becoming among the first few American ships to trade with such foreign ports as St. Petersburg, Russia, among others. Not surprisingly, a posthumous portrait of Derby shows him charting courses on a map while sitting in an office, outside the window of which are two floating ships, perhaps weighing anchor to sail for the West Indies or the Cape of Good Hope or India or China, perhaps returning from such a voyage.[3] The American Revolution made it possible for Derby to become a shipping magnate and blaze oceanic trails, establishing a prosperous though short-lived trade between the United States and Russia.

Derby operated a small fleet at the onset of the Revolution and attempted to trade with Jamaica, Haiti, and Dominica, with whom he conducted business prior to 1776. He was not insensible of the dangers. The British occupied Boston with a stranglehold on the harbor. In February 1776, he notified one of his ship's commanders to wait for further

1. James R. Fichter, *So Great a Proffit* (Harvard University Press, 2010), 133.
2. Anthony Dane Morrison & Nancy Schultz, *Salem: Place, Myth, and Memory* (Northeastern University Press, 2004), 189.
3. Portrait of Elias Hasket Derby by James Frothingham, Peabody Essex Museum, Salem, Massachusetts. c. 1800–1825.

instruction to sail north given the dangers presented by the British occupation, telling told Nathaniel Silsbee "I have Rote you a long letter
& hope you will fully know my Mind by it wich is for you to keep most
of the Interest in Your hands till You think the Danger not so much as
at this time."[4]

Indeed, British naval superiority threatened his business, intercept-
ing his ships and impounding their cargoes of rum and sugar[5] so that
"his trade was ruined, and his property seriously impaired."[6] To combat
the British and improve his mercantile affairs, Derby "united with his
townsmen, and took a prominent part in the equipment of at least 158
armed vessels, fitted out from Salem during the Revolution, mounting
more than 2,000 cannon, and manned by the gallant seamen of Salem
and the contiguous ports of Beverly and Marblehead."[7]

On June 13, 1776, Derby's schooner *Sturdy Beggar*, burthen ninety
tons, was outfitted with six guns that fired three-pound balls, twenty-
four men and four months of provisions, "for the purpose of making
reprisals on the Enemies of the United Colonies of North America."[8]
These armed privateers proved successful in not only safeguarding
Derby's ships but also in helping him turn a modest profit; his sloop
Revenge, armed with ten guns, took an enemy ship with 733 hogsheads
of sugar and other assorted cargo.[9] As the war progressed, privateers
were provided letters of marque. This allowed Derby to legally capture
enemy ships and retain any goods. Under this legal protection the *Revenge* struck again, commandeering an enemy ship near Jamaica, taking
334 hogsheads of sugar, 143 puncheons of rum, 40 pipes of Madeira
wine, various West Indian goods, in addition to 27 cannon of four to
nine pounds.[10]

By 1778, Derby was in control of ships larger and more powerful
than the likes of *Sturdy Beggar*. One such brig, called *Franklin*, burthen
200 tons, carried eighteen cannon that fired six-pound projectiles, and
was and was manned by a crew of over 100 who required 120 barrels
of beef and pork, and 3,000 pounds of bread.[11]

4. Elias Hasket Derby to Nathaniel Silsbee, February 23, 1776, in William Bell Clark, et,
al, ed., *Naval Documents of the American Revolution* (Washington, DC: U.S. Government
Printing Office, 1969), 4: 44–46 (*Naval Documents*).
5. Freeman Hunt, *Lives of American Merchants* (Derby & Jackson, 1858), 2: 30.
6. Ibid.
7. Ibid., 2: 33.
8. Journal of the Massachusetts Council, June 13, 1776, *Naval Documents*, 5: 506.
9. Hunt, *Lives of American Merchants*, 2: 34.
10. Richard Cranch to John Adams, July 22, 1776, *Naval Documents*, 5: 1177-1178.
11. Petition of Elias Hasket Derby, Fancis Cabot, and Job Prince, Jr., to Massachusetts
Council, April 18, 1778, *Naval Documents*, 12: 148-149.

Victory was secured for the American cause in 1783. News of peace was brought from France aboard *Astrea*, a ship belonging to none other than Elias Hasket Derby.[12]

Derby's dabbling in privateering was more lucrative in the long run than in the short. He owned four ships and three brigs, all seven of which were augmented for the wartime necessities of size and speed. "His ships had outgrown the humble trade he pursued before the war. They were no longer adapted to a small business, or the slow carriage of lumber, live-stock, and fish to the West Indies."[13] The war had required larger vessels which obsoleted the smaller ones Derby had been accustomed to using for commercial purposes. Larger ships meant larger cargo holds to fill, a higher volume of goods to sell, and plenty of cargo accumulation for the return trip. The West Indies were ill-suited for the sizable demands of ships like *Astrea*, or Derby's even larger *Grand Turk*, a 300-ton vessel. Expenses rose. Profits were hardly guaranteed.

Less than a year after a peace treaty was signed by the British and the Americans, Derby established trade relations between the United States and Russia, specifically in the port city of St. Petersburg. Sailing for Russia was an experiment for Derby and a pecuniary risk. He tended to buy his cargo in full, placing a greater financial burden and risk on him with each voyage should damage befall the ship. "Derby's barque *Light Horse* opened New England trade with St. Petersburg, leaving port June 15, 1784."[14]

Sailors brought back commodities such as iron, hemp, and a fine linen canvas called duck.[15] The prominent merchant and Boston Brahmin, George Cabot, wrote "the hemp, iron, and duck brought from Russia have been to our fisheries and navigation like seed to a crop."[16] Duck could be used to weave sails. Iron could produce nails to peg and reinforce wood. In return, American vessels carried abroad such products as tar, turpentine, and rice from the southern states; tea, spices and pepper from those ships which reached far East ports like Canton in China; and rum and other assorted provisions from New England.[17]

12. Richard H. McKey, Jr., "Elias Hasket Derby and the Founding of the Eastern Trade (Part I)," *Essex Institute Historical Collections* v. xcvii (Newcomb & Gauss, Co., 1962), 1.
13. Hunt, *Lives of American Merchants*, 2: 52.
14. *Bulletin of the Essex Institute* v. xv (The Salem Press, 1881), 44.
15. William Babcock Weeden, *Economic and Social History of New England, 1620–1789* (Houghton Mifflin, 1890), 825.
16. Justin Winsor, *The Memorial History of Boston: Including Suffolk County, Massachusetts, 1630–1880* (James R. Osgood and Company, 1881), 4: 223.
17. James Duncan Phillips, "Salem Opens American Trade with Russia," *The New England Quarterly* v. 14 no. 4 (1941), 689.

An early nineteenth-century portait of Elias Hasket Derby by James Frothingham. (*Peabody Essex Museum*)

And Russian ships began sailing across the sea to unload their stores in Boston. "The ship *Thomas and Nancy* arrived at Boston from St. Petersburg Aug. 31, 1786; and the ship *Garrick* Nov. 15, 1787."[18] The importation of Russian iron was a boon for manufacturing nails domestically which in turn stoked the carpentry industry. Houses and furniture made of abundantly supplied wood were fastened and secured easily with iron nails and the widespread want for nails, not just by the wealthy but commoners as well, catalyzed further innovation. "Jacob Perkins, a wonderful inventor of Newburyport, started a machine for cutting and heading [nails], in Amesbury, about 1790. In the following decade, 23 patents were granted in the United States for improving this excellent device for elevating the condition of mankind."[19] The same year Perkins was reinventing nail production, twenty-two American ships dropped anchor in the port of St. Petersburg; seven were from Boston, three from Salem, and one each from Beverly and Gloucester.[20]

Elias Hasket Derby died in 1799 a man of considerable wealth. His true legacy, though, was establishing trade with Russia in addition to the East Indies and China. From 1790 until his death, "Derby domi-

18. Winsor, *The Memorial History of Boston*, 4: 223.
19. Weeden, *Economic and Social History of New England*, 856.
20. Walther Kirchner, *Studies in Russian-American Commerce: 1820–1860* (Leiden: E. J. Brill, 1975), 14.

nated American trade in the Indian Ocean from his Isle of France depot. One-fifth of all American ships to visit the Isle of France in the decade from 1789 to 1799 were Derby's; almost one-third of all Salem ships to round the Cape of Good Hope were his ... Some of his methods changed but never his fortunes, which only increased."[21]

By the early 1800s, the trade between New England and St. Petersburg "assumed large proportions. Captain Swain, who arrived from St. Petersburg at Boston in the brig *Betsey*, in the autumn of 1803, gave a list of ninety American vessels which had arrived at that port between February 28 and July 24, and of these fifty-four belonged to Massachusetts."[22] Of the fifty-four ships from Massachusetts, twenty-one were from Salem, fourteen from Boston, eight from Newburyport, five from Marblehead, four from Gloucester, and one from New Bedford.[23] In Marblehead, annual customs duties rose from $22,300 in 1801 to $156,000 in 1807, fueled in large part by the Russia trade and other ports around the Baltic.[24]

But it wasn't long before some American merchants became disenchanted with the trade. Cabot wrote in an 1806 letter to the former secretary of state and then-sitting senator, Timothy Pickering, that he found himself at a disadvantage when it came to Russian relations. He was buying from them more than he was selling. His vessels were selling in Spain, but at a loss. They would arrive in Russia carrying little cargo, the empty space of which he had to pay for. He couldn't, though, help but acknowledge usefulness of Russian imports:

> In Russia, we sell little or nothing, and buy to a great amount. We go there dead freighted, and pay all in case or rather in bills on London, better to us than money, having cost us a considerable premium in Spain or elsewhere; yet who, among those that think no trade is important to the buyer as to the seller, will dare to deny that the trade with Russia since 1783 has been for its amount the most useful trade to the country?[25]

Despite a one-sided trade, where American merchants carried more of the burden, Russian ships began arriving in American ports. Many

21. McKey, "Elias Hasket Derby and the Founding of the Eastern Trade (Part II)," 83.
22. Hamilton Andrews Hill, *The Trade and Commerce of Boston: 1630–1890* (Boston: Damrell & Upham, 1895), 127.
23. Samuel Eliot Morison, *The Maritime History of Massachusetts: 1783–1860* (Houghton Mifflin, 1921), 179.
24. Ibid., 140.
25. George Cabot to Timothy Pickering, March 29, 1806, in Henry Cabot Lodge, *The Life and Letters of George Cabot* (Little Brown and Company, 1877), 358.

voyages, though, were marred with misfortune. Two ships left Russia for New England in 1806, one from St. Petersburg and the other from Archangel. "One returned to Kronstadt 'with rich freight.' The other, coming from Boston, was lost near the Danish coast, and only part of its cargo of 3,600 bottles of liquor was saved and reached Reval . . . The third ship was sent in 1809, but never reached the United States, having presumably floundered, at a loss to [merchant, K.A.] Anfilatov, estimated at 450,000 rubles."[26]

Cabot wrote his letter as the Napoleonic Wars raged in Europe. Britain and France were belligerent nations and the ocean was a theater of war between which American merchant ships were caught. The British were engaging American ships suspected of carrying British military deserters and impressing those men into British service, even Americans if they were unable to prove then and there that they weren't British. This was seen by the United States as the British forcing foreigners into their service.

As president, Thomas Jefferson relayed the actions of the British to Congress:

> On the impressment of our seamen, our remonstrances have never been intermitted. A hope existed at one moment of an arrangement which might have been submitted to, but it soon passed away, and the practice, though relaxed at times in the distant seas, has been constantly pursued in those in our neighborhood. The grounds on which the reclamations on this subject have been urged, will appear in an extract from instructions to our minister at London now communicated.[27]

The American response would culminate with the Embargo Act of 1807—an attempt to remain neutral between the two European powers, uphold the safety of U. S. sailors, and promote domestic commerce and industry. The embargo lasted for little over a year but its effect was felt in every corner of the nation. In 1807, Massachusetts exported $20,112,125 worth of goods; the entire United States, $180,343,150. In 1808, at the height of the embargo, those sums plummeted to $4,128,333 and $22,430,960, respectively—declines of approximately 75 percent and 80 percent.[28]

---

26. Kirchner, *Studies in Russian-American Commerce*, 15.

27. Thomas Jefferson, January 17, 1806, in *Journal of the Senate of the United States of America: 1789–1873*, 23.

28. J. Van Fenstermaker & John E. Filer, "The U.S. Embargo Act of 1807: Its Impact on New England Money, Banking, and Economic Activity," *Economic Inquiry* v.28 no. 1 (1990), 165.

Once the embargo was lifted and foreign trade rekindled, "American trade in the Baltic surged, bringing in huge profits to American merchants. One vessel, the *Catherine* of Boston, cleared $115,000 on a single voyage in 1809."[29] But the surge was fleeting. The War of 1812, followed by westward expansion, the adoption of the railroad as a primary mode of domestic transportation, and the development of native manufactories in the Baltic region all had a hand in the decline of the Russia trade. Like a high-wattage light bulb, it was bright and vibrant and quickly burned out.

The importance of the Russia trade, short-lived though it was, should not be underestimated. It generated large sums of money and influence for men and cities. It survived war and hardships, opening up the fledgling United States to new and untapped foreign markets, and provided the new nation a foothold in the international arena.

29. David W. McFadden, "John Quincy Adams, American Commercial Diplomacy, and Russia: 1809–1825," *The New England Quarterly* v. 66 no. 4 (1993), 618.

Jefferson's Reckoning: The Sage of Monticello's Haunting Final Years

❦ GEOFF SMOCK ❦

It was a mountaintop idyll; a luxuriant bath in the affirming glow of acclaim; a sunset valediction.

Or so it was to Saul K. Padover, who described the retired Thomas Jefferson as "that most rare of human species, a balanced and harmonious man capable of viewing the world with detached compassion and serene wisdom." Cushioned upon the laurels thrown his way by a grateful nation, "few men in history ever achieved such philosophical balance and spiritual harmony as did Jefferson in his later—his postpolitical—years."[1]

This was certainly the picture Jefferson painted for the outside world. Having run his race, he would spend his retirement years loathe to descend from his Monticellan paradise. Content in the bosom of his farm, family, books, and wine, "and having gained the harbor" safe from the public affairs of his country, the days remaining would be spent looking upon his "friends still buffeting the storm . . . with anxiety indeed, but not with envy." Intended by nature for "the tranquil pursuits of science," he was at long last living the life he had always desired, but that the "enormities of the times" had prevented: as a hermit atop his mountain.[2]

An intensely private man, his intensely public life—"twenty years of labor and solicitude"—had worn the statesman down. Safe finally

---

1. Saul K. Padover, *Jefferson: A Great American's Life & Ideas* (New York: Mentor, 1952), 159.
2. "Thomas Jefferson to P.S. Dupont de Nemours, 2 March 1809," in Merrill D. Peterson, ed., *Thomas Jefferson: Writings* (New York: The Library of America, 1984), 1203-1204.

in his study, Jefferson lamented that the "hand of time presses heavily on me. I am become feeble in body, inert in mind, and much retired from the society of the world to that of my own fire-side."[3] His daughter Martha had been there at Monticello to meet him on his final return from Washington, and it was she who assumed the domestic leadership of her father's household through the rest of his life. With her were over a dozen of the sage's grandchildren and great-grandchildren, and amongst this miniature polity Jefferson lived "like a patriarch of old."[4]

His daily routine began with a few hours of horseback riding throughout his plantations; the rest were mostly spent secluded in his study with the library and scientific instruments he had spent a lifetime accumulating. From this he would descend for the evening meal, take coffee, visit with family and perhaps visitors, and then retire strictly at nine o'clock.[5] Within this sheltered milieu, the "summum bonum" of his sunset years was, in his telling, an "Epicurean ease of body and tranquility of mind."[6]

The only acknowledged blemish on this arcadia was the constant stream of correspondence invading his private study - the "affliction of my life."[7] An old wrist injury sustained chasing (literally) a paramour during his time as minister in France made writing all the more taxing, yet however determined he was to leave the public, the public was equally determined not to leave him.[8] Up to eight hours of each day were spent with his correspondence, and "no office I ever was in has been so laborious as my supposed state of retirement at Monticello."[9]

3. "Thomas Jefferson to Madame de Corny, 2 March 1817," *Founders Online*, National Archives, last modified February 1, 2018, http://founders.archives.gov/documents/Jefferson/03-11-02-0115.

4. Thomas Jefferson to Maria Hadfield Cosway, December 27, 1820," *Founders Online*, National Archives, founders.archives.gov/documents/Jefferson/98-01-02-1711.

5. "Daniel Webster, Notes of Conversation with Thomas Jefferson, 1824," in John P. Kaminski, ed., *The Founders on the Founders: Word Portraits from the American Revolutionary Era* (Charlottesville: University of Virginia Press, 2008), 318.

6. Jefferson to John Adams, June 27, 1813," *Founders Online*, founders.archives.gov/documents/Adams/99-02-02-6076.

7. Jefferson to Charles Willson Peale, March 16, 1817," *Founders Online*, founders.archives.gov/documents/Jefferson/03-11-02-0155.

8. For a brief discussion of the romance between Jefferson and Maria Cosway in France, see Fawn M. Brodie, *Thomas Jefferson: An Intimate History* (New York: W.W. Norton & Company, 1974), 29. For the feelings Jefferson had for Mrs. Cosway, see his famous "Dialogue Between My Head and My Heart" epistle in Jefferson to Cosway, October 12, 1786," *Founders Online*, founders.archives.gov/documents/Jefferson/01-10-02-0309.

9. Jefferson to William A. Burwell, February 6, 1817," *Founders Online*, founders.archives.gov/documents/Jefferson/03-11-02-0038.

Much of this incoming epistolary wave solicited his opinion or involvement on various public issues. Except in rare instances, he refused, attesting to a "general aversion from the presumption of intruding on the public an opinion on works offered to their notice."[10]

Situated, often literally, atop the clouds at Monticello, Jefferson insisted that his time amongst the world and the affairs of men should and had passed—that his last role was to watch with unruffled serenity the next generation continue the inevitable progress his had begun in the revolutions of 1776 and 1800.[11] Having famously declared to his friend and favored lieutenant James Madison that "the earth belongs in usufruct to the living," he believed that, for all intents and purposes, he was no longer amongst the living, and must not meddle in a world that no longer belonged to him.[12] "I withdraw from all contest of opinion, and resign everything cheerfully to the generation now in place. They are wiser than we were, and their successor will be wiser than they, from the progressive advance of science."[13]

To ensure that wisdom and progress, he took a leading role in creating the University of Virginia—an institution he had begun to envision in his years as president and that would become the "Hobby" of his final years.[14] Such a university would be based on the "illimitable freedom of the human mind," and would be designed to "improving the virtue and science of their country," thus insuring that succeeding

10. Jefferson to Joseph Delaplaine, December 25, 1816 (first letter)," *Founders Online,* founders.archives.gov/documents/Jefferson/03-10-02-0475.

11. Jefferson would always insist that his and the Democratic-Republicans' sweeping victories in the election of 1800 was every bit the victory over monarchists and "Anglomen" the War of Independence had been. To him, the "revolution of 1800" was "as real a revolution in the principles of our government as that of 1776 was in its form." See "To Judge Spencer Roane, September 6, 1819," in Jean M. Yarbrough, ed., *The Essential Jefferson* (Indianapolis: Hackett Publishing Company, Inc., 2006), 250. See also "Jefferson to Governor John Langdon, March 5, 1810," in Peterson, ed., *Writings*, 1218.

12. Jefferson to James Madison, September 6, 1789," *Founders Online,* founders. archives.gov/documents/Jefferson/01-15-02-0375-0003. See also, "Jefferson to Major John Cartwright, June 5, 1824," in Petersen, ed., *Writings*, 1493. Technically, Jefferson attempted one last foray into public affairs in the last year of his life: a response written on behalf of Virginia rejecting President John Quincy Adams' proposed internal improvements on Constitutional grounds. Submitted to Madison for approval, his former lieutenant and successor advised him not to make it public. See Jefferson to Madison, December 24, 1825," *Founders Online,* founders.archives.gov/documents/Jefferson/98-01-02-5763.

13. For comments on earth belonging "to the living", see Jefferson to Madison, September 6, 1789," *Founders Online,* founders.archives.gov/documents/Jefferson/01-15-02-0375-0003. For his determination to defer to the "generation now in place," see "To Roane," in Yarbrough, ed., *Essential Jefferson*, 252.

14. "Jefferson to John Adams, October 12, 1823," in Peterson, ed., *Writings*, 1479.

generations had the manners and modes of thinking necessary for the perpetuation of republican government.[15] Jefferson would eventually gaze upon the university near his home with paternal pride; so much so that "Father of the University of Virginia" would be one of three accomplishments he requested etched into his epitaph.[16]

Aside from this, the founding father emeritus would be seen only by the family and slaves living with him at Monticello and those who visited him there—and even then only if they were fortunate. (Such was his determined isolation that Chief Justice John Marshall quipped he was "the great Lama of the mountains."[17])

When the elevated placement of Monticello and the carefully-constructed architecture within were not enough to insure Jefferson's privacy, he would retreat further still to his Poplar Forest property in nearby Bedford County—a property in some ways preferable to Monticello as being "more proportioned to the faculties of a private person."[18]

Yes, to all outward appearances, Jefferson was indeed in a self-proclaimed apotheosis of sorts. Surrounded by all that he cherished, he had already begun the ascent from a leader in the Revolutionary generation to historical immortality, all the while committing himself "cheerfully to the watch and care of those for whom, in my turn, I have watched and cared."[19]

The final climb atop his little mountain after the presidency was but the first step in this ultimate journey; a time to enjoy the comforts of a beloved patriarch while looking down upon the inevitable course of progress he and others had sacrificed so much to begin. "I have much confidence that we shall proceed successfully for ages to come." As the new nation grew westward, so too would the rights and freedoms of man, for "it will be seen that the larger the extent of the country, the more firm its republican structure, if founded . . . in principles of compact and equality." Others, but especially elder statesmen like himself, had nothing to gain from fear for the future anyway, for "the flatteries of hope are as cheap, and pleasanter than the gloom of despair."[20]

15. Thomas Jefferson to William Roscoe, December 27, 1820, *Founders Online*, founders. archives.gov/documents/Jefferson/98-01-02-1712. Jefferson to Cosway, October 24, 1822, *Founders Online*, founders.archives.gov/documents/Jefferson/98-01-02-3111.

16. "Epitaph [1826]," in Peterson, ed., *Writings*, 706-707.

17. John Marshall to Joseph Story, September 18, 1821, in Kaminski, ed., *Founders on the Founders*, 316.

18. Jefferson to John Wayles Eppes, September 18, 1812, *Founders Online*, founders. archives.gov/documents/Jefferson/03-05-02-0292.

19. Jefferson to Benjamin Waterhouse, March 3, 1818, in Kaminski, ed., *Founders on the Founders*, 316.

20. Jefferson to Francois de Marbois, June 14, 1817, in Peterson, ed., *Writings*, 1410-1411.

Thomas Sully's portrait of Thomas Jefferson at age 78, begun in 1821 and finished in 1830.

Yet as Jefferson entered the final decade of his life, this putative hope and serenity began to sink under the weight of a darkening melancholy. The trait that had most separated him from the other most famous Founding Fathers was the idealistic lens through which he viewed the world he and they inhabited. In his personal life, he had interpreted his existence as a utopia of domestic felicity, illustrated most in the descriptive images he painted of his own retirement atop Monticello: as a contented father and grandfather living out his days in familial bliss, as a student of the Enlightenment ensconced in his library, as a dinner-host promoting the natural harmony between people over bottles of the world's best wines.[21] This romantic optimism extended to his conception of human nature and the age in which he lived:

> I am among those who think well of the human character generally.
> I consider man as formed for society, and endowed by nature with those dispositions which fit him for society. I believe also . . . that his mind is perfectible to a degree of which we cannot as yet form any conception.[22]

To him, mankind had only just entered an epoch of the sublime—a harmonious age of human interaction and illimitable scientific

21. Geoff Smock, "Exploring Thomas Jefferson's Love of Wine," *Journal of the American Revolution*, August 28, 2016, accessed April 09, 2018, allthingsliberty.com/2016/08/thomas-jefferson-love-wine/.
22. Jefferson to William Green Munford, June 18, 1799, in Yarbrough, ed., *Essential Jefferson*, 194.

progress, freed at long last from a Plato's cave of chained oppression and shadowy ignorance. Human history was now a symphony only in its first sonata.

But for Jefferson to preserve these dogmas intact inside himself required a lifetime of either ignoring or explaining away any nagging cacophonies that could have contradicted them. Many of these beliefs were castles constructed in the sky, built and maintained by borrowing against reality—or in ignoring it altogether. In the final ten years of his life, these debts would at long last come due, and it was in finally being forced to reckon with them that the illusion of his personal euphony would give way to an increasing, acute despair.[23]

Paramount among these metaphorical personal debts was his very real, very crushing financial debt. Living a life conformed to his ideals—of meticulously constructed and reconstructed estates, of libraries lined with books, of cellars stocked with fine wines—had required him to spend far beyond his means. His insolvency had always been a specter looming just within his periphery, but he had managed to keep it at bay by convincing himself that liquidating a select few of his properties, or selling "one or two full crops," would relieve all of his burdens.[24]

It was but one of the sweet little lies he would comfort himself with throughout his life—one to which the progression of time slowly, but surely, contradicted. As his own time began to run out, it was a lie he could no longer maintain.

Having long insisted that not only did the earth "belong to the living," and that debts contracted by one generation must be settled by that generation, he was rendered despondent at the idea of bequeathing a ruined estate to his children and grandchildren. "My own debts had become considerable," he would complain to Madison. But instead of taking personal responsibility, he would place the blame on the need to bail out friends, on the "maintenance of my family," and the "abject depression" of the agricultural market. To make matters worse, his saving grace—property—had "lost its character of being a resource for debts."

In the end, he faced the prospect of selling Monticello and everything on it, and to "move thither with my family, where I have not even

23. For an authoritative interpretation of the dichotomy between the ideals and realities in Jefferson's life, and how he maintained them, see Joseph J. Ellis, *American Sphinx: The Character of Thomas Jefferson* (New York: Vintage Books, 1998).
24. Brodie, *An Intimate History*, 455-457. For his stated assurance that he could solve his debt through his agricultural products at Monticello, see Jefferson to Archibald Robertson, April 25, 1817, *Founders Online*, founders.archives.gov/documents/Jefferson/03-11-02-0247.

a log hut to put my head into, and whether ground for burial, will depend on the depredations which, under the form of sales, shall have been committed my property."[25]

Rivalling the lamentations of Job, these lachrymose sentiments came not only five months before his death, but at the end of multiple, previously unthinkable, and ultimately unsuccessful attempts to save his estate. Selling bits and pieces of his property, including slaves, had barely made a dent, and to add insult to injury, his fiscal woes were becoming increasingly public. Confronted with unavoidable failure, he was eventually left no other option than to take the humiliating step of petitioning the Virginia legislature to open a subscription lottery for his estate.[26] This not only entailed discussing the history of lotteries in Virginia, but the base need to recount his list of services on behalf of state and country.[27]

The petition was rejected.[28]

Jefferson's debt troubles further aggravated tensions inside his own family, within which tragedy had always been close at hand. Of his six children, four had died before reaching the age of seven and a fifth, Maria (or "Polly"), had died only months after giving birth to her third child. His wife, Martha, enfeebled by a lifetime of poor health, had died shortly after the birth of their last child, Elizabeth, who herself would die three years later. These losses sent the strongest tremors through Jefferson's carefully-maintained, idealistic world—the shocks of which often manifested themselves through extended, debilitating migraines.[29]

It was a few short years after his wife's death that Jefferson had left his sorrows behind and sailed to France as U.S. minister. For nearly the next twenty years of public service he would mostly be an absentee paterfamilias—briefly at home, occasionally visited by daughter and grandchildren, always willing to provide written paternal counsel, but usually absent.

Upon his return to Monticello, he was confronted with a family shaken not only by the previous deaths of Martha and the children, but

25. Jefferson to James Madison, February 17, 1826, in Peterson, ed., *Writings*, 1514-1515.

26. See "Broadside: A Plea for Financial Assistance by Subscription for Thomas Jefferson, 1825, December 31, 1825," *Founders Online*, founders.archives.gov/documents/Jefferson/98-01-02-5787.

27. Thomas Jefferson's Thoughts on Lotteries, ca. January 20, 1826, *Founders Online*, founders.archives.gov/documents/Jefferson/98-01-02-5845.

28. Thomas Jefferson Randolph to Jefferson, February 3, 1826, *Founders Online*, founders.archives.gov/documents/Jefferson/98-01-02-5875.

29. Ellis, *Sphinx*, 52.

abuse, depression, mental illness, alcoholism, and debt. His relationship with his son-in-law, Thomas Mann Randolph, had long been complicated. A vivid contrast in personalities (Jefferson was serene and reserved; Randolph loquacious and demonstrative), Randolph was known to grow enraged in the presence of his wife and suffered from bouts of mental illness throughout their marriage.[30] Every bit in debt as Jefferson, father- and son-in-law were able to commiserate over poor harvests and the malevolence of banks, but shared little else in common.[31] Randolph chafed under the pressure of living in the shadow of his illustrious father-in-law, while Jefferson likely resented, albeit privately, Randolph's quarrelsomeness, alcoholism, and behavior towards Martha and the children. So poor were relations between husband and wife that Martha and their eleven children would live with Jefferson at Monticello for the remainder of his life.[32]

Always on the brink, Randolph's life came crashing in around him after assuming the governorship of Virginia. By 1825, Jefferson's penultimate year on earth, Randolph was not only completely gripped by alcoholism, but both personally and financially ruined.

Jefferson endeavored to bring his prodigal son-in-law back within the family fold. "I hope that to your other pains has not been added that of a moment's doubt that you can ever want a necessary or comfort of life while I possess any thing," he wrote. "All I have is devoted to the comfortable maintenance of yourself and the family, and to a future provision for them."[33] Randolph could yet turn back from the path he had gone down and find happiness "by returning to the bosom of those who love and respect you, rather than to continue in solitude, brooding over your misfortunes, & encouraging their ravages on your mind."[34]

These pleas would go unanswered, and Randolph would remain estranged from his wife and family for the rest of Jefferson's life.

Seemingly possessed of all the qualities his father lacked, Jefferson's grandson, Thomas Jefferson Randolph, would grow to become his grandfather's favorite. Both hard-working and devoted, "Jeff" would

30. Brodie, *An Intimate History*, 280-281.
31. "There seems to be so general a sickening at the effects of the banks," Jefferson would write to him, "that I hope the country is ripe for suppressing them by degrees." Jefferson to Thomas Mann Randolph, August 9, 1819, *Founders Online*, founders.archives.gov/documents/Jefferson/98-01-02-0673.
32. Brodie, *An Intimate History*, 457-458.
33. Jefferson to Thomas Mann Randolph, June 5 1825, *Founders Online*, founders.archives.gov/documents/Jefferson/98-01-02-5282.
34. Jefferson to Thomas Mann Randolph, July 9, 1825, *Founders Online*, founders.archives.gov/documents/Jefferson/98-01-02-5369.

eventually offer to personally take over the elder Jefferson's increasingly-insolvent estate.

It came as some shock then in 1819 when Jefferson received word that Jeff had been stabbed in the streets by his grandson-in-law, Charles Lewis-Bankhead—who, like his father-in-law, Thomas Randolph, was known to abuse both alcohol and his family. Virtually estranged from the family himself, and having already been involved in a drunken altercation with Thomas Randolph at Monticello sometime before, tensions had been high between him and Jeff for some time.

No longer speaking to each other, Bankhead had nevertheless written to Jeff's wife—an insult in the gentlemen's code of early-nineteenth century society. When the two met in the streets of Charlottesville, Jeff's demand for an explanation quickly resulted in a physical altercation. By the time the two were separated, Jeff was copiously bleeding and had to be carried to nearby rooms.

When Jefferson received word of Jeff's condition that same evening, he disregarded the pleas of Martha and the grandchildren and raced via horseback to the bedside of his grandson. Once there, and seeing his feverish condition, Jefferson broke down and wept. His family, like his grandson in the bed before him, lay riven and bleeding in ways that would never fully heal. Jeff would ultimately recover; Bankhead would skip bail and abscond with his wife to a neighboring county.[35]

While dysfunction continued to shred the veneer of Jefferson's family paradise, so too were national developments jolting the vision of America he had spent his public life maintaining—to others and to himself. In his mind, his and the Democratic-Republicans' victory in the election of 1800 had insured that America would be an "empire of liberty," so long as there was ample western land in which to expand. If provided this, men would be "disposed to live honestly," provided "the means of doing so are open to them."[36]

Jefferson had envisioned this expansion happening in a structured, patriarchal manner. One of the major ideological pet projects of his retirement years had been a "ward republic" system, whereby counties and townships in the growing republic would be divided into hundreds. In each would be a central school for the children, a justice of the peace,

---

35. Alan Pell Crawford, *Twilight at Monticello: The Final Years of Thomas Jefferson* (New York: Random House, Inc., 1998), xxiii-xxvi; 162-169.

36. For Jefferson's "empire of liberty" quote, see Jefferson to Benjamin Chambers, December 28, 1805, *Founders Online,* founders.archives.gov/documents/Jefferson/99-01-02-2910. For his Americans being "disposed to live honestly" see "Jefferson to Francois de Marbois, June 14, 1817," in Peterson, ed., *Writings,* 1410-1411.

a constable, and a militia captain—who in their corporate whole would
be charged with managing "all its concerns." He was convinced that it
was a measure of organization "without which no republic can maintain
itself in strength." Each ward would essentially be "a small republic
within itself, and every man in the state would thus become an acting
member of the common government, transacting in person a great portion of its rights and duties."[37]

It was also an extension of the family structure practiced at Monticello (in theory, at least): a patriarchal figure at the head benevolently
caring for the affairs of children, children-in-law, and grandchildren
below him.[38]

Yet as with his family, socio-political realities in the United States
disappointed Jefferson's expectations. Instead of a republic of mini-re-
publics governed by enlightened patriarchs akin to himself, American
democracy in the first decades of the nineteenth century was becoming
a rough-and-tumble, coarsened expression of the ordinary man. Less
and less was it a Jeffersonian "empire of liberty" governed by genteel,
wine-sipping, enlightened patriarchs; but more the bristly, whiskey-
swilling common-man that would come to represent Jacksonian
democracy—or rapacious northern, urban, speculators, bankers, and
money-men akin to his old foe Hamilton.[39]

By his final decade, the man who had entered retirement expressing
a serene assurance about the next generation could hardly contain his
disdain for it. Not only was the federal government encroaching upon
the states, but America's young men, "who, having nothing in them of
the feelings or principles of '76, now look to a single and splendid government of an aristocracy, founded on banking institutions, and mon-
eyed incorporations under the guise and cloak of their favored branches
of manufactures, commerce and navigation."[40] Aiding and abetting this
was an anti-republican judiciary, "a subtle corps of sappers and miners
constantly working under ground to undermine the foundations of our
confederated fabric."[41]

37. Jefferson to John Cartwright, June 5, 1824, *Founders Online*, founders. archives.gov/doc-
uments/Jefferson/98-01-02-4313.
38. For an exemplary examination of Jefferson's patriarchal conceptions of both familial
and political society, see Annette Gordon-Reed and Peter S. Onuf, *"Most Blessed of Patriarchs": Thomas Jefferson and the Empire of Imagination* (New York: Liveright Publishing
Corp., 2016).
39. Gordon S. Wood, *Revolutionary Characters: What Made the Founders Different* (New
York: The Penguin Press, 2006), 114-115.
40. To William Branch Giles, December 26, 1825, in Yarbrough, ed., *Essential Jefferson*,
271.
41. To Thomas Ritchie, December 25, 1820, in Peterson, ed., *Writings*, 1446.

Of greatest alarm to Jefferson was the increasingly toxic nexus between one of his most cherished articles and his life's most obvious contradiction—between western expansion and slavery. Shattering the veneer of national comity and the "Era of Good Feeling," Missouri's petition to enter the Union as a slave state at long last brought to the forefront the issue the founding generation had worked tirelessly to delay.

This had suited no one more than Jefferson, who never missed an opportunity to lament slavery's existence and hope for its abolition—but who also was personally dependent on the labor and value that "species of property" provided him.[42] For his entire life, no one had wished "more ardently to see a good system commenced for raising the condition both of [slaves'] body & mind to what it ought to be."[43] But though emancipation would always be his most "fervent prayer," he had always foresworn any personal efforts to see its fulfillment.[44] Reassured that "the hour of emancipation is advancing, in the march of time," he avowed a gradualist approach—emancipating slaves born after a certain day—which would "lessen the severity of the shock which an operation so fundamental cannot fail to produce."[45] This path would also have the singular advantage of taking place long after he was gone.

The "Missouri Question" eviscerated this idea, and was received "like a fire bell in the night." So alarmed was Jefferson that he "considered it at once as the knell of the Union." Despite his long-held belief that allowing slavery to spread into the incoming western territories and states would gradually diffuse it, it brought to the surface all the gaping cleavages between north and south swept under the rug for the previous four decades. As it stood now, he complained that "we have the wolf by the ears, and we can neither hold him, nor safely let him go. Justice is in one scale, and self-preservation in the other." The generation he had long placed such assured faith in was now responsible for the impending demise of the union he had helped create. "I regret now that I am to die in the belief, that the useless sacrifice of themselves of the

---

42. The phrase "that species of property" was a common euphemism used by the leading members to refer to the institution of slavery. See Jefferson to Charles Clay, July 1, 1816, *Founders Online,* founders.archives.gov/documents/Jefferson/03-10-02-0112. George Washington would use the phrase in his correspondence several times. See George Washington to John Francis Mercer, December 5, 1786, *Founders Online,* founders.archives. gov/documents/Washington/04-04-02-0380; and Washington to Benjamin Dulany, July 15, 1799, *Founders Online,* http://founders.archives.gov/documents/ Washington/06-04-02-0156.
43. To Benjamin Banneker, August 30, 1791, in Yarbrough, ed., *Essential Jefferson,* 181.
44. To James Heaton, May 20, 1826, in Peterson, ed., *Writings,* 1516.
45. To Edward Coles, August 25, 1814, ibid., 1345.

generation of 1776 . . . is to be thrown away by the unwise and unworthy passions of their sons."[46]

The last cornerstone in Jefferson's castle in the sky had begun to crumble, and with it came the very structure itself. No longer able to hear only the harmonies of domestic utopias, an enlightened posterity, and an expanding empire of liberty, America's aging apostle of liberty was being mugged by harsh realities and impatient contradictions. He could no longer pay these illusions forward any more than he could his own debts, and the sorrow therein began to come out through his correspondence as much as the traditional Jeffersonian themes.

As the Missouri crisis passed and America once again managed to push the issue of slavery further into the future, Jefferson slowly walked back from his apocalyptic bodings.[47] But the bloom had fallen, and a naïve innocence he had maintained for most of his life had been lost forever. In those final years of his life, he had had to confront the bitter reality that the world—his world—did not exist as he would have had it exist in the spaces between his own mind and his voluminous writings. In this personal, painful reckoning, Jefferson's last years were much less a fulfillment of the Jeffersonian vision he left us on paper, and had convinced himself of through the course of his eight decades, than an intensely painful, private funeral for the death of his own grand illusions.

Thomas Jefferson gave his last breath on the fiftieth anniversary of the Declaration of Independence—surrounded by the books, slaves, and contradictions he had always tried to keep at bay. Those contradictions, most especially that between the America he envisioned in the Declaration and the one that truly existed, would live on for far longer.

46. To John Holmes, April 20, 1820, ibid., 1434. See also, Jefferson to William Short, April 13m 1820, *Founders Online*, founders.archives.gov/documents/Jefferson/98-01-02-1218.
47. See To Henry Lee, May 8, 1825, in Yarbrough, ed., *Essential Jefferson,* 267-268; and To Roger C. Weightman, June 24, 1826, in Peterson, ed., *Writings*, 1516-1517.

AUTHOR BIOGRAPHIES

J. L. BELL

J. L. Bell, an associate editor of the *Journal of the American Revolution*, maintains Boston1775.net, a popular website dedicated to history, analysis, and unabashed gossip about the start of the American Revolution in New England. His is author of *The Road to Concord: How Four Stolen Cannon Ignited the Revolutionary War* (Westholme, 2016) and *Gen. George Washington's Home and Headquarters–Cambridge, Massachusetts*, a comprehensive study for the National Park Service. He has also contributed to Todd Andrlik's *Reporting the Revolutionary War* (Sourcebooks, 2012), James Marten's *Children in Colonial America* (New York University Press, 2007), and many journals and magazines. He has been elected a Fellow of the Massachusetts Historical Society, a Member of the American Antiquarian Society, and a Member of the Colonial Society of Massachusetts.

JOHN CONCANNON

John Concannon is historian for the Gaspee Days Committee in Warwick, Rhode Island, and webmaster of the Gaspee Virtual Archives at http://gaspee.org. In his other life Dr. Concannon is a practicing pediatrician in Cranston, Rhode Island.

KEN DAIGLER

Ken Daigler is a retired CIA operations officer. He has also consulted for the Department of Defense in the counterintelligence field. He received a B.A. in history from Centre College of Kentucky and an M.A. in history from the Maxwell School at Syracuse University, and served in the U.S. Marine Corps during the Vietnam War. Ken has focused his studies on American intelligence activities in the 1765 to 1865 period. He had written numerous articles for various journals within the U.S. intelligence community and is author of *Spies, Patriots and Traitors* (Georgetown University Press, 2014).

NICK DELUCA

Nick DeLuca is a New England native, writer by trade, and history enthusiast. He has written articles, blogs, and social media content for organizations ranging from nonprofits to news outlets to the John F. Kennedy Presidential Library. He earned his B.A. in English from UMass Boston and currently lives in Western Massachusetts where he is pursuing an M.A. in Public History from UMass Amherst.

Larrie D. Ferreiro

Larrie D. Ferreiro is the 2017 Pulitzer Prize finalist for History, for his book *Brothers at Arms: American Independence and the Men of France and Spain Who Saved It*, which was also the JAR Book of the Year for 2016. He received his Ph.D. in history of science and technology from Imperial College, London. He teaches history and engineering at George Mason University in Virginia, Georgetown University in Washington, DC, and the Stevens Institute of Technology in New Jersey. He has served for almost forty years in the U.S. Navy, U.S. Coast Guard, and Department of Defense, and was an exchange engineer in the French Navy. He lives with his wife and their sons in Virginia.

Charles R. Foy

Charles R. Foy is Associate Professor, Emeritus, Eastern Illinois University. His scholarship focuses on eighteenth-century Black maritime culture. A former fellow at the National Maritime Museum & Mystic Seaport Museum, he has published more than a dozen articles on Black mariners (see http://works.bepress.com/charles_foy) and is the creator of the Black Mariner Database, a dataset of more than 28,000 eighteenth-century Black Atlantic mariners. He is completing a book manuscript, "Liberty's Labyrinth: Freedom in the Eighteenth-Century Black Atlantic," that details the nature of freedom in the eighteenth century through an analysis of the lives of Black mariners.

Katie Turner Getty

Katie Turner Getty is a Boston lawyer, writer, and independent researcher. She earned her J.D. from New England Law Boston, cum laude, holds a B.A. from Wellesley College with a focus on revolutionary America, and is a graduate of Bunker Hill Community College. For more information, visit her website, www.katieturnergetty.com

John Grady

John Grady was the communications director of the Association of the United States Army for seventeen years and managing editor of *Navy Times* for more than eight years. He is the author of *Matthew Fontaine Maury: Father of Oceanography*, a nominee for the Library of Virginia's 2016 non-fiction award. He has contributed to *Sea History*, *Naval History*, the *New York Times* "Disunion" series, and *Civil War Monitor* and was a blogger for the U.S. Navy's sesquicentennial of the Civil War website.

Don N. Hagist

Don N. Hagist, managing editor of *Journal of the American Revolution*, is an independent researcher specializing in the British army in the American Revolution. His books include *The Revolution's Last Men: the Soldiers Behind the Photographs* (Westholme Publishing, 2015), *British Soldiers, American War*

(Westholme Publishing, 2012), *A British Soldier's Story: Roger Lamb's Narrative of the American Revolution* (Ballindalloch Press, 2004), *General Orders: Rhode Island* (Heritage Books, 2001) and *Wives, Slaves, and Servant Girls* (Westholme Publishing, 2016).

PATRICK H. HANNUM

Patrick H. Hannum is a professor serving at the Joint and Combined Warfighting School, Joint Forces Staff College, National Defense University, Norfolk, Virginia, where he specializes in operational-level warfare and Phase II Joint Professional Military Education. He is a Marine Corps Veteran with twenty-nine years of active service as a ground combat officer; his service included battalion command. He holds a doctorate in education and advocates for the staff ride method of instruction, specializing in the Yorktown Campaign of 1781.

LARS HEDBOR

Lars Hedbor is a prolific author of historical novels of the American Revolution, focusing on the everyday experiences of ordinary people. The most recently released novel of the ten to date in his "Tales from a Revolution" series, *The Tree*, sheds light on an explosive early incident of violence in New Hampshire in the build up to the Revolution. Hedbor resides in the Pacific Northwest with his wife and four of his six daughters. For more information, visit his website at larsdhhedbor.com.

STEVEN C. HERTLER

Steven C. Hertler is a licensed examining psychologist with a research program centering on personality, using behavioral genetics, evolutionary biology, and behavioral ecology to alternatively explain classic character types. His writings, such as *Life History Evolution: A Biological Meta-Theory for the Social Sciences*, center on comparative psychology, cross-cultural psychology, biome distribution, and climate as it affects evolved behavior and human nature. Additional publications deal with what might be called "biohistory," where early and late modern group competition, war, and demography are studied from a biocultural perspective.

SIMON HILL

Simon Hill is a lecturer in history at Liverpool John Moores University and Visiting Lecturer in History at the University of Chester, England. He has written on how the American Revolution affected the British port-town of Liverpool in *Journal of Imperial and Commonwealth History* and *Journal for Eighteenth Century Studies*.

DAVID D. KINDY

David D. Kindy researches and writes about various history topics for the *Journal of the American Revolution*, *Smithsonian.com*, *Military History*, *American History*, and *World War II* magazines. He is a former vice president of the Pilgrim Society, which operates Pilgrim Hall Museum, the oldest continuously operating public museum in the country. He lives a stone's throw from Plymouth Rock in, of course, Plymouth with his wife Elynor and black Lab Harry.

JOHN KNIGHT

John Knight received a joint honours degree in American History/Politics from Warwick University, England. He was a fine art valuer for a number of London-based auction houses, including Christie's and Bonhams, before taking up writing and lecturing full time. He writes on American culture, society, and history at his website, www.englishmanlovesamerica.com

GEORGE KOTLIK

George Kotlik was born and raised in the Finger Lakes of Upstate New York. As a child, George and his father, who is also named George, traveled frequently to historical battlefields and forts. It is on these trips where his passion for history really took form. Over the years, he nurtured his historical interests to encompass subjects like the Great War for Empire, eighteenth-century colonial history, and the American War for Independence. Apart from reading, writing, and learning about history, George likes to play chess and spend time with his father.

BLAKE MCGREADY

Blake McGready is a Park Guide at Valley Forge National Historical Park. (The views and conclusions in his essay in this volume are those of the author and should not be interpreted as representing the opinions or policies of the National Park Service or the United States Government.) He holds degrees in history from SUNY New Paltz and Villanova University, and has worked at historic sites in his home state of New York and in Pennsylvania. He is particularly interested in the American Revolution, cultural memory, and environmental history. He is currently at work on a project about the battle of Princeton in American memory.

LOUIS ARTHUR NORTON

Louis Arthur Norton, a professor emeritus at the University of Connecticut, has published extensively on maritime history topics, including *Joshua Barney: Hero of the Revolutionary War* (Naval Institute, 2000) and *Captains Contentious: The Dysfunctional Sons of the Brine* (University of South Carolina Press, 2009). Two of his articles were awarded the 2002 and 2006 Gerald E. Morris Prize for maritime historiography in the Mystic Seaport Museum's LOG.

JIM PIECUCH

Jim Piecuch earned his Ph.D. at the College of William and Mary. He is an associate editor with the *Journal of the American Revolution*. He is editor of *Cavalry of the American Revolution* (Westholme Publishing, 2012) and author of *The Battle of Camden: A Documentary History* (History Press, 2006), *Three Peoples, One King: Loyalists, Indians, and Slaves in the Revolutionary South* (University of South Carolina Press, 2008), and *"The Blood Be Upon Your*

Head": Tarleton and the Myth of Buford's Massacre (Southern Campaigns of the American Revolution, 2010).

C. E. Pippenger

C. E. Pippenger (Pip) is a semi-retired clinical neuropharmacologist, and is an adjunct professor at the University of Vermont, Larner College of Medicine. His avocation is researching less well-known moments in history, particularly Benedict Arnold's adventures.

Gene Procknow

Gene Procknow's research includes interpreting the lives and leadership of Revolutionary generals, widening our understanding of the Revolution from a global perspective, and assessing the contributions of Ethan Allen and the creation of Vermont. Gene has written over 25 articles for the *Journal of the American Revolution* and has delivered the keynote address at gatherings commemorating the American Revolution. He maintains the website www.researchingtheamericanrevolution.com to assist in understanding Revolutionary War historiography and primary sources and is the author of the *Mad River Gazetteer*, which traces the naming of prominent Vermont place names to Revolutionary War patriots.

Chaim M. Rosenberg

Practicing as a psychiatrist in and around Boston, Chaim M. Rosenberg became interested in the abandoned nineteenth-century textile and shoe mills, the people who built them, and the people who worked in them. Among his books are *The Life and Times of Francis Cabot Lowell; 1775-1817; Goods for Sale: Products and Advertising in the Massachusetts Industrial Age; America at the Fair: Chicago's 1893 World's Columbian Exposition, Yankee Colonies Across America,* and *Losing America, Conquering India.*

Bob Ruppert

Bob Ruppert is a retired high school administrator from the greater Chicagoland area. He received his undergraduate degree from Loyola University and his graduate degree from the University of Illinois. He has been researching the American Revolution, the War for Independence, and the Federal Period for more than fifteen years. His interest began in 1963 when he was eight years old. His parents took the whole family, by car, to Newport Beach, Virginia and a small town that was slowly being restored to its eighteenth-century prominence: Williamsburg.

John L. Smith, Jr.

John L. Smith, Jr. earned a B.S. degree from the University of South Florida and an M.B.A. from the University of Tampa. He is a Vietnam-era veteran and holds honorable discharges from the U.S. Air Force Reserve and the U.S. Army Reserve. His historical work has been featured by *Knowledge Quest, National Review,* CNN, and *Smithsonian Magazine.* Most recently, he was interviewed on Sirius XM about the American invasion of Canada, 1775-1776.

Geoff Smock

Geoff Smock is a native of western Washington. He received a degree in history from Pacific Lutheran University and a M.Ed. from the University of Washington. He currently teaches eighth grade social studies and literacy near Seattle.

Eric Sterner

Eric Sterner is a national security and aerospace consultant. He held senior staff positions for the Committees on Armed Services and Science in the House of Representatives and served in the Department of Defense and as NASA's Associate Deputy Administrator for Policy and Planning. He earned a B.A. from American University and two M.A.s from George Washington University.

David O. Stewart

David O. Stewart, formerly a lawyer, writes books of history and historical fiction. *The Summer of 1787: The Men Who Invented the Constitution* won the Washington Writing Award as Best Book of 2007. Later works include *Impeached: The Trial of President Andrew Johnson, American Emperor: Aaron Burr's Challenge to Jefferson's America*, and *Madison's Gift: Five Partnerships That Built America*. He has also won the History Prize of the Society of the Cincinnati and the William H. Prescott Award of the National Society of Colonial Dames of America.

Daniel P. Stone

Daniel P. Stone earned a Ph.D. in American religious history from Manchester Metropolitan University (United Kingdom) and is the author of *William Bickerton: Forgotten Latter Day Prophet* (Signature Books, 2018). He has taught history courses at the University of Detroit Mercy and Florida Atlantic University and currently works as a research archivist for a private library/archive in Detroit, Michigan.

William Harrison Taylor

William Harrison Taylor earned his Ph.D. from Mississippi State University and is currently an associate professor of history at Alabama State University. His research primarily concentrates on the religious history of the Anglo-American world during the eighteenth century. He is the author of *Unity in Christ and Country: American Presbyterians in the Revolutionary Era, 1758–1801* (University of Alabama Press, 2017, winner of the 2018 A. Donald MacLeod Award in Presbyterian History) as well as the co-editor of *Faith and Slavery in the Presbyterian Diaspora* (Lehigh University Press, 2016).

Richard J. Werther

Richard J. Werther is a retired CPA and history enthusiast living in Novi, Michigan. He studied business management at Bucknell University in Lewisburg, Pennsylvania.

JOSEPH WROBLEWSKI

Joseph Wroblewski, received a B.A. and M.A. in Social Studies from Trenton State College (now the College of New Jersey) and earned an Ed.D. from Temple University. He served in the Peace Corps in Western Samoa, worked for the School District of Philadelphia in the Office of Research and Evaluation, and taught social studies at the S. A. Douglas High School. At present he is a volunteer docent at Morven (Princeton, New Jersey), the home of Richard Stockton.

INDEX